THE
CREATIVE
ENCOUNTER

THE
CREATIVE
ENCOUNTER

ROSEMARY HOLSINGER

West Valley College

CAMILLE JORDAN

Stanford University

LEON LEVENSON

San Jose City College

SCOTT, FORESMAN AND COMPANY
GLENVIEW, ILLINOIS   LONDON

Library of Congress Catalog Number: 79–104310
Copyright © 1971 by Scott, Foresman and Company, Glenview, Illinois 60025.
Philippines Copyright 1971 by Scott, Foresman and Company.
All Rights Reserved.
Printed in the United States of America.
Regional offices of Scott, Foresman are located in Dallas, Oakland, N. J.,
  Palo Alto, and Tucker, Ga.

Acknowledgments

"The Conditions for Creativity" by William H. Alamshah. From *Journal of Creative Behavior,* Vol. 1, No. 3, Summer 1967. Reprinted by permission of the publisher, Creative Education Foundation, Inc., and the author.   "Ecstatic Living" by Thad and Rita Ashby. From *The Oracle of Southern California,* October 1967. Reprinted by permission of the publisher.   "The Golden Section" by Sylvia Ashton-Warner. From *Teacher* by Sylvia Ashton-Warner. Copyright © 1963, by Sylvia Ashton-Warner. Reprinted by permission of Simon & Schuster, Inc.   "The Conjurer" by Ingmar Bergman. From *4 Screen Plays of Ingmar Bergman* by Ingmar Bergman (where this essay is titled "Bergman Discusses Film-Making"). Copyright © 1960, by Ingmar Bergman. Reprinted by permission of Simon & Schuster, Inc.
"The Veldt" by Ray Bradbury. Copyright 1953 by Ray Bradbury. Reprinted by permission of Harold Matson Company, Inc.   "The Creative Mind" by Jacob Bronowski. "The Creative Mind" from *Science and Human Values* by J. Bronowski. Copyright © 1956, 1965 by J. Bronowski. Reprinted by permission of Julian Messner, A Division of Simon & Schuster, Inc.   "The Historian and His Facts" by Edward Hallet Carr. From *What Is History?,* by Edward Hallet Carr. Copyright © 1961 by Edward Hallet Carr. Reprinted by permission of Alfred A. Knopf, Inc.
"Why All of Us May Be Hippies Someday" by Fred Davis. From *TRANS-action,* Vol. 5, No. 2, Dec. 1967. Copyright © December 1967 by TRANS-action, Inc. New Brunswick, New Jersey. Reprinted by permission of the publisher.
From "Pasteur and the Mad Dog" by Paul de Kruif. From *Microbe Hunters,* copyright, 1926, 1954, by Paul de Kruif. Reprinted by permission of Harcourt Brace Jovanovich, Inc.   "What Is a Social Fact?" by Emile Durkheim. Reprinted with permission of The Macmillan Company from *The Rules of Sociological Method* by Emile Durkheim, translated by George G. Catlin. Copyright 1938 by George G. Catlin, renewed 1966 by Sarah A. Solovag, John H. Muller & George G. Catlin.
From *Invisible Man* by Ralph Ellison. Copyright 1947 by Ralph Ellison. Reprinted from *Invisible Man,* by Ralph Ellison, by permission of Random House, Inc.
"Salt Crystals, Spider Webs, and Words" by Paul Engle. From the book *On Creative Writing* edited by Paul Engle. Copyright, ©, 1963, 1964 by Paul Engle. Reprinted by permission of E. P. Dutton & Co., Inc., publishers.   "The Productive Orientation" by Erich Fromm. From *Man for Himself* by Erich Fromm. Copyright 1947 by Erich Fromm. Reprinted by permission of Holt, Rinehart and Winston, Inc.
"The Politics of 'The Movement'" by Tom Hayden. From *The Radical Papers,* ed. Irving Howe (New York: Doubleday, 1966). Copyright © 1966 by Tom Hayden. Reprinted by permission of Cyrilly Abels.   From *The Art of Teaching* by Gilbert Highet. Condensed from *The Art of Teaching,* by Gilbert Highet. Copy-

PREFACE

The composer of the *Eroica,* the painter of "Three Musicians," the inventor of method acting, and, finally, the student who has written a good essay—all share one trait: creativity. The have taken the materials of observation, of experience, and of learning, and under the heat of creative energy forged them into something new. Each in his separate way has become a creator of something valuable either because of its beauty or its use.

The editors of this anthology of essays and stories have chosen creativity for its theme because we believe that college students may not understand or appreciate the role of creativity in all of living and often do not attempt to use the creative ability they possess. With Jean Jacques Rousseau, we believe that "Man's diverse powers are stirred by the same instinct." From a common thrust arises the instinct to live, to learn, and to create, with one's mind as well as with one's body. All of us have the potential for creativity in some field or area of life. And all of us can develop the ability to express our creativity in writing.

We cannot explain to students the mystery of creation any more than one can explain the feelings of hunger or of love. We hope merely to show that the creative capacity is as normal as are the capacities for hunger and love. It may be less recognizable and in most people it is less urgent, but it is there. Of course there are degrees of creativity, and we shall always stand in awe before the works that seem to go beyond the bounds of human talent. But it is necessary that every individual develop whatever talents he possesses. For what besides creativity can conquer the problems of over-population, air pollution, racism, and poverty? Indeed, if more creativity is not brought to bear to solve the national and international conflicts of the hydrogen-atomic era, there may be no one left to stand in awe before the triumph of art.

We acknowledge the fact that creativity is a painful process. It is the manifestation of the life force of the universe. Whether in nature, in individual man, or in human society, it is a movement from chaos to order, a movement which is inherently violent. And a new chaos may result, requiring a new creation. Inevitably a new idea or a new object brings changes in life—unleashes new forces and new problems while it provides solutions for old problems. Like many another process in nature, creation is continuous if it is vital. Creativity is the savage rain that gives life on earth; it is also the rainbow that says how beautiful was the life-giving rain.

In the Age of Technology, we dare to create rain. The editors of this anthology propose to create creativity. Since we believe creativity to be innate but often blocked in most people, our first section of essays presents theoretical discussions of the manifestations of creativity. From them it is hoped that a student will learn not only the necessity to accept the painful tensions of creativity but how he might better create the psychological atmosphere conducive to creativity—what attitudes toward himself, toward others, and towards the ideas of others which are new to him are the most favorable to being a creative person. From theoretical discussions of creativity we move to the subject-matter areas in which a college student is called upon to be creative. For the disciplines of Science, Art, Education, and the Social Sciences, there are essays and short stories which are creative works in themselves but which also explain some of the goals, problems, and techniques of being creative within that discipline. Our last two sections leave academic concerns and focus upon life, in which the student may have an academic interest but must surely have a personal interest. What does it mean to be a creative leader in society? Section VI, "The Revolutionary," gives some answers. Furthermore, when one is involved in the private, non-role-playing aspects of living—when one is a member of the crowd or alone with himself—how can he tell if he is confronting life or escaping life? Our final section, "The Individual," offers material with which to consider this question. Throughout all six sections of this book we direct a reader to confront the paradox of creativity: we pay dearly for it, but the cost is even dearer if we lack it.

ROSEMARY HOLSINGER
CAMILLE JORDAN
LEON LEVENSON

CONTENTS

*He who can no longer pause to wonder
and stand rapt in awe is as good as dead.*

—ALBERT EINSTEIN

I. CREATIVITY

The four articles in this opening section present an overview of the subject of creativity. The authors present definitions of the term, pose favoring and unfavoring social conditions, and, perhaps most important, set forth emotional and intellectual prerequisites. Despite differences in terminology and focus of interest, the articles agree closely on certain fundamentals. To *express* creativity a person must live in an environment which not only allows but rewards exploration toward new artistic forms and new solutions to old and new problems. But to *be* creative, the individual must also be open within himself, must have the ability to draw upon all of his inner resources. Provided with such exterior and interior freedom, any and all of us can attempt to resolve our personal disequilibriums, to "actualize" ourselves, to put our powers to productive use, or more simply, to be creative.

from
TOWARD A THEORY OF CREATIVITY

Carl R. Rogers

I maintain that there is a desperate social need for the creative behavior of creative individuals. It is this which justifies the setting forth of a tentative theory of creativity—the nature of the creative act, the conditions under which it occurs, and the manner in which it may constructively be fostered. Such a theory may serve as a stimulus and guide to research studies in this field.

THE SOCIAL NEED

Many of the serious criticisms of our culture and its trends may best be formulated in terms of a dearth of creativity. Let us state some of these very briefly:

In education we tend to turn out conformists, stereotypes, individuals whose education is "completed," rather than freely creative and original thinkers.

In our leisure-time activities, passive entertainment and regimented group action are overwhelmingly predominant, whereas creative activities are much less in evidence.

In the sciences, there is an ample supply of technicians, but the number who can creatively formulate fruitful hypotheses and theories is small indeed.

In industry, creation is reserved for the few—the manager, the designer, the head of the research department—whereas for the many life is devoid of original or creative endeavor.

In individual and family life the same picture holds true. In the clothes we wear, the food we eat, the books we read, and the ideas we hold, there is a strong tendency toward conformity, toward stereotypy. To be original or different is felt to be "dangerous."

Why be concerned over this? If, as a people, we enjoy conformity rather than creativity, shall we not be permitted this choice? In my estimation such a choice would be entirely reasonable were it not for one great shadow which hangs over all of us. In a time when knowledge, constructive and destructive, is advancing by the most incredible leaps and bounds into a fantastic atomic age, genuinely creative adaptation seems to represent the only possibility that man can keep abreast of the kaleidoscopic change in his world. With scientific discovery and invention proceeding, we are told, at a geometric rate of progression, a generally passive and culture-bound people cannot cope with the multiplying issues and problems. Unless individuals, groups, and nations can imagine, construct, and creatively revise new ways of relating to these complex changes, the lights will go out. Unless man can make new and original adaptations to his environment as rapidly as his science can change the environment, our culture will perish. Not only individual maladjustment and group tensions but international annihilation will be the price we pay for a lack of creativity.

Consequently it would seem to me that investigations of the process of creativity, the conditions under which this process occurs, and the ways in which it may be facilitated, are of the utmost importance.

It is in the hope of suggesting a conceptual structure under which such investigations might go forward, that the following sections are offered.

THE CREATIVE PROCESS

There are various ways of defining creativity. In order to make more clear the meaning of what is to follow, let me present the elements which, for me, are a part of the creative process, and then attempt a definition.

In the first place, for me as scientist, there must be something observable, some product of creation. Though my fantasies may be extremely novel, they cannot usefully be defined as creative unless they eventuate in some observable product—unless they are symbolized in words, or written in a poem, or translated into a work of art, or fashioned into an invention.

These products must be novel constructions. This novelty grows out of the unique qualities of the individual in his interaction with the materials of experience. Creativity always has the stamp of the individual upon its product, but the product is not the individual, nor his materials, but partakes of the relationship between the two.

Creativity is not, in my judgment, restricted to some particular content. I am assuming that there is no fundamental difference in the creative process as it is evidenced in painting a picture, composing a symphony, devising new instruments of killing, developing a scientific theory, discovering new procedures in human relationships, or creating new formings of one's own personality as in psychotherapy. (Indeed it is my experience in this last field, rather than in one of the arts, that has given me special interest in creativity and its facilitation. Intimate knowledge of the way in which the individual remolds himself in the therapeutic relationship, with originality and effective skill, gives one confidence in the creative potential of all individuals.)

My definition, then, of the creative process is that it is the emergence in action of a novel relational product, growing out of the uniqueness of the individual on the one hand, and the materials, events, people, or circumstances of his life on the other.

Let me append some negative footnotes on this definition. It makes no distinction between "good" and "bad" creativity. One man may be discovering a way of relieving pain, whereas another is devising a new and more subtle form of torture for political prisoners. Both these actions seem to me creative, even though their social value is very different. Although I shall comment on these social valuations later, I have avoided putting them in my definition because they are so fluctuating. Galileo and Copernicus made creative discoveries which in their own day were evaluated as blasphemous and wicked, and in our day as basic and constructive. We do not want to cloud our definition with terms which rest in subjectivity.

Another way of looking at this same issue is to note that to be regarded historically as representing creativity, the product must be acceptable to some group at some point of time. This fact is not helpful to our definition, however, both because of the fluctuating valuations already mentioned and because many creative products have undoubtedly never been socially noticed, have disappeared without ever having been evaluated. So this concept of group acceptance is also omitted from our definition.

In addition, it should be pointed out that our definition makes no distinction regarding the degree of creativity, since this too is a value judgment extremely variable in nature. The action of the child inventing a new game with his playmates; Einstein formulating a theory of relativity; the housewife devising a new sauce for the meat; a young author writing his first novel; all of these are, in terms of our definition, creative, and there is no attempt to set them in some order of more or less creative.

THE MOTIVATION FOR CREATIVITY

The mainspring of creativity appears to be the same tendency which we discover so deeply as the curative force in psychotherapy—*man's tendency to actualize himself, to become his potentialities.* By this I mean the directional trend which is evident in all organic and human life—the urge to expand, extend, develop, mature—the tendency to express and activate all the capacities of the organism, to the extent that such activation enhances the organism or the self. This tendency may become deeply buried under layer after layer of encrusted psychological defenses; it may be hidden behind elaborate façades which deny its existence; it is my belief however, based on my experience, that it exists in every individual and awaits only the proper conditions to be released and expressed. It is this tendency which is the primary motivation for creativity as the organism forms new relationships to the environment in its endeavor most fully to be itself.

Let us now attempt to deal directly with this puzzling issue of the social value of a creative act. Presumably few of us are interested in facilitating creativity which is socially destructive. We do not wish, knowingly, to lend our efforts to developing individuals whose creative genius works itself out in new and better ways of robbing, exploiting, torturing, killing other individuals; or developing forms of political organization or art forms which lead humanity into paths of physical or psychological self-destruction. Yet how is it possible to make the necessary discriminations such that we may encourage a constructive creativity and not a destructive?

The distinction cannot be made by examining the product. The very essence of the creative is its novelty, and hence we have no standard by which to judge it. Indeed history points up the fact that the more original the product, and the more far-reaching its implications, the more likely it is to be judged by contemporaries as evil. The genuinely significant creation, whether an idea, or a work of art, or a scientific discovery, is most likely to be seen at first as erroneous, bad, or foolish. Later it may be seen as obvious, something self-evident to all. Only still later does it receive its final evaluation as a creative contribution. It seems clear that no contemporary mortal can satisfactorily evaluate a creative product at the time that it is formed, and this statement is increasingly true the greater the novelty of the creation.

Nor is it of any help to examine the purposes of the individual participating in the creative process. Many, perhaps most, of the creations and discoveries which have proved to have great social value, have been motivated by purposes having more to do with personal interests than with social value, while on the other hand history records a somewhat sorry outcome for many of those creations (various Utopias, Prohibition, etc.) which had as their avowed purpose the achievement of the social good. No, we must face the fact that the individual creates primarily because it is satisfying to him, because this behavior is felt to be self-actualizing, and we get nowhere by trying to differentiate "good" and "bad" purposes in the creative process.

Must we then give over any attempt to discriminate between creativity which is potentially constructive, and that which is potentially destructive? I do not believe this pessimistic conclusion is justified. It is here that recent clinical findings from the field of psychotherapy give us hope. It has been found that when the individual is "open" to all of his experience (a phrase which will be defined more fully), then his behavior will be creative, and his creativity may be trusted to be essentially constructive.

The differentiation may be put very briefly as follows. To the extent that the individual is denying to awareness (or repressing, if you prefer that term) large areas of his experience, then his creative formings may be pathological or socially evil, or both. To the degree that the individual is open to all aspects of his experience, and has available to his awareness all the varied sensings and perceivings which are going on within his organism, then the novel products of his interaction with his environment will tend to be constructive both for himself and others. To illustrate, an individual with paranoid tendencies may creatively develop a most novel theory of the relationship between himself and his environment, seeing evidence for his theory in all sorts of minute clues. His theory has little social value, perhaps because there is an enormous range of experience which this individual cannot permit in his awareness. Socrates, on the other hand, although also regarded as "crazy" by his contemporaries, developed novel ideas which have proven to be socially constructive. Very possibly this was because he was notably nondefensive and open to his experience.

The reasoning behind this will perhaps become more clear in the remaining sections of this paper. Primarily however it is based upon the discovery in psychotherapy:

> . . . that if we can add to the sensory and visceral experiencing which is characteristic of the whole animal kingdom the gift of a free and undistorted awareness of which only the human animal seems fully capable, we have an organism which is aware of the demands of the culture as it is of its own physiological demands for food or sex; which is just as aware of its desire for friendly relationships as it is of its desire to aggrandize itself; which is just as aware of its delicate and sensitive tenderness toward others as it is of its hostilities toward others. When man's unique capacity of awareness is thus functioning freely and fully, we find that we have, not an animal whom we must fear, not a beast who must be controlled, but an organism able to achieve, through the remarkable integrative capacity of its central nervous system, a balanced, realistic, self-enhancing, other-enhancing behavior as a resultant of all these elements of awareness. To put it another way, when man is less than fully man—when he denies to awareness various aspects of his experience—then indeed we have all too often reason to fear him and his behavior, as the present world situation testifies. But when he is most fully man, when he is his complete organism, when awareness of experience, that peculiarly human attribute, is most fully operating, then he is to be trusted, then his behavior is constructive. It is not always conventional. It will not always be conforming. It will be individualized. But it will also be socialized (Rogers, 1953).

THE INNER CONDITIONS OF CONSTRUCTIVE CREATIVITY

What are the conditions within the individual which are most closely associated with a potentially constructive creative act? I see these as possibilities.

A. *Openness to experience: extensionality.* This is the opposite of psychological defensiveness, when to protect the organization of the self certain experiences are prevented from coming into awareness except in distorted fashion. In a person who is open to experience each stimulus is freely relayed through the nervous system, without being distorted by any process of defensiveness. Whether the stimulus originates in the environment, in the impact of form, color, or sound, on the sensory nerves, or whether it originates in the viscera, or as a memory trace in the central nervous system, it is available to awareness. This means that instead of perceiving in predetermined categories (trees are green; college education is good; modern art is silly) the individual is aware of this existential moment as *it* is, thus being alive to many experiences which fall outside the usual categories (*this* tree is lavender; *this* college education is damaging; *this* modern sculpture has a powerful effect on me).

This last suggests another way of describing openness to experience. It means lack of rigidity and permeability of boundaries in concepts, beliefs, perceptions, and hypotheses. It means a tolerance for ambiguity where ambiguity exists. It means the ability to receive much conflicting information without forcing closure upon the situation. It means what the general semanticist calls the "extensional orientation."

This complete openness of awareness to what exists at this moment is, I believe, an important condition of constructive creativity. In an equally intense but more narrowly limited fashion it is no doubt present in all creativity. The deeply maladjusted artist who cannot recognize or be aware of the sources of unhappiness in himself may nevertheless be sharply and sensitively aware of form and color in his experience. The tyrant (whether on a petty or grand scale) who cannot face the weaknesses in himself may nevertheless be completely alive to and aware of the chinks in the psychological armor of those with whom he deals. Because there is the openness to one phase of experience, creativity is possible; because the openness is *only* to one phase of experience, the product of this creativity may be potentially destructive of social values. The more the individual has available to himself a sensitive awareness of all phases of his experience, the more sure we can be that his creativity will be personally and socially constructive.

B. *An internal locus of evaluation.* Perhaps the most fundamental condition of creativity is that the source or locus of evaluative judgment is internal. The value of his product is, for the creative person, established not by the praise or criticism of others, but by himself. Have I created something satisfying to *me?* Does it express a part of me—my feeling or my thought, my pain or my ecstasy? These are the only questions which really matter to the creative person, or to any person when he is being creative.

This does not mean that he is oblivious to, or unwilling to be aware of, the judgments of others. It is simply that the basis of evaluation lies within himself, in his own organismic reaction to and appraisal of his product. If to the person it has the "feel" of being "me in action," of being an actualization of potentialities in himself which heretofore have not existed and are now emerging into existence, then it is satisfying and creative, and no outside evaluation can change that fundamental fact.

C. *The ability to toy with elements and concepts.* Though this is probably less important than A or B, it seems to be a condition of creativity. Associated with the openness and lack of rigidity described under A is the ability to play spontaneously with ideas, colors, shapes, relationships—to juggle elements into impossible juxtapositions, to shape wild hypotheses, to make the given problematic, to express the ridiculous, to translate from one form to another, to transform into improbable equivalents. It is from this spontaneous toying and exploration that there arises the hunch, the creative seeing of life in a new and significant way. It is as though out of the wasteful spawning of thousands of possibilities there emerges one or two evolutionary forms with the qualities which give them a more permanent value.

THE CREATIVE ACT AND ITS CONCOMITANTS

When these three conditions obtain, constructive creativity will occur. But we cannot expect an accurate description of the creative act, for by its very nature it is indescribable. This is the unknown which we must recognize as unknowable until it occurs. This is the improbable that becomes probable. Only in a very general way can we say that a creative act is the natural behavior of an organism which has a tendency to arise when that organism is open to all of its inner and outer experiencing, and when it is free to try out in flexible fashion all manner of relationships. Out of this multitude of half-formed possibilities the organism, like a great computing machine, selects this one which most effectively meets an inner need, or that one which forms a more effective relationship with the environment, or this other one which discovers a more simple and satisfying order in which life may be perceived.

There is one quality of the creative act which may, however, be described. In almost all the products of creation we note a selectivity, or emphasis, an evidence of discipline, an attempt to bring out the essence. The artist paints surfaces or textures in simplified form, ignoring the minute variations which exist in reality. The scientist formulates a basic law of relationships, brushing aside all the particular events or circumstances which might conceal its naked beauty. The writer selects those words and phrases which give unity to his expression. We may say that this is the influence of the specific person, of the "I." Reality exists in a multiplicity of confusing facts, but "I" bring a structure to my relationship to reality; I have "my" way of perceiving reality, and it is this (unconsciously?) disciplined personal selectivity or abstraction which gives to creative products their esthetic quality.

Although this is as far as we can go in describing any aspect of the creative act, there are certain of its concomitants in the individual which may be mentioned. The first is what we may call the Eureka feeling—"This is *it!*" "I have discovered!" "This is what I wanted to express!"

Another concomitant is the anxiety of separateness.[1] I do not believe that many significantly creative products are formed without the feeling, "I am alone. No one has ever done just this before. I have ventured into territory where no one has been. Perhaps I am foolish, or wrong, or lost, or abnormal."

Still another experience which usually accompanies creativity is the desire to communicate. It is doubtful whether a human being can create, without wishing to share his creation. It is the only way he can assuage the anxiety of separateness and assure himself that he belongs to the group. He may confide his theories only to his private diary. He may put his discoveries in some cryptic code. He may conceal his poems in a locked drawer. He may put away his paintings in a closet. Yet he desires to communicate with a group which will understand him, even if he must imagine such a group. He does not create in order to communicate, but once having created he desires to share this new aspect of himself-in-relation-to-his-environment with others.

CONDITIONS FOSTERING CONSTRUCTIVE CREATIVITY

Thus far I have tried to describe the nature of creativity, to indicate that quality of individual experience which increases the likelihood that creativity will be constructive, to set forth the necessary conditions for the creative act and to state some of its concomitants. But if we are to make progress in meeting the social need which was presented initially, we must know whether constructive creativity can be fostered, and if so, how.

From the very nature of the inner conditions of creativity it is clear that they cannot be forced, but must be permitted to emerge. The farmer cannot make the germ develop and sprout from the seed; he can only supply the nurturing conditions which will permit the seed to develop its own potentialities. So it is with creativity. How can we establish the external conditions which will foster and nourish the internal conditions described above? My experience in psychotherapy leads me to believe that by setting up conditions of psychological safety and freedom, we maximize the likelihood of an emergence of constructive creativity. Let me spell out these conditions in some detail, labeling them as X and Y.

X. *Psychological Safety.* This may be established by three associated processes:

---

[1] For this and the idea in the following paragraph I am specifically indebted to my student and colleague, Mr. Robert Lipgar.

1. *Accepting the individual as of unconditional worth.* Whenever a teacher, parent, therapist, or other person with a facilitating function feels basically that this individual is of worth in his own right and in his own unfolding, no matter what his present condition or behavior, he is fostering creativity. This attitude can probably be genuine only when the teacher, parent, etc., senses the potentialities of the individual and thus is able to have an unconditional faith in him, no matter what his present state.

The effect on the individual as he apprehends this attitude is to sense a climate of safety. He gradually learns that he can be whatever he is, without sham or façade, since he seems to be regarded as of worth no matter what he does. Hence he has less need of rigidity, can discover what it means to be himself, can try to actualize himself in new and spontaneous ways. He is, in other words, moving toward creativity.

2. *Providing a climate in which external evaluation is absent.* When we cease to form judgments of the other individual from our own locus of evaluation, we are fostering creativity. For the individual to find himself in an atmosphere where he is not being evaluated, not being measured by some external standard, is enormously freeing. Evaluation is always a threat, always creates a need for defensiveness, always means that some portion of experience must be denied to awareness. If this product is evaluated as good by external standards, then I must not admit my own dislike of it. If what I am doing is bad by external standards, then I must not be aware of the fact that it seems to be me, to be part of myself. But if judgments based on external standards are not being made then I can be more open to my experience, can recognize my own likings and dislikings, the nature of the materials and of my reaction to them, more sharply and more sensitively. I can begin to recognize the locus of evaluation within myself. Hence I am moving toward creativity.

To allay some possible doubts and fears in the reader, it should be pointed out that to cease evaluating another is not to cease having reactions. It may, as a matter of fact, free one to react. "I don't like your idea" (or painting, or invention, or writing), is not an evaluation, but a reaction. It is subtly but sharply different from a judgment which says, "What you are doing is bad (or good), and this quality is assigned to you from some external source." The first statement permits the individual to maintain his own locus of evaluation. It holds the possibility that I am unable to appreciate something which is actually very good. The second statement, whether it praises or condemns, tends to put the person at the mercy of outside forces. He is being told that he cannot simply ask himself whether this product is a valid expression of himself; he must be concerned with what others think. He is being led away from creativity.

3. *Understanding empathically.* It is this which provides the ultimate in psychological safety, when added to the other two. If I say that I "accept" you, but know nothing of you, this is a shallow acceptance indeed, and you realize that it may change if I actually come to know you.

But if I understand you, empathically, see you and what you are feeling and doing from your point of view, enter your private world and see it as it appears to you—and still accept you—then this is safety indeed. In this climate you can permit your real self to emerge, and to express itself in varied and novel formings as it relates itself to the world. This is a basic fostering of creativity.

Y. *Psychological freedom.* When a teacher, parent, therapist, or other facilitating person permits the individual a complete freedom of symbolic expression, creativity is fostered. This permissiveness gives the individual complete freedom to think, to feel, to be, whatever is most inward within himself. It fosters the openness, and the playful and spontaneous juggling of percepts, concepts, and meanings, which is a part of creativity.

Note that it is complete freedom of *symbolic* expression which is described. To express in behavior all feelings, impulses, and formings may not in all instances be freeing. Behavior may in some instances be limited by society, and this is as it should be. But symbolic expression need not be limited. Thus, to destroy a hated object (whether one's mother or a rococo building) by destroying a symbol of it, is freeing. To attack it in reality may create guilt and narrow the psychological freedom which is experienced. (I feel unsure of this paragraph, but it is the best formulation I can give at the moment which seems to square with my experience.)

The permissiveness which is being described is not softness or indulgence or encouragement. It is permission to be *free,* which also means that one is responsible. The individual is as free to be afraid of a new venture as to be eager for it; free to bear the consequences of his mistakes as well as of his achievements. It is this type of freedom responsibly to be oneself which fosters the development of a secure locus of evaluation within oneself, and hence tends to bring about the inner conditions of constructive creativity. . . .

QUESTIONS FOR DISCUSSION

1) Do you agree with Rogers that there is a "desperate social need" for more creative behavior in our society? Explain.

2) Rogers' definition of creativity permits him to say that there is no "fundamental difference" between creating a new work of art or scientific theory and "devising new instruments of killing." Do you agree with this view? Explain.

3) Why do you think individuals make the effort to be creative? Taking the reverse of this, why do some individuals not make the effort?

4) Rogers stresses the need for psychological "openness to experience." Are there influences toward which unlimited openness is not desirable? For instance, what about openness to destructive ideas or pressures?

5) Summarize the conditions which, according to Rogers, guarantee psychological safety and freedom. Is it possible to provide children and adults with these conditions in everyday life? How often are people provided with them? Explain.

from
THE PRODUCTIVE ORIENTATION

Erich Fromm

From the time of classic and medieval literature up to the end of the nineteenth century a great deal of effort was expended in describing the vision of what the good man and the good society ought to be. Such ideas were expressed partly in the form of philosophical or theological treatises, partly in the form of utopias. The twentieth century is conspicuous for the absence of such visions. The emphasis is on critical analysis of man and society, in which positive visions of what man ought to be are only implied. While there is no doubt that this criticism is of utmost significance and a condition for any improvement of society, the absence of visions projecting a "better" man and a "better" society has had the effect of paralyzing man's faith in himself and his future (and is at the same time the result of such a paralysis).

Contemporary psychology and particularly psychoanalysis are no exception in this respect. Freud and his followers have given a splendid analysis of the neurotic character. Their clinical description of the nonproductive character (in Freud's terms, the pregenital character) is exhaustive and accurate—quite regardless of the fact that the theoretical concepts they used are in need of revision. But the character of the normal, mature, healthy personality has found scarcely any consideration. This character, called the genital character by Freud, has remained a rather vague and abstract concept. It is defined by him as the character structure of a person in whom the oral and anal libido has lost its dominant position and functions under the supremacy of genital sexuality, the aim of which is sexual union with a member of the opposite sex. The description of the genital character does not go far beyond the statement that it is the character structure of an individual who is capable of functioning well sexually and socially.

In discussing the *productive character* I venture beyond critical analysis and inquire into the nature of the fully developed character that is the aim of human development and simultaneously the ideal of humanistic ethics. It may serve as a preliminary approach to the concept of productive orientation to state its connection with Freud's genital character. Indeed, if we do not use Freud's term literally in the context of his libido theory but *symbolically,* it denotes quite accurately the meaning of productiveness. For the stage of sexual maturity is that in which man has the capacity of natural production; by the union of the sperm and the egg new life is produced. While this type of production is common to man and to animals, the capacity for material production is specific for man. Man is not only a rational and social animal. He can also be defined as a producing animal, capable of transforming the materials which he finds at hand, using his reason and imagination. Not only *can* he produce, he *must* produce in order to live. Material production, however, is but the most frequent symbol for productiveness as an aspect of character. The "productive orientation"[1] of personality refers to a fundamental attitude, a *mode of relatedness* in all realms of human experience. It covers mental, emotional, and sensory responses to others, to oneself, and to things. Productiveness is man's ability to use his powers and to realize the potentialities inherent in him. If we say *he* must use *his* powers we imply that he must be free and not dependent on someone who controls his powers. We imply, furthermore, that he is guided by reason, since he can make use of his powers only if he knows what they are, how to use them, and what to use them for. Productiveness means that he experiences himself as the embodiment of his powers and as the "actor"; that he feels himself one with his powers and at the same time that they are not masked and alienated from him.

In order to avoid the misunderstandings to which the term "productiveness" lends itself, it seems appropriate to discuss briefly what is not meant by productiveness.

Generally the word "productiveness" is associated with creativeness, particularly artistic creativeness. The real artist, indeed, is the most convincing representative of productiveness. But not all artists are productive; a conventional painting, e.g., may exhibit nothing more than the technical skill to reproduce the likeness of a person in photographic fashion on a canvas. But a person can experience, see, feel, and think productively without having the gift to create something visible or communicable. *Productiveness is an attitude which every human being is capable of, unless he is mentally and emotionally crippled.*

The term "productive" is also apt to be confused with "active," and "productiveness" with "activity." While the two terms can be synonymous (for instance, in Aristotle's concept of activity), activity in modern usage frequently indicates the very opposite of productiveness. Activity is usually defined as behavior which brings about a change in an existing situation by an expenditure of energy. In contrast, a person is described as passive if he is unable to change or overtly influence an existing situation and is influenced or moved by forces outside himself. This current concept of activity takes into account only the actual expenditure of energy and the

---

[1] Productiveness as used in this book is meant as an expansion of the concept of spontaneity described in *Escape from Freedom*.

change brought about by it. It does not distinguish between the underlying psychic conditions governing the activities.

An example, though an extreme one, of nonproductive activity is the activity of a person under hypnosis. The person in a deep hypnotic trance may have his eyes open, may walk, talk, and do things; he "acts." The general definition of activity would apply to him, since energy is spent and some change brought about. But if we consider the particular character and quality of this activity, we find that it is not really the hypnotized person who is the actor, but the hypnotist who, by means of his suggestions, acts through him. While the hypnotic trance is an artificial state, it is an extreme but characteristic example of a situation in which a person can be active and yet not be the true actor, his activity resulting from compelling forces over which he has no control.

A common type of nonproductive activity is the reaction to anxiety, whether acute or chronic, conscious or unconscious, which is frequently at the root of the frantic preoccupations of men today. Different from anxiety-motivated activity, though often blended with it, is the type of activity based on submission to or dependence on an authority. The authority may be feared, admired, or "loved"—usually all three are mixed—but the cause of the activity is the command of the authority, both in a formal way and with regard to its contents. The person is active because the authority wants him to be, and he does what the authority wants him to do. This kind of activity is found in the authoritarian character. To him activity means to act in the name of something higher than his own self. He can act in the name of God, the past, or duty, but not in the name of himself. The authoritarian character receives the impulse to act from a superior power which is neither assailable nor changeable, and is consequently unable to heed spontaneous impulses from within himself.[2]

Resembling submissive activity is automaton activity. Here we do not find dependence on overt authority, but rather on anonymous authority as it is represented by public opinion, culture patterns, common sense, or "science." The person feels or does what he is supposed to feel or do; his activity lacks spontaneity in the sense that it does not originate from his own mental or emotional experience but from an outside source.

Among the most powerful sources of activity are irrational passions. The person who is driven by stinginess, masochism, envy, jealousy, and all other forms of greed is compelled to act; yet his actions are neither free nor rational but in opposition to reason and to his interests as a human being. A person so obsessed repeats himself, becoming more and more stereotyped. He is active, but he is not productive.

---

[2] But the authoritarian character does not only tend to submit but also wishes to dominate others. In fact, both the sadistic and the masochistic sides are always present, and they differ only in degree of their strength and their repression respectively. (See the discussion of the authoritarian character in *Escape from Freedom*, pp. 141 ff.)

Although the source of these activities is irrational and the acting persons are neither free nor rational, there can be important practical results, often leading to material success. In the concept of productiveness we are not concerned with activity *necessarily* leading to practical results but with an attitude, with a mode of reaction and orientation toward the world and oneself in the process of living. We are concerned with *man's character, not with his success.*[3]

Productiveness is man's realization of the potentialities characteristic of him, the use of his *powers*. But what is "power"? It is rather ironical that this word denotes two contradictory concepts: *power of* = capacity and *power over* = domination. This contradiction, however, is of a particular kind. Power = domination results from the paralysis of power = capacity. *"Power over" is the perversion of "power to."* The ability of man to make productive use of his powers is his potency; the inability is his impotence. With his power of reason he can penetrate the surface of phenomena and understand their essence. With his power of love he can break through the wall which separates one person from another. With his power of imagination he can visualize things not yet existing; he can plan and thus begin to create. Where potency is lacking, man's relatedness to the world is perverted into a desire to dominate, to exert power over others as though they were things. Domination is coupled with death, potency with life. Domination springs from impotence and in turn reinforces it, for if an individual can force somebody else to serve him, his own need to be productive is increasingly paralyzed.

How is man related to the world when he uses his powers productively?

The world outside oneself can be experienced in two ways: *reproductively* by perceiving actuality in the same fashion as a film makes a literal record of things photographed (although even mere reproductive perception requires the active participation of the mind); and *generatively* by conceiving it, by enlivening and re-creating this new material through the spontaneous activity of one's own mental and emotional powers. While to a certain extent everyone does react in both ways, the respective weight of each kind of experience differs widely. Sometimes either one of the two is atrophied, and the study of these extreme cases in which the reproductive or the generative mode is almost absent offers the best approach to the understanding of each of these phenomena.

The relative atrophy of the generative capacity is very frequent in

[3] An interesting although incomplete attempt to analyze productive thinking is Max Wertheimer's posthumously published work, *Productive Thinking* (New York: Harper & Brothers, 1945). Some of the aspects of productiveness are dealt with by Munsterberg, Natorp, Bergson, and James; in Brentano's and Husserl's analysis of the psychic "act"; in Dilthey's analysis of artistic production and in O. Schwarz, *Medizinische Anthropologie* (Leipzig: Hirzel, 1929), pp. iii ff. In all these works, however, the problem is not treated in relation to character.

our culture. A person may be able to recognize things as they are (or as his culture maintains them to be), but he is unable to enliven his perception from within. Such a person is the perfect "realist," who sees all there is to be seen of the surface features of phenomena but who is quite incapable of penetrating below the surface to the essential, and of visualizing what is not yet apparent. He sees the details but not the whole, the trees but not the forest. Reality to him is only the sum total of what has already materialized. This person is not lacking in imagination, but his is a calculating imagination, combining factors all of which are known and in existence, and inferring their future operation.

On the other hand, the person who has lost the capacity to perceive actuality is insane. The psychotic person builds up an inner world of reality in which he seems to have full confidence; he lives in his own world, and the common factors of reality as perceived by all men are unreal to him. When a person sees objects which do not exist in reality but are entirely the product of his imagination, he has hallucinations; he interprets events in terms of his own feelings, without reference to, or at least without proper acknowledgment of, what goes on in reality. A paranoid person may believe that he is being persecuted, and a chance remark may indicate a plan to humiliate and ruin him. He is convinced that the lack of any more obvious and explicit manifestation of such intention does not prove anything; that, although the remark may appear harmless on the surface, its real meaning becomes clear if one looks "deeper." For the psychotic person actual reality is wiped out and an inner reality has taken its place.

The "realist" sees only the surface features of things; he sees the manifest world, he can reproduce it photographically in his mind, and he can act by manipulating things and people as they appear in this picture. The insane person is incapable of seeing reality as it is; he perceives reality only as a symbol and a reflection of his inner world. Both are sick. The sickness of the psychotic who has lost contact with reality is such that he cannot function socially. The sickness of the "realist" impoverishes him as a human being. While he is not incapacitated in his social functioning, his view of reality is so distorted because of its lack of depth and perspective that he is apt to err when more than manipulation of immediately given data and short-range aims are involved. *"Realism" seems to be the very opposite of insanity and yet it is only its complement.*

The true opposite of both "realism" and insanity is productiveness. The normal human being is capable of relating himself to the world simultaneously by perceiving it as it is and by conceiving it enlivened and enriched by his own powers. If one of the two capacities is atrophied, man is sick; but the normal person has both capacities even though their respective weights differ. The presence of both reproductive and generative capacities is a precondition for productiveness; they are opposite poles whose interaction is the dynamic source of productiveness. With the last statement I want to emphasize that productiveness is not the sum or combination of both capacities but that it is something new which springs from this interaction.

We have described productiveness as a particular mode of relatedness to the world. The question arises whether there is anything which the productive person *produces* and if so, what? While it is true that man's productiveness can create material things, works of art, and systems of thought, *by far the most important object of productiveness is man himself.*

Birth is only one particular step in a continuum which begins with conception and ends with death. All that is between these two poles is a process of giving birth to one's potentialities, of bringing to life all that is potentially given in the two cells. But while physical growth proceeds by itself, if only the proper conditions are given, the process of birth on the mental plane, in contrast, does not occur automatically. It requires productive activity to give life to the emotional and intellectual potentialities of man, to give birth to his self. It is part of the tragedy of the human situation that the development of the self is never completed; even under the best conditions only part of man's potentialities is realized. Man always dies before he is fully born. . . .

QUESTIONS FOR DISCUSSION

1) In this selection, Fromm is concerned with a concept of creativity in which the chief result or object is oneself. What is "the productive orientation," and what powers in himself must a person utilize to achieve it?

2) What is the difference between "productiveness" and "activity"? What are some common forms of nonproductive activity in our society?

3) What are the traits of "the authoritarian character"? Fromm labels the desire to dominate others as "impotence." Do you agree? Explain.

4) Why is "productiveness" the opposite of both "realism" and insanity? Discuss.

CREATIVITY AS INTRA- AND INTER-PERSONAL PROCESS

Morris I. Stein

Let us start with a definition. The creative work is a novel work that is accepted as tenable or useful or satisfying by a significant group of others at some point in time.

By "novel" I mean that the creative product did not exist previously in precisely the same form. It stems from a *reintegration* of already existing materials or knowledge, but when it is completed, it contains elements that are new. The novelty of the work depends on the degree to which it deviates from that which exists. It is a measure of the distance between what has been achieved and what existed previously.

While novelty is a critical feature of creativity, if we attend solely to it we overlook the fact that creativity is not a single act but a *process*. Creativity results from both intra-personal[1] and inter-personal processes. It is the purpose of this paper to comment on several characteristics of the dynamic factors involved in both areas.

The stages of the creative process as they manifest themselves or as they have been inferred from behavior have been described in various ways. Some attend to the development of ideas and others concern themselves more with the individual's personality characteristics that are correlated with these developments. Both are involved in what I have called the intra-personal aspects of the creative process.

Wallas (1926) was one of the first to describe the processes involved in the development of creative ideas in terms which are now rather well known. For Wallas the creative process consists of the following stages: (a) Preparation—the stage in which the problem is investigated from all directions; (b) Incubation—the stage during which the individual is not consciously thinking about the problem; (c) Illumination—the stage during which the "happy idea" occurs, together with the psychological factors that immediately preceded and accompanied its appearance; (d) Verification—in which the validity of the idea is tested, and the idea is reduced to exact form. The psychoanalyst Kris (1952, 1953) described the process

---

[1] The psychological and psychiatric literature on this topic is summarized by Stein and Heinze (1960) in *Creativity and the Individual*.

as consisting of two major phases, inspiration and elaboration. During the inspiration phase the creative individual is described as "driven; he is in an exceptional state. Thoughts or images tend to flow, things appear in his mind of which he never seemed to have known." The second phase, elaboration, is characterized by labor, concentration and endeavor. Reichenbach, (1938) the philosopher, distinguished between the context of discovery and the context of justification to differentiate between "the thinker's way of finding [his] theorem and his way of presenting it before a public." I prefer to describe the creative process as consisting of three major phases, hypothesis formation, hypothesis testing and the communication of results, which will be further elaborated on in the course of this paper. Whether authors use "stages" or synonymous terms to describe the creative process they acknowledge the fact that the characteristics of the process are not separate or distinct but they overlap.

What are the personality and other psychological characteristics that the individual manifests as he proceeds through the course of the creative process? In the early stages of the process, the individual experiences a state of disequilibrium. One might say that homeostasis has been disturbed, that there is a lack of closure or that there is a lack of satisfaction with the existing state of affairs. The creative individual may actively seek to disturb the equilibrium he previously attained or he may be responsive to disequilibria already existing in the environment. Creativity may be initiated through an active or a reactive process. On studying the individual one might learn those historical factors or present needs and personality characteristics which are related to his motivation to seek new levels of equilibria or which predisposed him or sensitized him to the lack of closure in his present environment.

The creative individual also has the capacity to *tolerate ambiguity* (Frenkel-Brunswik, 1949). He has the capacity to exist in a state in which he does not comprehend all that he perceives or feels. Nevertheless, he continues to seek resolution of the problem confronting him. Some persons find this lack of structure intolerable and when they experience it they become too anxious for constructive work. They either retreat from the ambiguity or they impulsively grasp hold of any means that provides them with structure.

The creative individual possesses permeable boundaries between the regions within the self. This permeability is related to his capacity for developing a series of hypotheses for future testing. Just as there needs to be communication between the individual and his environment to initiate the creative process so there needs to be communication between the inner personal regions if the creative process is to be continued. This permeability may be self-induced by a process that the psychoanalysts call "regression in the service of the ego" (Hartmann, 1958), by selecting specific working environments, by taking drugs, drinking liquor, or it may occur when the person is distracted or devoting himself to activities other than those that are specifically relevant to his creative work.[2]

The inner personal regions that are permeable vary with the nature of the work. For one person, it may involve flexibility in the intellectual sphere, while for another, it may involve greater flexibility in the emotional or affective sphere. These are relative statements, since for creativity in all areas interaction between both intellect and affect is vital. Rigidity in one sphere may well impede developments in the other and sidetrack the creative process. The significance of this interaction and some of its hazards are well illustrated in Schiller's response to a friend who complained of his lack of creative power. To this friend Schiller said:

> *The reason for your complaint lies, it seems to me, in the constraint which your intellect imposes upon your imagination. Here I will make an observation, and illustrate it by an allegory. Apparently, it is not good—and indeed it hinders the creative work of the mind—if the intellect examines too closely the ideas already pouring in, as it were, at the gates. Regarded in isolation, an idea may be quite insignificant, and venturesome in the extreme, but it may acquire importance from an idea which follows it; perhaps, in a certain collocation with other ideas, which may seem equally absurd, it may be capable of furnishing a very serviceable link. The intellect cannot judge all these ideas unless it can retain them until it has considered them in connection with these other ideas. In the case of a creative mind, it seems to me, the intellect has withdrawn its watchers from the gates, and the ideas rush in pell-mell, and only then does it review and inspect the multitude. You worthy critics, or whatever you may call yourselves, are ashamed or afraid of the momentary and passing madness which is found in all creators, the longer or shorter duration of which distinguishes the thinking artist from the*

---

[2] Creative individuals have utilized a variety of such techniques. Levey (1940) reports that ". . . in order to produce a state of inspiration, Schiller kept rotten apples in his desk; Shelley and Rousseau remained bareheaded in the sunshine; Bossuet worked in a cold room with his head wrapped in furs; Milton, Descartes, Leibniz and Rossini lay stretched out; Tycho Brahe and Leibniz secluded themselves for very long periods, Thoreau built his hermitage, Proust worked in a cork-lined room, Carlyle in a noise-proof chamber, and Balzac wore a monkish working garb; Grétry and Schiller immersed their feet in ice-cold water; Guido Reni could paint, and de Musset could write poetry, only when dressed in magnificent style; Mozart, following exercise; Lamennais, in a room of shadowy darkness, and D'Annunzio, Farnol and Frost only at night. The aesthetician, Baumgarten, advised poets seeking inspiration to ride on horseback, to drink wine in moderation, and, provided they were chaste, to look at beautiful women."

> *dreamer. Hence your complaints of unfruitfulness, for you reject too soon and discriminate too severely. (Freud, 1938)*

The "momentary and passing madness" that Schiller speaks of is, I believe, a function of the permeability of the boundaries in the inner personal regions that are usually blocked from consciousness. Its intensity is likely correlated with the depth to which the experience goes. It is out of this experience that new structures and new directions are developed. As Zervos, in discussing Picasso's creative process, says:

> *His only wish has been desperately to be himself; in fact, he acts according to suggestions which come to him from beyond his own limits. He sees descending upon him a superior order of exigencies, he has a very clear impression that something compels him imperiously to empty his spirit of all that he has only just discovered, even before he has been able to control it, so that he can admit other suggestions. Hence his torturing doubts. But this anguish is not a misfortune for Picasso. It is just this which enables him to break down all his barriers, leaving the field of the possible free to him, and opening up to him the perspectives of the unknown. (Read, 1948)*

The number and variety of hypotheses that the creative individual entertains may give one the impression that the process is haphazard or disorganized. As one studies these hypotheses, however, one discovers common threads. One also finds that the creative individual, oriented toward the future, himself senses a feeling of direction and possesses some conception of the characteristics of the final product he is seeking. The hypotheses do not come forth in a logical and systematic fashion. Logic and systematization occur later. Einstein's thought processes while working on the theory of relativity are an example of what I have in mind.

> *Before the discovery that the crucial point, the solution, lay in the concept of time, more particularly in that of simultaneity, axioms played no role in the thought process—of this Einstein is sure. (The very moment he saw the gap, and realized the relevance of simultaneity, he knew this to be the crucial point for the solution.) But even afterward, the final five weeks, it was not the axioms that came first. "No really productive man thinks in such a paper fashion," said Einstein. (Wertheimer, 1945)*

Later, he added:

> *"During all those years there was a feeling of direction,*
> *of going straight toward something concrete. It is, of*
> *course, very hard to express that feeling in words; but it*
> *was decidedly the case, and clearly to be distinguished*
> *from later considerations about the rational form of the*
> *solution. Of course, behind such a direction there is always*
> *something logical; but I have it in a kind of survey, in a*
> *way visually." (Wertheimer, 1945)*

During the course of the creative process, the individual may experience depression, anxiety, feelings of inadequacy, etc. These feelings may have many sources. They may arise as consequences of momentary lack of direction. They may arise from the individual's inability to communicate his ideas to others. Or, they may be related to the relaxation of inner personal regions which permitted old unresolved tensions, residues of previous life experiences wherein the individual also felt inadequate, to come to the surface and to impinge upon his consciousness. Recollection of these earlier experiences reinforces the existing feelings. For the creative individual, this is only one point in a sequence of events, for he somehow overcomes these problems; but for others it may spell the end of the creative process.

After the development of various hypotheses, the creative process continues with the testing of hypotheses. It may involve the construction of practical models, long periods of observation and experimentation. In any event it involves a shift in attitude and behavior from that which was characteristic of the initial stages of the creative process. Initially, criticism and evaluation may have been absent for the most part. But, as the creative process proceeds they play more significant roles. They give form and substance to ideas, ". . . fantasy becomes art only when it is externalized and controlled by the responsible, realistic, and logical ego . . . imagination must submit its work to the scrutiny of the critical faculties. The artistry lies in the care and judgment with which the critical task is performed, as much as in the richness of the creative materials available for criticism. Without both, the work is either as formless and unintelligible as the so-called 'art' of the insane, or as mechanical and superficial as the formulas of the skillful hack." (Kaplan, 1957)

During the time that criticism and evaluation are characteristic of the creative process, the creative individual assumes a new role. In addition to creator he is also audience. Psychologically, and at times physically when the artist stands back from his canvas or when the scientist takes a "second look" at his experiment, he distances himself from what he has done and observes and considers whether what he has said communicates what he intended. In so doing he represents not only himself but also the larger audience with whom he will be communicating and it is here that the inter-personal aspects of the creative process become evident. Communication with the self alone is insufficient for it may be too idiosyncratic and may have no significance and meaning to other persons. Individuals may think of all sorts of novel ideas, but unless they can communicate these in a way acceptable to others they have no significance as creative contributions. As Freud (1931) has said,

> *The hysteric is undoubtedly a poet, though he represents his phantasies essentially by mimicry, without considering whether other people understand them or not. The ceremonials and prohibitions of obsessional patients force us to conclude that they have created a private religion for themselves; and even the delusions of the paranoiac show an unwelcome external similarity and inner relationship to the systems of our philosophers. We cannot get away from the impression that patients are making, in an asocial manner, the same attempts at a solution of their conflicts and an appeasement of their urgent desires which, when carried out in a manner acceptable to a large number of persons, are called poetry, religion and philosophy.*

In the process of communicating with others the creative person also eliminates the difficulties he experienced in the course of arriving at his final product. The audience is not expected to re-experience all the problems and difficulties that were involved in arriving at the final product.

Einstein, for example, said:

> *The way the two triple sets of axioms are contrasted in the Einstein-Infeld book is not at all the way things happened in the process of actual thinking. This was merely a later formulation of the subject matter, just a question of how the thing could afterwards best be written. The axioms express essentials in a condensed form. Once one has found such things one enjoys formulating them in that way; but in this process they did not grow out of any manipulation of axioms. (Wertheimer, 1945)*

It should be indicated that at times the creative person may present his work so well to others after his evaluation that they may regard it as "obvious," "simple," and wonder why they never thought of it. But as John Milton said, "so easy it seemed/ Once found, which yet unfound most would have thought/ Impossible!"

On completion of the creative product, the creative individual experiences a feeling of satisfaction with the final work. He has a feeling of exhilaration, part of which is related to the release of previously pent-up feelings and part of which is related to the aesthetic experience of having developed the good gestalt, the good form, in the final product. The experience at this time also reflects the goodness of fit, the "oneness," between the creative individual and that which he has created.

The fact that the individual has completed his work does not mean that the total creative process is at an end. To complete the creative process the final product, as was suggested previously, *needs* to be presented to and accepted by a group of significant *others* as tenable, useful or satisfying. The terms "tenable," "useful," and "satisfying" were selected to cover the areas of ideas, objects, and aesthetic experiences respectively. The phrase "significant group of others" refers to a formally or informally organized group of persons which is recognized as capable of evaluating developments in its own field. The size and composition of the group may vary. At times it may consist only of a small group on the "left bank," Greenwich Village, or the small number of persons who first gathered around Freud and Einstein. At other times it may include a large segment of society or all of society. The smaller groups, which may be called "psyche" groups, provide the individual with feedback so that he can clarify or alter his work and make better progress in the future. They also serve as filters for the broader society.

In a complex society there are groups of "intermediaries" who stand between the creative individual and the broader society. The intermediaries consist of members of scientific and professional organizations but also art critics, drama critics, curators of museums, literary agents, committees that make research grants, etc. They play critical roles in the creative process as I have conceived of it here. On the one hand, they provide the creative individual with a studied evaluation of the work from which he might profit. On the other hand, they also serve as selective filters by virtue of the fact that their evaluations do at times provide some individuals with recognition for what they have done while others are not so reinforced. Some intermediaries are also shapers of public opinion and while the acceptance by the large audience is more relevant to popularity than creativity there are instances where the lack of popular support may adversely affect an individual's future opportunities and progress. Relatively little systematic work has been done on the role of the intermediaries in the creative process, the potency of their positions and factors related to and affecting their decision-making processes. Much of what is known in this area is largely anecdotal.

When the final product has been accepted as tenable, useful, or satisfying by a group of significant others, it provides the creative individual with significant psychological feedback. By accepting the product and by regarding it as creative the group indicates that it accepts and implicitly approves of the needs which initially motivated the creative person to deviate from accepted patterns and to probe the unknown. In the process of accepting the creative product the group manifests similarity and identification between its own wishes and those of the creative individual (Lee, 1950; Sachs, 1951) and that it has, in a sense, joined the individual in the creative process and become co-creator (Kris, 1952). For the group the creative product has fulfilled or given expression to certain needs. The creative product "says" things that the group has wanted to say but has been unable to. The creative product may also give new direction to the experience and behavior of the group.

We come now to the last part of our definition, that the creative product is "accepted at some point in time." The historical point of view reflected by this phrase is to call attention to the fact that societies and their values undergo change. Consequently their criteria for what they regard as creative will also change. It suggests that there is no "absolute" definition of creativity and what is regarded as creative at any one point in time is a function of many factors operative in the society. It also focuses our attention on social forces for understanding why some individuals were not regarded as creative in their own lifetimes but had to be discovered at some later date.

My discussion to this point has concerned itself primarily with sketching the creative process as it begins with the individual and as it culminates with a communication to a group. Before closing I would like to discuss several additional interpersonal factors involved in the creative process, focusing my attention now on the society or culture in which it occurs.

If what was said above regarding the sensitivity of the creative individual to his external and internal environments is valid, then it may be said that a culture fosters creativity to the extent that it provides an individual with the opportunity to experience its many facets. A culture that limits a person's freedom to work, study, or experience one or more of its features restricts his opportunity for exposure to the gaps that exist, keeps him from learning the necessary media through which he might communicate his feelings and ideas to others and consequently decreases the probability of creative contributions.

A culture fosters creativity to the extent that it encourages openness to internal and external experience. Orientations that result in rigid inner personal boundaries and that lead to passivity and the expectation that ready-made solutions are available for new problems hamper creativity. Creativity depends on autonomy and independent inquiry.

Society also encourages creativity to the extent that its value system includes a positive regard for change and novelty. And, it discourages creativity to the extent that social pressures to conformity are so intense that deviations are punished directly or indirectly through social isolation and ostracism. Similarly creativity is fostered by affording creative individuals high status and by rewarding them in a fashion congruent with their pursuits and not in a manner that may cause them to leave their specific lines of endeavor. In so doing creative individuals are encouraged to continue their inquiries and they become models to younger generations as they embark on their own developments.

These are some of the ways in which the society provides an atmosphere for creativity. And it is through some combination of this atmosphere and individuals who are capable of embarking on the intra-personal aspects of the creative process that novel developments occur. Creativity, in the final analysis, is a function of the transactional relationships between the individual and the environment in which he lives.

REFERENCES

FRENKEL-BRUNSWIK, ELSA, "Intolerance of Ambiguity as an Emotional and Perceptual Personality Variable," in J. S. Bruner and D. Krech, eds., *Perception and Personality,* Durham, Duke Univ. Press, 1949.

FREUD, S., *The Basic Writings of Sigmund Freud,* ed. by A. A. Brill, New York, Random House, 1938.

FREUD, S., Preface to T. Reik, *Ritual—Psychoanalytic Studies,* London, Hogarth Press, 1931.

HARTMANN, H., *Ego Psychology and the Problems of Adaptation,* New York, International Univ. Press, 1958.

KAPLAN, A., "Freud and Modern Philosophy," in B. Nelson, ed., *Freud and the 20th Century,* New York, Meridian Books, 1957.

KRIS, E., *Psychoanalytic Explorations in Art,* New York, International Univ. Press, 1952.

KRIS, E., "Psychoanalysis and the Study of Creative Imagination," *Bull. New York Acad. Med.,* Vol. XXIX, 1953, pp. 334–351.

LEE, H. B., "The Values of Order and Vitality in Art," in G. Róheim, ed., *Psychoanalysis and the Social Sciences,* New York, International Univ. Press, 1958, Vol. II.

LEVEY, H. B., "A Theory Concerning Free Creation in the Inventive Arts," *Psychiatry,* Vol. III, 1940, pp. 229–293.

READ, H., *Art Now,* New York, Pitman Publ. Co., 1948.

REICHENBACH, H., *Experience and Prediction,* Chicago, Univ. of Chicago Press, 1938.

SACHS, H., *The Creative Unconscious,* 2nd ed., Cambridge, Sci-Art Publishers, 1951.

STEIN, M. I., and HEINZE, SHIRLEY J., *Creativity and the Individual,* Chicago, Free Press, 1960.

WALLAS, G., *The Art of Thought,* New York, Harcourt, Brace, 1926.

WERTHEIMER, M., *Productive Thinking,* New York, Harper & Bros., 1945.

QUESTIONS FOR DISCUSSION

1) The standard terms for the stages of the creative process are those of Wallas. Stein cites these: a) Preparation, b) Incubation, c) Illumination, d) Verification. How different are Stein's own terms? Are they an improvement? Discuss.

2) Name some of Stein's "personality and other psychological requirements" for the artist. Compare these to the ones set forth by Rogers.

3) The focus in this article is not on creativity as an attitude but as the production of something new which can be recognized and accepted or rejected by others. One of Stein's main ideas is that creation of something involves not only the individual operating as a single unit, but also the interaction of the individual with "significant others." What is the meaning of this last term? Do you agree that Stein's last stage, the presentation of the product to a group, should be counted as part of the creative process? What are Stein's reasons for this inclusion?

4) What are the ways in which a culture may encourage creative activity? (See Rogers and Alamshah for additional favoring factors.) How well does our culture do in these matters? Does it seem to value some forms of creativity more than others, perhaps overvaluing some, undervaluing others? Explain.

THE CONDITIONS FOR CREATIVITY

William H. Alamshah

Much has been written on the process of creativity (often described as preparation, incubation, illumination, and verification). In addition, those who have concerned themselves with this aspect of creativity have attempted to view this process *as a whole*.[1] Similar claims cannot be made regarding the *conditions* necessary for creativity: not a great deal has been written on this aspect of the problem, nor have there been attempts to view it *as a whole*.[2] I will try here (a) to discuss those conditions that may be necessary if creativity is to manifest itself, and (b) to do this in a general but nonetheless inclusive manner. The conditions relevant to creativity, in general, may be identified as (1) motivation; (2) self-limitation; (3) receptivity (or what Carl Rogers calls "openness"); and (4) competence.

THE CONDITION CALLED MOTIVATION

When we speak of having the motivation for creativity we may have in mind something *inherent* in human beings, or, something that has to be *acquired*. The inherent motivation for creativity consists of various needs; these may be identified, on the one hand, as *security* needs and, on the other hand, those that might be called *cultural*.

Security and Cultural Needs

The security needs refer to biological tensions natural to us (classified often as sensory, activity, and visceral), as well as various psychological tensions inherent in our makeup (conceived here as the need to belong, the need to be loved, the need to be important, the need to believe in

---

[1] Cf. the ideas of such writers as Helmholtz, Wallas, Young (J. W.), Rossman (Joseph), and Osborn (Alex).

[2] Lyman Bryson, Margaret Mead, Rudolf Arnheim, Milton Nahm, in discussing "The Conditions of Creativity" (*The Creative Mind*, J. D. Sommerfeld, New York: Russell & Russell, 1964, p. 105 f.) argue that two such conditions are (1) freedom and (2) "whatever is truly creative must come out of the experience of the creator"; Maslow mentions "mental health"; Haefele refers to the "encouragement to be spontaneous" and "to express one's self," permissiveness, and selectivity, as conditions which tend to sponsor creativity; Rogers (Carl) speaks of "openness to experience," the willingness to act as the "internal focus of evaluation," and the "ability to toy with elements and concepts"; but these, and other references that could be cited, do not appear as *systematic* approaches to the conditions of creativity.

something or someone, and the need to be productive of various personal or group valuings). The cultural needs may be identified as the need to understand, the need to love, and the need for beauty. Granting the existence of such needs (and we are not arguing here for their existence as something inherent) they can and do serve as motivations for creativity.[3]

Acquired Motivation and Creativity

Motivation, however, may also be *acquired*. Such motivation is, indeed, complex and varied. It may be neuropsychic in nature, which means that one can acquire various traits and attitudes essential for creativity (industriousness, persistence, adventurousness, independence).[4] It may mean the adoption and internationalization of some social or institutional role (parent, friend, "elder statesman," etc.). It may mean the acquisition of a certain office. (J. F. Kennedy once said he wanted the Presidency because he could do more *creatively* if he had it.) Or, finally, it may mean the acquisition of a certain type of character. Pavlov's remark that it takes a "dedicated character" to carry on the work of creativity is to the point here; as is Frank Barron's contention that creativity requires an individual who is "willing to stake his life on the meaning of his work."[5] Acquired motivation can involve the acquisition and internalization of any *one* or *all* of these personality characteristics or social structures. Any or all of these may be said to be significant for, and essential to, creativity.

Motivational Push and Pull

These two general types of motivation relate to each other in a dynamic and complementary manner. The inherent motivations (the needs) may be said to provide the "push" toward creativity, while the acquired motivations provide the "pull." For example, one who thinks of being creative in the field of art is indulging in that type of thinking called "fanciful" if he does not possess the minimal "push" that comes from strong sensory needs and the need for beauty, as well as the "pull"

---

[3] On the negative side, L. Kubie (*Neurotic Distortion and the Creative Process*, Kansas University Press, 1958) refers to distortions which enter into creative thinking from *"unconscious* needs and purposes." (p. 32).

[4] R. S. Crutchfield ("The Creative Process," Berkeley: University of California Press, 1962, Part VI, p. 14) identifies various "cognitive capacities," "distinctive approaches," and "emotional and motivational dispositions" as *"common* characteristics of creative persons"; see also Anne Roe, ("The Psychology of the Scientist," *The New Scientist*, P. C. Obler and H. A. Estrin, (eds.), p. 90 f., New York: Doubleday, 1962) for "personality traits" attributed to creative scientists.

[5] *The Creative Person*, Berkeley: University of California, 1961, Part II, p. 9.

that may be identified with such acquired motivations as a craving for the "solitary life," that "great love of people and things" (of which Ben Shahn speaks),[6] or the "dedication" (which Pavlov mentions) to things aesthetic. These motivations, inherent and acquired, can function in a complementary fashion to furnish the adequate "push" and "pull" required for artistic creativity.

FURTHER RESEARCH NEEDED IN MOTIVATION

There are, of course, a number of problems (not yet resolved) in comprehending this first condition for creativity: some researchers do not even acknowledge the existence of those inherent motivations (needs) of which we have spoken. If such be the case, what, it may be asked, constitutes sufficient *acquired* motivations necessary for creativity? Again, regarding acquired motivation, there is some general agreement that creative activity requires adventurousness, independence, sensitivity (certain *traits*),[7] and, certain *attitudes,* such as a willingness to take risks (McClelland), or a high tolerance for ambiguity and complexity. Are these *all* of the traits and attitudes necessary for creativity? What part, if any, could the *acquisition and internalization of an "office"* (editor, manager, director) play as acquired motivation for creativity? Again, is the acquisition of a certain type of *character* relevant as acquired motivation for creativity? If any, or all, of these acquired characteristics are relevant as conditional factors in motivation, how can we induce or encourage individuals to acquire them? These and other problems seem pertinent to the whole question of motivation.

THE CONDITION OF SELF-LIMITATION

This demand or requirement for creativity is little discussed. But the logic for its inclusion as a necessary condition for creativity is both clear and cogent. Creativity requires time; humans do not have unlimited time; hence, the necessity to *limit* our creative activity to that area (or areas) toward which our talents and energies, our valuing system, our character, and our goals or purposes propel us.

---

[6] "The Biography of a Painting," *Creativity in the Arts,* Englewood Cliffs, N.J.: Prentice-Hall, 1964, p. 28.
[7] Although I. A. Taylor asserts that creative people exhibit *contradictory* traits (humorous—serious, attentive—non-attentive, industrious—lazy, etc.). That is, the creative person is "not a composite of trait-points but personal dimensions." (Cf. J. L. Steinberg (Ed.), "Creativity Research for Future Creativity," in *Implications of Creativity Research,* Los Angeles: Los Angeles State College and Chouinard Art Institute, 1962, p. 82.

Self-Limitation and Individual Abilities

Since, in these respects, each individual is unique we cannot generalize as to how this condition is to be met. For example, the talents and energies of individuals are not the same: a Da Vinci could undertake creative projects in the arts, in science, and even in certain philosophical areas with a high degree of success. But most men are not as talented, nor are their energies to be likened to those of Da Vinci. For each individual, then, the fulfillment of this condition of self-limitation must be decided (at least in part) by reference to the unique talents and energies he possesses.

The Personal Valuing-System

But this is only one familiar aspect of the problem. The exercise of self-limitation or selectivity for creativity involves more than a concern for one's talents and energies: it includes (as suggested above) a consideration for one's valuing-system or "world-view,"[8] one's character,[9] and one's goals or purposes. We can be aided in our effort to understand the way things stand with us in these respects by taking aptitude tests, answering questionnaires designed to specify our valuings, and still others designed to identify our temperament. But these are not in themselves sufficient to effect our direction for creativity. For example, an aptitude test may tell us that we are able to identify mathematical relationships with better-than-average comprehension. But this does not mean that we wish to expend our creative energies in this direction. A given individual may exhibit great aptitude in mathematics and yet find himself strongly attracted to, and challenged by, a vocation in social welfare (where, presumably, marked aptitude for mathematics would be an incidental requirement). There is good reason for this. The whole question of what to do with ourselves creatively involves additional considerations to which we have just alluded, namely, the kind of valuing system or "world-view" which we have adopted; the kind of character we have developed; or the kinds of problems we believe are worthy of being called *important* problems (our goals or purposes). All of these factors impinge upon and are relevant to the area chosen by an individual for creative effort. Hence our mythical person may say with all seriousness: "I'd rather be a second-rate social worker than a first class mathematician." In other words, in choosing a

---

[8] D. W. Taylor holds that evidence obtained in research indicates that "important for creativity are the values which the individual acquires in the environment in which he grows up." Cf. *The Creative Person,* Part VIII, p. 9; Lasswell, H. D., ("The Social Setting of Creativity," *Creativity and Its Cultivation,* H. H. Anderson, (Ed.), New York: Harper Bros., 1959,) speaks of "value emphases" as one of the five factors of creativity in the social milieu.

[9] *Ibid.,* A. H. Maslow ("Creativity in Self-Actualizing People," pp. 94–95) identifies certain "characterological qualities" such as "boldness, courage, freedom, spontaneity, perspicuity, integration, and self-acceptance."

vocation many individuals are not too concerned with what they have already learned and are manifestly *able to do,* but with what they wish and believe they *ought to be.* If this is to the point of living a creative life, then our contention that tests of various kinds are not in themselves sufficient to effect selectivity for creativity is also to the point.

Valuing-Systems May or May Not Encourage Creativity

The principle of self-limitation involves other concerns in addition to those mentioned above. These should at least be mentioned in passing. We must attempt to identify, for example, those valuing-systems which tend to encourage the exercise of this principle and those which do not. For, if this notion of selectivity or self-limitation be conceived as a condition for creativity, then those valuing-systems which do not encourage selectivity militate against our entering effectively into the creative life. Again, we must learn, in connection with our institutional life (in the home, the school), to encourage our spouses, our children, our students, etc., to acquire that "inner-directedness" with which this principle is so closely allied. For it is clear that each individual must ultimately be responsible for the choice of that area of creativity in which he believes he belongs. Negatively stated, this means that entering a certain field of work because our father or mother had chosen it (for themselves or for us) may be of dubious worth with respect to one's real or lasting creative concerns. This consideration may, of course, require a change in our way of thinking regarding husband-wife, student-teacher, parent-child relationships. Hence, it may well be asked: "How do we go about effecting such changes? What new ways of thinking must we introduce to bring this about?"

It would seem, even from such a cursory discussion of selectivity, that we have much to learn regarding its demands as a condition for creativity.

THE CONDITION OF RECEPTIVITY

Carl Rogers calls this "openness" (which, indeed, may be a more apt term). But, whatever our term for it, this condition involves the life-blood of creativeness: being open or receptive to new ideas, new aesthetic forms, new feelings and attitudes. Indeed, receptivity may be likened to pouring wine from a bottle: before the wine can be poured, it is necessary first to remove the cork from the bottle and, secondly, to be prepared for the pouring by having an empty glass which will contain the wine.

Openness and Overcoming Prejudices

Removing the cork from the wine bottle corresponds to the first step in the development of receptivity. This action or process has been called by various names: the willingness to give up certain biases or prejudices;

"confessing our ignorance" (Socrates); "dying to the old man in us, in order that the young man may be born." This is, however, more easily said than done. How do we get at ourselves in order to discover what, in our valuing-system or world-view, constitutes undesirable bias, prejudice, or misconception?

One suggestion that seems worthy of consideration is to expose ourselves to more and more data or stimuli relevant to our creative interests. For it can and does happen that in such exposure we meet with ideas or viewpoints which unduly unsettle us. In our unsettlement it may happen that we are made aware of certain prejudices or areas of ignorance of which previously we were unaware. If such experience takes place we may thus be afforded the opportunity of acknowledging our prejudices or areas of ignorance.

Learning to Be Quiet

The "empty glass" into which the wine is to be poured symbolizes what some writers choose to call "the capacity to be quiet"; what other writers have called "purity of heart." Both expressions are useful in attempting to comprehend receptivity. "To be quiet" is, first of all, the opposite of allowing or entertaining a variety of "internal noises" (feelings of resentment, mental arguments with real or imaginary antagonists, or prejudgments). Hence, "quietness" denotes a *listening* posture, rather than a *talking* posture.[10] We are receptive because we are *waiting to hear* what we hope will be forthcoming in furthering our understanding of the creative project at hand. Thus, if we are "quiet" we go to a lecture, or pick up a book, and find ourselves actually listening to the ideas being set forth rather than pursuing ideas that have arisen impulsively from prior stimuli or data.

Singleness of Intent

In addition, "purity of heart,"[11] as Kierkegaard conceives it, consists in "the capacity to will one thing." This means that in the pursuit of beauty, for example, we seek beauty and are not preoccupied with other things that may issue from such a search (fame, fortune, social position). The same principle would apply if our search is aimed at knowledge, or at social betterment. The posture of receptivity, it would seem, tends to make us "hollow and smooth inside." For as Emerson (who used this phrase) suggests, this is what we must do if we would draw on our "vital energies."

---

[10] Harold Rugg, (*Imagination*, New York: Harper and Row, 1963) refers to a "quiet mind of intuition" exercised by both scientists and artists (p. 28).
[11] B. Ghiselin prefers the expression "purity of motive."

THE CONDITION OF COMPETENCE OR FITNESS

Varieties of Apprenticeship

Most everyone agrees that we cannot be creative if we do not master the tools required by the work at hand. The first step in achieving such mastery is very often called "apprenticeship." "Apprenticeship" will, of course, mean something different in each of the modes of creativity. For example, in the field of creative art "apprenticeship" can mean "copying for a long time and imitating for a long time" (this according to Emile Chartier, whom Maurois refers to as his teacher in creative writing). Such copying and imitating will, of course, be directed to the art form which one desires to master (music, painting, sculpture). In the field of scientific and philosophic creativity (the mode which this writer calls *creative intelligence*) it will mean learning the vocabulary, the basic propositions (or formulas), or the methodology already established in the chosen area of concentration. In the mode of creativity which may be called *creative living* (the kind of creativity possible in interpersonal relationships), "apprenticeship" will involve such things as learning the language, the customs, the history, or the valuing system of the individual or group with whom one wishes to become involved.

Love and Competence

But apprenticeship, any one would acknowledge, is only the first step to competence. Hopefully, our apprenticeship will serve to awaken a genuine love for whatever interests us. This is tied to that "purity of heart" of which we have just spoken. We come to love the object of our creative efforts for *itself* and are not actively concerned with what material or social rewards it can bring us. This, indeed, tends to develop competence because to love something for its own sake brings us into more intimate contact with that object; we come to know it more deeply and hence more truly. This is true whether the object of our interest be physics, engineering, human beings or God.

The Ideals of Creative Intelligence

Finally, competence may be said to find its fulfillment in the formulation of the ideal for which apprenticeship and love of the object has prepared us. This claim argues against those who say that ideals tend to defeat the development of competence. The grain of truth in this latter claim stems from observing those who formulate an ideal without first having subjected themselves to the discipline of "apprenticeship" and love of the object pursued. However, when such discipline has been satisfied the formulation of an ideal is but another way of saying that we envision new possibilities, new achievements, new relationships relevant to the creative work at hand. Indeed, historically the formulation and pursuits of ideals in all of the modes of creativity is characteristic, rather than foreign, to man's development of competence: Classicism, Romanticism, or Impressionism are not merely names for various "schools" of art, but ideal ways for viewing aesthetic relations. Freedom, Justice, and Love are not merely valuings that are prized in creative living but ideal ways of viewing interpersonal relations. Again, knowledge and truth are more than end products of scientific and philosophic creativity: they are ideals suited to creative intelligence.

SUMMARY

The conditions for creativity as outlined here are basically, and at a minimum, *motivation, self-limitation, selectivity* or *receptivity,* and *competence.* These conditions are worthy of study not only in themselves but also as they impinge upon the *process* and the *modes* of creativity. We need to understand these conditions more fully if we are to achieve greater effectiveness in what we call the *process* of creativity (preparation, incubation, illumination, verification). The same holds true if we are to comprehend better the *modes* of creativity (creative art, creative intelligence, and creative living). For, the conditions for creativity, more fully understood, may be likened to the man who chose to build his house on solid rock and found that when the winds and rains came the house did, indeed, stand.

QUESTIONS FOR DISCUSSION

1) Alamshah seems to allow more importance to "motivation" than to "competence." Do you agree with this? Should a person who would "rather be a second-rate social worker than a first class mathematician" be encouraged or discouraged in this wish? Why?

2) What is meant by the terms "push" and "pull" in the discussion about motivation? What are some of the personality traits which Alamshah associates with creativity?

3) What are the steps, according to Alamshah, which an individual must take to establish or improve his "receptivity"?

4) Alamshah discusses the matter of apprenticeship. Is a period of apprenticeship important or necessary to creative success? (Creativity here means the creation of a new product.) Discuss.

II. SCIENCE

We live in the age of science. There can be no doubt that man must now live or die by the results of his scientific creativity—the outpouring of two brief but frenzied centuries. Further, now that the early optimistic stages of this revolution have passed, the depth and complexity of the problems it has brought with it are frightening to even the wisest and bravest. The supposedly mastered environment flashes urgent warnings of exhaustion and pollution. Our own bright inventions threaten us with overpopulation on the one hand, genetic damage on the other. And other less dramatic difficulties may in the long run be no less serious.

Can man really adjust to the crowded, super-organized society both instituted and required by the machine? Will art, religion, and philosophy survive their contemporary suffocation—those flickering lamps, which, unsteady or not, must not fail because they give man the faith and hope to build his machines? Still, whatever happens in the humanities, it is the men of science, the Galileos, the Huxleys, and the Shockleys, who must provide our immediate salvation. We cannot dismantle what we have begun. The present generation cannot lose the passion to explore, to uncover new dimensions and new potentialities, whether of the moon, the electron, the earth, or of man himself.

THE METHOD OF SCIENTIFIC INVESTIGATION

Thomas Henry Huxley

The method of scientific investigation is nothing but the expression of the necessary mode of working of the human mind. It is simply the mode at which all phenomena are reasoned about, rendered precise and exact. There is no more difference, but there is just the same kind of difference, between the mental operations of a man of science and those of an ordinary person as there is between the operations and methods of a baker or of a butcher weighing out his goods in common scales and the operations of a chemist in performing a difficult and complex analysis by means of his balance and finely graduated weights. It is not that the action of the scales in the one case and the balance in the other differ in the principles of their construction or manner of working; but the beam of one is set on an infinitely finer axis than the other and of course turns by the addition of a much smaller weight.

You will understand this better, perhaps, if I give you some familiar example. You have all heard it repeated, I dare say, that men of science work by means of induction and deduction, and that by the help of these operations they, in a sort of sense, wring from nature certain other things which are called natural laws and causes, and that out of these, by some cunning skill of their own, they build up hypotheses and theories. And it is imagined by many that the operations of the common mind can be by no means compared with these processes, and that they have to be acquired by a sort of special apprenticeship to the craft. To hear all these large words you would think that the mind of a man of science must be constituted differently from that of his fellow men; but if you will not be frightened by terms, you will discover that you are quite wrong and that all these terrible apparatus are being used by yourselves every day and every hour of your lives.

There is a well-known incident in one of Molière's plays where the author makes the hero express unbounded delight on being told that he had been talking prose during the whole of his life. In the same way I trust that you will take comfort and be delighted with yourselves on the discovery that you have been acting on the principles of inductive and deductive philosophy during the same period. Probably there is not one here who has not in the course of the day had occasion to set in motion a complex train of reasoning of the very same kind, though differing of course in degree, as that which a scientific man goes through in tracing the causes of natural phenomena.

A very trivial circumstance will serve to exemplify this. Suppose you go into a fruiterer's shop, wanting an apple. You take up one, and on biting it you find it is sour; you look at it and see that it is hard and green. You take up another one, and that too is hard, green, and sour. The shopman offers you a third; but before biting it you examine it and find that it is hard and green, and you immediately say that you will not have it, as it must be sour like those that you have already tried.

Nothing can be more simple than that, you think; but if you will take the trouble to analyze and trace out into its logical elements what has been done by the mind, you will be greatly surprised. In the first place you have performed the operation of induction. You found that in two experiences hardness and greenness in apples go together with sourness. It was so in the first case, and it was confirmed by the second. True, it is a very small basis, but still it is enough to make an induction from; you generalize the facts, and you expect to find sourness in apples where you get hardness and greenness. You found upon that a general law that all hard and green apples are sour; and that, so far as it goes, is a perfect induction. Well, having got your natural law in this way, when you are offered another apple which you find is hard and green, you say, "All hard and green apples are sour; this apple is hard and green; therefore this apple is sour." That train of reasoning is what logicians call a syllogism and has all its various parts and terms—its major premise, its minor premise, and its conclusion. And by the help of further reasoning, which if drawn out would have to be exhibited in two or three other syllogisms, you arrive at your final determination, "I will not have that apple." So that, you see, you have, in the first place, established a law by induction, and upon that you have founded a deduction and reasoned out the special conclusion of the particular case. Well now, suppose, having got your law, that at some time afterwards you are discussing the qualities of apples with a friend. You will say to him, "It is a very curious thing, but I find that all hard and green apples are sour!" Your friend says to you, "But how do you know that?" You at once reply, "Oh, because I have tried them over and over again and have always found them to be so." Well, if we were talking science instead of common sense, we should call that an experimental verification. And if still opposed you go further and say, "I have heard from the people in Somersetshire and Devonshire, where a large number of apples are grown, that they have observed the same thing. It is also found to be the case in Normandy and in North America. In short, I find it to be the universal experience of mankind wherever attention has been directed to the subject." Whereupon, your friend, unless he is a very unreasonable man, agrees with you and is convinced that you are quite right in the conclusion you have drawn. He believes, although perhaps he does not know he believes it, that the more extensive verifications are, that the more frequently experiments have been made and results of the same kind arrived at, that the more varied the conditions under which the same results have been attained the more certain is the ultimate conclusion, and he disputes the question no further. He sees that the experiment has been tried under all sorts of conditions as to time, place, and people with the same result; and he says with you, therefore, that the law you have laid down must be a good one and he must believe it.

In science we do the same thing; the philosopher exercises precisely the same faculties, though in a much more delicate manner. In scientific inquiry it becomes a matter of duty to expose a supposed law to every possible kind of verification, and to take care, moreover, that this is done intentionally and not left to mere accident as in the case of the apples. And in science, as in common life, our confidence in a law is in exact proportion to the absence of variation in the result of our experimental verifications. For instance, if you let go your grasp of an article you may have in your hand, it will immediately fall to the ground. That is a very common verification of one of the best established laws of nature, that of gravitation. The method by which men of science established the existence of that law is exactly the same as that by which we have established the trivial proposition about the sourness of hard and green apples. But we believe it in such an extensive, thorough, and unhesitating manner because the universal experience of mankind verifies it, and we can verify it ourselves at any time; and that is the strongest possible foundation on which any natural law can rest.

So much by way of proof that the method of establishing laws in science is exactly the same as that pursued in common life. Let us now turn to another matter (though really it is but another phase of the same question), and that is the method by which from the relations of certain phenomena we prove that some stand in the position of causes towards the others.

I want to put the case clearly before you, and I will therefore show you what I mean by another familiar example. I will suppose that one of you, on coming down in the morning to the parlor of your house, finds that a teapot and some spoons which had been left in the room on the previous evening are gone; the window is open, and you observe the mark of a dirty hand on the window-frame; and perhaps, in addition to that, you notice the impress of a hobnailed shoe on the gravel outside. All these phenomena have struck your attention instantly, and before two seconds have passed you say, "Oh, somebody has broken open the window, entered the room, and run off with the spoons and the teapot!" That speech is out of your mouth in a moment. And you will probably add, "I know there has; I am quite sure of it." You mean to say exactly what you know; but in reality what you have said has been the expression of what is, in all essential particulars, an hypothesis. You do not *know* it at all; it is nothing but an hypothesis rapidly framed in your own mind! And it is an hypothesis founded on a long train of inductions and deductions.

What are those inductions and deductions, and how have you got at this hypothesis? You have observed, in the first place, that the window is open; but by a train of reasoning involving many inductions and deductions, you have probably arrived long before at the general law—and a very good one it is—that windows do not open of themselves; and you therefore conclude that something has opened the window. A second general law that you have arrived at in the same way is that teapots and spoons do not go out of a window spontaneously, and you are satisfied that, as they are not now where you left them, they have been removed. In the third place, you look at the marks on the window and the shoe marks outside, and you say that in all previous experience the former kind of mark has never been produced by anything else but the hand of a human being; and the same experience shows that no other animal but man at present wears shoes with hobnails on them such as would produce the marks in the gravel. I do not know, even if we could discover any of those "missing links" that are talked about, that they would help us to any other conclusion! At any rate the law which states our present experience is strong enough for my present purpose. You next reach the conclusion that as these kinds of marks have not been left by any other animal than man, or are liable to be formed in any other way than by a man's hand and shoe, the marks in question have been formed by a man in that way. You have, further, a general law founded on observation and experience, and that too is, I am sorry to say, a very universal and unimpeachable one—that some men are thieves; and you assume at once from all these premises—and that is what constitutes your hypothesis—that the man who made the marks outside and on the window sill opened the window, got into the room, and stole your teapot and spoons. You have now arrived at a *vera causa;* you have assumed a cause which it is plain is competent to produce all the phenomena you have observed. You can explain all these phenomena only by the hypothesis of a thief. But that is an hypothetical conclusion, of the justice of which you have no absolute proof at all; it is only rendered highly probable by a series of inductive and deductive reasonings.

I suppose your first action, assuming that you are a man of ordinary common sense and that you have established this hypothesis to your own satisfaction, will very likely be to go off for the police and set them on the track of the burglar with the view to the recovery of your property. But just as you are starting with this object, some person comes in and on learning what you are about says, "My good friend, you are going on a great deal too fast. How do you know that the man who really made the marks took the spoons? It might have been a monkey that took them, and the man may have merely looked in afterwards." You would probably reply,

"Well, that is all very well, but you see it is contrary to all experience of the way teapots and spoons are abstracted; so that, at any rate, your hypothesis is less probable than mine." While you are talking the thing over in this way, another friend arrives, one of that good kind of people that I was talking of a little while ago.

And he might say, "Oh, my dear sir, you are certainly going on a great deal too fast. You are most presumptuous. You admit that all these occurrences took place when you were fast asleep, at a time when you could not possibly have known anything about what was taking place. How do you know that the laws of nature are not suspended during the night? It may be that there has been some kind of supernatural interference in this case." In point of fact, he declares that your hypothesis is one of which you cannot at all demonstrate the truth and that you are by no means sure that the laws of nature are the same when you are asleep as when you are awake.

Well, now, you cannot at the moment answer that kind of reasoning. You feel that your worthy friend has you somewhat at a disadvantage. You will feel perfectly convinced in your own mind, however, that you are quite right, and you will say to him, "My good friend, I can only be guided by the natural probabilities of the case, and if you will be kind enough to stand aside and permit me to pass, I will go and fetch the police." Well, we will suppose that your journey is successful and that by good luck you meet with a policeman; that eventually the burglar is found with your property on his person and the marks correspond to his hand and to his boots. Probably any jury would consider those facts a very good experimental verification of your hypothesis touching the cause of the abnormal phenomena observed in your parlor, and would act accordingly.

Now, in this supposititious case I have taken phenomena of a very common kind in order that you might see what are the different steps in an ordinary process of reasoning, if you will only take the trouble to analyze it carefully. All the operations I have described, you will see, are involved in the mind of any man of sense in leading him to a conclusion as to the course he should take in order to make good a robbery and punish the offender. I say that you are led, in that case, to your conclusion by exactly the same train of reasoning as that which a man of science pursues when he is endeavoring to discover the origin and laws of the most occult phenomena. The process is, and always must be, the same; and precisely the same mode of reasoning was employed by Newton and Laplace in their endeavors to discover and define the causes of the movements of the heavenly bodies as you, with your own common sense, would employ to detect a burglar. The only difference is that, the nature of the inquiry being more abstruse, every step has to be most carefully watched so that there may not be a single crack or flaw in your hypothesis. A flaw or crack in many of the hypotheses of daily life may be of little or no moment as affecting the general correctness of the conclusions at which we may arrive; but in a scientific inquiry a fallacy, great or small, is always of importance and is sure to be in the long run constantly productive of mischievous if not fatal results.

Do not allow yourselves to be misled by the common notion that an hypothesis is untrustworthy simply because it is an hypothesis. It is often urged in respect to some scientific conclusion that, after all, it is only an hypothesis. But what more have we to guide us in nine-tenths of the most important affairs of daily life than hypotheses, and often very ill-based ones? So that in science, where the evidence of an hypothesis is subjected to the most rigid examination, we may rightly pursue the same course. You may have hypotheses and hypotheses. A man may say, if he likes, that the moon is made of green cheese; that is an hypothesis. But another man, who has devoted a great deal of time and attention to the subject and availed himself of the most powerful telescopes and the results of the observations of others, declares that in his opinion it is probably composed of materials very similar to those of which our own earth is made up; and that is also only an hypothesis. But I need not tell you that there is an enormous difference in the value of the two hypotheses. That one which is based on sound scientific knowledge is sure to have a corresponding value; and that which is a mere hasty random guess is likely to have but little value. Every great step in our progress in discovering causes has been made in exactly the same way as that which I have detailed to you. A person observing the occurrence of certain facts and phenomena asks, naturally enough, what kind of operation known to occur in nature applied to the particular case, will unravel and explain the mystery. Hence you have the scientific hypothesis; and its value will be proportionate to the care and completeness with which its basis has been tested and verified. It is in these matters as in the commonest affairs of practical life: the guess of the fool will be folly, while the guess of the wise man will contain wisdom. In all cases you see that the value of the result depends on the patience and faithfulness with which the investigator applies to his hypothesis every possible kind of verification.

QUESTIONS FOR DISCUSSION

1) Huxley's article demonstrates the essential simplicity of the thought processes involved in the scientific method and suggests the rigor and care necessary for great scientific discoveries. Does the necessity for methodical procedure rule out creativity in science? Explain.

2) Explain the following terms, showing their interrelationships: "induction," "deduction," and "syllogism."

3) What is the function of a hypothesis in scientific investigation?

4) Huxley begins his essay with an important premise: "The method of scientific investigation is nothing but the expression of the necessary mode of working of the human mind." Explain what Huxley means by this, and state whether or not you agree, paying particular attention to the word "necessary" in the statement.

5) What, in your judgment, are the limitations of the scientific method of reasoning? For example, would the scientific method be applicable to writing a poem? Explain.

THE CREATIVE MIND

Jacob Bronowski

On a fine November day in 1945, late in the afternoon, I was landed on an airstrip in Southern Japan. From there a jeep was to take me over the mountains to join a ship which lay in Nagasaki Harbor. I knew nothing of the country or the distance before us. We drove off; dusk fell; the road rose and fell away, the pine woods came down to the road, straggled on and opened again. I did not know that we had left the open country until unexpectedly I heard the ship's loudspeakers broadcasting dance music. Then suddenly I was aware that we were already at the center of damage in Nagasaki. The shadows behind me were the skeletons of the Mitsubishi factory buildings, pushed backwards and sideways as if by a giant hand. What I had thought to be broken rocks was a concrete power house with its roof punched in. I could now make out the outline of two crumpled gasometers; there was a cold furnace festooned with service pipes; otherwise nothing but cockeyed telegraph poles and loops of wire in a bare waste of ashes. I had blundered into this desolate landscape as instantly as one might wake among the mountains of the moon. The moment of recognition when I realized that I was already in Nagasaki is present to me as I write, as vividly as when I lived it. I see the warm night and the meaningless shapes; I can even remember the tune that was coming from the ship. It was a dance tune which had been popular in 1945, and it was called "Is You Is Or Is You Ain't Ma Baby?"

This book, which I have called *Science and Human Values*, was born at that moment. For the moment I have recalled was a universal moment; what I met was, almost as abruptly, the experience of mankind. On an evening like that evening, some time in 1945, each of us in his own way learned that his imagination had been dwarfed. We looked up and saw the power of which we had been proud loom over us like the ruins of Nagasaki.

The power of science for good and for evil has troubled other minds than ours. We are not here fumbling with a new dilemma; our subject and our fears are as old as the tool-making civilizations. Men have been killed with weapons before now: what happened at Nagasaki was only more massive (for 40,000 were killed there by a flash which lasted seconds) and more ironical (for the bomb exploded over the main Christian community of Japan). Nothing happened in 1945 except that we changed the scale of our indifference to man; and conscience, in revenge, for an instant became immediate to us. Before this immediacy fades in a sequence of televised atomic tests, let us acknowledge our subject for what it is: civilization face to face with its own implications. The implications are both the industrial slum which Nagasaki was before it was bombed, and the ashy desolation which the bomb made of the slum. And civilization asks of both ruins: "Is You Is Or Is You Ain't Ma Baby?"

The man whom I imagine to be asking this question, wryly with a sense of shame, is not a scientist; he is civilized man. It is of course more usual for each member of civilization to take flight from its consequences by protesting that others have failed him. Those whose education and perhaps tastes have confined them to the humanities protest that the scientists alone are to blame, for plainly no mandarin ever made a bomb or an industry. The scientists say, with equal contempt, that the Greek scholars and the earnest explorers of cave paintings do well to wash their hands of blame; but what in fact are they doing to help direct the society whose ills grow more often from inaction than from error?

This absurd division reached its *reductio ad absurdum,* I think, when one of my teachers, G. H. Hardy, justified his great life work on the ground that it could do no one the least harm—or the least good. But Hardy was a mathematician; will humanists really let him opt out of the conspiracy of scientists? Or are scientists to forgive Hardy because, protest as he might, most of them learned their indispensable mathematics from his books?

There is no comfort in such bickering. When Shelley pictured science as a modern Prometheus who would wake the world to a wonderful dream of Godwin, he was alas too simple. But it is as pointless to read what has happened since as a nightmare. Dream or nightmare, we have to live our experience as it is, and we have to live it awake. We live in a world which is penetrated through and through by science and which is both whole and real. We cannot turn it into a game simply by taking sides.

And this make-believe game might cost us what we value most: the human content of our lives. The scholar who disdains science may speak in fun, but his fun is not quite a laughing matter. To think of science as a set of special tricks, to see the scientist as the manipulator of outlandish skills—this is the root of the poison mandrake which flourishes rank in the comic strips. There is no more threatening and no more degrading doctrine than the fancy that somehow we may shelve the responsibility for making the decisions of our society by passing it to a few scientists armored with a special magic. This is another dream, the dream of H. G. Wells, in which the tall elegant engineers rule, with perfect benevolence, a humanity which has no business except to be happy. To H. G. Wells this was a dream of heaven—a modern version of the idle, harp-resounding heaven of other childhood pieties. But in fact it is the picture of a slave society and should make us shiver whenever we hear a man of sensibility dismiss science as someone else's concern. The world today is made, it is powered by science; and for any man to abdicate an interest in science is to walk with open eyes towards slavery.

My aim in this book is to show that the parts of civilization make a whole: to display the links which give society its coherence and, more, which give it life. In particular, I want to show the place of science in the canons of conduct which it has still to perfect.

This subject falls into three parts. The first is a study of the nature of the scientific activity, and with it of all those imaginative acts of understanding which exercise *The Creative Mind*. After this it is logical to ask what is the nature of the truth, as we seek it in science and in social life, and to trace the influence which this search for empirical truth has had on conduct. This influence has prompted me to call the second part *The Habit of Truth*. Last I shall study the conditions for the success of science and find in them the values of man which science would have had to invent afresh if man had not otherwise known them: the values which make up *The Sense of Human Dignity*.

This, then, is a high-ranging subject which is not to be held in the narrow limits of a laboratory. It disputes the prejudice of the humanist who takes his science sourly and, equally, the petty view which many scientists take of their own activity and that of others. When men misunderstand their own work, they cannot understand the work of others; so that it is natural that these scientists have been indifferent to the arts. They have been content, with the humanists, to think science mechanical and neutral; they could therefore justify themselves only by the claim that it is practical. By this lame criterion, they have of course found poetry and music and painting at least unreal and often meaningless. I challenge all these judgments.

There is a likeness between the creative acts of the mind in art and in science. Yet, when a man uses the word science in such a sentence, it may be suspected that he does not mean what the headlines mean by science. Am I about to sidle away to those riddles in the Theory of Numbers which Hardy loved, or to the heady speculations of astrophysicists, in order to make claims for abstract science which have no bearing on its daily practice?

I have no such design. My purpose is to talk about science as it is, practical and theoretical. I define science as the organization of our knowledge in such a way that it commands more of the hidden potential in nature. What I have in mind therefore is both deep and matter of fact; it reaches from the kinetic theory of gases to the telephone and the suspension bridge and medicated toothpaste. It admits no sharp boundary between knowledge and use. There are of course people who like to draw a line between pure and applied science; and oddly, they are often the same people who find art unreal. To them, the word useful is a final arbiter, either for or against a work; and they use this word as if it can mean only what makes a man feel heavier after meals.

There is no sanction for confining the practice of science in this or another way. True, science is full of useful inventions. And its theories have often been made by men whose imagination was directed by the uses to which their age looked. Newton turned naturally to astronomy because it was the subject of his day; and it was so because finding one's way at sea had long been a practical preoccupation of the society into which he was born. It should be added, mischievously, that astronomy also had some standing because it was used very practically to cast horoscopes. (Kepler used it for this purpose; in the Thirty Years' War, he cast the horoscope of Wallenstein which wonderfully told his character, and he predicted a universal disaster for 1643 which proved to be the murder of Wallenstein.

In a setting which is more familiar, Faraday worked all his life to link electricity with magnetism because this was the glittering problem of his day; and it was so because his society, like ours, was on the lookout for new sources of power. Consider a more modest example today: the new mathematical methods of automatic control, a subject sometimes called cybernetics, have been developed now because this is a time when communication and control have in effect become forms of power. These inventions have been directed by social needs, and they are useful inventions; yet it was not their usefulness which dominated and set light to the minds of those who made them. Neither Newton nor Faraday, nor yet Professor Norbert Weiner, spent their time in a scramble for patents.

What a scientist does is compounded of two interests: the interest of his time and his own interest. In this his behavior is no different from any other man's. The need of the age gives its shape to scientific progress as a whole. But it is not the need of the age which gives the individual scientist his sense of pleasure and of adventure and that excitement which keeps him working late into the night when all the useful typists have gone home at five o'clock. He is personally involved in his work, as the poet is in his and as the artist is in the painting. Paints and painting, too, must have been made for useful ends; and language was developed, from whatever beginnings, for practical communication. Yet you cannot have a man handle paints or language or the symbolic concepts of physics, you cannot even have him stain a microscope slide, without instantly waking in him a pleasure in the very language, a sense of exploring his own activity. This sense lies at the heart of creation.

The sense of personal exploration is as urgent, and as delightful, to the practical scientist as to the theoretical. Those who think otherwise are confusing what is practical with what is humdrum. Good humdrum work without originality is done every day by every one, theoretical scientists as well as practical, and writers and painters too, as well as truck drivers and bank clerks. Of course the unoriginal work keeps the world going; but it is not therefore the monopoly of practical men. And neither need the practical man be unoriginal. If he is to break out of what has been done before, he must bring to his own tools the same sense of pride and discovery which the poet brings to words. He cannot afford to be less radical in conceiving and less creative in designing a new turbine than a new world system.

And this is why in turn practical discoveries are not made only by practical man. As the world's interest has shifted, since the Industrial Revolution, to the tapping of new springs of power, the theoretical scientist has shifted his interests too. His speculations about energy have been as abstract as once they were about astronomy; and they have been profound now as they were then, because the man loved to think. The Carnot cycle and the dynamo grew equally from this love, and so did nuclear physics and the German V weapons and Kelvin's interest in low temperatures. Man does not invent by following either use or tradition; he does not invent even a new form of communication by calling a conference of communication engineers. Who invented the television set? In any deep sense, it was Clerk Maxwell who foresaw the existence of radio waves, and Heinrich Hertz who proved it, and J. J. Thomson who discovered the electron. This is not said in order to rob any practical man of the invention, but from a sad sense of justice; for neither Maxwell nor Hertz nor J. J. Thomson would take pride in television just now.

Man masters nature not by force but by understanding. This is why science has succeeded where magic failed: because it has looked for no spell to cast on nature. The alchemist and the magician in the Middle Ages thought, and the addict of comic strips is still encouraged to think, that nature must be mastered by a device which outrages her laws. But in four hundred years since the Scientific Revolution we have learned that we gain our ends only *with* the laws of nature; we control her only by understanding her laws. We cannot even bully nature by any insistence that our work shall be designed to give power over her. We must be content that power is the by-product of understanding. So the Greeks said that Orpheus played the lyre with such sympathy that wild beasts were tamed by the hand on the strings. They did not suggest that he got this gift by setting out to be a lion tamer.

What is the insight with which the scientist tries to see into nature? Can it indeed be called either imaginative or creative? To the literary man the question may seem merely silly. He has been taught that science is a large collection of facts; and if this is true, then the only seeing which scientists need do is, he supposes, seeing the facts. He pictures them, the colorless professionals of science, going off to work in the morning into the universe in a neutral, unexposed state. They then expose themselves like a photographic plate. And then in the darkroom or laboratory they develop the image, so that suddenly and startlingly it appears, printed in capital letters, as a new formula for atomic energy.

Men who have read Balzac and Zola are not deceived by the claims of these writers that they do no more than record the facts. The readers of Christopher Isherwood do not take him literally when he writes: "I am a camera." Yet the same readers solemnly carry with them from their school days this foolish picture of the scientist fixing by some mechanical process the facts of nature. I have had, of all people, a historian tell me that science is a collection of facts, and his voice had not even the irony of one filing cabinet reproving another.

It seems impossible that this historian had ever studied the beginnings of a scientific discovery. The Scientific Revolution can be held to begin in the year 1543 when there was brought to Copernicus, perhaps on his death-bed, the first printed copy of the book he had written about a dozen years earlier. The thesis of this book is that the earth moves around the sun. When did Copernicus go out and record this fact with his camera? What appearance in nature prompted his outrageous guess? And in what odd sense is this guess to be called a neutral record of fact?

Less than a hundred years after Copernicus, Kepler published (be-tween 1609 and 1619) the three laws which describe the paths of the planets. The work of Newton and with it most of our mechanics spring from these laws. They have a solid, matter-of-fact sound. For example, Kepler says that if one squares the year of a planet, one gets a number which is proportional to the cube of its average distance from the sun. Does any one think that such a law is found by taking enough readings and then squaring and cubing everything in sight? If he does then, as a scientist, he is doomed to a wasted life; he has as little prospect of making a scientific dis-covery as an electronic brain has.

It was not this way that Copernicus and Kepler thought, or that sci-entists think today. Copernicus found that the orbits of the planets would look simpler if they were looked at from the sun and not from the earth. But he did not in the first place find this by routine calculation. His first step was a leap of imagination—to lift himself from the earth, and put him-self wildly, speculatively into the sun. "The earth conceives from the sun," he wrote; and "the sun rules the family of stars." We catch in his mind an image, the gesture of the virile man standing in the sun, with arms out-stretched, overlooking the planets. Perhaps Copernicus took the picture from the drawings of the youth with outstretched arms which the Renais-sance teachers put into their books on the proportions of the body. Perhaps he knew Leonardo's drawings of his loved pupil Salai. I do not know. To me, the gesture of Copernicus, the shining youth looking outward from the sun, is still vivid in a drawing which William Blake about 1800 based on all these: the drawing which is usually called *Glad Day*.

Kepler's mind, we know, was filled with just such fanciful analogies; and we know what they are. Kepler wanted to relate the speeds of the planets to the musical intervals. He tried to fit the five regular solids into their orbits. None of these likenesses worked, and they have been forgot-ten; yet they have been and they remain the stepping stones of every crea-tive mind. Kepler felt for his laws by way of metaphors, he searched mys-tically for likenesses with what he knew in every strange corner of nature. And when among these guesses he hit upon his laws, he did not think of their numbers as the balancing of a cosmic bank account, but as a revela-tion of the unity in all nature. To us, the analogies by which Kepler listened for the movement of the planets in the music of the spheres are far-fetched; but are they more so than the wild leap by which Rutherford and Bohr found a model for the atom in, of all places, the planetary system?

No scientific theory is a collection of facts. It will not even do to call a theory true or false in the simple sense in which every fact is either so or not so. The Epicureans held that matter is made of atoms two thousand years ago and we are now tempted to say that their theory was true. But if we do so, we confuse their notion of matter with our own. John Dalton in 1808 first saw the structure of matter as we do today, and what he took from the ancients was not their theory but something richer, their image: the atom. Much of what was in Dalton's mind was as vague as the Greek notion, and quite as mistaken. But he suddenly gave life to the new facts of chemistry and the ancient theory together, by fusing them to give what neither had: a coherent picture of how matter is linked and built up from different kinds of atoms. The act of fusion is the creative act.

All science is the search for unity in hidden likenesses. The search may be on a grand scale, as in the modern theories which try to link the fields of gravitation and electro-magnetism. But we do not need to be brow-beaten by the scale of science. There are discoveries to be made by snatching a small likeness from the air too, if it is bold enough. In 1932 the Japanese physicist Yukawa wrote a paper which can still give heart to a young scientist. He took as his starting point the known fact that waves of light can sometimes behave as if they were separate pellets. From this he reasoned that the forces which hold the nucleus of an atom together might sometimes also be observed as if they were solid pellets. A schoolboy can see how thin Yukawa's analogy is, and his teacher would be severe with it. Yet Yukawa without a blush calculated the mass of the pellet he expected to see, and waited. He was right; his meson was found, and a range of other mesons, neither the existence nor the nature of which had been suspected before. The likeness had borne fruit.

The scientist looks for order in the appearances of nature by exploring such likenesses. For order does not display itself of itself; if it can be said to be there at all, it is not there for the mere looking. There is no way of pointing a finger or a camera at it; order must be discovered and, in a deep sense, it must be created. What we see, as we see it, is mere disorder.

This point has been put trenchantly in a fable by Professor Karl Popper. Suppose that someone wished to give his whole life to science. Suppose that he therefore sat down, pencil in hand, and for the next twenty, thirty, forty years recorded in notebook after notebook everything that he could observe. He may be supposed to leave out nothing: today's humidity, the racing results, the level of cosmic radiation and the stock market prices and the look of Mars, all would be there. He would have compiled the most careful record of nature that has ever been made; and, dying in the calm certainty of a life well spent, he would of course leave his notebooks to the Royal Society. Would the Royal Society thank him for the treasure of a lifetime of observation? It would not. It would refuse to open his notebooks at all, because it would know without looking that they contain only a jumble of disorderly and meaningless items.

Science finds order and meaning in our experience, and sets about this in quite a different way. It sets about it as Newton did in the story which he himself told in his old age, and of which the schoolbooks give only a caricature. In the year 1665, when Newton was twenty-two, the plague broke out in southern England, and the University of Cambridge was closed. Newton therefore spent the next eighteen months at home, removed from traditional learning, at a time when he was impatient for knowledge and, in his own phrase: "I was in the prime of my age for invention." In this eager, boyish mood, sitting one day in the garden of his widowed mother, he saw an apple fall. So far the books have the story right; we think we even know the kind of apple; tradition has it that it was Flower of Kent. But now they miss the crux of the story. For what struck the young Newton at the sight was not the thought that the apple must be drawn to the earth by gravity; that conception was older than Newton. What struck him was the conjecture that the same force of gravity, which reaches to the top of the tree, might go on reaching out beyond the earth and its air, endlessly into space. Gravity might reach the moon: this was Newton's new thought; and it might be gravity which holds the moon in her orbit. There and then he calculated what force from the earth would hold the moon, and compared it with the known force of gravity at tree height. The forces agreed; Newton says laconically: "I found them answer pretty nearly." Yet they agreed only nearly: the likeness and the approximation go together, for no likeness is exact. In Newton's sentence modern science is full grown.

It grows from a comparison. It has seized a likeness between two unlike appearances; for the apple in the summer garden and the grave moon overhead are surely as unlike in their movements as two things can be. Newton traced in them two expressions of a single concept, gravitation: and the concept (and the unity) are in that sense his free creation. The progress of science is the discovery at each step of a new order which gives unity to what had long seemed unlike. Faraday did this when he closed the link between electricity and magnetism. Clerk Maxwell did it when he linked both with light. Einstein linked time with space, mass with energy, and the path of light past the sun with the flight of a bullet; and spent his dying years in trying to add to these likenesses another, which would find a single imaginative order between the equations of Clerk Maxwell and his own geometry of gravitation.

When Coleridge tried to define beauty, he returned always to one deep thought: beauty, he said, is "unity in variety." Science is nothing else than the search to discover unity in the wild variety of nature—or more exactly, in the variety of our experience. Poetry, painting, the arts are the same search, in Coleridge's phrase, for unity in variety. Each in its own way looks for likenesses under the variety of human experience. What is a poetic image but the seizing and the exploration of a hidden likeness, in holding together two parts of a comparison which are to give depth each to the other? When Romeo finds Juliet in the tomb, and thinks her dead, he uses in his heartbreaking speech the words:

Death, that hath suck'd the honey of thy breath.

The critic can only haltingly take to pieces the single shock which this image carries. The young Shakespeare admired Marlowe, and Marlowe's Faustus had said of the ghostly kiss of Helen of Troy that it sucked forth his soul. But that is a pale image; what Shakespeare has done is to fire it with the single word honey. Death is a bee at the lips of Juliet, and the bee is an insect that stings; the sting of death was a commonplace phrase when Shakespeare wrote. The sting is there, under the image; Shakespeare has packed it into the word honey; but the very word rides powerfully over its own undertones. Death is a bee that stings other people, but it comes to Juliet as if she were a flower; this is the moving thought under the instant image. The creative mind speaks in such thoughts.

The poetic image here is also, and accidentally, heightened by the tenderness which town dwellers now feel for country ways. But it need not be; there are likenesses to conjure with, and images as powerful, within the man-made world. The poems of Alexander Pope belongs to this world. They are not countrified, and therefore readers today find them unemotional and often artificial. Let me then quote Pope: here he is in a formal satire face to face, towards the end of his life, with his own gifts. In eight lines he looks poignantly forward towards death and back to the laborious years which made him famous.

> *Years foll'wing Years, steal something ev'ry day,*
> *At last they steal us from our selves away;*
> *In one our Frolicks, one Amusements end,*
> *In one a Mistress drops, in one a Friend:*
> *This subtle Thief of Life, this paltry Time,*
> *What will it leave me, if it snatch my Rhime?*
> *If ev'ry Wheel of that unweary'd Mill*
> *That turn'd ten thousand Verses, now stands still.*

The human mind had been compared to what the eighteenth century called a mill, that is to a machine, before; Pope's own idol Bolingbroke had compared it to a clockwork. In these lines the likeness goes deeper, for Pope is thinking of the ten thousand Verses which he had translated from Homer: what he says is sad and just at the same time, because this really had been a mechanical and at times a grinding task. Yet the clockwork is present in the image too; when the wheels stand still, time for Pope will stand still for ever; we feel that we already hear, over the horizon, the defiance of Faust which Goethe had not yet written—let the clock strike and stop, let the hand fall, and time be at an end.

> *Werd ich zum Augenblicke sagen:*
> *Verweile doch! du bist so schön!*
> *Dann magst du mich in Fesseln schlagen,*
> *Dann will ich gern zugrunde gehn!*
> *Dann mag die Totenglocke schallen,*
> *Dann bist du deines Dienstes frei,*
> *Die Uhr mag stehn, der Zeiger fallen,*
> *Es sei die Zeit für mich vorbei!*[1]

I have quoted Pope and Goethe because their metaphor here is not poetic; it is rather a hand reaching straight into experience and arranging it with new meaning. Metaphors of this kind need not always be written in words. The most powerful of them all is simply the presence of King Lear and his Fool in the hut of a man who is shamming madness, while lightning rages outside. Or let me quote another clash of two conceptions of life, from a modern poet. In his later poems, W. B. Yeats was troubled by the feeling that in shutting himself up to write, he was missing the active pleasures of life; and yet it seemed to him certain that the man who lives for these pleasures will leave no lasting work behind him. He said this at times very simply, too:

> *The intellect of man is forced to choose*
> *Perfection of the life, or of the work.*

This problem, whether man fulfills himself in work or in play, is of course more common than Yeats allowed; and it may be more commonplace. But it is given breadth and force by the images in which Yeats pondered it.

> *Get all the gold and silver that you can,*
> *Satisfy ambition, or animate*
> *The trivial days and ram them with the sun,*

---

[1] If ever I say to the moment
"Stay! You are so beautiful!"
Then may you clap me in chains,
Then will I gladly perish!
Then may the death-knell ring,
Then are you free from your servitude;
Let the clock stop, its hand fall,
Let time for me be at an end.
                              —*Faust*, Part I

And yet upon these maxims meditate:
All women dote upon an idle man
Although their children need a rich estate;
No man has ever lived that had enough
Of children's gratitude or woman's love.

The love of women, the gratitude of children: the images fix two philosophies as nothing else can. They are tools of creative thought, as coherent and as exact as the conceptual images with which science works: as time and space, or as the proton and the neutron.

The discoveries of science, the works of art are explorations—more, are explosions, of a hidden likeness. The discoverer or the artist presents in them two aspects of nature and fuses them into one. This is the act of creation, in which an original thought is born, and it is the same act in original science and original art. But it is not therefore the monopoly of the man who wrote the poem or who made the discovery. On the contrary, I believe this view of the creative act to be right because it alone gives a meaning to the act of appreciation. The poem or the discovery exists in two moments of vision: the moment of appreciation as much as that of creation; for the appreciator must see the movement, wake to the echo which was started in the creation of the work. In the moment of appreciation we live again the moment when the creator saw and held the hidden likeness. When a simile takes us aback and persuades us together, when we find a juxtaposition in a picture both odd and intriguing, when a theory is at once fresh and convincing, we do not merely nod over someone else's work. We re-enact the creative act, and we ourselves make the discovery again. At bottom, there is no unifying likeness there until we too have seized it, we too have made it for ourselves.

How slipshod by comparison is the notion that either art or science sets out to copy nature. If the task of the painter were to copy for men what they see, the critic could make only a single judgment: either that the copy is right or that it is wrong. And if science were a copy of fact, then every theory would be either right or wrong, and would be so forever. There would be nothing left for us to say but this is so or is not so. No one who has read a page by a good critic or a speculative scientist can ever again think that this barren choice of yes or no is all that the mind offers.

Reality is not an exhibit for man's inspection, labeled: "Do not touch." There are no appearances to be photographed, no experiences to be copied, in which we do not take part. We re-make nature by the act of discovery, in the poem or in the theorem. And the great poem and the deep theorem are new to every reader, and yet are his own experiences, because he himself re-creates them. They are the marks of unity in variety; and in the instant when the mind seizes this for itself, in art or in science, the heart misses a beat.

QUESTIONS FOR DISCUSSION

1) "All science is the search for unity in hidden likenesses," says Bronowski. And what are poetry, painting and the other arts but different forms of this same effort? Thus does Bronowski seek to dispel the notion that because science is based upon the laws of deduction and induction it is not creative. The original scientific thinker, he points out, far from following painstaking procedures, often seizes upon or is inspired with sudden, often imprecise, notions. Some of the scientists of this type he mentions are Copernicus, John Dalton, Yukawa, and Newton. How well do the discoveries of these men serve to illustrate the accuracy of Bronowski's idea? (See "Newton, the Man," for example, which follows.)

2) This article begins with an insight the author gained at the ruins of Nagasaki. What was this insight? How does it relate to Bronowski's idea of the similarity of artistic and scientific creativity?

3) In what sense is this essay a negation of Huxley's essay?

4) Three of Bronowski's subsidiary theses are contrary to popular belief. One is that there is no real distinction between "pure" and "applied" science. Another is that science is not objective, like a camera's eye. And another: the spectator of a creation—whether it be a conclusion of science or a work of art —is also its creator. What kind of reasoning is used in each of these arguments? Are the arguments convincing? Explain.

NEWTON, THE MAN

John Maynard Keynes

It is with some diffidence that I try to speak to you in his own home of Newton *as he was himself*. I have long been a student of the records and had the intention to put my impressions into writing to be ready for Christmas Day 1942, the tercentenary of his birth. The war has deprived me both of leisure to treat adequately so great a theme and of opportunity to consult my library and my papers and to verify my impressions. So if the brief study which I shall lay before you to-day is more perfunctory than it should be, I hope you will excuse me.

One other preliminary matter. I believe that Newton was different from the conventional picture of him. But I do not believe he was less great. He was less ordinary, more extraordinary, than the nineteenth century cared to make him out. Geniuses *are* very peculiar. Let no one here suppose that my object to-day is to lessen, by describing, Cambridge's greatest son. I am trying rather to see him as his own friends and contemporaries saw him. And they without exception regarded him as one of the greatest of men.

In the eighteenth century and since, Newton came to be thought of as the first and greatest of the modern age of scientists, a rationalist, one who taught us to think on the lines of cold and untinctured reason.

I do not see him in this light. I do not think that any one who has pored over the contents of that box which he packed up when he finally left Cambridge in 1696 and which, though partly dispersed, have come down to us, can see him like that. Newton was not the first of the age of reason. He was the last of the magicians, the last of the Babylonians and Sumerians, the last great mind which looked out on the visible and intellectual world with the same eyes as those who began to build our intellectual inheritance rather less than 10,000 years ago. Isaac Newton, a posthumous child born with no father on Christmas Day, 1642, was the last wonderchild to whom the Magi could do sincere and appropriate homage.

Had there been time, I should have liked to read to you the contemporary record of the child Newton. For, though it is well known to his biographers, it has never been published *in extenso*, without comment, just as it stands. Here, indeed, is the makings of a legend of the young magician, a most joyous picture of the opening mind of genius free from the uneasiness, the melancholy and nervous agitation of the young man and student.

For in vulgar modern terms Newton was profoundly neurotic of a not unfamiliar type, but—I should say from the records—a most extreme example. His deepest instincts were occult, esoteric, semantic—with profound shrinking from the world, a paralyzing fear of exposing his thoughts, his beliefs, his discoveries in all nakedness to the inspection and criticism of the world. 'Of the most fearful, cautious and suspicious temper that I ever knew,' said Whiston, his successor in the Lucasian Chair. The too well-known conflicts and ignoble quarrels with Hooke, Flamsteed, Leibnitz are only too clear an evidence of this. Like all his type he was wholly aloof from women. He parted with and published nothing except under the extreme pressure of friends. Until the second phase of his life, he was a wrapt, consecrated solitary, pursuing his studies by intense introspection with a mental endurance perhaps never equalled.

I believe that the clue to his mind is to be found in his unusual powers of continuous concentrated introspection. A case can be made out, as it also can with Descartes, for regarding him as an accomplished experimentalist. Nothing can be more charming than the tales of his mechanical contrivances when he was a boy. There are his telescopes and his optical experiments. These were essential accomplishments, part of his unequalled all-round technique, but not, I am sure, his *peculiar* gift, especially amongst his contemporaries. His peculiar gift was the power of holding continuously in his mind a purely mental problem until he had seen straight through it. I fancy his pre-eminence is due to his muscles of intuition being the strongest and most enduring with which a man has ever been gifted. Anyone who has ever attempted pure scientific or philosophical thought knows how one can hold a problem momentarily in one's mind and apply all one's powers of concentration to piercing through it, and how it will dissolve and escape and you find that what you are surveying is a blank. I believe that Newton could hold a problem in his mind for hours and days and weeks until it surrendered to him its secret. Then being a supreme mathematical technician he could dress it up, how you will, for purposes of exposition, but it was his intuition which was pre-eminently extraordinary—'so happy in his conjectures,' said de Morgan, 'as to seem to know more than he could possibly have any means of proving.' The proofs, for what they are worth, were, as I have said, dressed up afterwards—they were not the instrument of discovery.

There is the story of how he informed Halley of one of his most fundamental discoveries of planetary motion. 'Yes,' replied Halley, 'but how do you know that? Have you proved it?' Newton was taken aback— 'Why, I've known it for years,' he replied. 'If you'll give me a few days, I'll certainly find you a proof of it'—as in due course he did.

Again, there is some evidence that Newton in preparing the *Principia* was held up almost to the last moment by lack of proof that you could treat a solid sphere as though all its mass was concentrated at the centre, and only hit on the proof a year before publication. But this was a truth which he had known for certain and had always assumed for many years.

Certainly there can be no doubt that the peculiar geometrical form in which the exposition of the *Principia* is dressed up bears no resemblance at all to the mental processes by which Newton actually arrived at his conclusions.

His experiments were always, I suspect, a means, not of discovery, but always of verifying what he knew already.

Why do I call him a magician? Because he looked on the whole universe and all that is in it *as a riddle,* as a secret which could be read by applying pure thought to certain evidence, certain mystic clues which God had laid about the world to allow a sort of philosopher's treasure hunt to the esoteric brotherhood. He believed that these clues were to be found partly in the evidence of the heavens and in the constitution of elements (and that is what gives the false suggestion of his being an experimental natural philosopher), but also partly in certain papers and traditions handed down by the brethren in an unbroken chain back to the original cryptic revelation in Babylonia. He regarded the universe as a cryptogram set by the Almighty—just as he himself wrapt the discovery of the calculus in a cryptogram when he communicated with Leibnitz. By pure thought, by concentration of mind, the riddle, he believed, would be revealed to the initiate.

He *did* read the riddle of the heavens. And he believed that by the same powers of his introspective imagination he would read the riddle of the Godhead, the riddle of past and future events divinely fore-ordained, the riddle of the elements and their constitution from an original undifferentiated first matter, the riddle of health and of immortality. All would be revealed to him if only he could persevere to the end, uninterrupted, by himself, no one coming into the room, reading, copying, testing—all by himself, no interruption for God's sake, no disclosure, no discordant breakings in or criticism, with fear and shrinking as he assailed these half-ordained, half-forbidden things, creeping back into the bosom of the Godhead as into his mother's womb. 'Voyaging through strange seas of thought *alone,*' not as Charles Lamb 'a fellow who believed nothing unless it was as clear as the three sides of a triangle.'

And so he continued for some twenty-five years. In 1687, when he was forty-five years old, the *Principia* was published.

Here in Trinity it is right that I should give you an account of how he lived amongst you during these years of his greatest achievement. The east end of the Chapel projects farther eastwards than the Great Gate. In the second half of the seventeenth century there was a walled garden in the free space between Trinity Street and the building which joins the Great Gate to the Chapel. The south wall ran out from the turret of the Gate to a distance overlapping the Chapel by at least the width of the present pavement. Thus the garden was of modest but reasonable size. This was Newton's garden. He had the Fellow's set of rooms between the Porter's Lodge and the Chapel—that, I suppose, now occupied by Professor Broad. The garden was reached by a stairway which was attached to a veranda raised on wooden pillars projecting into the garden from the range of buildings. At the top of this stairway stood his telescope— not to be confused with the observatory erected on the top of the Great Gate during Newton's lifetime (but after he had left Cambridge) for the use of Roger Cotes and Newton's successor, Whiston. This wooden erection was, I think, demolished by Whewell in 1856 and replaced by the stone bay of Professor Broad's bedroom. At the Chapel end of the garden was a small two-storied building, also of wood, which was his elaboratory. When he decided to prepare the *Principia* for publication he engaged a young kinsman, Humphrey Newton, to act as his amanuensis (the MS. of the *Principia,* as it went to the press, is clearly in the hand of Humphrey). Humphrey remained with him for five years—from 1684 to 1689. When Newton died Humphrey's son-in-law Conduitt wrote to him for his reminiscences, and among the papers I have is Humphrey's reply.

During these twenty-five years of intense study mathematics and astronomy were only a part, and perhaps not the most absorbing, of his occupations. Our record of these is almost wholly confined to the papers which he kept and put in his box when he left Trinity for London.

Let me give some brief indications of their subject. They are enormously voluminous—I should say that upwards of 1,000,000 words in his handwriting still survive. They have, beyond doubt, no substantial value whatever except as a fascinating sidelight on the mind of our greatest genius.

Let me not exaggerate through reaction against the other Newton myth which has been so sedulously created for the last two hundred years. There was extreme method in his madness. All his unpublished works on esoteric and theological matters are marked by careful learning, accurate method and extreme sobriety of statement. They are just as *sane* as the *Principia,* if their whole matter and purpose were not magical. They were nearly all composed during the same twenty-five years of his mathematical studies. They fall into several groups.

Very early in life Newton abandoned orthodox belief in the Trinity. At this time the Socinians were an important Arian sect amongst intellectual circles. It may be that Newton fell under Socinian influences, but I think not. He was rather a Judaic monotheist of the school of Maimonides. He arrived at this conclusion, not on so-to-speak rational or sceptical grounds, but entirely on the interpretation of ancient authority. He was persuaded that the revealed documents give no support to the Trinitarian doctrines which were due to late falsifications. The revealed God was one God.

But this was a dreadful secret which Newton was at desperate pains to conceal all his life. It was the reason why he refused Holy Orders, and therefore had to obtain a special dispensation to hold his Fellowship and

Lucasian Chair and could not be Master of Trinity. Even the Toleration Act of 1689 excepted anti-Trinitarians. Some rumours there were, but not at the dangerous dates when he was a young Fellow of Trinity. In the main the secret died with him. But it was revealed in many writings in his big box. After his death Bishop Horsley was asked to inspect the box with a view to publication. He saw the contents with horror and slammed the lid. A hundred years later Sir David Brewster looked into the box. He covered up the traces with carefully selected extracts and some straight fibbing. His latest biographer, Mr More, has been more candid. Newton's extensive anti-Trinitarian pamphlets are, in my judgment, the most interesting of his unpublished papers. Apart from his more serious affirmation of belief, I have a completed pamphlet showing up what Newton thought of the extreme dishonesty and falsification of records for which St Athanasius was responsible, in particular for his putting about the false calumny that Arius died in a privy. The victory of the Trinitarians in England in the latter half of the seventeenth century was not only as complete, but also as extraordinary, as St Athanasius's original triumph. There is good reason for thinking that Locke was a Unitarian. I have seen it argued that Milton was. It is a blot on Newton's record that he did not murmur a word when Whiston, his successor in the Lucasian Chair, was thrown out of his professorship and out of the University for publicly avowing opinions which Newton himself had secretly held for upwards of fifty years past.

That he held this heresy was a further aggravation of his silence and secrecy and inwardness of disposition.

Another large section is concerned with all branches of apocalyptic writings from which he sought to deduce the secret truths of the Universe —the measurements of Solomon's Temple, the Book of David, the Book of Revelations, an enormous volume of work of which some part was published in his later days. Along with this are hundreds of pages of Church History and the like, designed to discover the truth of tradition.

A large section, judging by the handwriting amongst the earliest, relates to alchemy—transmutation, the philosopher's stone, the elixir of life. The scope and character of these papers have been hushed up, or at least minimized, by nearly all those who have inspected them. About 1650 there was a considerable group in London, round the publisher Cooper, who during the next twenty years revived interest not only in the English alchemists of the fifteenth century, but also in translations of the medieval and post-medieval alchemists.

There is an unusual number of manuscripts of the early English alchemists in the libraries of Cambridge. It may be that there was some continuous esoteric tradition within the University which sprang into activity again in the twenty years from 1650 to 1670. At any rate, Newton was clearly an unbridled addict. It is this with which he was occupied 'about 6 weeks at spring and 6 at the fall when the fire in the elaboratory scarcely went out' at the very years when he was composing the *Principia* —and about this he told Humphrey Newton not a word. Moreover, he was almost entirely concerned, not in serious experiment, but in trying to read the riddle of tradition, to find meaning in cryptic verses, to imitate the alleged but largely imaginary experiments of the initiates of past centuries. Newton has left behind him a vast mass of records of these studies. I believe that the greater part are translations and copies made by him of existing books and manuscripts. But there are also extensive records of experiments. I have glanced through a great quantity of this— at least 100,000 words, I should say. It is utterly impossible to deny that it is wholly magical and wholly devoid of scientific value; and also impossible not to admit that Newton devoted years of work to it. Some time it might be interesting, but not useful, for some student better equipped and more idle than I to work out Newton's exact relationship to the tradition and MSS. of his time.

In these mixed and extraordinary studies, with one foot in the Middle Ages and one foot treading a path for modern science, Newton spent the first phase of his life, the period of life in Trinity when he did all his real work. Now let me pass to the second phase.

After the publication of the *Principia* there is a complete change in his habit and way of life. I believe that his friends, above all Halifax, came to the conclusion that he must be rooted out of the life he was leading at Trinity which must soon lead to decay of mind and health. Broadly speaking, of his own motion or under persuasion, he abandons his studies. He takes up University business, represents the University in Parliament; his friends are busy trying to get a dignified and remunerative job for him— the Provostship of King's, the Mastership of Charterhouse, the Controllership of the Mint.

Newton could not be Master of Trinity because he was a Unitarian and so not in Holy Orders. He was rejected as Provost of King's for the more prosaic reason that he was not an Etonian. Newton took this rejection very ill and prepared a long legalistic brief, which I possess, giving reasons why it was not unlawful for him to be accepted as Provost. But, as ill-luck had it, Newton's nomination for the Provostship came at the moment when King's had decided to fight against the right of Crown nomination, a struggle in which the College was successful.

Newton was well qualified for any of these offices. It must not be inferred from his introspection, his absent-mindedness, his secrecy and his solitude that he lacked aptitude for affairs when he chose to exercise it. There are many records to prove his very great capacity. Read, for example, his correspondence with Dr Covell, the Vice-Chancellor when, as the University's representative in Parliament, he had to deal with the delicate question of the oaths after the revolution of 1688. With Pepys and Lowndes he became one of the greatest and most efficient of our civil servants. He was a very successful investor of funds, surmounting the crisis of the South Sea Bubble, and died a rich man. He possessed in exceptional degree almost every kind of intellectual aptitude—lawyer, historian, theologian, not less than mathematician, physicist, astronomer.

And when the turn of his life came and he put his books of magic back into the box, it was easy for him to drop the seventeenth century behind him and to evolve into the eighteenth-century figure which is the traditional Newton.

Nevertheless, the move on the part of his friends to change his life came almost too late. In 1689 his mother, to whom he was deeply attached, died. Somewhere about his fiftieth birthday on Christmas Day 1692, he suffered what we should now term a severe nervous breakdown. Melancholia, sleeplessness, fears of persecution—he writes to Pepys and to Locke and no doubt to others letters which lead them to think that his mind is deranged. He lost, in his own words, the 'former consistency of his mind.' He never again concentrated after the old fashion or did any fresh work. The breakdown probably lasted nearly two years, and from it emerged, slightly 'gaga,' but still, no doubt, with one of the most powerful minds of England, the Sir Isaac Newton of tradition.

In 1696 his friends were finally successful in digging him out of Cambridge, and for more than another twenty years he reigned in London as the most famous man of his age, of Europe, and—as his powers gradually waned and his affability increased—perhaps of all time, so it seemed to his contemporaries.

He set up house with his niece Catharine Barton, who was beyond reasonable doubt the mistress of his old and loyal friend Charles Montague, Earl of Halifax and Chancellor of the Exchequer, who had been one of Newton's intimate friends when he was an undergraduate at Trinity. Catharine was reputed to be one of the most brilliant and charming women in the London of Congreve, Swift and Pope. She is celebrated, not least for the broadness of her stories, in Swift's *Journal to Stella*. Newton puts on rather too much weight for his moderate height. 'When he rode in his coach one arm would be out of his coach on one side and the other on the other.' His pink face, beneath a mass of snow-white hair, which 'when his peruke was off was a venerable sight,' is increasingly both benevolent and majestic. One night in Trinity after Hall he is knighted by Queen Anne. For nearly twenty-four years he reigns as President of the Royal Society. He becomes one of the principal sights of London for all visiting intellectual foreigners, whom he entertains handsomely. He liked to have clever young men about him to edit new editions of the *Principia*—and sometimes merely plausible ones as in the case of Facio de Duillier.

Magic was quite forgotten. He has become the Sage and Monarch of the Age of Reason. The Sir Isaac Newton of orthodox tradition—the eighteenth-century Sir Isaac, so remote from the child magician born in the first half of the seventeenth century—was being built up. Voltaire returning from his trip to London was able to report of Sir Isaac—''twas his peculiar felicity, not only to be born in a country of liberty, but in an Age when all scholastic impertinences were banished from the World. Reason alone was cultivated and Mankind cou'd only be his Pupil, not his Enemy.' Newton, whose secret heresies and scholastic superstitions it had been the study of a lifetime to conceal!

But he never concentrated, never recovered 'the former consistency of his mind.' 'He spoke very little in company.' 'He had something rather languid in his look and manner.'

And he looked very seldom, I expect, into the chest where, when he left Cambridge, he had packed all the evidences of what had occupied and so absorbed his intense and flaming spirit in his rooms and his garden and his elaboratory between the Great Gate and Chapel.

But he did not destroy them. They remained in the box to shock profoundly any eighteenth- or nineteenth-century prying eyes. They became the possession of Catharine Barton and then of her daughter, the Countess of Portsmouth. So Newton's chest, with many hundreds of thousands of words of his unpublished writings, came to contain the 'Portsmouth Papers.'

In 1888 the mathematical portion was given to the University Library at Cambridge. They have been indexed, but they have never been edited. The rest, a very large collection, were dispersed in the auction room in 1936 by Catharine Barton's descendant, the present Lord Lymington. Disturbed by this impiety, I managed gradually to reassemble about half of them, including nearly the whole of the biographical portion, that is, the 'Conduitt Papers,' in order to bring them to Cambridge which I hope they will never leave. The greater part of the rest were snatched out of my reach by a syndicate which hoped to sell them at a high price, probably in America, on the occasion of the recent tercentenary.

As one broods over these queer collections, it seems easier to understand—with an understanding which is not, I hope, distorted in the other direction—this strange spirit, who was tempted by the Devil to believe at the time when within these walls he was solving so much, that he could reach all the secrets of God and Nature by the pure power of mind—Copernicus and Faustus in one.

QUESTIONS FOR DISCUSSION

1) Keynes here gives us a startlingly different picture of Newton from that which is ordinarily presented. For instance, Keynes asserts that Newton was "the last of the magicians." What does he mean by this?

2) Keynes cites several of Newton's traits, such as his being "neurotic," "solitary," and "absent-minded," and concludes that "Geniuses *are* very peculiar." From what you may know of geniuses, do you agree? Are "creative" people also "peculiar"? Explain.

3) Keynes speaks of Newton's "unusual powers of continuous concentrated introspection" and of his "muscles of intuition," observing that Newton often *knew* the answers to questions before he could prove his answers were correct. Comment on this aspect of Newton as an aspect of creativity in general.

4) Does Keynes seem to be saying that all of Newton's work on "esoteric and theological matters" was a waste of time and a sign that Newton was "neurotic"? Or is the point that a man's life must be seen as a whole, and that the capacity to hold a wide range of beliefs in one's mind at the same time is a mark of creativity? Explain.

5) Discuss the allusions in the last sentence: that Newton was "Copernicus and Faustus in one."

PASTEUR AND
THE MAD DOG

Paul de Kruif

And now Pasteur began—God knows why—to stick little hollow glass tubes into the gaping mouths of dogs writhing mad with rabies. While two servants pried apart and held open the jowls of a powerful bulldog, Pasteur stuck his beard within a couple of inches of those fangs whose snap meant the worst of deaths, and, sprinkled sometimes with a maybe fatal spray, he sucked up the froth into his tube—to get a specimen in which to hunt for the microbe of hydrophobia. I wish to forget, now, everything that I have said about his showmanship, his unsearcherlike go-gettings. This business of his gray eyes looking that bulldog in the mouth—this was no grandstand stuff.

Why did Pasteur set out to trap the germ of rabies? That is a mystery, because there were a dozen other serious diseases, just then, whose microbes had not yet been found, diseases that killed many more people than rabies had ever put to death, diseases that were not nearly so surely deadly to an adventurous experimenter as rabies would be—if one of those dogs should get loose. . . .

It must have been the artist, the poet in him that urged him on to this most hard and dangerous hunting, for Pasteur himself said: "I have always been haunted by the cries of those victims of the mad wolf that came down the street of Arbois when I was a little boy. . . ." Pasteur knew the way the yells of a mad dog curdle the blood of every one. He remembered that less than a hundred years before in France, laws had to be passed against the poisoning, the strangling, the shooting of wretched people whom frightened fellow-townsmen just suspected of having rabies. Doubtless he saw himself the deliverer of men from such crazy fear—such hopeless suffering.

And then, in this most magnificent and truest of all his searchings, Pasteur started out, as he so often did, by making mistakes. In the saliva of a little child dying from hydrophobia he discovered a strange motionless germ that he gave the unscientific name of "microbe-like-an-eight." He read papers at the Academy that hinted about this figure-eight germ having something to do with the mysterious cause of hydrophobia. But in a little while this trail proved to be a blind one, for with Roux and Chamberland he found—after he had settled down and got his teeth into this search—that this eight-microbe could be found in the mouths of many healthy people who had never been anywhere near a mad dog.

Presently, late in 1882, he ran on to his first clew. "Mad dogs are scarce just now, old Bourrel the veterinarian brings me very few of them, and people with hydrophobia are still harder to get hold of—we've got to produce this rabies in animals in our laboratory and keep it going there —otherwise we won't be able to go on studying it steadily," he pondered.

He was more than sixty, and he was tired.

Then one day, a lassoed mad dog was brought into the laboratory; dangerously he was slid into a big cage with healthy dogs and allowed to bite them. Roux and Chamberland fished froth out of the mouth of this mad beast and sucked it up into syringes and injected this stuff into rabbits and guinea-pigs. Then they waited eagerly to see this menagerie develop the first signs of madness. Sometimes—alas—the experiment worked, but other very irritating times it did not; four healthy dogs had been bitten and six weeks later they came in one morning to find two of these creatures lashing about their cages, howling—but for months after that the other two showed no sign of rabies; there was no rime or reason to this business, no regularity, confound it! this was not *science!* And it was the same with the guinea-pigs and rabbits; two of the rabbits might drag out their hind legs with a paralysis—then die in dreadful convulsions, but the other four would go on chewing their greens as if there were no mad-dog virus within a million miles of them.

Then one day a little idea came to Pasteur, and he hurried to tell it to Roux.

"This rabies virus that gets into people by bites, it settles in their brains and spinal cords. . . . All the symptoms of hydrophobia show that it's the nervous system that this virus—this bug we can't find—attacks. . . .

"That's where we have to look for the unknown microbe . . . that's where we can grow it maybe, even without seeing it . . . maybe we could use the living animal's brain instead of a bottle of soup . . . a funny culture-bottle that would be, but. . . .

"When we inject it under the skin—the virus may get lost in the body before it can travel to the brain—if I could only stick it right into a dog's brain . . . !"

Roux listened to these dreamings of Pasteur, he listened bright-eyed to these fantastic imaginings. . . . Another man than Roux might have thought Pasteur completely crazy. . . . The brain of a dog or rabbit instead of a bottle of broth, indeed! What nonsense! But not to Roux!

"But why not put the virus right into a dog's brain, master, I can trephine a dog—I can drill a little hole in his skull—without hurting him —without damaging his brain at all . . . it would be easy . . ." said Roux.

Pasteur shut Roux up, furiously. He was no doctor, and he did not know that surgeons can do this operation on human beings even, quite safely. "What! bore a hole right through a dog's skull—why, you'd hurt the poor beast terribly . . . you would damage his brain . . . you would paralyze him . . . No! I will not permit it!"

So near was Pasteur, by reason of his tender-heartedness, so close was he to failing completely in winning to the most marvelous of his gifts to men. He quailed before the stern experiment that his weird idea demanded. But Roux—the faithful, the now almost forgotten Roux—saved him by disobeying him.

For, a few days later when Pasteur left the laboratory to go to some meeting or other, Roux took a healthy dog, put him easily out of pain with a little chloroform, and bored a hole in the beast's head and exposed his palpitating, living brain. Then up into a syringe he drew a little bit of the ground-up brain of a dog just dead with rabies: "This stuff must be swarming with those rabies microbes that are maybe too small for us to see," he pondered; and through the hole in the sleeping dog's skull went the needle of the syringe, and into the living brain Roux slowly, gently shot the deadly rabid stuff. . . .

Next morning Roux told Pasteur about it—— "What!" shouted Pasteur. "Where is the poor creature . . . he must be dying . . . paralyzed. . . ."

But Roux was already down the stairs, and in an instant he was back, his operated dog prancing in ahead of him, jumping up against Pasteur, sniffing 'round among the old broth bottles under the laboratory benches. Then Pasteur realized Roux's cleverness—and the new road of experiment that lay before him, and though he was not fond of dogs, his joy made him fuss over this one: "Good dog, excellent beast!" Pasteur said, and dreamed: "This beast will show that my idea will work. . . ."

Sure enough, less than two weeks later the good creature began to howl mournful cries and tear up his bed and gnaw at his cage—and in a few days more he was dead, and this brute died, as you will see, so that thousands of mankind might live.

Now Pasteur and Roux and Chamberland had a sure way, that worked one hundred times out of one hundred, of giving rabies to their dogs and guinea-pigs and rabbits. "We cannot find the microbe—surely it must be too tiny for the strongest microscope to show us—there's no way to grow it in flasks of soup . . . but we can keep it alive—this deadly virus—in the brains of rabbits . . . that is the only way to grow it," you can hear Pasteur telling Roux and Chamberland.

Never was there a more fantastic experiment in all of microbe hunting, or in any science, for that matter; never was there a more unscientific feat of science than this struggling, by Pasteur and his boys, with a microbe they couldn't see—a weird bug of whose existence they only knew by its invisible growth in the living brains and spinal cords of an endless succession of rabbits and guinea-pigs and dogs. Their only knowledge that there was such a thing as the microbe of rabies was the convulsive death of the rabbits they injected, and the fearful cries of their trephined dogs. . . .

Then Pasteur and his assistants started on their outlandish—any wise man would say their impossible—adventure of taming this vicious virus that they could not see. There were little interruptions; Roux went with Thuillier to fight the cholera in Egypt and there, you will remember, Thuillier died; and Pasteur went out into the rural pig-sties of France to discover the microbe and find a vaccine against a disease that was just then murdering French swine. But Pasteur stopped getting entangled in those vulgar arguments which were so often to his discredit, and the three of them locked themselves in their laboratory in the Rue d'Ulm with their poor paralyzed and dangerous animals. They sweat through endless experiments.

Pasteur mounted guard over his young men and kept their backs bent over their benches as if they were some higher kind of galley slave. He watched their perilous experiments with one eye and kept the other on the glass door of the workroom, and when he saw some of Roux's and Chamberland's friends approaching, to ask them maybe to come out for a glass of beer on the terrace of a near-by café, the master would hurry out and tell the interlopers: "No. No! Not now! Cannot you see? They are busy—it is a most important experiment they are doing!"

Months—gray months went by during which it seemed to all of them that there was no possible way of weakening the invisible virus of rabies. . . . One hundred animals, alas, out of every hundred that they injected—died. You would think that Roux and Chamberland, still youngsters, would have been the indomitable ones, the never-say-die men of this desperate crew. But on the contrary!

"It's no go, master," said they, making limp waves of their hands toward the cages with their paralyzed beasts—toward the tangled jungles of useless tubes and bottles. . . .

Then Pasteur's eyebrows cocked at them, and his thinning gray hair seemed to stiffen: "Do the same experiment over again—no matter if it failed last time—it may look foolish to you, but the important thing is not to leave the subject!" Pasteur shouted, in a fury. So it was that this man scolded his monkish disciples and prodded them to do useless tests over and over and over—with no reasons, with complete lack of logic. With every fact against him Pasteur searched and tried and failed and tried again with that insane neglect of common sense that sometimes turns hopeless causes into victories.

Indeed, why wasn't this setting out to tame the hydrophobia virus—why wasn't it a nonsensical wild-goose chase? There was in all human history no single record of any man or beast getting better from this horrible malady, once the symptoms had declared themselves, once the mysterious messengers of evil had wormed their unseen way into the spinal cord and brain. It was this kind of murderous stuff that Pasteur and his men balanced on the tips of their knives, sucked up into their glass pipettes within an inch from the lips—stuff that was separated from their mouths by a thin little wisp of cotton. . . .

Then, one exciting day, the first sweet music of encouragement came to these gropers in the dark—one of their dogs inoculated with the surely fatal stuff from a rabid rabbit's brain—this dog came down with his weird barkings and portentous shiverings and slatherings—and then miraculously got completely better! Excitedly, a few weeks later, they shot this first of all recovered beasts with a deadly virus, directly into his brain they injected the wee murderers. The little wound on his head healed quickly—anxiously Pasteur waited for his doomful symptoms to come on him, but these signs never came. For months the dog romped about his cage. He was absolutely immune!

"Now we know it—we know we have a chance. . . . When a beast once has rabies and gets better from it, there will be no recurrence. . . . We must find a way to *tame* the virus now," said Pasteur to his men, who agreed, but were perfectly certain that there was no way to tame that virus.

But Pasteur began inventing experiments that no god would have attempted; his desk was strewn with hieroglyphic scrawls of them. And at eleven in the morning, when the records of the results of the day before had been carefully put down, he would call Roux and Chamberland, and to them he would read off some wild plan for groping after this unseen unreachable virus—some fantastic plan for getting his fingers on it *inside* the body of a rabbit—to weaken it.

"Try this experiment to-day!" Pasteur would tell them.

"But that is technically impossible!" they protested.

"No matter—plan it any way you wish, provided you do it well," Pasteur replied. (He was, those days, like old Ludwig van Beethoven writing unplayable horn parts for his symphonies—and then miraculously discovering hornblowers to play those parts.) For, one way or another, the ingenious Roux and Chamberland devised tricks to do those crazy experiments. . . .

And at last they found a way of weakening the savage hydrophobia virus—by taking out a little section of the spinal cord of a rabbit dead of rabies, and hanging this bit of deadly stuff up to dry in a germ-proof bottle for fourteen days. This shriveled bit of nervous tissue that had once been so deadly they shot into the brains of healthy dogs—and those dogs did not die. . . .

"The virus is dead—or better still very much weakened," said Pasteur, jumping at the latter conclusion with no sense or reason. "Now we'll try drying other pieces of virulent stuff for twelve days—ten days—eight days—six days, and see if we can't just give our dogs a *little* rabies . . . then they ought to be immune. . . ."

Savagely they fell to this long will o' the wisp of an experiment. For fourteen days Pasteur walked up and down the bottle and microscope and cage-strewn unearthly workshop and grumbled and fretted and made scrawls in that everlasting notebook of his. The first day the dogs were dosed with the weakened—the almost extinct virus that had been dried for fourteen days; the second day they received a shot of the slightly stronger nerve stuff that had been thirteen days in its bottle; and so on until the fourteenth day—when each beast was injected with one-day-dried virus that would have surely killed a not-inoculated animal.

For weeks they waited—hair graying again—for signs of rabies in these animals, but none ever came. They were happy, these ghoulish fighters of death! Their clumsy terrible fourteen vaccinations had not hurt the dogs—but were they immune?

Pasteur dreaded it—if this failed all of these years of work had gone for nothing, and "I am getting old, old . . ." you can hear him whispering to himself. But the test had to be made. Would the dogs stand an injection of the most deadly rabid virus—right into their brains—a business that killed an ordinary dog one hundred times out of one hundred?

Then one day Roux bored little holes through the skulls of two vaccinated dogs—and two not vaccinated ones: and into all four went a heavy dose of the most virulent virus. . . .

One month later, Pasteur and his men, at the end of three years of work, knew that victory over hydrophobia was in their hands. For, while the two vaccinated dogs romped and sniffed about their cages with never a sign of anything ailing them—the two that had not received the fourteen protective doses of dried rabbit's brain—these two had howled their last howls and died of rabies. . . .

QUESTIONS FOR DISCUSSION

1) When de Kruif argues that Pasteur became interested in discovering a cure for rabies because of the "artist" in him, what definition, or characteristics, of the artist does he have in mind? Would the writers on creativity represented in this anthology agree with de Kruif? Explain.

2) De Kruif also aspires to show that Pasteur was artistic in his method as well as in his motive. His emphasis is on the "accidental" elements in Pasteur's discoveries and on Pasteur's defiance of logic. Is this evidence sufficient for de Kruif's argument? Explain.

3) Does the account of Pasteur's conquest of rabies support Huxley's definition of the scientific method or Bronowski's definition? Explain.

OBSERVATIONS ON
THE DEVELOPMENT
OF THE TRANSISTOR[1]

William Shockley

Perhaps the one thing that I bring to this meeting is a background in creativity in the transistor field. But I thought that rather than trying to give a detailed history that would hit all the aspects that might bear on this, I would try to give a once-over-lightly of about five minutes and then see if these aspects would turn up responsible questions.

Before I start, there are one or two things I feel like saying at this point about why I am here at this meeting.

There are at least two reasons. The decisive one is that I had a personal debt of gratitude to Allen Wallis. If somebody else had asked me to take time to come to a meeting of this sort, I might very well not have done it, simply because I could perfectly well see other things I should be spending my time on.

I will say there's another aspect though, and that is that this is a real stimulating affair. I've enjoyed the discussion and I enjoy the type of thing that goes on. I have more confidence in this group of people than I would ordinarily have and, therefore, my guard is up somewhat less. I can talk about myself more than I would under similar circumstances in groups of this size. So this is something about background.

Now somehow I see myself as a sort of guinea pig in this setup. I qualify as being an intelligent and creative person. I can count patents. I can read what is being said about me. (I have had the unusual experience of reading my biography recently, and there are things which people say about me which I would never have had the nerve to say, you know, myself. But there they are, and I can say I am a pretty creative guy with a lot of originality and effectiveness. Whether I would have said that if I hadn't seen it in writing where I could quote it, I don't know.)

But saying something more about myself here: A lot of things that have been said by some of the people speaking about the psychology of creative people strikes home. I am looking at this reprint which Frank Barron just handed out to us. It says we're "likely to have more than the usual amount of respect for the forces of the irrational in ourselves and

---

[1] An interview at a seminar conducted by the Graduate School of Business of the University of Chicago on February 2 and 3, 1962, under a grant from the McKinsey Foundation for Management Research, Inc.

in others." I think this is true. And I would think maybe this other paragraph: "They have exceptionally broad, flexible awareness of themselves. The self is strongest when it can regress, admit primitive fantasies, naïve ideas, crude impulses, inner consciousness and behavior, and yet return to a high degree of rationality and self-criticism. The creative person is both more primitive, more cultured, more destructive and more constructive, crazier and saner than the average person." I don't know, but I would be inclined to buy this kind of thing in reading about myself.

Something else in my background is this: I am a person with very mixed self-esteem and I am aware of this. It doesn't solve all your problems to win a Nobel Prize. You still go around wondering if you are any good, every now and then, and you do various things which may not be really necessary for any demonstration, you see. I would have felt somewhat distressed if I hadn't worked out this generalization of the end links in the chain. I enjoy showing off. I have a need to feel I'm making contributions to things.

Well, I thought I would run through things historically.

CHRONOLOGY

I'll start out with 1936, which was the year I came with Bell Telephone Laboratories as a fresh Ph.D. from M.I.T. There was a conversation that I had at M.I.T. which I think may be significant in what went on in my career. It was a conversation with M. J. Kelly—whom many of you probably know by name—who was then research director and who subsequently became president. Kelly talked about the objective of an electronic telephone exchange; that is, where everything is done electronically, with no relays.

Well, then, there's a period of about 1939 to 1940 in the course of which I had some ideas of trying to make a solid state amplifier. (That is what the transistor is.) But I got involved in doing some things like trying to make other amplifiers that didn't have vacuum tubes in them. One of them involved using a piezo-electric crystal. It was a thoroughly lousy idea, I think, but you never can tell. These things may come back if somebody does it better and finds a use for it. But as far as I can tell now, it is a lousy idea. Nevertheless, the intent was right.

From '41 to '45, there was a war, at which time I was a radar designer and in operations research work.

From '45 to '48, I was co-head of a solid state research group. The areas dealt with in the solid state group were formalized by Mervin Kelly. That covered chiefly four general areas: (1) magnetic materials; (2) piezo-electric crystals; (3) semiconductors; and (4) dielectrics of insulators.

Semiconductors are the crystalline materials that transistors are made of; of course, at that time there were no transistors but a number of other useful electronic functions were performed by semiconductors. In particular, copper oxide rectifiers were used to make so-called "click reducers"; these protect the subscribers by limiting the maximum amount of noise that may come out of the earphone in the event of some malfunction of a telephone circuit. All of the subjects selected for areas of research by the solid state group had to do with the transmission of electrical signals over wires and were related directly to major problems of the telephone business. In this area, I had a very free hand.

From 1946 to 1948, I cooked up some additional ideas about amplifiers. These led to certain difficulties; certain new lines of research started, out of which came the transistor.

The first transistor was not an idea of mine. (The point-contact transistor is a different kind of thing.) But at the same time, I cooked up the idea of the junction transistor, which is the patent under which practically every transistor made now is made.

From '51 to '54, there were various kinds of writing and other transistor ideas. I have the patents on at least two other principles, which are important principles in getting amplification out of semiconductors that are quite distinct from junction transistors.

From '54 to '55, I got tagged at the Pentagon again in the weapons systems evaluation group in an activity which led to the setting up of a corporation group, which some of you may know, is called the Institute for Defense Analysis.

From '56 to '62, I've been involved in a new venture of trying to set up a business. There are about 130 people and we are part of Clevite Transistor, a division of the Clevite Corporation.

SCIENTIFIC ASPECTS OF PRACTICAL PROBLEMS

There are some interesting aspects about this: I think I've formulated a sort of research objective in this activity which I will try to describe by the phrase "respect for scientific aspects of practical problems." That is, if we can't make a transistor of some sort, or if we can't make a process work (after we've done a reasonable amount of messing about and trying), then we turn around and say: What is nature telling us? What does it mean? We forget about solving the problem for the time being. We try to understand the science of what is going on. This I think may represent an important trend in creativity in modern industry, which would not have been appropriate in the time of Edison. At the time of Edison, it was better to try things, because the fundamental understanding was not there. There is now enough fundamental understanding in these things, and once you understand this, it is pretty likely you'll find answers.

DISCUSSION: PRACTICAL ASPECTS OF SCIENTIFIC PROBLEMS

OGILVY. Who owns the patents you mentioned? Do you get royalties on them or does Bell?

SHOCKLEY. Bell owns all the patents, and I can't see a better way of handling it. I would just love to have my hooks in this thing, of course. This is obvious. But, on the other hand, any other scheme would make an unlivable place. I would not like to work in an organization nor try to run an organization in which a man received outstanding awards for his patent contributions.

If you have such an arrangement, you will find six people sitting down in a conference to discuss something, some problem. Now suppose there is a high award for an invention, and I have an idea. I'll say to myself, "Gee, maybe this idea is really an invention, but I don't quite see it yet." So I will keep my mouth shut, I'll go back to my desk, I will work for a day on the thing, and I'll get it written down and witnessed before I bring it out in front of anybody who might be able to out-think me on it.

PETERSON. What about the problem of the discovery of the problem to be tackled, as contrasted with the solutions? How do you select problems?

SHOCKLEY. Well, you see, in '39 and '40, I think they did a very good job in my conditioning at Bell Laboratories. They stuck me to the vacuum tube department for a while there, but then when I indicated that I wanted to get into more scientific things, no bar was put up to my getting back and doing more basic work in solid state physics.

Well, I then had ideas that you might be able to make an amplifying device not using a vacuum tube. There is a thing called the old crystal detector which some of you are old enough to know about—the galena, cat's whisker—which does the same job as a certain kind of vacuum tube. What De Forest, the father of electronics, did was to take the rectifier and put a grid in it. Now, the cat's whisker, galena detector did a job like a vacuum tube diode, which Edison had a lot to do with discovering, by the way. He put a grid in this which is a handle, a valve handle which gave a valve-controlled electrical flow. People had an idea somehow that you could stick a valve handle into this crystal detector. That idea was not original with me.

But back in 1940, I had an idea which in principle is sound. It doesn't violate any laws in physics to do this job. In about '45 to '46, I had another idea which was sounder and which now works, though it didn't work then. Now, I'm not saying any more about this because I just suspect that if we get into any of the technical aspects it will take too much time.

But there is an aspect of pattern in there, from '45 to '48, that I think is worth mentioning. Taking this idea of how an amplifier might be made to work based on sound physics, but which so far did not, I persuaded at least three different experimenters, all of whom were competent, to try to do this and make a measurable observation. Nothing measurable came out of this.

It was at that point that Bardeen came up with a physical explanation that there were some new physical phenomena occurring here, not generally recognized, which was preventing this thing from working. This was his theory of surface states, a subject still of active scientific interest in semiconductors. We started to investigate that aspect, and this led us to new experimental configurations, more understanding of nature, and in turn, in the course of these experimental configurations, to some situations which appeared to give us more control. It was in the course of following those up that Bardeen and Brattain came out with the first point-contact amplifying device, the first point-contact transistor.

At the same time, in part stimulated by these things and stimulated also by some earlier work I had done on how semiconductors work, I came out with the more generally useful idea of the junction transistor, which was filed as a patent application in 1948. I published extensive papers on the theory in 1949. It was first made to work effectively in 1950.

I reported on this at one of the first international semiconductor meetings in Reading. It was a non-scheduled paper, and it made so little impression that it never got into the proceedings of that meeting.

Then in 1950—this is an interesting sideline—I got involved with the Pentagon; I was shipped off to Korea in an operations research activity. In the course of this, I got involved with being consultant for the Quartermaster General, and I discovered the proximity fuse situation. And one thing that was perfectly obvious was that what one should try to do was to make proximity fuses which were transistorized.

When I tried to promote a program of that sort, the best electronics man I could find at Bell Laboratories to make a transistorized amplifier to go on a proximity fuse said, "Look, if you could really make a really good junction transistor, this would be an awful lot better than a point-contact transistor." During this period, there had been some more development on techniques and we had another crack at making a junction transistor, and then we made the first really striking transistors. These were announced in 1951, and it was really in '51 that the transistor field took on something of clear and major technical and economic importance. These junction transistors, made as a result of this military stimulus, were of a much lower power, with much higher quality and much higher operating efficiencies, than the then existing point-contact transistors.

BRUNER. Do you recall what your own psychological reaction was at the time with respect to the experimental tests? Certain groups and good experimenters had failed and then Bardeen subsequently came up with the reason why you're not getting the effect you should get. You were building a little sub-theory, I gather, from this disparity. But, prior to Bardeen's contribution, how did you feel about your idea after good men had failed to get the effect?

SHOCKLEY. Well, I was having self-esteem problems, frustration, confusion, and a whole bunch of things. I was not really depressed about this, but—

BRUNER. Did your confidence in the basic conception go under attrition?

SHOCKLEY. Well, this took some attrition all right, yes; but all the same, one says, "Damn it all, here are the things of which there is pretty good evidence, and according to these this ought to work, but there is something in here which is messing it up. What is it?"

BRUNER. It is a fascinating problem, whether there is any personality trait that distinguishes people who rightly stick to their guns, as opposed to people who stick to their guns unsoundly, when the facts start piling up against them.

SHOCKLEY. Well, this junction transistor idea and the patent application were sound. But, in the course of this, we tried various ways of making good PN junctions. Morgan Sparks tried dropping molten N-type germanium on solid P-type germanium; these things came out lousy. I can remember being shaken by some fellow who said the only way to make a good rectifier was to form it while applying voltage when it is being made. The physics of the situation—there was no reason to think it would work —but I can remember after enough failures taking this man's objections a damn sight more seriously than they deserved.

BRUNER. Are these colleagues of yours evokers or just co-creators?

SHOCKLEY. I am said to be the chief evoker in this; I set this goal and went after it. These colleagues of mine, one way or another, accomplish essential things to make it go. But I can recall one electrical engineer in our group who said, "Well, this other device, the point-contact, might be called a transistor, but if you ever make this junction transistor, it should be called the *per*sistor, because that is what you are doing about it."

OGILVY. Are you a better creator or evoker?

SHOCKLEY. Myself? I do both things. No modesty.

OGILVY. You keep going back and forth from one road to the other?

SHOCKLEY. Myself? I think so. There is only so much you can do yourself with your own hands. I do things which involve pencil and paper and tight quantitative thinking simply because I don't have anyone else that can do these things as well as I can.

I tell people what I think I want. I want a man who is going to work on the best idea there is around. I expect him to take mine into account, and his own, and everybody else's you see. But I have trouble that I can specifically pin onto a couple of kinds of people: the fellow who says, "Well, you told me to do this," and he goes and does a lousy job at it, and it doesn't work. And the fellow who, by God, will not do what I tell him. He's got to prove he can do something which is his own idea.

IMPLICATIONS FOR REWARD SYSTEMS

MERTON. Dr. Shockley, isn't this an instance of the type of relation between personality variables and organizational variables? You said earlier that you were opposed to the notion of giving awards to the men who made patentable inventions. You went on to explain that a reward system of this kind could be dysfunctional. The result might be the hoarding of experience, secrecy. This would cut down the rate of innovation in the organization.

Here you are talking about an organizational variable, the reward system, and how it is going to affect behavior. Ten minutes later, when you were asked whether you were a creator or an evoker, you decided that you probably were both. Now, if we consider that as an aspect of your personality, then you are not the type of individual who is secretive. You are willing to share your ideas and to get others to follow them up.

And now we start to raise the question, you see, of the connection between types of personality and types of reward systems. Some men would tend to be fairly secretive under any reward system. They can be found in the history of science. They are the men who would not make their ideas available until they had worked them out as fully as they could, even if the reward system was not of the kind that you mentioned. Every time we get down to concrete cases, we find that we cannot even describe the case adequately without examining the interplay between personality and organizational variables.

SHOCKLEY. Let me say that, in my own case, I'm conscious of the points you make, and I'm conscious that I may actually make an evaluation at a moment as to what I am going to do. That is, if I'm in a discussion and I have an idea which I might bring out, I may actually go through this evaluation and say: What am I likely to add to make the discussion go? What will this add to the organization? What will I get out of it if I do it another way? And then I come to a decision, and what has gone into this decision, I don't know. I might decide in that case to be secretive, either for selfish reasons or because I think that this one will lead the whole discussion more astray; we might not get to the end and then for more straightforward organizational reasons it wouldn't pay off, you see.

NO "SWEEPING PRINCIPLES"

I would comment on one aspect about a lot of what has gone on here yesterday and today: I distrust, by and large, the availability and applicability of any great number of sweeping principles. I lean more to being a believer of low cunning and expediency. As an illustration: How do you go about starting a scientific job? Certainly you have the people who read everything; they don't get anywhere. And the people who read nothing —well, by and large, they don't get anywhere, either. Or the people who go around and ask everybody, and the people who ask nobody. I say to my own people, "Well, I don't know how you start a project, but maybe you can ask your boss. See if he knows someone in another company whom he can phone up and ask. Or go and look at the literature. Or step out and do an experiment." You see, there is one principle here, and that is that you don't first start on something which is going to take six man-months before you get to the answer. You can always find something in which, in a few hours of effort, you will have made some little steps, so there is certainly some kind of a small step before a big-scale effort—well, that's such an elementary general principle, but short of ones as elementary as that, I'm not sure I have much confidence that you can enunciate too many of them.

QUESTIONS FOR DISCUSSION

1) In this interview we learn more about William Shockley than about his discovery, the junction transistor. Does his personality run along the lines laid down for creative people by the writers in the Creativity section? Explain. (Stein's article is especially relevant in this case.)

2) How important a part do group recognition and reward appear to play in the efforts of creative scientists? Shockley is a firm advocate of group efforts. Why?

3) Do the accounts of the work of Pasteur and of Shockley reveal any significant differences between scientific research in the 19th century and in the 20th century? Explain.

THE VELDT

Ray Bradbury

"George, I wish you'd look at the nursery."

"What's wrong with it?"

"I don't know."

"Well, then."

"I just want you to look at it, is all, or call a psychologist in to look at it."

"What would a psychologist want with a nursery?"

"You know very well what he'd want." His wife paused in the middle of the kitchen and watched the stove busy humming to itself, making supper for four.

"It's just that the nursery is different now than it was."

"All right, let's have a look."

They walked down the hall of their soundproofed Happylife Home, which had cost them thirty thousand dollars installed, this house which clothed and fed and rocked them to sleep and played and sang and was good to them. Their approach sensitized a switch somewhere and the nursery light flicked on when they came within ten feet of it. Similarly, behind them, in the halls, lights went on and off as they left them behind, with a soft automaticity.

"Well," said George Hadley.

They stood on the thatched floor of the nursery. It was forty feet across by forty feet long and thirty feet high; it had cost half again as much as the rest of the house. "But nothing's too good for our children," George had said.

The nursery was silent. It was empty as a jungle glade at hot high noon. The walls were blank and two dimensional. Now, as George and Lydia Hadley stood in the center of the room, the walls began to purr and recede into crystalline distance, it seemed, and presently an African veldt appeared, in three dimensions, on all sides, in color, reproduced to the final pebble and bit of straw. The ceiling above them became a deep sky with a hot yellow sun.

George Hadley felt the perspiration start on his brow.

"Let's get out of this sun," he said. "This is a little too real. But I don't see anything wrong."

"Wait a moment, you'll see," said his wife.

Now the hidden odorophonics were beginning to blow a wind of odor at the two people in the middle of the baked veldtland. The hot straw smell of lion grass, the cool green smell of the hidden water hole, the great rusty smell of animals, the smell of dust like a red paprika in the hot air. And now the sounds: the thump of distant antelope feet on grassy sod, the papery rustling of vultures. A shadow passed through the sky. The shadow flickered on George Hadley's upturned, sweating face.

"Filthy creatures," he heard his wife say.

"The vultures."

"You see, there are the lions, far over, that way. Now they're on their way to the water hole. They've just been eating," said Lydia. "I don't know what."

"Some animal." George Hadley put his hand up to shield off the burning light from his squinted eyes. "A zebra or a baby giraffe, maybe."

"Are you sure?" His wife sounded peculiarly tense.

"No, it's a little late to be sure," he said, amused. "Nothing over there I can see but cleaned bone, and the vultures dropping for what's left."

"Did you hear that scream?" she asked.

"No."

"About a minute ago?"

"Sorry, no."

The lions were coming. And again George Hadley was filled with admiration for the mechanical genius who had conceived this room. A miracle of efficiency selling for an absurdly low price. Every home should have one. Oh, occasionally they frightened you with their clinical accuracy, they startled you, gave you a twinge, but most of the time what fun for everyone, not only your own son and daughter, but for yourself when you felt like a quick jaunt to a foreign land, a quick change of scenery. Well, here it was!

And here were the lions now, fifteen feet away, so real, so feverishly and startlingly real that you could feel the prickling fur on your hand, and your mouth was stuffed with the dusty upholstery smell of their heated pelts, and the yellow of them was in your eyes like the yellow of an exquisite French tapestry, the yellows of lions and summer grass, and the sound of the matted lion lungs exhaling on the silent noontide, and the smell of meat from the panting, dripping mouths.

The lions stood looking at George and Lydia Hadley with terrible green-yellow eyes.

"Watch out!" screamed Lydia.

The lions came running at them.

Lydia bolted and ran. Instinctively, George sprang after her. Outside, in the hall, with the door slammed, he was laughing and she was crying, and they both stood appalled at the other's reaction.

"George!"

"Lydia! Oh, my dear poor sweet Lydia!"

"They almost got us!"

"Walls, Lydia, remember; crystal walls, that's all they are. Oh, they look real, I must admit—Africa in your parlor—but it's all dimensional, superreactionary, supersensitive color film and mental tape film behind glass screens. It's all odorophonics and sonics, Lydia. Here's my handkerchief."

"I'm afraid." She came to him and put her body against him and cried steadily. "Did you see? Did you *feel*? It's too real."

"Now, Lydia . . ."

"You've got to tell Wendy and Peter not to read any more on Africa."

"Of course—of course." He patted her.

"Promise?"

"Sure."

"And lock the nursery for a few days until I get my nerves settled."

"You know how difficult Peter is about that. When I punished him a month ago by locking the nursery for even a few hours—the tantrum he threw! And Wendy too. They *live* for the nursery."

"It's got to be locked, that's all there is to it."

"All right." Reluctantly he locked the huge door. "You've been working too hard. You need a rest."

"I don't know—I don't know," she said, blowing her nose, sitting down in a chair that immediately began to rock and comfort her. "Maybe I don't have enough to do. Maybe I have time to think too much. Why don't we shut the whole house off for a few days and take a vacation?"

"You mean you want to fry my eggs for me?"

"Yes." She nodded.

"And darn my socks?"

"Yes." A frantic, watery-eyed nodding.

"And sweep the house?"

"Yes, yes—oh, yes!"

"But I thought that's why we bought this house, so we wouldn't have to do anything?"

"That's just it. I feel like I don't belong here. The house is wife and mother now, and nursemaid. Can I compete with an African veldt? Can I give a bath and scrub the children as efficiently or quickly as the automatic scrub bath can? I cannot. And it isn't just me. It's you. You've been awfully nervous lately."

"I suppose I have been smoking too much."

"You look as if you didn't know what to do with yourself in this house, either. You smoke a little more every morning and drink a little more every afternoon and need a little more sedative every night. You're beginning to feel unnecessary too."

"Am I?" He paused and tried to feel into himself to see what was really there.

"Oh, George!" She looked beyond him, at the nursery door. "Those lions can't get out of there, can they?"

He looked at the door and saw it tremble as if something had jumped against it from the other side.

"Of course not," he said.

At dinner they ate alone, for Wendy and Peter were at a special plastic carnival across town and had televised home to say they'd be late, to go ahead eating. So George Hadley, bemused, sat watching the dining-room table produce warm dishes of food from its mechanical interior.

"We forgot the ketchup," he said.

"Sorry," said a small voice within the table, and ketchup appeared.

As for the nursery, thought George Hadley, it won't hurt for the children to be locked out of it awhile. Too much of anything isn't good for anyone. And it was clearly indicated that the children had been spending a little too much time on Africa. That *sun*. He could feel it on his neck, still, like a hot paw. And the *lions*. And the smell of blood. Remarkable how the nursery caught the telepathic emanations of the children's minds and created life to fill their every desire. The children thought lions, and there were lions. The children thought zebras, and there were zebras. Sun—sun. Giraffes—giraffes. Death and death.

That *last*. He chewed tastelessly on the meat that the table had cut for him. Death thoughts. They were awfully young, Wendy and Peter, for death thoughts. Or, no, you were never too young, really. Long before you knew what death was you were wishing it on someone else. When you were two years old you were shooting people with cap pistols.

But this—the long, hot African veldt—the awful death in the jaws of a lion. And repeated again and again.

"Where are you going?"

He didn't answer Lydia. Preoccupied, he let the lights glow softly on ahead of him, extinguish behind him as he padded to the nursery door. He listened against it. Far away, a lion roared.

He unlocked the door and opened it. Just before he stepped inside, he heard a faraway scream. And then another roar from the lions, which subsided quickly.

He stepped into Africa. How many times in the last year had he opened this door and found Wonderland, Alice, the Mock Turtle, or Aladdin and his Magical Lamp, or Jack Pumpkinhead of Oz, or Dr. Doolittle, or the cow jumping over a very real-appearing moon—all the delightful contraptions of a make-believe world. How often had he seen Pegasus flying in the sky ceiling, or seen fountains of red fireworks, or heard angel voices singing. But now, this yellow hot Africa, this bake oven with murder in the heat. Perhaps Lydia was right. Perhaps they needed a little vacation from the fantasy which was growing a bit too real for ten-year-old children. It was all right to exercise one's mind with gymnastic fantasies, but when the lively child mind settled on *one* pattern . . . ? It seemed that, at a distance, for the past month, he had heard lions roaring, and smelled their strong odor seeping as far away as his study door. But, being busy, he had paid it no attention.

George Hadley stood on the African grassland alone. The lions looked up from their feeding, watching him. The only flaw to the illusion was the open door through which he could see his wife, far down the dark hall, like a framed picture, eating her dinner abstractedly.

"Go away," he said to the lions.

They did not go.

He knew the principle of the room exactly. You sent out your thoughts. Whatever you thought would appear.

"Let's have Aladdin and his lamp," he snapped.

The veldtland remained; the lions remained.

"Come on, room! I demand Aladdin!" he said.

Nothing happened. The lions mumbled in their baked pelts.

"Aladdin!"

He went back to dinner. "The fool room's out of order," he said. "It won't respond."

"Or——"

"Or what?"

"Or it *can't* respond," said Lydia, "because the children have thought about Africa and lions and killing so many days that the room's in a rut."

"Could be."

"Or Peter's set it to remain that way."

"Set it?"

"He may have got into the machinery and fixed something."

"Peter doesn't know machinery."

"He's a wise one for ten. That I.Q. of his——"

"Nevertheless——"

"Hello, Mom. Hello, Dad."

The Hadleys turned. Wendy and Peter were coming in the front door, cheeks like peppermint candy, eyes like bright blue agate marbles, a smell of ozone on their jumpers from their trip in the helicopter.

"You're just in time for supper," said both parents.

"We're full of strawberry ice cream and hot dogs," said the children, holding hands. "But we'll sit and watch."

"Yes, come tell us about the nursery," said George Hadley.

The brother and sister blinked at him and then at each other. "Nursery?"

"All about Africa and everything," said the father with false joviality.

"I don't understand," said Peter.

"Your mother and I were just traveling through Africa with rod and reel; Tom Swift and his Electric Lion," said George Hadley.

"There's no Africa in the nursery," said Peter simply.

"Oh, come now, Peter. We know better."

"I don't remember any Africa," said Peter to Wendy. "Do you?"

"No."

"Run see and come tell."

She obeyed.

"Wendy, come back here!" said George Hadley, but she was gone. The house lights followed her like a flock of fireflies. Too late, he realized he had forgotten to lock the nursery door after his last inspection.

"Wendy'll look and come tell us," said Peter.

"She doesn't have to tell *me*. I've seen it."

"I'm sure you're mistaken, Father."

"I'm not, Peter. Come along now."

But Wendy was back. "It's not Africa," she said breathlessly.

"We'll see about this," said George Hadley, and they all walked down the hall together and opened the nursery door.

There was a green, lovely forest, a lovely river, a purple mountain, high voices singing, and Rima, lovely and mysterious, lurking in the trees with colorful flights of butterflies, like animated bouquets, lingering in her long hair. The African veldtland was gone. The lions were gone. Only Rima was here now, singing a song so beautiful that it brought tears to your eyes.

George Hadley looked in at the changed scene. "Go to bed," he said to the children.

They opened their mouths.

"You heard me," he said.

They went off to the air closet, where a wind sucked them like brown leaves up the flue to their slumber rooms.

George Hadley walked through the singing glade and picked up something that lay in the corner near where the lions had been. He walked slowly back to his wife.

"What is that?" she asked.

"An old wallet of mine," he said.

He showed it to her. The smell of hot grass was on it and the smell of a lion. There were drops of saliva on it, it had been chewed, and there were blood smears on both sides.

He closed the nursery door and locked it, tight.

In the middle of the night he was still awake and he knew his wife was awake. "Do you think Wendy changed it?" she said at last, in the dark room.

"Of course."

"Made it from a veldt into a forest and put Rima there instead of lions?"

"Yes."

"Why?"

"I don't know. But it's staying locked until I find out."

"How did your wallet get there?"

"I don't know anything," he said, "except that I'm beginning to be sorry we bought that room for the children. If children are neurotic at all, a room like that———"

"It's supposed to help them work off their neuroses in a healthful way."

"I'm starting to wonder." He stared at the ceiling.

"We've given the children everything they ever wanted. Is this our reward—secrecy, disobedience?"

"Who was it said, 'Children are carpets, they should be stepped on occasionally'? We've never lifted a hand. They're insufferable—let's admit it. They come and go when they like; they treat us as if we were offspring. They're spoiled and we're spoiled."

"They've been acting funny ever since you forbade them to take the rocket to New York a few months ago."

"They're not old enough to do that alone, I explained."

"Nevertheless, I've noticed they've been decidedly cool toward us since."

"I think I'll have David McClean come tomorrow morning to have a look at Africa."

"But it's not Africa now, it's *Green Mansions* country and Rima."

"I have a feeling it'll be Africa again before then."

A moment later they heard the screams.

Two screams. Two people screaming from downstairs. And then a roar of lions.

"Wendy and Peter aren't in their rooms," said his wife.

He lay in his bed with his beating heart. "No," he said. "They've broken into the nursery."

"Those screams—they sound familiar."

"Do they?"

"Yes, awfully."

And although their beds tried very hard, the two adults couldn't be rocked to sleep for another hour. A smell of cats was in the night air.

"Father?" said Peter.

"Yes."

Peter looked at his shoes. He never looked at his father any more, nor at his mother. "You aren't going to lock up the nursery for good, are you?"

"That all depends."

"On what?" snapped Peter.

"On you and your sister. If you intersperse this Africa with a little variety—oh, Sweden perhaps, or Denmark or China———"

"I thought we were free to play as we wished."

"You are, within reasonable bounds."

"What's wrong with Africa, Father?"

"Oh, so now you admit you have been conjuring up Africa, do you?"

"I wouldn't want the nursery locked up," said Peter coldly. "Ever."

"Matter of fact, we're thinking of turning the whole house off for about a month. Live sort of a carefree one-for-all existence."

"That sounds dreadful! Would I have to tie my own shoes instead of letting the shoe tier do it? And brush my own teeth and comb my hair and give myself a bath?"

"It would be fun for a change, don't you think?"

"No, it would be horrid. I didn't like it when you took out the picture painter last month."

"That's because I wanted you to learn to paint all by yourself, son."

"I don't want to do anything but look and listen and smell; what else *is* there to do?"

"All right, go play in Africa."

"Will you shut off the house sometime soon?"

"We're considering it."

"I don't think you'd better consider it any more, Father."

"I won't have any threats from my son!"

"Very well." And Peter strolled off to the nursery.

"Am I on time?" said David McClean.

"Breakfast?" asked George Hadley.

"Thanks, had some. What's the trouble?"

"David, you're a psychologist."

"I should hope so."

"Well, then, have a look at our nursery. You saw it a year ago when you dropped by; did you notice anything peculiar about it then?"

"Can't say I did; the usual violences, a tendency toward a slight paranoia here or there, usual in children because they feel persecuted by parents constantly, but, oh, really nothing."

They walked down the hall. "I locked the nursery up," explained the father, "and the children broke back into it during the night. I let them stay so they could form the patterns for you to see."

There was a terrible screaming from the nursery.

"There it is," said George Hadley. "See what you make of it."

They walked in on the children without rapping.

The screams had faded. The lions were feeding.

"Run outside a moment, children," said George Hadley. "No, don't change the mental combination. Leave the walls as they are. Get!"

With the children gone, the two men stood studying the lions clustered at a distance, eating with great relish whatever it was they had caught.

"I wish I knew what is was," said George Hadley. "Sometimes I can almost see. Do you think if I brought high-powered binoculars here and——"

David McClean laughed dryly. "Hardly." He turned to study all four walls. "How long has this been going on?"

"A little over a month."

"It certainly doesn't *feel* good."

"I want facts, not feelings."

"My dear George, a psychologist never saw a fact in his life. He only hears about feelings; vague things. This doesn't feel good, I tell you. Trust my hunches and my instincts. I have a nose for something bad. This is very bad. My advice to you is to have the whole damn room torn down and your children brought to me every day during the next year for treatment."

"Is it that bad?"

"I'm afraid so. One of the original uses of these nurseries was so that we could study the patterns left on the walls by the child's mind, study at our leisure, and help the child. In this case, however, the room has become a channel toward—destructive thoughts, instead of a release away from them."

"Didn't you sense this before?"

"I sensed only that you had spoiled your children more than most. And now you're letting them down in some way. What way?"

"I wouldn't let them go to New York."

"What else?"

"I've taken a few machines from the house and threatened them, a month ago, with closing up the nursery unless they did their homework. I did close if for a few days to show I meant business."

"Ah, ha!"

"Does that mean anything?"

"Everything. Where before they had a Santa Claus now they have a Scrooge. Children prefer Santas. You've let this room and this house replace you and your wife in your children's affections. This room is their mother and father, far more important in their lives than their real parents. And now you come along and want to shut it off. No wonder there's hatred here. You can feel it coming out of the sky. Feel that sun. George, you'll have to change your life. Like too many others, you've built it around creature comforts. Why, you'd starve tomorrow if something went wrong in your kitchen. You wouldn't know how to tap an egg. Nevertheless, turn everything off. Start new. It'll take time. But we'll make good children out of bad in a year, wait and see."

"But won't the shock be too much for the children, shutting the room up abruptly, for good?"

"I don't want them going any deeper into this, that's all."

The lions were finished with their red feast.

The lions were standing on the edge of the clearing watching the two men.

"Now *I'm* feeling persecuted," said McClean. "Let's get out of here. I never have cared for these damned rooms. Make me nervous."

"The lions look real, don't they?" said George Hadley. "I don't suppose there's any way——"

"What?"

"—that they could *become* real?"

"Not that I know."

"Some flaw in the machinery, a tampering or something?"

"No."

They went to the door.

"I don't imagine the room will like being turned off," said the father.

"Nothing ever likes to die—even a room."

"I wonder if it hates me for wanting to switch it off?"

"Paranoia is thick around here today," said David McClean. "You can follow it like a spoor. Hello." He bent and picked up a bloody scarf. "This yours?"

"No." George Hadley's face was rigid. "It belongs to Lydia."

They went to the fuse box together and threw the switch that killed the nursery.

The two children were in hysterics. They screamed and pranced and threw things. They yelled and sobbed and swore and jumped at the furniture.

"You can't do that to the nursery, you can't!"

"Now, children."

The children flung themselves onto a couch, weeping.

"George," said Lydia Hadley, "turn on the nursery, just for a few moments. You can't be so abrupt."

"No."

"You can't be so cruel."

"Lydia, it's off, and it stays off. And the whole damn house dies as of here and now. The more I see of the mess we've put ourselves in, the more it sickens me. We've been contemplating our mechanical, electronic navels for too long. My God, how we need a breath of honest air!"

And he marched about the house turning off the voice clocks, the stoves, the heaters, the shoe shiners, the shoe lacers, the body scrubbers and swabbers and massagers, and every other machine he could put his hand to.

The house was full of dead bodies, it seemed. It felt like a mechanical cemetery. So silent. None of the humming hidden energy of machines waiting to function at the tap of a button.

"Don't let them do it!" wailed Peter at the ceiling, as if he was talking to the house, the nursery. "Don't let Father kill everything." He turned to his father. "Oh, I hate you!"

"Insults won't get you anywhere."

"I wish you were dead!"

"We were, for a long while. Now we're going to really start living. Instead of being handled and massaged, we're going to *live*."

Wendy was still crying and Peter joined her again. "Just a moment, just one moment, just another moment of nursery," they wailed.

"Oh, George," said the wife, "it can't hurt."

"All right—all right, if they'll just shut up. One minute, mind you, and then off forever."

"Daddy, Daddy, Daddy!" sang the children, smiling with wet faces.

"And then we're going on a vacation. David McClean is coming back in half an hour to help us move out and get to the airport. I'm going to dress. You turn the nursery on for a minute, Lydia, just a minute, mind you."

And the three of them went babbling off while he let himself be vacuumed upstairs through the air flue and set about dressing himself. A minute later Lydia appeared.

"I'll be glad when we get away," she sighed.

"Did you leave them in the nursery?"

"I wanted to dress too. Oh, that horrid Africa. What can they see in it?"

"Well, in five minutes we'll be on our way to Iowa. Lord, how did we ever get in this house? What prompted us to buy a nightmare?"

"Pride, money, foolishness."

"I think we'd better get downstairs before those kids get engrossed with those damned beasts again."

Just then they heard the children calling, "Daddy, Mommy, come quick—quick!"

They went downstairs in the air flue and ran down the hall. The children were nowhere in sight. "Wendy? Peter!"

They ran into the nursery. The veldtland was empty save for the lions waiting, looking at them. "Peter, Wendy?"

The door slammed.

"Wendy, Peter!"

George Hadley and his wife whirled and ran back to the door.

"Open the door!" cried George Hadley, trying the knob. "Why, they've locked it from the outside! Peter!" He beat at the door. "Open up!"

He heard Peter's voice outside, against the door.

"Don't let them switch off the nursery and the house," he was saying.

Mr. and Mrs. George Hadley beat at the door. "Now, don't be ridiculous, children. It's time to go. Mr. McClean'll be here in a minute and . . ."

And then they heard the sounds.

The lions on three sides of them, in the yellow veldt grass, padding through the dry straw, rumbling and roaring in their throats.

The lions.

Mr. Hadley looked at his wife and they turned and looked back at the beasts edging slowly forward, crouching, tails stiff.

Mr. and Mrs. Hadley screamed.

And suddenly they realized why those other screams had sounded familiar.

"Well, here I am," said David McClean in the nursery doorway. "Oh, hello." He stared at the two children seated in the center of the open glade eating a little picnic lunch. Beyond them was the water hole and the yellow veldtland; above was the hot sun. He began to perspire. "Where are your father and mother?"

The children looked up and smiled. "Oh, they'll be here directly."

"Good, we must get going." At a distance Mr. McClean saw the lions fighting and clawing and then quieting down to feed in silence under the shady trees.

He squinted at the lions with his hand up to his eyes.

Now the lions were done feeding. They moved to the water hole to drink.

A shadow flickered over Mr. McClean's hot face. Many shadows flickered. The vultures were dropping down the blazing sky.

"A cup of tea?" asked Wendy in the silence.

QUESTIONS FOR DISCUSSION

1) One of the perennial questions about creativity is whether or not the social value of the act or product created is the measure of its creativity. Is a new torture chamber from which no victim escapes "creative"? Yes, Carl R. Rogers ("Toward a Theory of Creativity") might answer, for "there is no fundamental difference in the creative process as it is evidenced in painting a picture, composing a symphony, devising new instruments of killing, developing a scientific theory, discovering new procedures in human relationships, or creating new formings of one's own personality as in psychotherapy." Or, there can be constructive creativity and destructive creativity. The contrary view has been implied in Erich Fromm's writings, as in this statement from "The Creative Attitude": "to see . . . creatively means . . . to wake up fully to the awareness of reality, inside and outside of oneself." The builder of the torture chamber is not "fully aware" of the reality of human suffering and is therefore not "creative" in Fromm's sense of the term. Is it according to Rogers' definition of creativity, or Fromm's definition, or both definitions, that the parents in "The Veldt" are creative people? Which definition of creativity applies to the children? Explain.

2) If we accept social value as a hallmark of good art, and if we accept moral value as a species of social value, what must be our judgment of "The Veldt" as a short story? Explain.

III. ART

A nineteenth-century writer, John Ruskin, called art "the product of the whole spirit of man." The twentieth-century artist, seeking within himself to bring forth that spirit, has found it so battered and disjointed as to be virtually unrecognizable. His music is without melody, his painting rejects form, his literature is a "slice of life" without beginning or end. Serious art in our time often seems the reluctant embrace of a strident and confusing reality. But perhaps we are lucky to have this much, because the contemporary artist's failure to make aesthetic sense of himself and his environment furnishes a continuing index to the distance we have to go before our civilization becomes spiritually livable. For it is only the minor purpose of the artist to entertain with pleasing reflections. His main purpose, the goal which exalts him to his most difficult of all callings, is to spin out of his own being a pattern for the lives and aspirations of his fellow citizens; or to paraphrase the words of James Joyce, to forge in the smithy of his soul the uncreated conscience of humanity.

ART AND NEUROSIS

Lionel Trilling

The question of the mental health of the artist has engaged the attention of our culture since the beginning of the Romantic Movement. Before that time it was commonly said that the poet was "mad," but this was only a manner of speaking, a way of saying that the mind of the poet worked in different fashion from the mind of the philosopher; it had no real reference to the mental hygiene of the man who was the poet. But in the early nineteenth century, with the development of a more elaborate psychology and a stricter and more literal view of mental and emotional normality, the statement was more strictly and literally intended. So much so, indeed, that Charles Lamb, who knew something about madness at close quarters and a great deal about art, undertook to refute in his brilliant essay, "On the Sanity of True Genius," the idea that the exercise of the imagination was a kind of insanity. And some eighty years later, the idea having yet further entrenched itself, Bernard Shaw felt called upon to argue the sanity of art, but his cogency was of no more avail than Lamb's. In recent years the connection between art and mental illness has been formulated not only by those who are openly or covertly hostile to art, but also and more significantly by those who are most intensely partisan to it. The latter willingly and even eagerly accept the idea that the artist is mentally ill and go on to make his illness a condition of his power to tell the truth.

This conception of artistic genius is indeed one of the characteristic notions of our culture. I should like to bring it into question. To do so is to bring also into question certain early ideas of Freud's and certain conclusions which literary laymen have drawn from the whole tendency of the Freudian psychology. From the very start it was recognized that psychoanalysis was likely to have important things to say about art and artists. Freud himself thought so, yet when he first addressed himself to the subject he said many clumsy and misleading things. I have elsewhere and at length tried to separate the useful from the useless and even dangerous statements about art that Freud has made.[1] To put it briefly here, Freud had some illuminating and even beautiful insights into certain particular works of art which made complex use of the element of myth. Then, without specifically undertaking to do so, his "Beyond the Pleasure Principle" offers a brilliant and comprehensive explanation of our interest in tragedy.

---

[1] See "Freud and Literature" [in Mr. Trilling's *The Liberal Imagination*].

And what is of course most important of all—it is a point to which I shall return—Freud, by the whole tendency of his psychology, establishes the *naturalness* of artistic thought. Indeed, it is possible to say of Freud that he ultimately did more for our understanding of art than any other writer since Aristotle; and this being so, it can only be surprising that in his early work he should have made the error of treating the artist as a neurotic who escapes from reality by means of "substitute gratifications."

As Freud went forward he insisted less on this simple formulation. Certainly it did not have its original force with him when, at his seventieth birthday celebration, he disclaimed the right to be called the discoverer of the unconscious, saying that whatever he may have done for the systematic understanding of the unconscious, the credit for its discovery properly belonged to the literary masters. And psychoanalysis has inherited from him a tenderness for art which is real although sometimes clumsy, and nowadays most psychoanalysts of any personal sensitivity are embarrassed by occasions which seem to lead them to reduce art to a formula of mental illness. Nevertheless Freud's early belief in the essential neuroticism of the artist found an all too fertile ground—found, we might say, the very ground from which it first sprang, for, when he spoke of the artist as a neurotic, Freud was adopting one of the popular beliefs of his age. Most readers will see this belief as the expression of the industrial rationalization and the bourgeois philistinism of the nineteenth century. In this they are partly right. The nineteenth century established the basic virtue of "getting up at eight, shaving close at a quarter-past, breakfasting at nine, going to the City at ten, coming home at half-past five, and dining at seven." The Messrs. Podsnap who instituted this scheduled morality inevitably decreed that the arts must celebrate it and nothing else. "Nothing else to be permitted to these . . . vagrants the Arts, on pain of excommunication. Nothing else To Be—anywhere!"[2] We observe that the virtuous day ends with dinner—bed and sleep are naturally not part of the Reality that Is, and nothing must be set forth which will, as Mr. Podsnap put it, bring a Blush to the Cheek of a Young Person.

The excommunication of the arts, when it was found necessary, took the form of pronouncing the artist mentally degenerate, a device which eventually found its theorist in Max Nordau. In the history of the arts this is new. The poet was always known to belong to a touchy tribe—*genus irritabile* was a tag anyone would know—and ever since Plato the process of the inspired imagination, as we have said, was thought to be a special one of some interest, which the similitude of madness made somewhat intelligible. But this is not quite to say that the poet was the victim of actual mental aberration. The eighteenth century did not find the poet to be less than other men, and certainly the Renaissance did not. If he was a profes-

---

[2] From Dickens' *Our Mutual Friend* [editors' note].

sional, there might be condescension to his social status, but in a time which deplored all professionalism whatever, this was simply a way of asserting the high value of poetry, which ought not to be compromised by trade. And a certain good nature marked even the snubbing of the professional. At any rate, no one was likely to identify the poet with the weakling. Indeed, the Renaissance ideal held poetry to be, like arms or music, one of the signs of manly competence.

The change from this view of things cannot be blamed wholly on the bourgeois or philistine public. Some of the "blame" must rest with the poets themselves. The Romantic poets were as proud of their art as the vaunting poets of the sixteenth century, but one of them talked with an angel in a tree and insisted that Hell was better than Heaven and sexuality holier than chastity; another told the world that he wanted to lie down like a tired child and weep away this life of care; another asked so foolish a question as "Why did I laugh tonight?"; and yet another explained that he had written one of his best poems in a drugged sleep. The public took them all at their word—they were not as other men. Zola, in the interests of science, submitted himself to examination by fifteen psychiatrists and agreed with their conclusion that his genius had its source in the neurotic elements of his temperament. Baudelaire, Rimbaud, Verlaine found virtue and strength in their physical and mental illness and pain. W. H. Auden addresses his "wound" in the cherishing language of a lover, thanking it for the gift of insight it has bestowed. "Knowing you," he says, "has made me understand." And Edmund Wilson in his striking phrase, "the wound and the bow," has formulated for our time the idea of the characteristic sickness of the artist, which he represents by the figure of Philoctetes, the Greek warrior who was forced to live in isolation because of the disgusting odor of a suppurating wound and who yet had to be sought out by his countrymen because they had need of the magically unerring bow he possessed.

The myth of the sick artist, we may suppose, has established itself because it is of advantage to the various groups who have one or another relation with art. To the artist himself the myth gives some of the ancient powers and privileges of the idiot and the fool, half-prophetic creatures, or of the mutilated priest. That the artist's neurosis may be but a mask is suggested by Thomas Mann's pleasure in representing his untried youth as "sick" but his successful maturity as senatorially robust. By means of his belief in his own sickness, the artist may the more easily fulfill his chosen, and assigned, function of putting himself into connection with the forces of spirituality and morality; the artist sees as insane the "normal" and "healthy" ways of established society, while aberration and illness appear as spiritual and moral health if only because they controvert the ways of respectable society.

Then too, the myth has its advantage for the philistine—a double advantage. On the one hand, the belief in the artist's neuroticism allows the philistine to shut his ears to what the artist says. But on the other hand it allows him to listen. For we must not make the common mistake—the contemporary philistine does want to listen, at the same time that he wants to shut his ears. By supposing that the artist has an interesting but not always reliable relation to reality, he is able to contain (in the military sense) what the artist tells him. If he did not want to listen at all, he would say "insane"; with "neurotic," which hedges, he listens when he chooses.

And in addition to its advantage to the artist and to the philistine, we must take into account the usefulness of the myth to a third group, the group of "sensitive" people, who, although not artists, are not philistines either. These people form a group by virtue of their passive impatience with philistinism, and also by virtue of their awareness of their own emotional pain and uncertainty. To these people the myth of the sick artist is the institutional sanction of their situation; they seek to approximate or acquire the character of the artist, sometimes by planning to work or even attempting to work as the artist does, always by making a connection between their own powers of mind and their consciousness of "difference" and neurotic illness.

The early attempts of psychoanalysis to deal with art went on the assumption that, because the artist was neurotic, the content of his work was also neurotic, which is to say that it did not stand in a correct relation to reality. But nowadays, as I have said, psychoanalysis is not likely to be so simple in its transactions with art. A good example of the psychoanalytical development in this respect is Dr. Saul Rosenzweig's well-known essay, "The Ghost of Henry James."[3] This is an admirable piece of work, marked by accuracy in the reporting of the literary fact and by respect for the value of the literary object. Although Dr. Rosenzweig explores the element of neurosis in James's life and work, he nowhere suggests that this element in any way lessens James's value as an artist or moralist. In effect he says that neurosis is a way of dealing with reality which, in real life, is uncomfortable and uneconomical, but that this judgment of neurosis in life cannot mechanically be transferred to works of art upon which neurosis has had its influence. He nowhere implies that a work of art in whose genesis a neurotic element may be found is for that reason irrelevant or in any way diminished in value. Indeed, the manner of his treatment suggests, what is of course the case, that every neurosis deals with a real emotional situation of the most intensely meaningful kind.

Yet as Dr. Rosenzweig brings his essay to its close, he makes use of the current assumption about the causal connection between the psychic illness of the artist and his power. His investigation of James, he says, "reveals the aptness of the Philoctetes pattern." He accepts the idea of "the sacrificial roots of literary power" and speaks of "the unhappy sources of

---

[3] First published in *Character and Personality,* December 1943, and reprinted in *Partisan Review,* Fall, 1944.

James's genius." "The broader application of the inherent pattern," he says, "is familiar to readers of Edmund Wilson's recent volume *The Wound and the Bow*. . . . Reviewing the experience and work of several well-known literary masters, Wilson discloses the sacrificial roots of their power on the model of the Greek legend. In the case of Henry James, the present account . . . provides a similar insight into the unhappy sources of his genius. . . ."

This comes as a surprise. Nothing in Dr. Rosenzweig's theory requires it. For his theory asserts no more than that Henry James, predisposed by temperament and family situation to certain mental and emotional qualities, was in his youth injured in a way which he believed to be sexual; that he unconsciously invited the injury in the wish to identify himself with his father, who himself had been similarly injured—"castrated": a leg had been amputated—and under strikingly similar circumstances; this resulted for the younger Henry James in a certain pattern of life and in a preoccupation in his work with certain themes which more or less obscurely symbolize his sexual situation. For this I think Dr. Rosenzweig makes a sound case. Yet I submit that this is not the same thing as disclosing the roots of James's power or discovering the sources of his genius. The essay which gives Edmund Wilson's book its title and cohering principle does not explicitly say that the roots of power are sacrificial and that the source of genius is unhappy. Where it is explicit, it states only that "genius and disease, like strength and mutilation, may be inextricably bound up together," which of course, on its face, says no more than that personality is integral and not made up of detachable parts; and from this there is no doubt to be drawn the important practical and moral implication that we cannot judge or dismiss a man's genius and strength because of our awareness of his disease or mutilation. The Philoctetes legend in itself does not suggest anything beyond this. It does not suggest that the wound is the price of the bow, or that without the wound the bow may not be possessed or drawn. Yet Dr. Rosenzweig has accurately summarized the force and, I think, the intention of Mr. Wilson's whole book; its several studies do seem to say that effectiveness in the arts does depend on sickness.

An examination of this prevalent idea might well begin with the observation of how pervasive and deeply rooted is the notion that power may be gained by suffering. Even at relatively high stages of culture the mind seems to take easily to the primitive belief that pain and sacrifice are connected with strength. Primitive beliefs must be treated with respectful alertness to their possible truth and also with the suspicion of their being magical and irrational, and it is worth noting on both sides of the question, and in the light of what we have said about the ambiguous relation of the neurosis to reality, that the whole economy of the neurosis is based exactly on this idea of the *quid pro quo* of sacrificial pain: the neurotic person unconsciously subscribes to a system whereby he gives up some pleasure or power, or inflicts pain on himself in order to secure some other power or some other pleasure.

In the ingrained popular conception of the relation between suffering and power there are actually two distinct although related ideas. One is that there exists in the individual a fund of power which has outlets through various organs or faculties, and that if its outlet through one organ or faculty be prevented, it will flow to increase the force or sensitivity of another. Thus it is popularly believed that the sense of touch is intensified in the blind not so much by the will of the blind person to adapt himself to the necessities of his situation as, rather, by a sort of mechanical redistribution of power. And this idea would seem to explain, if not the origin of the ancient mutilation of priests, then at least a common understanding of their sexual sacrifice.

The other idea is that a person may be taught by, or proved by, the endurance of pain. There will easily come to mind the ritual suffering that is inflicted at the tribal initiation of youths into full manhood or at the admission of the apprentice into the company of journeyman adepts. This idea in sophisticated form found its way into high religion at least as early as Aeschylus, who held that man achieves knowledge of God through suffering, and it was from the beginning an important element of Christian thought. In the nineteenth century the Christianized notion of the didactic suffering of the artist went along with the idea of his mental degeneration and even served as a sort of countermyth to it. Its doctrine was that the artist, a man of strength and health, experienced and suffered, and thus learned both the facts of life and his artistic craft. "I am the man, I suffered, I was there," ran his boast, and he derived his authority from the knowledge gained through suffering.

There can be no doubt that both these ideas represent a measure of truth about mental and emotional power. The idea of didactic suffering expresses a valuation of experience and of steadfastness. The idea of natural compensation for the sacrifice of some faculty also says something that can be rationally defended: one cannot be and do everything and the wholehearted absorption in any enterprise, art for example, means that we must give up other possibilities, even parts of ourselves. And there is even a certain validity to the belief that the individual has a fund of undifferentiated energy which presses the harder upon what outlets are available to it when it has been deprived of the normal number.

Then, in further defense of the belief that artistic power is connected with neurosis, we can say that there is no doubt that what we call mental illness may be the source of psychic knowledge. Some neurotic people, because they are more apprehensive than normal people, are able to see more of certain parts of reality and to see them with more intensity. And many neurotic or psychotic patients are in certain respects in closer touch with the actualities of the unconscious than are normal people. Further, the expression of a neurotic or psychotic conception of reality is likely to be more intense than a normal one.

Yet when we have said all this, it is still wrong, I believe, to find the root of the artist's power and the source of his genius in neurosis. To the idea that literary power and genius spring from pain and neurotic sacrifice there are two major objections. The first has to do with the assumed uniqueness of the artist as a subject of psychoanalytical explanation. The second has to do with the true meaning of power and genius.

One reason why writers are considered to be more available than other people to psychoanalytical explanation is that they tell us what is going on inside them. Even when they do not make an actual diagnosis of their malaises or describe "symptoms," we must bear it in mind that it is their profession to deal with fantasy in some form or other. It is in the nature of the writer's job that he exhibit his unconscious. He may disguise it in various ways, but disguise is not concealment. Indeed, it may be said that the more a writer takes pains with his work to remove it from the personal and subjective, the more—and not the less—he will express his true unconscious, although not what passes with most for the unconscious.

Further, the writer is likely to be a great hand at personal letters, diaries, and autobiographies: indeed, almost the only good autobiographies are those of writers. The writer is more aware of what happens to him or goes on in him and often finds it necessary or useful to be articulate about his inner states, and prides himself on telling the truth. Thus, only a man as devoted to the truth of the emotions as Henry James was would have informed the world, despite his characteristic reticence, of an accident so intimate as his. We must not of course suppose that a writer's statements about his intimate life are equivalent to true statements about his unconscious, which, by definition, he doesn't consciously know; but they may be useful clues to the nature of an entity about which we can make statements of more or less cogency, although never statements of certainty; or they at least give us what is surely related to a knowledge of his unconscious— that is, an insight into his personality.[4]

But while the validity of dealing with the writer's intellectual life in psychoanalytical terms is taken for granted, the psychoanalytical explanation of the intellectual life of scientists is generally speaking not countenanced. The old myth of the mad scientist, with the exception of an occasional mad psychiatrist, no longer exists. The social position of science requires that it should cease, which leads us to remark that those partisans of art who insist on explaining artistic genius by means of psychic imbal-

---

[4] I am by no means in agreement with the statement of Dr. Edmund Bergler about "the" psychology of the writer, but I think that Dr. Bergler has done good service in warning us against taking at their face value a writer's statements about himself, the more especially when they are "frank." Thus, to take Dr. Bergler's notable example, it is usual for biographers to accept Stendhal's statements about his open sexual feelings for his mother when he was a little boy, feelings which went with an intense hatred of his father. But Dr. Bergler believes that Stendhal unconsciously used his consciousness of his love of his mother and of his hatred of his father to mask an unconscious love of his father, which frightened him. ("Psychoanalysis of Writers and of Literary Productivity" in *Psychoanalysis and the Social Sciences,* vol. 1.)

ance are in effect capitulating to the dominant mores which hold that the members of the respectable professions are, however dull they may be, free from neurosis. Scientists, to continue with them as the best example of the respectable professions, do not usually give us the clues to their personalities which writers habitually give. But no one who has ever lived observantly among scientists will claim that they are without an unconscious or even that they are free from neurosis. How often, indeed, it is apparent that the devotion to science, if it cannot be called a neurotic manifestation, at least can be understood as going very cozily with neurotic elements in the temperament, such as, for example, a marked compulsiveness. Of scientists as a group we can say that they are less concerned with the manifestations of personality, their own or others', than are writers as a group. But this relative indifference is scarcely a sign of normality—indeed, if we choose to regard it with the same sort of eye with which the characteristics of writers are regarded, we might say the indifference to matters of personality is in itself a suspicious evasion.

It is the basic assumption of psychoanalysis that the acts of *every* person are influenced by the forces of the unconscious. Scientists, bankers, lawyers, or surgeons, by reason of the traditions of their professions, practice concealment and conformity; but it is difficult to believe that an investigation according to psychoanalytical principles would fail to show that the strains and imbalances of their psyches are not of the same frequency as those of writers, and of similar kind. I do not mean that everybody has the same troubles and identical psyches, but only that there is no special category for writers.[5]

If this is so, and if we still want to relate the writer's power to his neurosis, we must be willing to relate all intellectual power to neurosis. We must find the roots of Newton's power in his emotional extravagances, and the roots of Darwin's power in his sorely neurotic temperament, and the roots of Pascal's mathematical genius in the impulses which drove him to extreme religious masochism—I choose but the classic examples. If we make the neurosis-power equivalence at all, we must make it in every field of endeavor. Logician, economist, botanist, physicist, theologian—no profession may be so respectable or so remote or so rational as to be exempt from the psychological interpretation.[6]

---

[5] Dr. Bergler believes that there is a particular neurosis of writers, based on an oral masochism which makes them the enemy of the respectable world, courting poverty and persecution. But a later development of Dr. Bergler's theory of oral masochism makes it *the* basic neurosis, not only of writers but of everyone who is neurotic.

[6] In his interesting essay, "Writers and Madness" (*Partisan Review,* January-February 1947), William Barrett has taken issue with this point and has insisted that a clear distinction is to be made between the relation that exists between the scientist and his work and the relation that exists between the artist and his work. The difference, as I understand it, is in the claims of the ego. The artist's ego makes a claim upon the

Further, not only power but also failure or limitation must be accounted for by the theory of neurosis, and not merely failure or limitation
in life but even failure or limitation in art. Thus it is often said that the
warp of Dostoevski's mind accounts for the brilliance of his psychological
insights. But it is never said that the same warp of Dostoevski's mind also
accounted for his deficiency in insight. Freud, who greatly admired Dostoevski, although he did not like him, observed that "his insight was entirely restricted to the workings of the abnormal psyche. Consider his
astounding helplessness before the phenomenon of love; he really only
understands either crude, instinctive desire or masochistic submission or
love from pity."[7] This, we must note, is not merely Freud's comment on
the extent of the province which Dostoevski chose for his own, but on his
failure to understand what, given the province of his choice, he might be
expected to understand.

And since neurosis can account not only for intellectual success and
for failure or limitation but also for mediocrity, we have most of society
involved in neurosis. To this I have no objection—I think most of society
is indeed involved in neurosis. But with neurosis accounting for so much,
it cannot be made exclusively to account for one man's literary power.

We have now to consider what is meant by genius when its source is
identified as the sacrifice and pain of neurosis.

In the case of Henry James, the reference to the neurosis of his personal life does indeed tell us something about the latent intention of his

world which is personal in a way that the scientist's is not, for the scientist, although he does indeed want prestige and thus "responds to one of the deepest urges
of his ego, it is only that his prestige may come to attend his person through the
public world of other men; and it is not in the end his own being that is exhibited
or his own voice that is heard in the learned report to the Academy." Actually,
however, as is suggested by the sense which mathematicians have of the *style* of
mathematical thought, the creation of the abstract thinker is as deeply involved
as the artist's—see *An Essay on the Psychology of Invention in the Mathematical
Field* by Jacques Hadamard, Princeton University Press, 1945—and he quite as much
as the artist seeks to impose *himself*, to *express* himself. I am of course not maintaining that the processes of scientific thought are the same as those of artistic
thought, or even that the scientist's creation is involved with his total personality *in
the same way* that the artist's is—I am maintaining only that the scientist's creation
is as *deeply* implicated with his total personality as is the artist's.

This point of view seems to be supported by Freud's monograph on Leonardo.
One of the problems that Freud sets himself is to discover why an artist of the highest endowment should have devoted himself more and more to scientific investigation,
with the result that he was unable to complete his artistic enterprises. The particular
reasons for this that Freud assigns need not be gone into here; all that I wish to
suggest is that Freud understands these reasons to be the working out of an inner
conflict, the attempt to deal with the difficulties that have their roots in the most
primitive situations. Leonardo's scientific investigations were as necessary and "compelled" and they constituted as much of a claim on the whole personality as anything the artist undertakes; and so far from being carried out for the sake of public
prestige, they were largely private and personal, and were thought by the public
of his time to be something very like insanity.
[7] From a letter quoted in Theodor Reik's *From Thirty Years With Freud*, p. 175.

work and thus about the reason for some large part of its interest for us. But if genius and its source are what we are dealing with, we must observe that the reference to neurosis tells us nothing about James's passion, energy, and devotion, nothing about his architectonic skill, nothing about the other themes that were important to him which are not connected with his unconscious concern with castration. We cannot, that is, make the writer's inner life exactly equivalent to his power of expressing it. Let us grant for the sake of argument that the literary genius, as distinguished from other men, is the victim of a "mutilation" and that his fantasies are neurotic.[8] It does not then follow as the inevitable next step that his ability to express these fantasies and to impress us with them is neurotic, for that ability is what we mean by his genius. Anyone might be injured as Henry James was, and even respond within himself to the injury as James is said to have done, and yet not have his literary power.

The reference to the artist's neurosis tells us something about the material on which the artist exercises his powers, and even something about his reasons for bringing his powers into play, but it does not tell us anything about the source of his power, it makes no causal connection between them and the neurosis. And if we look into the matter, we see that there is in fact no causal connection between them. For, still granting that the poet is uniquely neurotic, what is surely not neurotic, what indeed suggests nothing but health, is his power of using his neuroticism. He shapes his fantasies, he gives them social form and reference. Charles Lamb's way of putting this cannot be improved. Lamb is denying that genius is allied to insanity; for "insanity" the modern reader may substitute "neurosis." "The ground of the mistake," he says, "is, that men, finding in the raptures of the higher poetry a condition of exaltation, to which they have no parallel in their own experience, besides the spurious resemblance of it in dreams and fevers, impute a state of dreaminess and fever to the poet. But the true poet dreams being awake. He is not possessed by his subject but has dominion over it. . . . Where he seems most to recede from humanity, he will be found the truest to it. From beyond the scope of nature if he summon possible existences, he subjugates them to the law of her consistency. He is beautifully loyal to that sovereign directress, when he appears most to betray and desert her. . . . Herein the great and the little wits are differenced; that if the latter wander ever so little from nature or natural existence, they lose themselves and their readers. . . . They do not create, which implies shaping and consistency. Their imagina-

---

[8] I am using the word *fantasy*, unless modified, in a neutral sense. A fantasy, in this sense, may be distinguished from the representation of something that actually exists, but it is not opposed to "reality" and not an "escape" from reality. Thus the idea of a rational society, or the image of a good house to be built, as well as the story of something that could never really happen, is a fantasy. There may be neurotic or non-neurotic fantasies.

tions are not active—for to be active is to call something into act and form —but passive as men in sick dreams."

The activity of the artist, we must remember, may be approximated by many who are themselves not artists. Thus, the expressions of many schizophrenic people have the intense appearance of creativity and an inescapable interest and significance. But they are not works of art, and although Van Gogh may have been schizophrenic he was in addition an artist. Again, as I have already suggested, it is not uncommon in our society for certain kinds of neurotic people to imitate the artist in his life and even in his ideals and ambitions. They follow the artist in everything except successful performance. It was, I think, Otto Rank who called such people half-artists and confirmed the diagnosis of their neuroticism at the same time that he differentiated them from true artists.

Nothing is so characteristic of the artist as his power of shaping his work, of subjugating his raw material, however aberrant it be from what we call normality, to the consistency of nature. It would be impossible to deny that whatever disease or mutilation the artist may suffer is an element of his production which has its effect on every part of it, but disease and mutilation are available to us all—life provides them with prodigal generosity. What marks the artist is his power to shape the material of pain we all have.

At this point, with our recognition of life's abundant provision of pain, we are at the very heart of our matter, which is the meaning we may assign to neurosis and the relation we are to suppose it to have with normality. Here Freud himself can be of help, although it must be admitted that what he tells us may at first seem somewhat contradictory and confusing.

Freud's study of Leonardo da Vinci is an attempt to understand why Leonardo was unable to pursue his artistic enterprises, feeling compelled instead to advance his scientific investigations. The cause of this Freud traces back to certain childhood experiences not different in kind from the experiences which Dr. Rosenzweig adduces to account for certain elements in the work of Henry James. And when he has completed his study Freud makes this *caveat:* "Let us expressly emphasize that we have never considered Leonardo as a neurotic. . . . We no longer believe that health and disease, normal and nervous, are sharply distinguished from each other. We know today that neurotic symptoms are substitutive formations for certain repressive acts which must result in the course of our development from the child to the cultural man, that we all produce such substitutive formations, and that only the amount, intensity, and distribution of these substitutive formations justify the practical conception of illness. . . ." The statement becomes the more striking when we remember that in the course of his study Freud has had occasion to observe that Leonardo was both homosexual and sexually inactive. I am not sure that the statement that Leonardo was not a neurotic is one that Freud would have made at every point in the later development of psychoanalysis, yet it is in conformity with his continuing notion of the genesis of culture. And the *practical*, the quantitative or economic, conception of illness he insists on in a passage in the *Introductory Lectures*. "The neurotic symptoms," he says, ". . . are activities which are detrimental, or at least useless, to life as a whole; the person concerned frequently complains of them as obnoxious to him or they involve suffering and distress for him. The principal injury they inflict lies in the expense of energy they entail, and, besides this, in the energy needed to combat them. Where the symptoms are extensively developed, these two kinds of effort may exact such a price that the person suffers a very serious impoverishment in available mental energy which consequently disables him for all the important tasks of life. This result depends principally upon the amount of energy taken up in this way; therefore you will see that 'illness' is essentially a practical conception. But if you look at the matter from a theoretical point of view and ignore this question of degree, you can very well see that we are all ill, i.e., neurotic; for the conditions required for symptom-formation are demonstrable also in normal persons."

We are all ill: the statement is grandiose, and its implications—the implications, that is, of understanding the totality of human nature in the terms of disease—are vast. These implications have never been properly met (although I believe that a few theologians have responded to them), but this is not the place to attempt to meet them. I have brought forward Freud's statement of the essential sickness of the psyche only because it stands as the refutation of what is implied by the literary use of the theory of neurosis to account for genius. For if we are all ill, and if, as I have said, neurosis can account for everything, for failure and mediocrity—"a very serious impoverishment of available mental energy"—as well as for genius, it cannot uniquely account for genius.

This, however, is not to say that there is no connection between neurosis and genius, which would be tantamount, as we see, to saying that there is no connection between human nature and genius. But the connection lies wholly in a particular and special relation which the artist has to neurosis.

In order to understand what this particular and special connection is we must have clearly in mind what neurosis is. The current literary conception of neurosis as a *wound* is quite misleading. It inevitably suggests passivity, whereas, if we follow Freud, we must understand a neurosis to be an *activity*, an activity with a purpose, and a particular kind of activity, a *conflict*. This is not to say that there are no abnormal mental states which are not conflicts. There are; the struggle between elements of the unconscious may never be instituted in the first place, or it may be called off. As Freud says in a passage which follows close upon the one I last quoted, "If regressions do not call forth a prohibition on the part of the ego, no neurosis results; the libido succeeds in obtaining a real, although not a normal, satisfaction. But if the ego . . . is not in agreement with these regressions, conflict ensues." And in his essay on Dostoevski Freud says that "there are no neurotic complete masochists," by which he means that the ego which gives way completely to masochism (or to any other pathological excess) has passed beyond neurosis; the conflict has ceased, but at the cost of the defeat of the ego, and now some other name than that of neurosis must be given to the condition of the person who thus takes himself beyond the pain of the neurotic conflict. To understand this is to become aware of the curious complacency with which literary men regard mental disease. The psyche of the neurotic is not equally complacent; it regards with the greatest fear the chaotic and destructive forces it contains, and it struggles fiercely to keep them at bay.[9]

We come then to a remarkable paradox: we are all ill, but we are ill in the service of health, or ill in the service of life, or, at the very least, ill in the service of life-in-culture. The form of the mind's dynamics is that of the neurosis, which is to be understood as the ego's struggle against being overcome by the forces with which it coexists, and the strategy of this conflict requires that the ego shall incur pain and make sacrifices of itself, at the same time seeing to it that its pain and sacrifice be as small as they may.

But this is characteristic of all minds: no mind is exempt except those which refuse the conflict or withdraw from it; and we ask wherein the mind of the artist is unique. If he is not unique in neurosis, is he then unique in the significance and intensity of his neurosis? I do not believe that we shall go more than a little way toward a definition of artistic genius by answering this question affirmatively. A neurotic conflict cannot ever be either meaningless or merely personal; it must be understood as exemplifying cultural forces of great moment, and this is true of any neurotic conflict at all. To be sure, some neuroses may be more interesting than others, perhaps because they are fiercer or more inclusive; and no doubt the writer who makes a claim upon our interest is a man who by reason of the energy and significance of the forces in struggle within him

---

[9] In the article to which I refer in the note on page 101, William Barrett says that he prefers the old-fashioned term "madness" to "neurosis." But it is not quite for him to choose—the words do not differ in fashion but in meaning. Most literary people, when they speak of mental illness, refer to neurosis. Perhaps one reason for this is that the neurosis is the most benign of the mental ills. Another reason is surely that psychoanalytical literature deals chiefly with the neurosis, and its symptomatology and therapy have become familiar; psychoanalysis has far less to say about psychosis, for which it can offer far less therapeutic hope. Further, the neurosis is easily put into a causal connection with the social maladjustments of our time. Other forms of mental illness of a more severe and degenerative kind are not so widely recognized by the literary person and are often assimilated to neurosis with a resulting confusion. In the present essay I deal only with the conception of neurosis, but this should not be taken to imply that I believe that other pathological mental conditions, including actual madness, do not have relevance to the general matter of the discussion.

provides us with the largest representation of the culture in which we, with him, are involved; his neurosis may thus be thought of as having a connection of concomitance with his literary powers. As Freud says in the Dostoevski essay, "the neurosis . . . comes into being all the more readily the richer the complexity which has to be controlled by his ego." Yet even the rich complexity which his ego is doomed to control is not the definition of the artist's genius, for we can by no means say that the artist is preeminent in the rich complexity of elements in conflict within him. The slightest acquaintance with the clinical literature of psychoanalysis will suggest that a rich complexity of struggling elements is no uncommon possession. And that same literature will also make it abundantly clear that the devices of art—the most extreme devices of poetry, for example—are not particular to the mind of the artist but are characteristic of mind itself.

But the artist is indeed unique in one respect, in the respect of his relation to his neurosis. He is what he is by virtue of his successful objectification of his neurosis, by his shaping it and making it available to others in a way which has its effect upon their own egos in struggle. His genius, that is, may be defined in terms of his faculties of perception, representation, and realization, and in these terms alone. It can no more be defined in terms of neurosis than can his power of walking and talking, or his sexuality. The use to which he puts his power, or the manner and style of his power, may be discussed with reference to his particular neurosis, and so may such matters as the untimely diminution or cessation of its exercise. But its essence is irreducible. It is, as we say, a gift.

We are all ill: but even a universal sickness implies an idea of health. Of the artist we must say that whatever elements of neurosis he has in common with his fellow mortals, the one part of him that is healthy, by any conceivable definition of health, is that which gives him the power to conceive, to plan, to work, and to bring his work to a conclusion. And if we are all ill, we are ill by a universal accident, not by a universal necessity, by a fault in the economy of our powers, not by the nature of the powers themselves. The Philoctetes myth, when it is used to imply a causal connection between the fantasy of castration and artistic power, tells us no more about the source of artistic power than we learn about the source of sexuality when the fantasy of castration is adduced, for the fear of castration may explain why a man is moved to extravagant exploits of sexuality, but we do not say that his sexual power itself derives from his fear of castration; and further the same fantasy may also explain impotence or homosexuality. The Philoctetes story, which has so established itself among us as explaining the source of the artist's power, is not really an explanatory myth at all, it is a moral myth having reference to our proper behavior in the circumstances of the universal accident. In its juxtaposition of the wound and the bow, it tells us that we must be aware that weakness does not preclude strength nor strength weakness. It is therefore not irrelevant to the artist, but when we use it we will do well to keep in mind the other myths of the arts, recalling what Pan and Dionysius suggest of the relation of art to physiology and superabundance, remembering that to Apollo were attributed the bow and the lyre, two strengths together, and that he was given the lyre by its inventor, the baby Hermes—that miraculous infant who, the day he was born, left his cradle to do mischief: and the first thing he met with was a tortoise, which he greeted politely before scooping it from its shell, and, thought and deed being one with him, he contrived the instrument to which he sang "the glorious tale of his own begetting." These were gods, and very early ones, but their myths tell us something about the nature and source of art even in our grim, late human present.

QUESTIONS FOR DISCUSSION

1) Trilling gives a negative answer to the question of whether or not the artist creates because he is neurotic. Neurosis as the basis of artistic achievement has been a common belief since Freud announced it in his early writings on the origin of the artistic impulse. Basic to Trilling's disagreement with the Freudian belief is Trilling's definition of genius, given midway in this essay, but implied in the early paragraphs. What is Trilling's definition of genius, and how does his definition support his belief that the artist is not necessarily, or, at least, not merely a neurotic? Why is it better, rhetorically, that Trilling imply his position before stating it categorically?

2) Why, in Trilling's view, do artists and the public take comfort in the common conception of the artist as a neurotic? What harm is done to the artist, to his work, and to the common good?

3) How, according to Trilling, does Freud's own definition of neurosis refute Freud's theory of neurosis as the basis of the artistic impulse? Does Trilling see any artistic capital in an artist's neurosis? Explain.

from
Beethoven's Characteristics

J. W. N. Sullivan

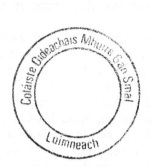

One of the most significant facts, for the understanding of Beethoven, is that his work shows an organic development up till the very end. The older Beethoven lived, the more and more profound was what he had to say. The greatest music Beethoven ever wrote is to be found in the last string quartets, and the music of every decade before the final period has greater music than its predecessor. Such sustained development, in the case of an artist who reaches years of maturity, is a rare and important phenomenon. Bach, for instance, who may be likened to Beethoven for the seriousness and maturity of his mind, lost himself at the end in the arid labyrinths of pure technique. Wagner, as the fever in his blood grew less, had nothing to express at the end but exhaustion and ineffectual longing. Beethoven's music continually developed because it was the expression of an attitude towards life that had within it the possibility of indefinite growth.

Some attitudes towards life are not susceptible of development. They may achieve greater richness and subtlety, but they are incapable of organic growth. The cynic, for example, may become more bitter and penetrating, but unless he suffers a catastrophic change he remains at the same distance from reality. The man who has sincerely accepted a religious scheme in which all the major problems of life are provided with solutions is likely to go through life without ever experiencing the direct impact of those problems. That is, in fact, the weakness of Bach as compared with Beethoven. Wagner, the great apostle of the pride of life, finds, as the bright world slips past him, that he is left alone with his yearning and his pain. The attitude of both Bach and Wagner towards life was not sufficient to support all their length of days. Beethoven, on his death-bed, could say, *Plaudite, amici, comœdia finita est*. But the "comedy" has been in play up to the last moment.

The chief characteristics of the fully mature Beethoven's attitude towards life are to be found in his realization of suffering and in his realization of the heroism of achievement. The character of life as suffering is an aspect that our modern civilization, mercifully for the great majority of people, does a great deal to obscure. Few men have the capacity fully to realize suffering as one of the great structural lines of human life. Bach, as we have said, escaped the problem with his religious scheme. Wagner, on the basis of a sentimental philosophy, finds the reason and anodyne of suffering in the pity it awakens. Mozart, with his truer instinct, is bewildered. The G minor quintet is the most poignant expression of his angelic anguish at his late discovery of this earth's pain. To Beethoven the character of life as suffering became a fundamental part of his outlook. The deep sincerity and *naïveté* of his nature, combined with the circumstances of his life, made this knowledge inevitable. The quality of this realization has nothing in common with the pessimism of such a man as Schopenhauer. It is the direct, simple and final acceptance of an obvious fact. This attitude of mind is perhaps rarer to-day than at any previous period in history. To the modern mind suffering is essentially remediable. Suffering is primarily due to physical and moral maladjustment, and with the spread of science and correct social theories we shall be able to abolish it. For an increasing number of people suffering is already practically abolished. They may go through life without meeting one problem they cannot evade until they reach their death-bed, while they find the sufferings of others easier to endure through their conviction that they are the temporary consequences of the imperfect state of society. But to the vast majority of people suffering is still one of the fundamental characteristics of life, and it is their realization that an experience of suffering, pure and profound, enters as an integral part into Beethoven's greatest work, that helps to give that work its unique place in the minds and hearts of men.

Beethoven's capacity for a deep and passionate realization of suffering necessitated, if he were not to be reduced to impotence, a corresponding capacity for endurance and an enormous power of self-assertion. No artist ever lived whose work gives a greater impression of indomitable strength than we find in some of Beethoven's most characteristic movements. The force that triumphs throughout the Scherzo of the ninth symphony, for example, is indeed indestructible, while the fugue of the Hammerclavier sonata is an almost insensate outburst of unconquerable self-assertion. As he grew older his force increased. "I will take Fate by the throat," he said as a young man, à propos of his increasing deafness, and there is plenty of the "will to victory" in the fifth symphony he proceeded to write. But a stronger, although a more subtle pulse, is to be found in some of the last string quartets. In his last years he had more to carry and he carried it more lightly.

The "personality" of such a man as Beethoven is a slowly developed synthetic whole. It is formed by the gradual combination of its constituent elements into an organic unity. For the development of a personality a rich and profound inner life is necessary, and for that reason it is usually only great artists and religious teachers who impress us as being complete persons. Amongst the elements constitutive of Beethoven's personality we must include his lack of malleability. This quality made him almost immune from purely external influences. Thus he was impervious to criticism; his manners were atrocious; he ignored conventions; he was permanently subject to no social passions, not even sexual love. The low standard of education he achieved seems to have been as much due to his lack of plasticity as to his lack of opportunities. He was not an educable man. He accepted none of the schemes of thought or conduct current in his time; it is doubtful whether he was even fully aware of their existence. He remained utterly faithful to his own experience. It is for this reason that his affirmative utterances, as in the Credo of the Mass in D, have such unexampled weight. Such utterances spring solely from his own personal and tested experience.

Beethoven's capacity for realizing the fundamental character of life in its two aspects of suffering and achievement, combined with his lack of flexibility, was the necessary condition for the development of his attitude towards life. That development takes the form of a synthesis. The Beethoven of the C minor symphony finds the meaning of life in achievement in spite of suffering. Fate is an enemy to be defied. The Beethoven of the last quartets finds that the highest achievement is reached through suffering. Suffering is accepted as a necessary condition of life, as an illuminating power. That the reconciliation he thus effected was genuine and complete is made evident by the music, for none of Beethoven's music is more obviously the expression of an authentic experience. The quality of this experience has led many writers to call this music "mystical" or "metaphysical." But whatever meanings these terms may be intended to convey, the music in question is really Beethoven's expression of the final synthesis he achieved between the primary elements of his experience. He did not turn away from life towards some mystical Nirvana. He forgot none of the joy, the effort, or the pain. He abandoned nothing. What he achieved is something much more wonderful than an old man's serenity. The life in the last string quartets is as full, varied and intense as anywhere in Beethoven's music. But those aspects of life that Beethoven formerly presented as contrasted he now presents as harmoniously flowering from a single stem. Life's experiences are still presented with all their diversity, but no longer as conflicting.

Within the iron framework of Beethoven's permanent attitude towards life flourished a highly sensitive and passionate emotional nature. Although his vision had the stern strength of the Puritan outlook it had none of its bleakness. He was fully alive to the countless lovely and tender things in life. No one's reaction to simple pastoral scenes, for example, was ever more intense and innocent that Beethoven's. He had none of the doubts that troubled the Victorian romantics after their acquaintance with the doctrine of the "struggle for existence," neither had he any of the eighteenth-century cultured affection of a "love for nature." His reaction was spontaneous, direct and unsophisticated. Only a man pure in heart could have written the Pastoral symphony. The same quality is shown in what may be called his love music. The Op. 78 sonata expresses that exquisite, shy and yet joyful tenderness, that only the truly chaste have ever achieved. In this it is typical. In spite of music's unexampled power of expressing eroticism, most powerfully exemplified by Wagner's work, there is no trace of this quality in Beethoven. He knows nothing, even in his most abandoned mood (as in the finale of the seventh symphony) of the ecstasy of sexual delirium. We know from Beethoven's own words that he was what is called a "moralist" in sexual matters, but we know from his music that this was due to no asceticism, to no principles, but to the presence of very strong feelings which could allow nothing inferior in that kind to co-exist with them. To the man of the world Beethoven's love for music may be that of a romantic; to the youth who is just awakening to the awe and rapture of this great experience Beethoven is one of the very few true poets of the heart. Beethoven's attitude towards sexual love never became sophisticated. This very intense and rich emotional nature was, in truth, very simple and very pure. There were no feigned or borrowed emotions, and nerve-storms never took the place of feelings. He had no need to complicate his joy with bitterness or to distort his rapture with cynicism. These are the devices of a man who wishes to come to terms with his suffering without facing it in all its starkness. But Beethoven had the innocence of his courage.

We have, then, in the person of Beethoven a musical genius with all the conditions for writing great music. He has a realization of the ultimate character of life, he has a force adequate to any trial, however arduous, his growth will be free from the distorting effects of mere convention, and his response is pure and sincere to a wide range of experience. No other musician who ever lived has united so many advantages. . . .

QUESTIONS FOR DISCUSSION

1) The article preceding this one, by Lionel Trilling, focuses on the relationship between artistic creativity and neurosis. How "abnormal" or "neurotic" does Beethoven appear to have been?

2) Sullivan believes that Beethoven's masterpieces grew out of his suffering and his attitude toward it. Would you agree that the great artist must suffer greatly? Explain. Is "suffering," or an awareness of suffering, the same thing as "neurosis"? Explain.

3) Openness to new experiences is one of the chief characteristics of creativity, as all writers on the subject agree. Ironically, this openness must coexist with an indomitable egoism—"an internal locus of evaluation," Carl Rogers calls it; "a sense of self . . . as the originator of one's acts," says Fromm. Something remains unchanged and unchangeable at the same time that something is ever ready to change. To what extent does Beethoven seem to have been open or closed to new experiences? Discuss.

CONVERSATION WITH PICASSO[1]

Christian Zervos

Last winter, I was with Picasso at his estate of Boisgeloup, for the purpose of choosing the works reproduced in this number [of Cahiers d'Art]. At the moment I had already in mind the examination of art, published in the first number of this year, and I focused my conversation on this subject. Picasso spoke to me simply, but with the emotion which he knows how to put into his words, when he speaks of art (he speaks about it rarely), and which gives to each word a direct sense that transcription cannot preserve.

I report his ideas here as accurately as my memory made possible on the very evening of my visit to Boisgeloup. They have not been read over by Picasso. To my proposal to show my notes to him, he answered: "You need not show them to me. The essential, in these times of moral misery, is to create enthusiasm. How many people have read Homer? Nevertheless everyone speaks of him. Thus the Homeric myth has been created. A myth of this kind creates a precious excitation. It is enthusiasm of which we have the most need, we and the young."

This conversation by fits and starts is then reproduced here without order or sequence, for fear of involuntarily distorting the sense.

Christian Zervos.

We can make over to fit the artist the quip of the man who said there is nothing more dangerous than instruments of war in the hands of generals. In the same way there is nothing more dangerous than justice in the hands of judges and paint brushes in the hands of the painter! Imagine the danger for a society! But today we haven't the spirit to banish the poets and painters, for we no longer have any idea of the danger of keeping them in the city.

To my distress and perhaps to my delight, I order things in accordance with my passions. What a sad thing for a painter who loves blondes but denies himself the pleasure of putting them in his picture because they don't go well with the basket of fruit! What misery for a painter who detests apples to have to use them all the time because they harmonize with the table cloth! I put in my pictures everything I like. So much the worse for the things—they have to get along with one another.

Heretofore pictures moved toward their completion by progression.

---

[1] Translated by Brewster Ghiselin.

Each day brought something new. A picture was a sum of additions. With me, a picture is a sum of destructions. I make a picture, and proceed to destroy it. But in the end nothing is lost; the red I have removed from one part shows up in another.

It would be very interesting to record photographically, not the stages of a painting, but its metamorphoses. One would see perhaps by what course a mind finds its way towards the crystallization of its dream. But what is really very curious is to see that the picture does not change basically, that the initial vision remains almost intact in spite of appearances. I see often a light and a dark, when I have put them in my picture, I do everything I can to "break them up," in adding a color that creates a counter effect. I perceive, when this work is photographed, that what I have introduced to correct my first vision has disappeared, and that after all the photographic image corresponds to my first vision, before the occurrence of the transformations brought about by my will.

The picture is not thought out and determined beforehand, rather while it is being made it follows the mobility of thought. Finished, it changes further, according to the condition of him who looks at it. A picture lives its life like a living creature, undergoing the changes that daily life imposes upon us. That is natural, since a picture lives only through him who looks at it.

When I am working on a picture, I think of a white and apply a white. But I cannot continue to work, think and apply a white; colors, like lineaments, follow the changes of emotion. You have seen the sketch I made of a picture with all the colors indicated. What is left? Still, the white I thought of, the green I thought of are in the picture; but not in the place foreseen, nor in the expected quantity. Naturally pictures can be made out of harmonizing patches, but they will have no dramatic quality.

I want to develop the ability to do a picture in such a way that no one can ever see how it has been done. To what end? What I want is that my picture should evoke nothing but emotion.

Work is a necessity for man.

A horse does not go by itself between the shafts.

Man invented the alarm clock.

At the beginning of each picture there is someone who works with me. Toward the end I have the impression of having worked without a collaborator.

When one begins a picture one often discovers fine things. One ought to beware of these, destroy one's picture, recreate it many times. On each destruction of a beautiful find, the artist does not suppress it, to tell the truth; rather he transforms it, condenses it, makes it more substantial. The issue is the result of rejected discoveries. Otherwise one becomes one's own admirer. I sell myself nothing!

In reality one works with few colors. What gives the illusion of many is that they have been put in the right place.

Abstract art is only painting. And drama?

There is no abstract art. One always has to begin with something. One can then remove all appearance of reality; one runs no risk, for the idea of the object has left an ineffaceable imprint. It is the thing that aroused the artist, stimulated his ideas, stirred his emotions. Ideas and emotions will ultimately be prisoners of his work; whatever they do, they can't escape from the picture; they form an integral part of it, even when their presence is no longer discernible. Whether he likes it or not, man is the instrument of nature; it imposes its character, its appearance, upon him. In my Dinard pictures, as in those of Pourville, I expressed almost the same vision. But you have seen yourself how different is the atmosphere of the pictures made in Brittany and in Normandy, since you have recognized the light of the cliffs of Dieppe. I did not copy this light, I didn't pay particular attention to it. I was simply bathed by it; my eyes saw and my subconscious registered their vision; my hand recorded my sensations. One cannot oppose nature. It is stronger than the strongest of men! We have all an interest in being on good terms with her. We can permit ourselves some liberties, but only in detail.

There is not, moreover, a figurative and a nonfigurative art. Everything appears to us in the form of figures. Even in metaphysics ideas are expressed by figures; thus you can understand how absurd it would be to think of painting without images of figures. A person, an object, a circle, are figures; they act upon us more or less intensely. Some are nearer to our sensations, produce emotions which concern our affective faculties; others appeal more especially to the intellect. They must all be accepted, for my spirit has as much need of emotion as my senses. Do you think it interests me that this picture represents two people? These two people once existed, but they exist no longer. The vision of them gave me an initial emotion, little by little their real presence became obscured, they became for me a fiction, then they disappeared, or rather were transformed into problems of all sorts. For me they aren't two people any more, but forms and colors, understand, forms and colors which sum up, however, the idea of the two people and conserve the vibration of their life.

I behave with my painting as I behave with things. I paint a window, just as I look through a window. If this window when open doesn't look good in my picture, I draw a curtain and close it as I would have done in my room. One must act in painting, as in life, directly. Admittedly painting has its conventions, of which it is necessary to take account, since one can't do otherwise. For this reason one must have constantly before one's eyes the very presence of life.

The artist is a receptacle of emotions come from no matter where: from the sky, the earth, a piece of paper, a passing figure, a cobweb. This is why one must not discriminate between things. There is no rank among them. One must take one's good where one finds it, except in one's own works. I have a horror of copying myself, but I have no hesitation, when I am shown for example a portfolio of old drawings, in taking from them whatever I want.

When we invented cubism, we had no intention of inventing cubism, but simply of expressing what was in us. Nobody drew up a program of action, and though our friends the poets followed our efforts attentively, they never dictated to us. The young painters of today often outline a program for themselves to follow and try to do their assignments correctly like well-behaved schoolboys.

The painter passes through states of fullness and of emptying. That is the whole secret of art. I take a walk in the forest of Fontainebleau. There I get an indigestion of greenness, I must empty this sensation into a picture. Green dominates in it. The painter paints as if in urgent need to discharge himself of his sensations and his visions. Men take possession of it as a means of covering their nakedness a little. They take what they can and as they can. I believe that finally they take nothing, they quite simply cut out a coat to the measure of their own incomprehension. They make in their own image everything from God to the picture. That is why the nail is the undoer of painting. Painting has always some importance, at least that of the man who made it. The day it is bought and hung on the wall it takes on an importance of another kind, and the painting is done for.

The academic teaching about beauty is false. We are deceived, but so well deceived that it is impossible to recover even the shadow of a truth. The beauties of the Parthenon, the Venuses, the Nymphs, the Narcissuses, are so many lies. Art is not the application of a canon of beauty, but what instinct and intellect can conceive independently of the canon. When one loves a woman one doesn't take instruments and measure her, one loves her with desire, and nevertheless everything has been done to introduce the canon even into love. To tell the truth the Parthenon is nothing but a farmhouse with a roof; colonnades and sculptures were added because in Athens there were people who worked and who wanted to express themselves. It is not what the artist does that counts, but what he is. Cézanne would never have interested me if he had lived and thought like Jacques-Emile Blanche, even if the apple he painted had been ten times as beautiful. What interests us is the uneasiness of Cézanne, the real teaching of Cézanne, the torments of van Gogh, that is to say the drama of the man. The rest is false.

Everybody wants to understand painting. Why is there no attempt to understand the song of birds? Why does one love a night, a flower, everything that surrounds a man, without trying to understand it all? While as for painting, one wants to understand. Let it be understood above all that the artist works by necessity, that he is, he too, a least element of the world, to which no more importance should be attached than to so many natural things which charm us but which we do not explain to ourselves. Those who try to explain a picture are most of the time on the wrong track. Gertrude Stein announced to me joyously some time ago that she had at last understood what my picture represented: three musicians. It was a still life!

How would you have a spectator live my picture as I have lived it? A picture comes to me from far off, who knows how far, I divined it, I saw it, I made it, and yet next day I myself don't see what I have done. How can one penetrate my dreams, my instincts, my desires, my thoughts, which have taken a long time to elaborate themselves and bring themselves to the light, above all seize in them what I brought about, perhaps, against my will?

With the exception of some painters who are opening new horizons to painting, the youth of today do not know any more where to go. Instead of taking up our researches in order to react sharply against us, they apply themselves to reanimating the past. Yet the world is open before us, everything is still to be done, and not to be done over again. Why hang on hopelessly to everything that has fulfilled its promise? There are kilometers of painting in the manner of; but it is rare to see a young man working in his own way.

Is there some notion abroad that man can't repeat himself? To repeat is to go against the laws of the spirit, its forward motion.

I am no pessimist, I do not dislike art, for I could not live without devoting all my hours to it. I love it as the whole end of my life. Everything I do in connection with art gives me a tremendous joy. Nevertheless I don't see why everybody busies himself about art, calls it to account, and on the subject gives vent freely to his own folly. The museums are so many lies, the people who occupy themselves with art are for the most part imposters. I don't understand why there should be more prejudices about art in the revolutionary countries than in the backward ones! We have imposed upon the pictures in the museums all our stupidities, our errors, the pretenses of our spirit. We have made poor ridiculous things of them. We cling to myths instead of sensing the inner life of the men who painted them. There ought to be an absolute dictatorship . . . a dictatorship of painters . . . the dictatorship of a painter . . . to suppress all who have deceived us, to suppress the tricksters, to suppress the matter of deception, to suppress habits, to suppress charm, to suppress history, to suppress a lot of other things. But good sense will always carry the day. One ought above all to make a revolution against good sense! The true dictator will always be vanquished by the dictatorship of good sense . . . Perhaps not!

QUESTIONS FOR DISCUSSION

1) Two theories of the origin of the artistic impulse are often presented. One theory is that art is a compensation for dissatisfaction in life; it gives art a negative origin. The other view gives art a positive origin; the artist, it says, has

118 THE CREATIVE ENCOUNTER

an exuberance of power that permits him to capitalize upon his experiences, whether they be painful or pleasurable, and make art of them. Which theory does Picasso accept? Explain.

2) What aspects of Picasso's descriptions of his procedures reveal the attitudes of a creative person?

3) Like many artists, perhaps like most artists, Picasso insists that art cannot be explained or understood, only experienced and loved. Do your experiences with learning about art confirm or deny this attitude? Explain.

4) What is Picasso's view of the relationship between artist, art, and audience? What aspects of the creative process are overlooked by Picasso?

SALT CRYSTALS, SPIDER WEBS, AND WORDS

Paul Engle

Writing is like making love—it is astonishing how far pure instinct (if it really is pure) will carry you. It is also true of both these lyrical forms of expression that a few things consciously learned will push toward perfection what might otherwise be an ordinary act.

And yet—can writing actually be taught? Is there much more you can give to a beginner beyond Flaubert's no-nonsense advice of a kiss on the brow and a kick in the behind?

In pointing out that a writer crystallizes a concept, as when he endows a woman with qualities she simply does not have, Stendhal produced an image that, however little it flatters the ladies, does dramatize the process by which persuasive words can turn a dull object into something glittering and gay. He observes that a dead branch, dark and ugly, if left overnight in the salt mines of Salzburg, will be covered with crystals and next day will glitter in the sunlight.

This image of the salt crystals on the branch wisely and attractively illustrates what the writer does with that curious and secret substance called his "material." What writer has not been stopped by an eager-eyed and bushy-tailed person who cries out despairingly, "I've got the greatest material for a book, if I could just *write!*"

The first and most important point about writing is that there is no such thing as material by itself, apart from the way in which a person sees it, feels toward it, and is able to give it organized form and expression in words. For a writer, form is a part of content, affecting it, realizing it. A man may go through the most dramatic and horrible experiences in war, but actually draw out of them less "material" for writing than shy Emily Dickinson in the second-floor room of an Amherst house, lowering notes in baskets out the window and thinking gently of death—or even (biographers speculate) of a man she knew but little, whom she might never see again.

Henry James said it first and beautifully when he wrote that experience is unlimited: "an immense sensibility, a kind of huge spider web of the finest silken threads suspended in the chamber of consciousness, and catching every air-borne particle in its tissue. It is the very atmosphere of the mind." This is crucial, for it is not what happens in the outside world that is of absolute significance, but what happens to that external event when it is discovered and then ordered by the internal power of a mind. James goes on to speak then of the creative aspect: "and when the mind is imaginative . . . it takes to itself the faintest hints of life, it converts the very pulse of the air into revelations."

By experience, then, a writer does not mean having adventures. In answering a critic who had complained about the novel that it is impossible to have one without bold action, James protested, "Why without adventure, more than without matrimony, or celibacy, or parturition, or cholera . . . ?"

Anything is suitable for fiction, which is not a record of incidents happening *to* men and women, but of the response they make within themselves to the incidents. This is because fiction deals with character, which determines action, and thus actions illustrate character. The conduct of a man in a ring fighting an enraged bull or the soft wave of a woman's hand are equally moving and suitable.

A thousand Frenchmen may walk down a Paris street and, turning a corner, forget the place. But Toulouse-Lautrec walking down the same street would see, with his shrewd eye, and remember, with his artist's force of retention, not bricks but visions. In this way the imagination works not only on the stuff that is stored in the mind, but also on the very act of experiencing. Like the pilot, the writer must see faster and more completely than the ordinary viewer of life.

Out of his practical skills in the writing of fiction, James described the process of the writer using his experience. "The power to guess the unseen from the seen," he said, "to trace the implication of things, to judge the whole piece by the pattern, the condition of feeling life in general so completely that you are well on your way to knowing any particular corner of it—this cluster of gifts may almost be said to constitute experience, and they occur in country and in town, and in the most differing stages of education. If experience consists of impressions, it may be said that impressions *are* experience, just as (have we not seen it?) they are the very air we breathe."

This is final wisdom about writing. The writer, when given an inch, takes an ell. Remember that an ell is forty-five inches. If that is the degree of heightening, then the eye of the writer must look at life with forty-five times as much perception. That is a marvelous degree of intensity, and in particular when it comes from the author of *Portrait of a Lady,* a book about which it has been remarked that, although it concerns the relationship between a man and a woman, there is only one kiss, and the heroine, poor thing, did not enjoy it.

But some will argue: writing, like all art, is intuitive, and any intrusion of the reason will destroy the lovely, natural thing. This is dead wrong. It reduces writing to the level of a child babbling without regard to the shape of what he is saying. It is, indeed, so much like the uninhibited confessions from the psychiatrist's couch, sodium amytal cheerfully flowing through the veins and breaking down shyness, that it would seem proper to give inhibition-removing drugs to the writer. He could sit there gaily listening to the rustlings of his unconscious. And of course the hallucinatory state would be the most creative of all.

It is quite possible that some good things could be thus spontaneously created. I met in India people who could induce visions. Yet surely the great and structured works of writing are done with the intelligence playing over against the intuition, each bracing the other, the mind giving form and sense, the intuition giving immediacy of impression, the stored-up memory, the deeply instinctive phrase.

To say that writing comes only from the intuition is to belittle it as coming from one narrow aspect of our lives alone. The opposite is true. The total life of the writer is the source of his work. All these go into his writing, in varying quantities: the senses, as of taste and touch, the rate of metabolism, the blood pressure, the digestion, the body temperature, the memory of things past, perhaps going back to the childhood not only of the writer but of the race itself, the liveliness and alertness of the brain, previous reading of books, shrewdness of insight into human character, the libido, the ear for the sound of language.

The writer, therefore, must not only have a more than ordinary capacity for life and the power to retain what he experiences in a readily available memory but he must also have an astonishing degree of self-knowledge. Unless he is aware of his material, he cannot use it, save for the always present quantity that flows up from the deep well of the unconscious recollection. Without access to knowledge of self, the writer can make dreams but not art. Dr. Lawrence S. Kubie says that without self-knowledge, "we can have the neurotic raw material of literature, but not mature literature. We can have no adults, but only aging children who are armed with words."

By self-knowledge I do not mean self-expression. Although all good writing always bears the individual mark, sound, and motion of the writer, he is not trying to put his own self into words, but to create a piece of writing. Often, the less of his own self involved or expressed, the better. His own personality ought to be dissolved into the images or characters of his book. The writer is offering us not reality, but his reaction to whatever reality he has experienced.

Yet the ego is important. It must be that within the creative person there is a constant tension between an awareness of the reality around him, a thrusting up of the unconscious life and its memory, and the drive of the ego toward controlling these in a form that also heightens them. These are crude terms to describe subtle conditions, but the creation of any art is one of the most complex of human activities, involving every animal and human quality. The ego must shape the mortal impulses. It is here that something can indeed be taught about writing, for it is in this shaping that the individual's private events are turned into public forms. It is here that writing becomes an art and not merely a report on experience, and this is true of the best reporting.

How many boys have played around greenhouses? Swarms. But how many, on growing up, have put their feelings about that place into powerful poetry? Only Theodore Roethke. His account is proof.

Roethke asks what does it matter that he grew up in and around a beautiful greenhouse, hated school, worked in a pickle factory, lived sometimes quietly and sometimes foolishly and violently, and meant almost nothing to the people of his own state, the man in the street, but passionately desired their regard?

> All such details, and others like them [Roethke comments] seem particularly trivial and vulgar in my case because I have tried to put down in poems, as barely and honestly as possible, symbolically, what few nuggets of observation and, let us hope, spiritual wisdom I have managed to seize upon in the course of a conventional albeit sometimes disordered existence. I have tried to transmute and purify my "life," the sense of being defiled by it in both small and formal and somewhat blunt short poems, and latterly, in longer poems which try in their rhythms to catch the very movement of the mind itself, to trace the spiritual history of a protagonist (not "I" personally) of all haunted and harried men; to make in this series (now probably finished) a true and not arbitrary order which will permit many ranges of feeling, including humor. . . .

And then he says in verse:

> My heart sways with the world.
> I am that final thing,
> A man learning to sing.

Although this may suggest a self-consciousness not shared by all poets, it is further evidence of that deep need for self-knowledge that is a strength and a source. Roethke knew *what* he was trying to do in those moving and often tortured poems, and this awareness, far from inhibiting the imaginative freedom of the verse, enriched it. The cool mind, curiously enough, it seems, really can express a warm feeling.

Once the writer has a sense of his experience and of his own self, without illusion, and can be tough-minded about his own weakness and vulgarity, what else can he possibly learn? What can he *do* to make his writing better, assuming that he is not trapped in the conviction that writing is a wholly automatic outburst from underground?

He can examine the knowledge of their own writing habits great men have made available. It is odd the things writers have done. The German poet Schiller used to keep rotting apples under the lid of his desk because their smell helped him write. Pilots on the river at Rouen would see the light in Flaubert's study very late at night as he utterly shut himself away from the world to worry two pages of prose a week into the ruthlessly purified and perfected shape he demanded. Why this enormous care? The old wisecrack says that a physician who fails can always bury his patient out of sight. Frank Lloyd Wright remarked that an architect who fails can at least urge his client to plant vines. The writer, however, once his work is in print, can do nothing. There the text is, black on the page; any errors and ugliness will show forever. There are rare exceptions, of course, like William Butler Yeats, who, in his old age (with that marvelous lyrical mind hardened by the criticism of others), went back to the poems of his youth and cut out much of the sentimentality and soft, vague language.

Reticent as always, William Faulkner said that the tools of the writer's trade are paper, tobacco, food, and whiskey. Of these, the most dangerous is not tobacco or whiskey (writers are famous for abusing them), but paper. One of the most terrifying sights is that waiting, threatening blank sheet. Its force is proved by the Japanese writer who, after much success, could not, for a long time, push ahead with his writing. One autumn—and this is a true story—he disappeared. The next spring his body was found, after the snow had melted, high up in the mountains. Pinned to his jacket was a note only the suffering writer could have written: "I have done this because I could no longer endure the sight of the empty page."

All those writers who have commented on their craft agree that a work of art is work. How could the joining of passion and idea in slippery words be anything but a labor? That first really modern novel, *Madame Bovary,* was composed by Gustave Flaubert with the deliberation of a medieval monk illuminating a manuscript. The French novelist could write quickly and fluently, as his early books and his lively letters show, but he would never give up a sentence until it was beyond improving. To get his description of the landscape correct, he sat all day on a balcony looking through pieces of different-colored glass in order to note the changes in shape of fields and roads and trees hour by hour.

Never was a writer more emotionally involved with what he was writing than Flaubert. When he described Emma Bovary poisoning herself, he was so moved that he could taste arsenic on his own tongue and felt so poisoned himself that he vomited his dinner. And yet when he finally finished that scene, he had engineered it onto the page with an almost fanatical control. Once again, the writer's talent had produced an immortal passage out of passionate deliberation.

Flaubert would begin a single paragraph by setting down its general idea, with perhaps a few images (a risk always, for a brilliant image-making faculty he had; he wrote that he was devoured by metaphors as by vermin and spent his time crushing them). Then he wrote a first draft, reading it aloud for sound and sense (always read any sort of text out loud, the surest way to catch the feeble phrase, the trite adjective, the outworn image, the dull rhythm, the phony speech). Then he would rewrite, again and again, as a fine craftsman polishes over and over the same increasingly brilliant piece of maple or mahogany. Every word that did not act with energy was thrown away, until the paragraph was lean, tough, expressive. *Madame Bovary's* final version was written on 1,788 pages, but these were only the latest of many times that number of pages actually written. At times fifteen or twenty pages would be reduced to four. Thus, when Flaubert said that he spent a week over two pages, he meant over the two finally perfected pages out of many more.

Flaubert may be the only man in history who told his girl friend, "You should write more coldly." This was a part of his advice that "we must be on our guard against that kind of intellectual overheating called inspiration, which often consists more largely of nervous emotion than of muscular strength . . . my brow is burning, sentences keep rushing into my head. . . . Instead of one idea I have six, and where the most simple type of exposition is called for I find myself writing similes and metaphors. I could keep going until tomorrow noon without fatigue." And yet he could follow such an outburst with the blunt advice, brief, wise, but taking most writers a lifetime to learn: "Everything should be done coldly, with poise." When putting down the word "hysterics" one day he was so carried away that he bellowed loudly and felt so sharply what Emma Bovary was going through that he was afraid of having hysterics himself.

Can it be that the French, more than any other people, are able to balance heat and cold, desire and deliberation, and make a single intense but controlled utterance? The modern poet, Paul Valéry, wrote that poetry must be a holiday of the mind and then said, with greater calm, that when he writes, "I proceed like a surgeon who sterilizes his hands and prepares the area to be operated on . . . clearing up the verbal situation."

The English seem more practical, if a little less dedicated to perfection. Novelist Joyce Cary described his process thus:

> *A finished book of mine starts usually perhaps ten years before as a character sketch and a bit of description; it goes on to an incident or so, it gathers subsidiary characters, and then perhaps I grow interested in it, and set out to give it form as a book. I sketch a plan; I may write the end, the middle, and the beginning and very often just in this order. That is, I decide how and where the book shall end, which is just as important to a book as to a play, and then I ask myself where are the most difficult turns in the book. Then I may write one of these difficult passages to*

see if it is viable. . . . I may stop there. But if it does
work, then I may devise a beginning and finish the book.

How contrary to the old notion of inspiration to find Cary devising
a beginning of a novel of which he has written bits in various parts and
without order. This is evidence that what the writer is really doing is not
so much writing a poem or play or story that he has firmly in mind, but
rather is using his writing to discover what it truly is he is trying to say.
Often he will not know until the final revision of the last page what he had
been trying to do from the start.

One would hardly guess the zest and liveliness of Chekhov's mind
if he had only seen a moody performance of *The Sea Gull*. Commenting
on the new "decadent" writers he noted, "They're a lot of strong, healthy
young men: what they need is to be sentenced to a few months hard
labor! This new-art business is just a pack of nonsense. . . . There's
nothing new in art except talent." Chekhov constantly wrote subjects for
stories in moments taken from his medical practice ("Medicine is my lawful wife, literature my mistress. When I am tired of the one, I spend a
night with the other"). One notebook contained 100 entries. Some of
these are diverting: A building contractor of great frugality loathed paying
repair bills. When he married, he chose an exceptionally healthy woman
so that he would have no repair bills with her.

A writer should be as objective as a chemist, he commented, and
have nothing to do with the subjective approach that most of us make in
our everyday lives. And when he wrote that the writer should never sit
down to his work until he felt cold as ice, he was remarkably like Flaubert.
Any reader of Chekhov's short stories will be amazed to find how very
simple were the original notes for two of the finest. "A cabdriver who has
just lost his son has to go on working just the same. He tries to speak
of his grief to his fares, but finds only indifference." Another equally
famous story began with three little sentences. "Some officers on maneu-
vers are invited to a house where there are several young women. One of
them kisses one of the officers, a shy and reserved young man, in the dark.
He looks for her, but in vain." These are the plain, experienced reality,
but the stories written out of them are the heightened overreality.

Poor Chekhov, tending the sick with his own fatal illness corrupting
his lungs. When he died in Germany, his coffin was taken to Moscow
in a baggage car marked "Oysters." Yet he never allowed a scrap of self-
pity to interfere with the absolute integrity of his dedication to writing:

My own experience is that once a story has been
written, one has to cross out the beginning and the end.
It is there that we authors do most of our lying. . . . One
must always tear up the first half. I mean that seriously.

> *Young writers begin by, as one says, "placing the story"*
> *—whereas the reader ought, on the contrary, to be able to*
> *grasp what it is all about by the way it is told, without any*
> *explanations from the author, from the conversation and*
> *the actions of the characters. . . . One must ruthlessly*
> *suppress everything that is not concerned with the subject.*
> *If, in the first chapter, you say there is a gun hanging on*
> *the wall, you should make quite sure that it is going to be*
> *used further on in the story.*

Chekhov felt strongly the distinction between direct reality as it is lived and the imagined reality of art. In 1898 he went to a rehearsal of *The Sea Gull* at the Moscow Art Theater and was told by an actor that backstage there would be sounds of frogs croaking, grasshoppers scraping, and dogs barking. He asked why, and was told this would be realistic. But the theatre is not realism, it is art, he argued. If you put a real nose into a painting of a face, the nose will be realistic but the picture will be ruined. You do not use fiction to resolve the existence of God; you exhibit characters conducting lives and show the way in which they discuss God.

Similarly Tolstoy remarked that *Anna Karenina,* that massive novel, was just a simple story about a married woman who falls in love with an officer. This sort of reducing of any piece of writing to its essence is a part of that control over material which is indispensable to the practicing writer. Such definition comes out of enormous and confusing reaches of experience. No one has more imaginatively stated the mysterious and at the same time gritty nature of human existence than Virginia Woolf when she wrote that "life is a luminous halo, a semitransparent envelope surrounding us from the beginning."

Virginia Woolf also wrote a paragraph defining the nature of this envelope more precisely:

> *Examine for a moment an ordinary mind on an or-*
> *dinary day. The mind receives myriad impressions—triv-*
> *ial, fantastic, evanescent, or engraved with the sharpness*
> *of steel. From all sides they come, an incessant shower of*
> *innumerable atoms; and as they fall, as they shape them-*
> *selves into the life of Monday or Tuesday, the accent falls*
> *differently from of old; the moment of importance came not*
> *here but there; so that, if the writer were a freeman and*
> *not a slave, if he could write what he chose, not what he*
> *must, if he could base his work upon his own feeling and*
> *not upon convention, there would be no plot, no comedy,*
> *no tragedy, no love interest, or catastrophe in the accepted*
> *style.*

The simple, often gruntlike puffs of air which we call words must be used by the writer with such skill that they can bring to a reader, who cannot even hear whatever tone of voice the writer would give them, a form and sense that will move him. This is by no means so easy as lifting bricks all day or breaking stone. Flaubert testifies to that: "My head reels and my throat aches with chasing after, slogging over, delving into, turning 'round, groping after, and bellowing, in a hundred thousand different ways, a sentence that I've at last finished. It's good . . ." One sentence!

No one knew better the tortures or the necessity of this sort of harsh self-discipline than that most exuberant and debauched poet, Baudelaire. In his *Flowers of Evil,* he wrote, there was a cold and sinister beauty. How did that beauty happen? This first of the beatniks differed from his later brothers not in his contempt for the vulgarity of middle-class life, nor in his concern for the flaunting immorality that repudiated such life, but in his attitude toward his art. Yearning to have his book appear so that it could prove to his mother, his formidable father-in-law General Aupick, and his friends that he was an authentic poet, he nevertheless kept the printer waiting several months while he revised a few lines into perfection. It may actually be that much writing is created into excellence and then revised into greatness. This is true of the play, the story, the novel, the poem, the article, of whatever form men choose to make words move other men.

QUESTIONS FOR DISCUSSION

1) Engle suggests that the writer is not as free to follow his intuitions and emotions as the painter. Why not?

2) Engle states that the particular experiences a writer may have are in themselves of no great importance to his art. What does he mean by this? Is this similar to Trilling's statement (see "Art and Neurosis," p. 94) that a writer may be neurotic, but that he must have the gift of writing as well? Explain.

3) How does Engle's account of Flaubert at work on *Madame Bovary* illustrate his thesis that only "the cool mind . . . can express warm feeling"?

4) How does Chekhov's theory of the relationship between art and reality support Engle's theory of the relationship between the artist and his materials?

A SUDDENLY DISCOVERED TALENT

Konstantin Stanislavsky

Our productions were few and far between and in the interim we suffered from having no artistic work to do. In order to assuage our artistic thirst we would engage in the following things. As soon as evening would arrive we would make ourselves up as beggars or drunkards and go to the station. There we would frighten everybody, and more than once the watchmen would chase us from the platform. The worse they treated us, the more we were satisfied. For in life one must be more subtle and truth-like than on the stage, where illusion is almost ready-made for you. If we were not good actors we would get into trouble. But since we were chased away, we must have played our parts well.

Our greatest success came to us in the rôles of gypsies. A passing gypsy camp that had stopped between our estate and the station gave us the proper clue for making costumes. Gypsy women and children could be seen on every road near the summer residences. One evening we expected a cousin, a beautiful young woman who was in love with a neighbor of ours and with whom all of us were in love. We knew that she liked to be told her fortune. Not long before her arrival a new governess appeared in our house, with whom our cousin was still unacquainted. The new governess told fortunes brilliantly. Having told her all the secrets of my cousin, I, she, and the small son of one of the maids secretly assumed the guise of gypsies. We walked on the road to the station, and meeting my cousin in her carriage, we started running after her, shouting something in a broken gypsy jargon. The young woman was frightened, and ordered the coachman to get her home as quickly as possible. Having reached the house, and told one of my brothers the secret, we waited near the gates. Soon the excited young woman and her family came to visit us. Putting her hand through a break in the fence she asked for her fortune to be told. She was told everything. The effect was indescribable,—then somebody suddenly cried that he had lost a ring.

"The gypsies stole it. Search them."

We began to run to the wood, followed by the entire crowd. But my cousin, pleased by what we had told her, had managed to put a small diamond pin in the hand of the governess. Next day, this pin suddenly appeared on my cousin's dress. Mystification, conversations, guesses, and then new mischief.

There was a time when we could not arrange any performances, but we wanted to play very much. And so we, that is, my two sisters, my friend and I, decided to rehearse by ourselves for the sake of practice two vaudeville skits translated from the French, "The Weak String" and "A Woman's Secret." Much later I learned that our precursors, the famous actors of the Russian stage, were not brought up in tragedies which force youth to tear passion to tatters and overstrain the abilities of the young novice, but in the simplest vaudeville skits. The French vaudeville act enjoyed special honor. But it demanded good technique, inner and outer agility, faultless diction, elegance, and a verve that gave the skit the necessary piquancy, just as sparkling gas gives champagne its taste. Without tearing passion to tatters, without straining the soul of youth, the old school first worked out its technique by means of the vaudeville skit. And only after that technique was present did it pass on to the more difficult problems of the spirit.

The vaudeville plots were simple indeed.

Two students love two grisettes, and seek for the weak strings in their souls in order to play on them and so win their love. But what is the weak string of a woman? A male canary beats a female, and the latter, after a good beating, kisses the former. Is not this the weak string of a woman? One must beat them. The students try it and receive strong slaps in return. But in the end they fall in love with each other and marry. Truly, is it not clear, pure, and naive?

And here is another simple subject. An artist and a student by the name of Megrio (I played Megrio) court a grisette. The artist loves the grisette, and the student helps him. But they have discovered a terrible secret—the grisette drinks—rum has been found in her room. Perplexity and sorrow! In the end it is proven that the grisette used the rum for her hair only. The rum is consumed by the student and the janitor, and the grisette falls in love with the artist. The latter two kiss in the finale, while the first two roll under a table and sing a funny duet.

An artist, a grisette, an attic, a student, Montmartre—in this there is style, enchantment, grace, and even romance.

Taking advantage of the fact that we lived all that summer in the village, we could rehearse as much as we pleased and then be able to play in a perfected manner. We would rise in the morning, bathe, and then rehearse one skit. Then we would breakfast and rehearse the other. After a walk we would repeat the first. In the evening if a guest came out to visit us, we would propose at once:

"Don't you want us to play for you?"

"Go right ahead," he would answer.

We would light a kerosene lamp, for the scenery was always set and ready, lower the curtain, and dress—one would get into a blouse, another into an apron, a bonnet, a kepi—and the performance would begin before our solitary listener. We considered such performances in the light of rehearsals at which we put before ourselves continually new problems in order to become perfect. Here the phrase that I had heard at random once, "the feeling of true measure," was studied from every angle. At last I inculcated the actors with such a feeling of true measure that our lonely spectator would fall asleep from boredom. "It is good, but rather—quiet," he would say in a confused manner.

This gave us a new problem—to speak louder. Another spectator would come and say that we were shouting. That meant that there was still no feeling of true measure and it was necessary to speak neither loudly nor softly, but find a middle road. This problem, so simple at first sight, we could not solve. The hardest thing on the stage is to speak neither louder nor softer than is necessary, and at the same time be simple and natural. But to speak softly means to wipe out the entire rôle, and so we were forced to speak louder than was necessary. Loudness for the sake of loudness is not a creative goal.

"The vaudeville skit must be played in full tempo, in full tone," said still another spectator.

"The act takes forty minutes to play," I said to myself. "When it takes only thirty minutes it will mean that we are playing at full tempo."

At last we reached thirty minutes.

"When it will take us twenty minutes, we will be doing well," I thought.

There was created a sort of a sport, to play for the sake of swiftness, and we reached twenty minutes.

It seemed to us that the skit was being played in the proper tempo at last, and in full tone, that is, loudly. But when our critic came again he refused to grant us any degree of success.

"I don't understand a single word you are saying, or anything that you are doing. This is a madhouse."

"This means that the business is to remain the same," I decided. "I won't allow another minute to be added to the time the skit takes on the stage, but it must be done so that every word, every gesture, and the entire plot of the skit is completely understood."

If we had been successful in solving this hardest of all problems, we might have become great vaudeville artists and comedians. But of course, we were not successful. Nevertheless we came to some results, and our work brought us a great deal of outer technical craftsmanship. We began to speak more clearly and to act more definitely. This in itself is a result not to be sneered at. Yet the swiftness was merely for the sake of swiftness, the loudness for the sake of loudness, the full tone for the sake of the full tone, the rapid tempo for the sake of the rapid tempo. All these four things existed, but they did not live *in* us. And the creativeness of an actor must come from within, while his voice and his body remain obedient instruments in the sure hands of a virtuoso. There is trouble when a violin has a false tone. No matter how well the violinist feels, he cannot interpret what he feels. A false instrument will mutilate and distort all the interpretative creativeness of the artist. Our instrument—the mutual assumption of voice and body—was distorted, and it was for this reason that we exaggerated and experienced a nervousness very much like that of a jockey who races for a prize.

At another time, wishing again to give a performance which would use only those who lived all summer together, after a long search for a suitable play, we decided that we were going to write the text and music of an operetta. As a basis for our new work we laid down a naive principle: each of the actors would invent a rôle to suit himself and explain what he wanted to play. Putting all these orders together, we would invent a plot that could be composed of the ordered rôles, write the text and the music, which last labor was undertaken by one of our friends. We, the newly baked writers and the composer, learned by experience all of the tortures of creation. We found out what it meant to create a musico-dramatic work for the stage and in what the difficulty of such a work lay. There is no doubt that some parts of the work were successful. They were suitable for the stage, joyous, and gave good material to the stage director and the actor. But when we tried to unite the separate parts and to tie them together into a plot, we found that the plot was bad, that it would not hold. There was no single basic idea which might lead the author to a definite goal. Just the opposite; there were many altogether differing ideas, a few from each of the actors, which tore the plot into many separate pieces. The parts in themselves were all right, but the play would not stick together. We did not really understand the reason for our literary failure, but the very fact that we had had to think of it ourselves was very useful.

It was necessary to decide whom I wanted to play. Of course I must be handsome, in order to sing tender love arias, be successful with the ladies, and resemble some famous singer whom I could copy in voice, singing, and in stage manner,—that I might imitate his qualities, and most of all his individual faults. I was in that stage of artistic development when the youth does not understand and does not want to recognize his special gifts. A short man wants to be tall, an ugly woman to be beautiful, an awkward lout agile, a man devoid of lyricism to act a sweet lover, a man devoid of passion to play Don Juan, a fool to play a philosopher, a coward to play a hero, an atheist to play Sophocles or Dostoyevsky, whose whole meaning lies in the search for God. Ask an amateur what part he wants to play most. You will be amazed by his choice. People are always attracted by what they have not, and actors often use the stage to receive there what they cannot get in real life. If a woman cannot be a beauty in life she wants to be beautiful at least on the stage. This is the logic of those who are completely ignorant of pure art. What can a performance that has no basic life element give to the artist? To be beautiful and successful is not a creative goal that can make a work of art. And the imitation of a favorite actor can only create an outer method, but not the soul, without which there can be no art. Such a performance only makes for bad craftsmanship and works out a ready-made manner of acting which at times becomes a mechanical habit. But the misunderstanding of one's true ability and calling in the art is the strongest obstacle in the further development of an actor. It is a blind alley which he enters for tens of years, and from which he cannot get out until he realizes his mistake and returns to the avenue that leads to the gates of pure art.

But even this performance proved to be interesting because of one very educative incident. My cousin, who was to play the leading part, and who came to live with us for the sake of playing the part, was forced to leave in the middle because she was needed at home. There was no one to take her place. It became necessary to give the part to my oldest sister. Until that time she had been a Cinderella who did only the rougher work around the stage, like preparing costumes, renewing scenery, and calling the actors when it was their turn to appear; she appeared on the stage only on the most extraordinary occasions in the rôle of a super or at most in a small part. And suddenly, the leading part was hers. She agreed to help us in a spirit of self-sacrifice that was worthy of admiration.

Not believing in the successful result of this change, I rehearsed her only because I had to, and often could not hide my bad feelings for her, although she was innocent and did not at all deserve any bad wishes. I tortured her, and at one of the rehearsals reached the last limit of her breaking patience. She could not make her own the strongest and most important moment of the rôle, without which all that followed would be incomprehensible. I decided not to go any further until she had reached success in the part. With tears of despair in her eyes, my sister played the most important scene so that we all became seriously affected. The ice had cracked and the water was at last free; the bars had dropped and the prisoner was at liberty. The timidity that had chained her was broken by her in her despair and the strong temperament of an artist found its way to the surface. With the same passion with which I had persecuted her, I now glorified her. Without letting her stop to dry her tears I begged her to continue. Encouraged and inspirited by me, experiencing the feeling of a soul opening, she continued to amaze us with her suddenly discovered talent. From that time on my sister began to believe in herself and tore out the thing that had corked up her soul. We had a great new artist, and I dreamed of only one thing—to show her to the public in a part that fitted her.

The performance of our operetta, which was called "Let Every Cricket Know his Hearth," was not very successful, and brought us more harm than good, but then it had given us a new actress for whose sake we began to look for a play.

My sister did not have a good singing voice, so we decided to choose a drama for her. Our choice fell on a rather weak play, "The Practical Man" by Potekhin, because it had good parts for me and for the rest of the amateurs who were living in the village that summer. Again rehearsals took place several times a day, and sometimes all day without a stop. Here is how we managed to do it.

In order to become better acquainted with a part and to enter into it, habit and continual practice are necessary,—so we decided. It was therefore agreed that on a given day we would live no longer as ourselves but as the people whom we were to play, and under the circumstances of the play in question. Whatever might happen on that day in the real life around us, whether we went for a walk, or gathered mushrooms or went boating, or strolled out of the house, or sat indoors, we were to be controlled by the circumstances of the play and to be dependent on the spiritual make-up of each of the rôles played. It was necessary to turn our real life into use for the sake of our rôles. For instance, in the play, the father and mother of my future bride forbade me strictly to see their daughter because I was poor, ugly, and a student. It was necessary to plot in order to meet my sweetheart without the knowledge of her parents. But here there comes my friend, who is to play her father. It was necessary to use all possible speed to part from my sister so that he might not notice us, or to explain our meeting and give some valid and logical reason for it. My friend in his turn was forced to act on these occasions not as if he were meeting us in real life, but as he would have acted if he were the practical man whose part he was playing, and whose double he was to be all of the day. The hardship lay in the fact that it was necessary to be not only an actor, but also the author of all sorts of impromptus. Often there were not enough words or subjects for conversation, and then we would leave our parts for a minute, consult as to what was supposed to happen to the *dramatis personæ* under the given circumstances, and decide what thoughts, words, actions and movements were to appear as the result of the living conditions we met on our way. After our consultations we returned to our rôles and continued our experiment.

As we practiced and gathered material, we found our work easier, and at last after long and obstinate trials, we reached the stage where it was very easy for us to go through all the circumstances into which we might place the characters. Apparently we were entering into our rôles.

Even here, according to my old habit, I began by imitating the well-known actor Sadovsky of the Imperial theatres, in the rôle of the student in the play "Talents and Admirers" by Ostrovsky. I worked out the same awkward, web-footed walk that was his, his short-sightedness, his clumsy hands, the habit of patting the almost growing hairs of my beard, and of righting the spectacles and the long hair that gathered in waves about my forehead. As I advanced towards an understanding of real life that surrounded us, this copying, unknown to me, began to pass into a habit, and later into a true experience. In the atmosphere of the stage, among properties and made-up people it was possible to conventionalize, but in the atmosphere of life where all was truth, it is impossible to lie. Perhaps this

forced me to play no longer for the sake of showing off myself, but so as
to persuade my audience of the truthfulness and faithfulness of my interpretations to life and reality. Apparently in this production I learned what
was the feeling of true measure. But alas, I could not force that feeling
into my consciousness at that time. It appeared in this rôle just as unexpectedly as it disappeared in others. But I do not doubt that the work we
then accomplished, although it was temporary and soon forgotten, nevertheless planted certain seeds of the future in our souls. What I had taken
from Sadovsky had at last become mine. This was the first part in which
I was praised by the spectators, especially those among them who understood the stage. But the young ladies said, "Isn't it a pity that you are so
ugly!"

It was pleasanter for me to believe the young ladies, and not those
who really knew, and I began to dream of being handsome on the stage
at my next appearance.

It was a pity. I had left a blind alley, and the broad highway was
already before me. And now I went back to the blind alley to try all
possible sorts of rôles except those which nature intended for me. Poor,
poor actors that have mistaken their calling on the stage! And as for you,
young men and women, try first of all to understand what your calling
really is.

QUESTIONS FOR DISCUSSION

1) In creating the musical operetta, what important lessons did Stanislavsky
learn?

2) Why did Stanislavsky feel it necessary to make his sister work so hard?
Discuss the result.

3) What important differences do there appear to be between the creator-as-
actor and, say, the creator-as-writer? What important similarities are there?

4) If you do not know much about Stanislavsky's "method" of acting, what
would you infer from your reading of this essay about the techniques Stanislavsky would encourage other actors to learn?

5) In terms of the essay as a whole, discuss the importance of the last sentence:
"And as for you, young men and women, try first of all to understand what
your calling really is." What implications does this statement have for creativity
in general?

THE CONJURER

Ingmar Bergman

During the shooting of *The Virgin Spring,* we were up in the northern province of Dalarna in May and it was early in the morning, about half past seven. The landscape there is rugged, and our company was working by a little lake in the forest. It was very cold, about 30 degrees, and from time to time a few snowflakes fell through the gray, rain-dimmed sky. The company was dressed in a strange variety of clothing—raincoats, oil slickers, Icelandic sweaters, leather jackets, old blankets, coachmen's coats, medieval robes. Our men had laid some ninety feet of rusty, buckling rail over the difficult terrain to dolly the camera on. We were all helping with the equipment—actors, electricians, make-up men, script girl, sound-crew —mainly to keep warm. Suddenly someone shouted and pointed toward the sky. Then we saw a crane floating high above the fir trees, and then another, and then several cranes, floating majestically in a circle above us. We all dropped what we were doing and ran to the top of a nearby hill to see the cranes better. We stood there for a long time, until they turned westward and disappeared over the forest. And suddenly I thought: this is what it means to make a movie in Sweden. This is what can happen, this is how we work together with our old equipment and little money, and this is how we can suddenly drop everything for the love of four cranes floating above the tree tops.

My association with film goes back to the world of childhood.

My grandmother had a very large old apartment in Uppsala. I used to sit under the dining-room table there, "listening" to the sunshine which came in through the gigantic windows. The cathedral bells went ding-dong, and the sunlight moved about and "sounded" in a special way. One day, when winter was giving way to spring and I was five years old, a piano was being played in the next apartment. It played waltzes, nothing but waltzes. On the wall hung a large picture of Venice. As the sunlight moved across the picture the water in the canal began to flow, the pigeons flew up from the square, people talked and gesticulated. Bells sounded, not those of Uppsala Cathedral but from the picture itself. And the piano music also came from that remarkable picture of Venice.

A child who is born and brought up in a vicarage acquires an early familiarity with life and death behind the scenes. Father performed funerals, marriages, baptisms, gave advice and prepared sermons. The devil was an early acquaintance, and in the child's mind there was a need to personify him. This is where my magic lantern came in. It consisted of a small metal box with a carbide lamp—I can still remember the smell of the hot metal—and colored glass slides: Red Riding Hood and the Wolf, and all the others. And the Wolf was the Devil, without horns but with a tail and a gaping red mouth, strangely real yet incomprehensible, a picture of wickedness and temptation on the flowered wall of the nursery.

When I was ten years old I received my first, rattling film projector, with its chimney and lamp. I found it both mystifying and fascinating. The first film I had was nine feet long and brown in color. It showed a girl lying asleep in a meadow, who woke up and stretched out her arms, then disappeared to the right. That was all there was to it. The film was a great success and was projected every night until it broke and could not be mended any more.

This little rickety machine was my first conjuring set. And even today I remind myself with childish excitement that I am really a conjurer, since cinematography is based on deception of the human eye. I have worked it out that if I see a film which has a running time of one hour, I sit through twenty-seven minutes of complete darkness—the blankness between frames. When I show a film I am guilty of deceit. I use an apparatus which is constructed to take advantage of a certain human weakness, an apparatus with which I can sway my audience in a highly emotional manner— make them laugh, scream with fright, smile, believe in fairy stories, become indignant, feel shocked, charmed, deeply moved or perhaps yawn with boredom. Thus I am either an impostor or, when the audience is willing to be taken in, a conjurer. I perform conjuring tricks with apparatus so expensive and so wonderful that any entertainer in history would have given anything to have it.

A film for me begins with something very vague—a chance remark or a bit of conversation, a hazy but agreeable event unrelated to any particular situation. It can be a few bars of music, a shaft of light across the street. Sometimes in my work at the theater I have envisioned actors made up for yet unplayed roles.

These are split-second impressions that disappear as quickly as they come, yet leave behind a mood—like pleasant dreams. It is a mental state, not an actual story, but one abounding in fertile associations and images. Most of all, it is a brightly colored thread sticking out of the dark sack of the unconscious. If I begin to wind up this thread, and do it carefully, a complete film will emerge.

This primitive nucleus strives to achieve definite form, moving in a way that may be lazy and half asleep at first. Its stirring is accompanied by vibrations and rhythms which are very special and unique to each film. The picture sequences then assume a pattern in accordance with these rhythms, obeying laws born out of and conditioned by my original stimulus.

If that embryonic substance seems to have enough strength to be made into a film, I decide to materialize it. Then comes something very complicated and difficult: the transformation of rhythms, moods, atmosphere, tensions, sequences, tones and scents into words and sentences, into an understandable screenplay.

This is an almost impossible task.

The only thing that can be satisfactorily transferred from that original complex of rhythms and moods is the dialogue, and even dialogue is a sensitive substance which may offer resistance. Written dialogue is like a musical score, almost incomprehensible to the average person. Its interpretation demands a technical knack plus a certain kind of imagination and feeling—qualities which are so often lacking, even among actors. One can write dialogue, but how it should be delivered, its rhythm and tempo, what is to take place between lines—all this must be omitted for practical reasons. Such a detailed script would be unreadable. I try to squeeze instructions as to location, characterization and atmosphere into my screenplays in understandable terms, but the success of this depends on my writing ability and the perceptiveness of the reader, which are not always predictable.

Now we come to essentials, by which I mean montage, rhythm and the relation of one picture to another—the vital third dimension without which the film is merely a dead product from a factory. Here I cannot clearly give a key, as in a musical score, nor a specific idea of the tempo which determines the relationship of the elements involved. It is quite impossible for me to indicate the way in which the film "breathes" and pulsates.

I have often wished for a kind of notation which would enable me to put on paper all the shades and tones of my vision, to record distinctly the inner structure of a film. For when I stand in the artistically devastating atmosphere of the studio, my hands and head full of all the trivial and irritating details that go with motion-picture production, it often takes a tremendous effort to remember how I originally saw and thought out this or that sequence, or what was the relation between the scene of four weeks ago and that of today. If I could express myself clearly, in explicit symbols, then this problem would be almost eliminated and I could work with absolute confidence that whenever I liked I could prove the relationship between the part and the whole and put my finger on the rhythm, the continuity of the film.

Thus the script is a very imperfect *technical* basis for a film. And there is another important point in this connection which I should like to mention. Film has nothing to do with literature; the character and substance of the two art forms are usually in conflict. This probably has something to do with the receptive process of the mind. The written word is read and assimilated by a conscious act of the will in alliance with the intellect; little by little it affects the imagination and the emotions. The process is different with a motion picture. When we experience a film, we consciously prime ourselves for illusion. Putting aside will and intellect, we make way for it in our imagination. The sequence of pictures plays directly on our feelings.

Music works in the same fashion; I would say that there is no art form that has so much in common with film as music. Both affect our emotions directly, not via the intellect. And film is mainly rhythm; it is inhalation and exhalation in continuous sequence. Ever since childhood, music has been my great source of recreation and stimulation, and I often experience a film or play musically.

It is mainly because of this difference between film and literature that we should avoid making films out of books. The irrational dimension of a literary work, the germ of its existence, is often untranslatable into visual terms—and it, in turn, destroys the special, irrational dimension of the film. If, despite this, we wish to translate something literary into film terms, we must make an infinite number of complicated adjustments which often bear little or no fruit in proportion to the effort expended.

I myself have never had any ambition to be an author. I do not want to write novels, short stories, essays, biographies, or even plays for the theater. I only want to make films—films about conditions, tensions, pictures, rhythms and characters which are in one way or another important to me. The motion picture, with its complicated process of birth, is my method of saying what I want to my fellow men. I am a film-maker, not an author.

Thus the writing of the script is a difficult period but a useful one, for it compels me to prove logically the validity of my ideas. In doing this, I am caught in a conflict—a conflict between my need to transmit a complicated situation through visual images, and my desire for absolute clarity. I do not intend my work to be solely for the benefit of myself or the few, but for the entertainment of the general public. The wishes of the public are imperative. But sometimes I risk following my own impulse, and it has been shown that the public can respond with surprising sensitivity to the most unconventional line of development.

When shooting begins, the most important thing is that those who work with me feel a definite contact, that all of us somehow cancel out our conflicts through working together. We must pull in one direction for the sake of the work at hand. Sometimes this leads to dispute, but the more definite and clear the "marching orders," the easier it is to reach the goal which has been set. This is the basis for my conduct as director, and perhaps the explanation of much of the nonsense that has been written about me.

While I cannot let myself be concerned with what people think and say about me personally, I believe that reviewers and critics have every right to interpret my films as they like. I refuse to interpret my work to others, and I cannot tell the critic what to think; each person has the right to understand a film as he sees it. Either he is attracted or repelled. A film is made to create reaction. If the audience does not react one way or another, it is an indifferent work and worthless.

I do not mean by this that I believe in being "different" at any price. A lot has been said about the value of originality, and I find this foolish. Either you are original or you are not. It is completely natural for artists to take from and give to each other, to borrow from and experience one another. In my own life, my great literary experience was Strindberg. There are works of his which can still make my hair stand on end—*The People of Hemsö,* for example. And it is my dream to produce *Dream Play* some day. Olof Molander's production of it in 1934 was for me a fundamental dramatic experience.

On a personal level, there are many people who have meant a great deal to me. My father and mother were certainly of vital importance, not only in themselves but because they created a world for me to revolt against. In my family there was an atmosphere of hearty wholesomeness which I, a sensitive young plant, scorned and rebelled against. But that strict middle-class home gave me a wall to pound on, something to sharpen myself against. At the same time they taught me a number of values— efficiency, punctuality, a sense of financial responsibility—which may be "bourgeois" but are nevertheless important to the artist. They are part of the process of setting oneself severe standards. Today as a film-maker I am conscientious, hard-working and extremely careful; my films involve good craftsmanship, and my pride is the pride of a good craftsman.

Among the people who have meant something in my professional development is Torsten Hammaren of Gothenburg. I went there from Hälsingborg, where I had been head of the municipal theater for two years. I had no conception of what theater was; Hammaren taught me during the four years I stayed in Gothenburg. Then, when I made my first attempts at film, Alf Sjöberg—who directed *Torment*—taught me a great deal. And there was Lorens Marmstedt, who really taught me film-making from scratch after my first unsuccessful movie. Among other things I learned from Marmstedt is the one unbreakable rule: you must look at your own work very coldly and clearly; you must be a devil to yourself in the screening room when watching the day's rushes. Then there is Herbert Grevenius, one of the few who believed in me as a writer. I had trouble with scriptwriting, and was reaching out more and more to the drama, to dialogue, as a means of expression. He gave me great encouragement.

Finally, there is Carl Anders Dymling, my producer. He is crazy enough to place more faith in the sense of responsibility of a creative artist than in calculations of profit and loss. I am thus able to work with an integrity that has become the very air I breathe, and one of the main reasons I do not want to work outside of Sweden. The moment I lose this freedom I will cease to be a film-maker, because I have no skill in the art of compromise. My only significance in the world of film lies in the freedom of my creativity.

Today, the ambitious film-maker is obliged to walk a tightrope without a net. He may be a conjurer, but no one conjures the producer, the bank director or the theater owners when the public refuses to go see a film and lay down the money by which producer, bank director, theater owner and conjurer can live. The conjurer may then be deprived of his magic wand; I would like to be able to measure the amount of talent, initiative and creative ability which has been destroyed by the film industry in its ruthlessly efficient sausage machine. What was play to me once has now become a struggle. Failure, criticism, public indifference all hurt more today than yesterday. The brutality of the industry is undisguised—yet that can be an advantage.

So much for people and the film business. I have been asked, as a clergyman's son, about the role of religion in my thinking and film-making. To me, religious problems are continuously alive. I never cease to concern myself with them; it goes on every hour of every day. Yet this does not take place on the emotional level, but on an intellectual one. Religious emotion, religious sentimentality, is something I got rid of long ago—I hope. The religious problem is an intellectual one to me: the relationship of my mind to my intuition. The result of this conflict is usually some kind of tower of Babel.

Philosophically, there is a book which was a tremendous experience for me: Eiono Kaila's *Psychology of the Personality*. His thesis that man lives strictly according to his needs—negative and positive—was shattering to me, but terribly true. And I built on this ground.

People ask what are my intentions with my films—my aims. It is a difficult and dangerous question, and I usually give an evasive answer: I try to tell the truth about the human condition, the truth as I see it. This answer seems to satisfy everyone, but it is not quite correct. I prefer to describe what I *would like* my aim to be.

There is an old story of how the cathedral of Chartres was struck by lightning and burned to the ground. Then thousands of people came from all points of the compass, like a giant procession of ants, and together they began to rebuild the cathedral on its old site. They worked until the building was completed—master builders, artists, laborers, clowns, noblemen, priests, burghers. But they all remained anonymous, and no one knows to this day who built the cathedral of Chartres.

Regardless of my own beliefs and my own doubts, which are unimportant in this connection, it is my opinion that art lost its basic creative drive the moment it was separated from worship. It severed an umbilical cord and now lives its own sterile life, generating and degenerating itself. In former days the artist remained unknown and his work was to the glory of God. He lived and died without being more or less important than other artisans; "eternal values," "immortality" and "masterpiece" were terms not applicable in his case. The ability to create was a gift. In such a world flourished invulnerable assurance and natural humility.

Today the individual has become the highest form and the greatest bane of artistic creation. The smallest wound or pain of the ego is examined under a microscope as if it were of eternal importance. The artist considers his isolation, his subjectivity, his individualism almost holy. Thus we finally gather in one large pen, where we stand and bleat about our loneliness without listening to each other and without realizing that we are smothering each other to death. The individualists stare into each other's eyes and yet deny the existence of each other. We walk in circles, so limited by our own anxieties that we can no longer distinguish between true and false, between the gangster's whim and the purest ideal.

Thus if I am asked what I would like the general purpose of my films to be, I would reply that I want to be one of the artists in the cathedral on the great plain. I want to make a dragon's head, an angel, a devil—or perhaps a saint—out of stone. It does not matter which; it is the sense of satisfaction that counts. Regardless of whether I believe or not, whether I am a Christian or not, I would play my part in the collective building of the cathedral.

QUESTIONS FOR DISCUSSION

1) Ingmar Bergman is one of the leading film-makers in the world. In this article he discusses the nature of the film as an art form, the influences which shaped his own career, and the goals he seeks to attain as an artist. How does Bergman get the ideas for his films? What processes must he go through to transform these ideas into films?

2) Why, according to Bergman, is film-making closer to music than to literature despite the use of dialogue in film-making? What are the special problems of this medium of story-telling that lead Bergman to call it "the impossible task"?

3) It might be said that Bergman was very "creative" in his attitude toward his family, in his attitude toward the environment in which he had to work, and in his attitude toward religion. Why?

4) Bergman writes that his "strict middle-class home" was an aid to him in that it gave him something to rebel against. Further, some of its "bourgeois" values are helpful to him as an artist. Do you think the artist needs something to rebel against in order to bring out his creativity? Explain.

5) Bergman uses a metaphor to explain his artistic purpose. What is this metaphor and what does it mean?

MAIN CURRENTS OF AMERICAN THOUGHT

Irwin Shaw

"Flacker: all right now, Kid, now you'd better talk," Andrew dictated. "Business: Sound of the door closing, the slow turning of the key in the lock. Buddy: You're never going to get me to talk, Flacker. Business: Sound of a slap. Flacker: Maybe that'll make you think different, Kid. Where is Jerry Carmichael? Buddy: (laughing) Wouldn't you like to know, Flacker? Flacker: Yeah. (Slowly, with great threat in his voice) And I'm going to find out. One way or another. See? Business: Siren fades in, louder, fades out. Announcer: Will Buddy talk? Will Flacker force him to disclose the whereabouts of the rescued son of the railroad king? Will Dusty Blades reach him in time? Tune in Monday at the same time, et cetera, et cetera . . ."

Andrew dropped onto the couch and put his feet up. He stretched and sighed as he watched Lenore finish scratching his dictation down in the shorthand notebook. "Thirty bucks," he said. "There's another thirty bucks. Is it the right length?"

"Uhuh," Lenore said. "Eleven and a half pages. This is a very good one, Andy."

"Yeah," Andrew said, closing his eyes. "Put it next to Moby Dick on your library shelf."

"It's very exciting," Lenore said, standing up. "I don't know what they're complaining about."

"You're a lovely girl," Andrew put his hands over his eyes and rubbed around and around. "I have wooden hinges on my eyelids. Do you sleep at night?"

"Don't do that to your eyes," Lenore started to put on her coat. "You only aggravate them."

"You're right." Andrew dug his fists into his eyes and rotated them slowly. "You don't know how right you are."

"Tomorrow. At ten o'clock?" Lenore asked.

"At ten o'clock. Dig me out of the arms of sleep. We shall leave Dusty Blades to his fate for this week and go on with the further adventures of Ronnie Cook and His Friends, forty dollars a script. I always enjoy writing Ronnie Cook much better than Dusty Blades. See what ten dollars does to a man." He opened his eyes and watched Lenore putting her hat on in front of the mirror. When he squinted, she was not so plain-looking. He felt very sorry for Lenore, plain as sand, with her flat-colored face and her hair pulled down like rope, and never a man to her name. She was putting on a red hat with a kind of ladder arrangement going up one side. It looked very funny and sad on her. Andrew realized that it was a new hat. "That's a mighty fine hat," he said.

"I thought a long time before I bought this hat," Lenore said, flushing because he'd noticed it.

"Har-*riet!*" The governess next door screamed in the alley to the next-door neighbor's little girl. "Harriet, get away from there this minute!"

Andrew turned over on his stomach on the couch and put a pillow over his head. "Have you got any ideas for Ronnie Cook and His Friends for tomorrow?" he asked Lenore.

"No. Have you?"

"No." He pulled the pillow tight around his head.

"You'll get them by tomorrow," Lenore said. "You always do."

"Yeah," said Andrew.

"You need a vacation," Lenore said.

"Get out of here."

"Good-bye," Lenore started out. "Get a good night's sleep."

"Anything you say."

Andrew watched her with one eye as she went off the porch on which he worked and through the living room and dining room, toward the stairs. She had nice legs. You were always surprised when a girl with a face like that had nice legs. But she had hair on her legs. She was not a lucky girl. "Oh, no," Andrew said as the door closed behind her, "you are not a lucky girl."

He closed his eyes and tried to sleep. The sun came in through the open windows and the curtains blew softly over his head and the sun was warm and comforting on his closed eyes. Across the street, on the public athletic field, four boys were shagging flies. There would be the neat pleasant crack of the bat and a long time later the smack of the ball in the fielder's glove. The tall trees outside, as old as Brooklyn, rustled a little from time to time as little spurts of wind swept across the baseball field.

"Har*riet!*" The governess called. "Stop that or I will make you stand by yourself in the corner all afternoon! Harriet! I demand you to stop it!" The governess was French. She had the only unpleasant French accent Andrew had ever heard.

The little girl started to cry, "Mamma! Mamma! Mamma, she's going to hit me!" The little girl hated the governess and the governess hated the little girl, and they continually reported each other to the little girl's mother. "Mamma!"

"You are a little liar," the governess screamed. "You will grow up, and you will be a liar all your life. There will be no hope for you."

"Mamma!" wailed the little girl.

They went inside the house and it was quiet again.

"Charlie," one of the boys on the baseball field yelled, "hit it to me, Charlie!"

The telephone rang, four times, and then Andrew heard his mother talking into it. She came onto the porch.

"It's a man from the bank," she said. "He wants to talk to you."

"You should've told him I wasn't home," Andrew said.

"But you are home," his mother said. "How was I to know that . . . ?"

"You're right." Andrew swung his legs over and sat up. "You're perfectly right."

He went into the dining room, to the telephone, and talked to the man at the bank.

"You're a hundred and eleven dollars overdrawn," said the man at the bank.

Andrew squinted at his mother, sitting across the room, on a straight chair, with her arms folded in her lap, her head turned just a little, so as not to miss anything.

"I thought I had about four hundred dollars in the bank," Andrew said into the phone.

"You are a hundred and eleven dollars overdrawn," said the man at the bank.

Andrew sighed. "I'll check it." He put the phone down.

"What's the matter?" his mother asked.

"I'm a hundred and eleven dollars overdrawn," he said.

"That's shameful," his mother said. "You ought to be more methodical."

"Yes." Andrew started back to the porch.

"You're awfully careless." His mother followed him. "You really ought to keep track of your money."

"Yes." Andrew sat down on the couch.

"Give me a kiss," his mother said.

"Why?"

"No particular reason." She laughed.

"O.K." He kissed her and she held him for a moment. He dropped down on the couch. She ran her finger under his eye.

"You've got rings under your eyes," she said.

"That's right."

She kissed him again and went to the rear of the house. He closed his eyes. From the rear of the house came the sound of the vacuum cleaner. Andrew felt his muscles getting stiff in protest against the vacuum cleaner. He got up and went to her bedroom, where she was running the machine back and forth under the bed. She was down on one knee and was bent over looking under the bed.

"Hey!" Andrew yelled. "Hey, Mom!"

She turned off the machine and looked up at him. "What's the matter?"

"I'm trying to sleep," he said.

"Well, why don't you sleep?"

"The vacuum cleaner. It's shaking the house."

His mother stood up, her face setting into stern lines. "I've got to clean the house, don't I?"

"Why do you have to clean the house while I'm trying to sleep?"

His mother bent down again. "I can't use it while you're working. I can't use it while you're reading. I can't use it until ten o'clock in the morning because you're sleeping." She started the machine. "When am I supposed to clean the house?" she called over the noise of the cleaner. "Why don't you sleep at night like everybody else?" And she put her head down low and vigorously ran the machine back and forth.

Andrew watched her for a moment. No arguments came to him. The sound of the cleaner so close to him made his nerves jump. He went out of the room, closing the door behind him.

The telephone was ringing and he picked it up and said, "Hello."

"Ahndrew?" his agent's voice asked. His agent was from Brooklyn, too, but he had a very broad A, with which he impressed actors and sponsors.

"Yes, this is Ahndrew." Andrew always made this straight-faced joke with his agent, but the agent never seemed to catch on. "You didn't have to call. The Dusty Blades scripts are all through. You'll get them tomorrow."

"I called about something else, Ahndrew," his agent said, his voice very smooth and influential on the phone. "The complaints're piling up on the Blades scripts. They're as slow as gum. Nothing ever happens. Ahndrew, you're not writing for the *Atlantic Monthly*."

"I know I'm not writing for the *Atlantic Monthly*."

"I think you've rather run out of material," his agent said lightly, soothingly. "I think perhaps you ought to take a little vacation from the Blades scripts."

"Go to hell, Herman," Andrew said, knowing that Herman had found somebody to do the scripts more cheaply for him.

"That's hardly the way to talk, Ahndrew," Herman said, his voice still smooth, but hurt. "After all, I have to stand in the studio and listen to the complaints."

"Sad, Herman," Andrew said. "That's a sad picture," and hung up.

He rubbed the back of his neck reflectively, feeling again the little lump behind his ear.

He went into his own room and sat at his desk looking blankly at the notes for his play that lay, neatly piled, growing older, on one side. He took out his check book and his last month's vouchers and arranged them in front of him.

"One hundred and eleven dollars," he murmured, as he checked back and added and subtracted, his eyes smarting from the strain, his hands shaking a little because the vacuum cleaner was still going in his mother's room. Out on the athletic field more boys had arrived and formed an infield and were throwing the ball around the bases and yelling at each other.

Dr. Chalmers, seventy-five dollars. That was for his mother and her stomach.

Eighty dollars rent. The roof over his head equaled two Ronnie Cook's and His Friends. Five thousand words for rent.

Buddy was in the hands of Flacker. Flacker could torture him for six pages. Then you could have Dusty Blades speeding to the rescue with Sam, by boat, and the boat could spring a leak because the driver was in Flacker's pay, and there could be a fight for the next six pages. The driver could have a gun. You could use it, but it wouldn't be liked, because you'd done at least four like it already.

Furniture, and a hundred and thirty-seven dollars. His mother had always wanted a good dining-room table. She didn't have a maid, she said, so he ought to get her a dining-room table. How many words for a dining-room table?

"Come on, Baby, make it two," the second baseman out on the field was yelling. "Double 'em up!"

Andrew felt like picking up his old glove and going out there and joining them. When he was still in college he used to go out on a Saturday at ten o'clock in the morning and shag flies and jump around the infield and run and run all day, playing in pickup games until it got too dark to see. He was always tired now and even when he played tennis he didn't move his feet right, because he was tired, and hit flatfooted and wild.

Spain, one hundred dollars. Oh, Lord.

A hundred and fifty to his father, to meet his father's payroll. His father had nine people on his payroll, making little tin gadgets that his father tried to sell to the dime stores, and at the end of every month Andrew had to meet the payroll. His father always gravely made out a note to him.

Flacker is about to kill Buddy out of anger and desperation. In bursts Dusty, alone. Sam is hurt. On the way to the hospital. Buddy is spirited away a moment before Dusty arrives. Flacker, very smooth and oily. Confrontation. "Where is Buddy, Flacker?" "You mean the little lad?" "I mean the little lad, Flacker!"

Fifty dollars to Dorothy's piano teacher. His sister. Another plain girl. She might as well learn how to play the piano. Then one day they'd come to him and say, "Dorothy is ready for her debut. All we're asking you to do is rent Town Hall for a Wednesday evening. Just advance the money." She'd never get married. She was too smart for the men who would want her and too plain for the men she'd want herself. She bought her dresses in Saks. He would have to support, for life, a sister who would only buy her dresses in Saks and paid her piano teacher fifty dollars a month every month. She was only twenty-four, she would have a normal life expectancy of at least forty more years, twelve times forty, plus dresses at Saks and Town Hall from time to time . . .

His father's teeth—ninety dollars. The money it cost to keep a man going in his losing fight against age.

The automobile. Nine hundred dollars. A nine-hundred-dollar check looked very austere and impressive, like a penal institution. He was going to go off in the automobile, find a place in the mountains, write a play. Only he could never get himself far enough ahead on Dusty Blades and Ronnie Cook and His Friends. Twenty thousand words a week, each week, recurring like Sunday on the calendar. How many words was Hamlet? Thirty, thirty-five thousand?

Twenty-three dollars to Best's. That was Martha's sweater for her birthday. "Either you say yes or no," Martha said Saturday night. "I want to get married and I've waited long enough." If you married you paid rent in two places, light, gas, telephone twice, and you bought stockings, dresses, toothpaste, medical attention, for your wife.

Flacker played with something in his pocket. Dusty's hand shoots out, grabs his wrist, pulls his hand out. Buddy's little penknife, which Dusty had given him for a birthday present, is in Flacker's hand. "Flacker, tell me where Buddy Jones is, or I'll kill you with my bare hands." A gong rings. Flacker has stepped on an alarm. Doors open and the room fills with his henchmen.

Twenty dollars to Macy's for books. Parrington, *Main Currents in American Thought*. How does Dusty Blades fit into the *Main Currents in American Thought*?

Ten dollars to Dr. Farber. "I don't sleep at night. Can you help me?"

"Do you drink coffee?"

"I drink one cup of coffee in the morning. That's all."

Pills, to be taken before retiring. Ten dollars. We ransom our lives from doctors' hands.

If you marry, you take an apartment downtown because it's silly to live in Brooklyn this way; and you buy furniture, four rooms full of furniture, beds, chairs, dishrags, relatives. Martha's family was poor and getting no younger and finally there would be three families, with rent and clothes and doctors and funerals.

Andrew got up and opened the closet door. In it, stacked in files were the scripts he had written in the last four years. They stretched from one end of a wide closet across to another, bridge from one wall to another of a million words. Four years' work.

Next script. The henchmen close in on Dusty. He hears the sounds of Buddy screaming in the next room . . .

How many years more?

The vacuum cleaner roared.

Martha was Jewish. That meant you'd have to lie your way into some hotels, if you went at all, and you never could escape from one particular meanness of the world around you; and when the bad time came there you'd be, adrift on that dangerous sea.

He sat down at his desk. One hundred dollars again to Spain. Barcelona had fallen and the long dusty lines were beating their way to the French border with the planes over them, and out of a sense of guilt at not being on a dusty road, yourself, bloody-footed and in fear of death, you gave a hundred dollars, feeling at the same time that it was too much and nothing you ever gave could be enough. Three-and-a-third The Adventures of Dusty Blades to the dead and dying of Spain.

The world loads you day by day with new burdens that increase on your shoulders. Lift a pound and you find you're carrying a ton. "Marry me," she says, "marry me." Then what does Dusty do? What the hell can he do that he hasn't done before? For five afternoons a week now, for a year, Dusty has been in Flacker's hands, or the hands of somebody else who is Flacker but has another name, and each time he has escaped. How now?

The vacuum roared in the hallway outside his room.

"Mom!" he yelled. "Please turn that thing off!"

"What did you say?" his mother called.

"Nothing."

He added up the bank balances. His figures showed that he was four hundred and twelve dollars overdrawn instead of one hundred and eleven dollars, as the bank said. He didn't feel like adding the figures over. He put the vouchers and the bank's sheet into an envelope for his income-tax returns.

"Hit it out, Charlie!" A boy called on the field. "Make it a fast one!"

Andrew felt like going out and playing with them. He changed his clothes and put on a pair of old spikes that were lying in back of the closet. His old pants were tight on him. Fat. If he ever let go, if anything happened and he couldn't exercise, he'd blow up like a house, if he got sick and had to lie in bed and convalesce. . . . Maybe Dusty has a knife in a holster up his sleeve. . . . How plant that? The rent, the food, the piano teacher, the people at Saks who sold his sister dresses, the nimble girls who painted the tin gadgets in his father's shop, the teeth in his father's mouth, the doctors, the doctors, all living on the words that would have to come out of his head. See here, Flacker, I know what you're up to. Business: Sound of a shot. A groan. Hurry, before the train gets to the crossing! Look! He's gaining on us! Hurry! Will he make it? Will Dusty Blades head off the desperate gang of counterfeiters and murderers in the race for the yacht? Will I be able to keep it up? The years, the years ahead. . . . You grow fat and the lines become permanent under your eyes and you drink too much and you pay more to the doctors because death is nearer and there is no stop, no vacation from life, in no year can you say, "I want to sit this one out, kindly excuse me."

His mother opened the door. "Martha's on the phone."

Andrew clattered out in his spiked shoes, holding the old, torn fielder's glove. He closed the door to the dining room to show his mother this was going to be a private conversation.

"Hello," he said. "Yes." He listened gravely. "No," he said. "I guess not. Good-bye. Good luck, Martha."

He stood looking at the phone. His mother came in and he raised his head and started down the steps.

"Andrew," she said, "I want to ask you something."

"What?"

"Could you spare fifty dollars, Andrew?"

"Oh, God!"

"It's important. You know I wouldn't ask you if it wasn't important. It's for Dorothy."

"What does she need it for?"

"She's going to a party, a very important party, a lot of very big people're going to be there and she's sure they'll ask her to play . . ."

"Do the invitations cost fifty dollars apiece?" Andrew kicked the top step and a little piece of dried mud fell off the spiked shoes.

"No, Andrew." His mother was talking in her asking-for-money voice. "It's for a dress. She can't go without a new dress, she says. There's a man there she's after."

"She won't get him, dress or no dress," Andrew said. "Your daughter's a very plain girl."

"I know," his mother's hands waved a little, helpless and sad. "But it's better if she at least does the best she can. I feel so sorry for her, Andrew . . ."

"Everybody comes to me!" Andrew yelled, his voice suddenly high. "Nobody leaves me alone! Not for a minute!"

He was crying now and he turned to hide it from his mother. She looked at him, surprised, shaking her head.

QUESTIONS FOR DISCUSSION

1) *Main Currents in American Thought* is a survey of American literature and thought written by the historian Vernon L. Parrington. Why has Shaw given his story almost this same title?

2) One of the themes of this story is the alienation of the artist from his family as well as from his society. Does the alienation here stem from the artist's failure to love and understand those about him, or is it the artist who is neither loved nor understood? Discuss.

3) Comment on the following statement: Andrew is not really a creative person or he would find the means to write his play.

IV. EDUCATION

Modern industrial society has required for some time that all men and women be literate. This requirement alone places upon schools an immense burden of providing facilities, training teachers, and devising methods for dealing with huge numbers of children. Now it is obvious that the goal of mere literacy is not nearly enough. The already burdened schools must cope further—with the responsibilities of two major props of society which have weakened, the church and the family. Accordingly, to a vastly heterogeneous population, the schools must somehow transmit a viable core of cultural values and assumptions. Even more important and difficult, they must provide special aid to the disadvantaged. They must stimulate, fortify, even subsidize those who would otherwise drop out of the schools and society both. Most important of all, however, the schools must now move toward stimulating creativity and independence among all their students. The thinkers and leaders of the future will come from the ranks in the public schools. These leaders will need to be creative, resourceful, flexible, and self-confident. They will not get that way unless the schools learn to motivate and engage where too many of them now coerce or stultify. Despite the terrible difficulty of it, the American school is going to have to become a center for personal liberation.

from

THE ART
OF TEACHING

Gilbert Highet

The best-known kind of teaching, and the most highly organized—although not the most important—is done in schools, in colleges, in universities, and in technical institutions. Everyone who is reading this book has had some of it, and knows what it is to be a pupil. Everyone owes something to professional teachers. Let us start, then, by looking at them. What kind of people are they, and how do they work?

The teacher has a very peculiar job. It is easy in some ways, and in others it is difficult. The easiest part about it is the spacious routine. There are not many teachers who, like business-men and professional people, are on duty forty-eight or fifty weeks a year every year, and there are still fewer who teach from nine to five every day, five or six days a week. Most schools and colleges run for only nine months in the year altogether, and there is seldom any necessity for a teacher to be on call every hour of the working day. Of course there is a great deal to be done outside teaching hours. Some of it is routine—preparing examinations, reading papers, interviewing pupils. Some of it is research and preparation. But much of this kind of work can be done in one's own time, at one's own home, or in the quiet of a book-room. The great advantage of this is that comparatively few teachers are tied to the desk, chained to the telephone which begins to ring at nine on Monday morning and is still chattering at noon on Saturday, or limited for vacations to a fortnight in July among the millions of exhausted factory-workers.

Leisure is one of the three greatest rewards of being a teacher. It is, unfortunately, the privilege which teachers most often misuse. But let us leave that point meanwhile: we can come back to it later, with some constructive suggestions. There is not too much leisure in the world.

The teacher's chief difficulty is poverty. He (or she) belongs to a badly paid profession. He cannot dress and live like a workman, but he is sometimes paid as little as an unskilled laborer. There are some big prizes at the top of the profession, and a few lucrative sidelines, but the average teacher in every land must be resigned to a life of genteel poverty. In some countries, where wealth is greatly admired as a symbol of success, this is a heavy sacrifice to make. In others, it is partly compensated by the rewards of prestige and respect. But it is always painful. Nevertheless, the job is secure, since there will always be young people who need teaching. A colleague of mine once told me that he lived better during the depression than ever before. In the roaring twenties, men who had been at Princeton with him pitied him for earning five thousand a year teaching when they were making fifty thousand a year selling bonds; but in 1932 he still had a job, and a salary which bought more at deflated prices, while they had neither. Still, even a safe poverty is galling, and many of the snarly bad-tempered teachers whom we remember with hatred were really nice people soured by years of anxiety and penny-pinching.

The teacher's second reward is that he is using his mind on valuable subjects. All over the world people are spending their lives either on doing jobs where the mind must be kept numb all day, or else on highly rewarded activities which are tedious or frivolous. One can get accustomed to operating an adding-machine for five and a half days a week, or to writing advertisements to persuade the public that one brand of cigarettes is better than another. Yet no one would do either of these things for its own sake. Only the money makes them tolerable. But if you really understand an important and interesting subject, like the structure of the human body or the history of the two World Wars, it is a genuine happiness to explain them to others, to feel your mind grappling with their difficulties, to welcome every new book on them, and to learn as you teach.

With this the third reward of teaching is very closely linked. That is the happiness of making something. When the pupils come to you, their minds are only half-formed, full of blank spaces and vague notions and over-simplifications. You do not merely insert a lot of facts, if you teach them properly. It is not like injecting 500 cc. of serum, or administering a year's dose of vitamins. You take the living mind, and mold it. It resists sometimes. It may lie passive and apparently refuse to accept any imprint. Sometimes it takes the mold too easily, and then seems to melt again and become featureless. But often it comes into firmer shape as you work, and gives you the incomparable happiness of helping to create a human being. To teach a boy the difference between truth and lies in print, to start him thinking about the meaning of poetry or patriotism, to hear him hammering back at you with the facts and arguments you have helped him to find, sharpened by himself and fitted to his own powers, gives the sort of satisfaction that an artist has when he makes a picture out of blank canvas and chemical colorings, or a doctor when he hears a sick pulse pick up and carry the energies of new life under his hands.

Some teachers, however, seldom or never have this experience. They are robbed of one of the rewards their job ought to bring them. Instead, they complain of an infliction almost as severe as poverty. They say the boys and girls hate them; and often they hate the boys and girls. Over a period of years, their hatred becomes known and builds up a barrier which they can never break down. I remember when I was eight I went into a class dominated by a female Fury. We were all terrified of her before she even entered the room. Whatever else we learnt that year, we certainly learnt to detest school, and grown-ups, and authority; and we got a fascinating insight into the power and horror of physical cruelty. On the other hand, no single teacher can ever be so devilish as a class of strong, badly disciplined children which has got out of hand. A few years later, in the same school, I recall helping to reduce an inoffensive master, with a good war record, almost to tears of rage and frustration; and I know a teacher in a city school who told me that her chief problem was to keep the boys in her class from attacking one another with furriers' knives.

Now, it is natural for a pupil to resist his teacher. It is healthy, and it can be invigorating for them both. The best works of art are created in difficult media: it is harder to shape marble than wax. Yet when the resistance is never broken down, but hardens into hostility, and when the teacher finds the same hostility—or at best a sniggering indifference— year after year, there is something very far wrong. Sometimes the pupils are wrong. Sometimes the teacher is wrong. Sometimes there is a deepseated dislocation in the community to which they both belong, and their hostility reflects it. (We shall be discussing this a little later, when we come to discipline.) But whatever its cause may be, it is a sore trial to the teacher. It is one of the two worst drawbacks in the job. It is bitter to be poor; but it is torture to spend your life's energy, year after year, trying to awaken understanding and appreciation of genuinely important things in what seems to be a collection of spoiled, ill-mannered boobies, smirking or scowling, yawning or chattering, whose ideals are gangsters, footballers, and Hollywood divorcees. It is like giving a blood transfusion, and then seeing your precious blood spilt on the ground and trodden into mud.

This can happen, in certain conditions, even to a good teacher. But it is more likely to happen to bad teachers. How can it be avoided?

In other words, what are the qualities of a good teacher?

First, and most necessary of all, he must know the subject. He must know what he teaches. This sounds obvious; yet it is not always practiced. It means that, if his job is teaching chemistry, he must know chemistry. It is not enough for a chemistry teacher to know just that amount of chemistry which is taught in schools and required for the final examinations. He must really understand the science of chemistry. Its upper regions must be clear to him, at least in outline; and he should know what are the most important new discoveries made every year. If a boy shows a gift for chemistry, the master must be able to encourage him, by throwing open window after window into the future, showing him what he can learn at the university, what types of chemistry are most vital in peace and war, which big problems still remain to be solved, and (this is always important) how the great chemists of the past and present have lived and worked.

Therefore teaching is inseparable from learning. Every good teacher will learn more about his subject every year—every month, every week if possible. If a girl chooses the career of teaching French in school, she should not hope to commit the prescribed texts and grammars to memory and then turn her mind to other things. She should dedicate part of her life to the French language, to the superb literature of France, to French art and history and civilization. To become a good teacher of French, she will build up a growing library of her own French books, spending one year (for instance) reading Balzac, the next year reading Proust, the next with Molière, and the next with Giraudoux, Cocteau, Romains, and the other modern playwrights. She will visit France, if and when she can save up enough money to do so—which will be fearfully difficult with salaries at their present low level. She may take summer courses in French at a university. Certainly she will see every available French film, and learn to enjoy Raimu's rich Marseillais accent, to guffaw with Fernandel. For it will not all be serious work and planned self-improvement. It will be living, and therefore it will contain enjoyments, and even frivolities, like the latest records by Lucienne Boyer and Charles Trenet. But it will be learning at the same time, and it will make better teaching.

You may ask why this is necessary. Why can a teacher not simply learn the rudiments of the subject, master them thoroughly, and then stop? A postman does not learn every street in the city. He learns only his own area. A French teacher in a small town may never have a pupil who will be able to understand Proust. Why should she trouble to read Proust's novels? Why should a schoolmaster teaching elementary chemistry keep up to date with the latest discoveries? The elements of chemistry are limited in number, and do not change.

There are two answers to this. The first is that one cannot understand even the rudiments of an important subject without knowing its higher levels—at least, not well enough to teach it. Every day the grossest and most painful blunders are made not only by teachers but by journalists and radio commentators and others who have the public ear, because they confidently state a half-truth which they have read in an encyclopedia article, or because they lay down as gospel a conjecture once uttered by an authority they admired. And many teachers, trying to explain certain problems in their own subject, fall into explanations suggested to them by a colleague or thrown up by their own imagination, which are nevertheless totally wrong, and which an extending knowledge of the field would have corrected long ago.

The second answer is that the human mind is infinitely capacious. We know the minimum diet which will keep a child alive. We know the maximum quantity of food he can absorb. But no one knows, no one can even guess how much knowledge a child will want and, if it is presented to him in the right way, will digest. Therefore it is simply useless to teach a child even the elements of a subject, without being prepared to answer his questions about the upper ranges and the inner depths of the subject. And from the teacher's point of view it is far more difficult to do so. A limited field of material stirs very few imaginations. It can be learnt off by heart, but seldom creatively understood and never loved. A subject that carries the mind out in limitless journeys will, if it is well taught, make the learner eager to master all the preliminary essentials and press on.

Young people hate grown-ups for many reasons. One of the reasons is that they feel grown-ups' minds are fixed and limited. Whenever they meet a man or a woman who does not always say what they expect, who tells them novel stories about strange aspects of the world, who throws unexpected lights on what they sadly know as ordinary dull life, who seems as completely alive, sensitive, energetic, and zestful as they themselves, they usually admire him or her. It is true that we cannot all be fountains of energy and novelty throughout every day, but we ought, if we are teachers, to be so keen on our own subjects that we can talk interestingly about unusual aspects of them to young people who would otherwise have been dully neutral, or—worse—eager but disappointed. A teacher must believe in the value and interest of his subject as a doctor believes in health. . . .

The first essential of good teaching, then, is that the teacher must know the subject. That really means that he must continue to learn it.

The second essential is that he must like it. The two are connected, for it is almost impossible to go on learning anything year after year without feeling a spontaneous interest in it. I have a friend who is a stockbroker. He learns more about the market every year. He can recite the high and low quotations on forty leading stocks as far back as 1922; he knows the names of all their directors; he is an encyclopedia of knowledge on unlisted securities, including a lot of rather peculiar South American issues. It would kill me. I could do it—but only with a tremendous effort, for some other reason, clearly indicated. He honestly enjoys it. When he is in France he reads the Bourse page just as eagerly, although he never deals in European stocks. Whether this interest is acquired or natural scarcely matters. By now it is perfectly genuine. The result is that he is a good stockbroker. His interest gives him a steadily increasing knowledge, his knowledge strengthens his judgment, and he is not only successful but happy.

Suppose he met a young man entering business, with the intention of becoming a stockbroker, and saw clearly from his conversation and his manner that he neither knew nor cared whether General Electric was changing its price-policy: he would advise him to give up Wall Street and try some other job. In just the same way, if a girl sets out to make a living (or even a living until marriage) teaching history, and really cares nothing whatever for politics, for biography, for reconstructing the manners and mentalities of other ages, and for the different interpretations that can be put on such important events as the Crusades or the Versailles Treaty, it is useless for her to go on. She will teach it badly to begin with, and worse as she goes on, for she will come to hate it more and more. Eventually she will become like the horse harnessed to the millstone, plodding round and round the same circle, without hope, day after day.

Of course nearly every teacher dislikes some part of his subject. Many a good history teacher shies away from the early Middle Ages, or shuns economic manuals showing the relation of rent to prices and wages at various periods. But she (or he) acknowledges that defect, learns the essentials of that part of the subject, and then, with all the more energy because of a feeling of guilty neglect, throws herself into the part she really enjoys. But to dislike the entire subject, to be a history teacher and be bored by history, to teach French and never open a French book at home, that must be either a constant pain or a numbing narcosis. Think how astonished you would be if your doctor told you that personally he really cared nothing about the art of healing, that he never read the medical journals and paid no attention to new treatments for common complaints, that apart from making a living he thought it completely unimportant whether his patients were sick or sound, and that his real interest was mountain-climbing. You would change your doctor. But the young cannot change their teachers—at least, not until they reach university age, sometimes not even then. They have sometimes to submit to being treated by doctors of the mind, who seem to believe the treatment useless and the patient worthless. No wonder they often distrust education.

The young dislike their elders for having fixed minds. But they dislike them even more for being insincere. They themselves are simple, single-minded, straightforward, almost painfully naïve. A hypocritical boy or girl is rare, and is always a monster or a spiritual cripple. They know grown-ups are clever, they know grown-ups hold the power. What they cannot bear is that grown-ups should also be deceitful. Thousands of boys have admired and imitated bandits and gunmen because they felt these were at least brave and resolute characters, who had simply chosen to be spades instead of diamonds; but few boys have ever admired a forger or a poisoner. So they will tolerate a parent or a teacher who is energetic and violent, and sometimes even learn a good deal from him; but they loathe and despise a hypocrite.

And the teacher who dislikes his subject or is indifferent to it always runs the risk of becoming a hypocrite. Think of the alternatives. Suppose you are teaching chemistry without thinking it worth learning. Either you can tell your pupils to learn it because you will punish them if they don't; or you can tell them to learn it because it will help to get them good jobs in the future; or you can pretend that you think it is too, too fascinating, and just watch what happens when a little H_2 is exploded along with some SO_4. In the first case they will learn grudgingly and perhaps inadequately—it depends largely on the area where you live. (A class in Germany would learn well, a class in Australia would learn badly.) In the second case some of them may believe you and learn well. In the third case none of them will believe you, and you will throw disgust into someone who might have become a good chemist.

But if you do enjoy the subject, it will be easy to teach even when you are tired, and delightful when you are feeling fresh. You will never be at a loss for a new illustration, for a topic of discussion, for an interesting point of view. Even if you do make a blunder, as every teacher does, if you forget a formula or mix up τύπτω with κρύπτω, you will not need to bluff your way out, you can admit that you have forgotten and even ask for the correct word (or, more wisely, promise to look it up), without sacrificing the respect and the attention of your class. For the young do not demand omniscience. They know it is unattainable. They do demand sincerity.

It follows from this that if you are going to be a teacher you must choose your subjects carefully. Of course, many schoolmasters have to take classes in anything and everything—at least to begin with. But even they can decide which are the really essential subjects, and guide their own interests in those directions; and they can mark out the type of subject they would like to teach later, when they get some seniority. . . .

The third essential of good teaching is to like the pupils. If you do not actually like boys and girls, or young men and young women, give up teaching.

It is easy to like the young because they are young. They have no faults, except the very ones which they are asking you to eradicate: ignorance, shallowness, and inexperience. The really hateful faults are those which we grown men and women have. Some of these grow on us like diseases, others we build up and cherish as though they were virtues. Ingrained conceit, calculated cruelty, deep-rooted cowardice, slobbering greed, vulgar self-satisfaction, puffy laziness of mind and body—these and the other real sins result from years, decades of careful cultivation. They show on our faces, they ring harsh or hollow in our voices, they have become bone of our bone and flesh of our flesh. The young do not sin in those ways. Heaven knows they are infuriatingly lazy and unbelievably stupid and sometimes detestably cruel—but not for long, not all at once, and not (like grown-ups) as a matter of habit or policy. They are trying to be energetic and wise and kind. When you remember this, it is difficult not to like them.

A teacher must not only like the young because they are young. He must enjoy their company in groups. There is a famous American definition of a good education. It consists, says the epigram, of Mark Hopkins on one end of a bench and the student on the other. Mark Hopkins was a fine teacher, but he did better when he put ten students on the bench and stood in front of them. Later we shall discuss the advantages of man-to-man teaching and of classes of various kinds. Meanwhile it is enough to point out that there are many more pupils than teachers in the world, so that the average teacher must spend several hours a day with a collection of ten to thirty youngsters. Unless he likes groups of young people, he will not teach them well. It will be useless for him to wish that there were only two or three, or that they were all more mature. They will always be young, and there will always be lots of them.

In certain institutions, and given certain rather special conditions, someone who hates large groups and is nervous among young people can still be accepted and admired as a teacher. A scholar, for instance, who has spent a generation learning a difficult subject may not know how to teach it, and may be embarrassed or repelled by having a youthful audience. But if his reputation and his knowledge are distinguished enough, they will hold the attention of a class even when he himself is dull and inaudible. Many of his hearers will go away stimulated, not by his teaching, but by the excitement of contact, however remote, with a distinguished mind. Many of the world's great universities contain such scholars. Usually they are shocking bad teachers during the first twenty or thirty years, and continue to be bad teachers when they reach their peak; but by the time they have mastered genetics or iconography, most of the work of teaching is done for them, by the accumulated power of their knowledge. Their classes sit silent, attentive, eager. Their thin flat voices are magnified by the attention of their pupils. Incomplete ideas are filled in, obscure trains of thought are illuminated, by the keenness of the audience. I have never heard Dr. Einstein speak, I do not believe he would put much vital energy into teaching, and I do not understand astrophysics; but I should go to hear him lecture, and I know I should learn something from it.

But for most of us, who cannot reasonably count on being savants with a self-illuminating reputation, it is essential to enjoy the conditions of teaching, to feel at home in a room containing twenty or thirty healthy young people, and to make our enjoyment of this group-feeling give us energy for our teaching. Every profession has its atmosphere, its setting, and those who practice it must feel at home there. It is silly to become an actor if you want a settled home and time to think. Do not enter journalism unless you like the bustle of a large noisy office, welcome travel and the unexpected, and hope to like it all the rest of your life. If you do not enjoy the prospect of facing the young in large groups, if you would always prefer working in a laboratory or reading in a library, you will never be a good teacher.

Of course nobody can bear young people all the time. One of the pleasures and the necessities of the teacher's life is to escape—into a cool library or a little garden—away from their noise and their devilish energy. Among the most difficult jobs in the profession are those which give very little respite and condemn the dean to be always on call, the housemaster to spend every day of his working life among the boys. Still, these jobs are not thrust upon us, but taken by choice. Those who hold them usually relish them. Remember, you must not armor yourself against the energies of the young. You must not be the policeman watching the mob. You must be the leader of a group—something higher than the actor with his audience, something lower than the priest with his congregation, something kindlier than the officer with his unit. You must always feel what the orator feels when he addresses an audience partly friendly and partly docile, and senses after a little that they are with him. Such a man is borne upwards and swept onwards by energy which flows into him from outside, from the group of which he is the heart and the voice. The good teacher feels that same flow of energy, constantly supplied by the young. If he can canalize it, he will never be tired. At least, not while he is teaching. . . .

We have seen, then, that the third essential of teaching in ordinary schools and colleges is to like the pupils. Is it also essential to know the pupils?

It depends largely on the method of teaching that is being used—class instruction, lecturing, laboratory work, or tutoring. The distinction between these methods will be discussed later. Here it is enough to say that there is only one of them in which it is genuinely necessary to know every individual pupil well: the tutorial system.

In the other systems, how much must the teacher know of his pupils?

To begin with, he must know the young. They are quite unlike adults. They are so different that it would be easier to understand them if they looked like animals. You know how a baby, before it is born, passes through the main stages of evolution. It begins by looking like an amœba, goes on to look like a fish, resembles a big-headed monkey for some time, and ends up at birth still looking remarkably like a little red blind clutching grimacing ape. I have often thought that in its first fifteen years of life it passes through another series of animal existences. Boys of nine and ten, for instance, are very like dogs. Watch a pack of them hot on the scent, yapping, running and jumping, bouncing aimlessly around full of unexpendable energy, kicking one another or breaking down a door as carelessly as a dog nips at its neighbor's flanks or bursts through a hedge. When they are really enjoying the chase, all their teeth and eyes gleam and their breath and laughter go "huh, huh, huh, huh" like a leash of fox-terriers. Girls in their middle teens are like horses, strong, nervous, given to sudden illnesses and inexplicable terrors, able to work remarkably hard if they are kept firmly in hand, but really happiest when they are thinking of nothing in particular and prancing about with their manes flying. Both dogs and horses are amiable creatures and can be domesticated, but it is a mistake to treat them as though they were human. It is also a mistake to treat horses as though they were dogs, or dogs like horses.

So, if you are interested in teaching, do not even expect the young to be like yourself and the people you know. Learn the peculiar patterns of their thought and emotions just as you would learn to understand horses or dogs—or other animals (for there are all kinds of different animals implicit in children: the very small ones are often more like birds)—and then you will find that many of the inexplicable things they do are easy to understand, many of the unpardonable things easy to forget.

How can you learn this? Chiefly by experience. Watch them and talk to them. Mix with them sometimes off duty. Give them a party now and then, or play games with them. Listen to them, not to eavesdrop, but to understand, by learning the random careless rhythm of their chatter, how their emotions and minds really work. But as well as doing this, you can learn a great deal about them by remembering your own youth. The more intensely you can think yourself back into those parts of it which seem furthest away from your present adult life, the better you can understand the young. Some of the least successful teachers on general work are men and women who, even when they were boys and girls, had an air of premature solemnity and unchildlike primness, who studied hard and seldom played rough or silly games, and whose parents kept them in cotton-wool. Often they enjoyed themselves best, not as boys among boys, or girls among girls, but when assuming the teacher's authority and omniscience. Such youngsters often earn good marks, and then shrink from going out into the rude world to make a living by adventurous competition. Then they take up teaching as a career, and are surprised when they dislike so much of it. Sometimes, indeed, they are extremely good with bright hardworking boys and girls who remind them of themselves. They project all their ambitions onto such pupils, training them to get good scholarships and pass difficult examinations. But they are rarely much good with the ordinary youngsters who fill the average class, because they themselves have never been either ordinary or young.

The teacher, then, must know the young as such. Next, he must know the names and faces of his pupils. Some people find this easy, some very difficult, but it is a *must*. I do it so badly myself that I cannot advise anyone how to do it. Still, I know it must be done. One of the gravest mistakes made by A. E. Housman as a teacher at London University was to boast of his inability to recognize his pupils. The girls hated it, particularly because he would put what felt like really personal venom and vitality into correcting their blunders, and would pass them on the street next day. In his farewell address, before departing for Cambridge, he told them he was sorry, adding: "If I had remembered all your faces, I might have forgotten more important things"—meaning that if he had burdened his memory with the distinction between Miss Jones and Miss Smith, he might have forgotten the difference between the second and the fourth declension. You can imagine how this bogus humility and pedantic arrogance was welcomed by the young women he had snubbed. There was of course a certain amount of truth in it. He meant that it would have been an extra expenditure of time and energy for him to learn the names of his pupils; but he also implied that the effort was unnecessary, and not really part of his job. And there, since he was taking money for teaching, he was wrong. The young are trying desperately hard to become real people, to be individuals. If you wish to influence them in any way, you must convince them that you know them as individuals. The first step towards this is memorizing their faces and their names.

But the teacher will find that, beyond this, it is seldom feasible to treat all his pupils as individuals. Even if it were possible, it would be unwise. For it would mean that the problem presented by each young man or girl would have to be approached as though it were unique. This would make it very difficult to solve, would be exhausting for the teacher, and would waste the profits of experience. The art of teaching, like the art of healing, consists partly in recognizing, within each individual, a particular type or combination of types. If a doctor is asked to visit a sick man, he does not attempt to work out all the items of his individuality—the facts that he is a Freemason, has been twice married, enjoys chess and bird-watching do not interest him. He is the reverse of the modern novelists like Joyce and Proust who endeavor to bring out every infinitesimal wrinkle, every memory which shades a thought or alters a decision. What the doctor sees is not Leopold Bloom or Monsieur Bergotte, but a case of lobar pneumonia one day old, in a man of fifty with good heart and blood-pressure but poor metabolism and a history of respiratory infections. The combination of these factors is his problem. If the patient also has individual attributes which are really relevant—if, for instance, he is a Christian Scientist and believes lobar pneumonia is a mental delusion—the doctor will take them also into account. But the success of his treatment will depend on the penetration with which he can *generalize* about this particular individual.

Similarly, the best way to know one's pupils is to divide them into types. This is a skill which the teacher can learn only by experience. He will begin, early in his career, by thinking they are all different. Then he will observe that Clark is rather like Johansen, and that Verney and Lennox react in very much the same way to difficulties, and even write similar essays. Then, after four or five years' teaching, he will notice another Clark in his class—a youth who looks the same (except that he has red hair) and laughs at the same kind of jokes and writes the same big square hand . . . only this boy is called Macdonald and comes from a different part of the country. Next year another Verney will turn up. And so on, until the teacher, if he learns well, will in ten or fifteen years assemble a little gallery of types which, singly or combined, will account for eighty-five per cent of the average class.

It is a complicated business, typing one's pupils. It must not be over-simplified. It would be frankly impossible in a very broad sampling of humanity. For instance, it was extremely difficult in the army, where one had great strong farmers, quick little city boys, grave youths from the small towns, and dozens of unexpected blends of character and background and physique, all in the same unit. But schools and universities do not function in mid-air. They are each attached to one group of traditions and supplied chiefly by two or three localities; also, schools and local society and youth itself do a great deal of uniformizing, so that a teacher can usually count on a fairly even distribution and recurrence of types. . . .

So far, we have said that a good teacher should know his subject, and, within limits, know his pupils. There is another necessary qualification. He or she should know much else. The good teacher is a man or woman of exceptionally wide and lively intellectual interests. It is useless to think of teaching as a business, like banking or insurance: to learn the necessary quota of rules and facts, to apply them day by day as the bank-manager applies his, to go home in the evening and sink into a routine of local gossip and middle-brow relaxation (radio, TV, the newspaper, and the detective-story), to pride oneself on being an average citizen, indistinguishable from the dentist and the superintendent of the gas-works—and then to hope to stimulate young and active minds. Teachers in schools and colleges must see more, think more, and understand more than the average man and woman of the society in which they live. This does not only mean that they must have a better command of language and know special subjects, such as Spanish literature and marine biology, which are closed to others. It means that they must know more about the world, have wider interests, keep a more active enthusiasm for the problems of the mind and the inexhaustible pleasures of art, have a keener taste even for some of the superficial enjoyments of life—yes, and spend the whole of their career widening the horizons of their spirit. Most people, as we see, stop growing between thirty and forty. They "settle down"—a phrase which implies stagnation—or at the utmost they "coast along," using their acquired momentum, applying no more energy, and gradually slowing down to a stop. No teacher should dream of doing this. His job is understanding a large and important area of the world's activity and achievement and making it viable for the young. He should expect to understand more and more of it as the years go by.

He has two special functions that make him different from other professional men and from the business-men and workers in his community.

The first of these is to make a bridge between school or college and the world. It is really very hard for the young to understand why they are shut up in classrooms and taught skills such as trigonometry, while the "real world" hums and clatters and shouts beyond the windows. They submit, poor creatures, but the pressure required to keep them there is intense. If they are allowed to think that school or college is an ingenious prison, a squirrel-cage in which they must whirl uselessly for a few years until they are let out, they will profit little or nothing from it. They may resent it bitterly. They cannot be told directly or convincingly how learning trigonometry will fit into their future existence: partly because no one knows which of them will turn out to be a bridge-engineer or will make some now unimagined discovery in ballistics, partly because they themselves cannot realize the value of mathematical thinking during their adolescence and youth, and partly because they cannot foresee even the outlines of their adult lives. But they should be given to understand in as many ways as possible that the two worlds are closely and necessarily connected, and that light and energy from one flow into the other.

This is often done by "making subjects relevant." Little German boys used to be trained in mathematics by getting problems about the number of pounds of explosive required to demolish a (non-German) viaduct. Some teachers of English use current magazines like *Time* to demonstrate vivid and concise writing. Certainly every teacher of a modern foreign language ought to use the newspapers and films produced in that language. But this idea cannot be applied to all subjects, nor to some of the most valuable subjects, while in others it often leads to superficiality and lowers intellectual standards.

The best way to do it is for the teacher to make *himself* relevant. Nine thousand times more pupils have learnt a difficult subject well because they felt the teacher's vitality and energy proved its value than because they chose the subject for its own sake. If a youth, sizing up the professor of medieval history, decides that he is a tremendous expert in the history of the Middle Ages and a deadly bore in everything else, he is apt to conclude that medieval history makes a man a deadly bore. If on the other hand he finds that the man is filled with lively interest in the contemporary world, that he actually knows more about it because, through his training, he understands it better, that the practice of the intellectual life, so far from making him vague and remote, has made him wise and competent, the youth will conclude without further evidence that medieval history is a valuable interest.

The good teacher is an interesting man or woman. As such, he or she will make the work interesting for the students, in just the same way as he or she talks interestingly and writes an interesting letter. Most teaching is done by talking. If your mind is full of lively awareness of the world, you will never be at a loss for new points of view on your own subject. Novel illustrations will constantly suggest themselves to you. You will discard outworn types of argument and find fresh ones. Allusions and reminiscences will brighten your talk and keep your audience from suffering the awful torture of feeling that it knows exactly what you are going to say next. Much teaching consists in explaining. We explain the unknown by the known, the vague by the vivid. The students usually know so little that they are delighted to hear you explain what you know and tie it up with what they are trying to understand. A colleague of mine in Paris used to have great difficulty, when discussing *Don Quixote,* in convincing his intelligent youngsters that Quixote was not merely a farcical old lunatic who should have been locked up. Then he described a series of bull-fights he had seen on a holiday in Seville, with their cruelty, their pride, their useless courage, which is an art in itself, and the oddity of sixteenth-century costumes in a Roman arena for a twentieth-century entertainment, which struck none of the Spaniards as odd; and he reminded them of the same Spanish pride and idealism as expressed in tragedy by the French master Corneille. Then his pupils began to understand that their own standards had not been complex enough for judging all the world's great books, and that Don Quixote's insanity might be a kind of strange sense. From that point the discussions used to develop in a dozen equally interesting and instructive directions.

The second function of the teacher is to make a bridge between youth and maturity. He has to interpret adult life to the young in such a way as to make them adults. To do this, he should belong to both worlds.

Many teachers find this extremely difficult. Some schoolmasters in Britain "live for the school." This means that their horizon is bounded at one edge by the preparatory institutions from which the youngsters come and on the other by the colleges to which they go. The great events of their lives are school cricket-matches and scholarship examinations. Like some officers of the regular army, they will talk for hours about the flap in Ingoldsby's unit, and "Whatever became of old Snoggins?" but they grow embarrassed when asked about new books or contemporary politics. At the other extreme are teachers who care less than nothing for the hopes and fears and gaieties of the young, who never open the college magazine or watch a school football game, who feel it is an infringement on their dignity to spend nearly every day with children and adolescents, and who would obviously be happier if all their pupils were fifty years old and graying at the temples.

Difficult though this bridge-building between two worlds may be, it is possible; it is necessary; it is done by the best teachers. After all, no one is entirely and exclusively thirty-three years old, or forty-eight, or whatever his legal age may be. Watch any group of people enjoying themselves, vividly interested, and you will see them growing decades younger. Within every one of us, not far from the surface, lie hidden many personalities, some of them as young as childhood, and only one as old as today. The good teacher will be able to draw vitality and variety from the younger layers of personality which are still alive within him, and to know what it is to be a youth again, or a boy, without ceasing to be a man.

For example, he will notice and remember not only the things that interest him as an adult, but those things which used to interest him as a youngster. If he does, and if he uses them to illustrate his teaching but discusses them from a mature level, his teaching will become easier and his explanations clearer. The young are not very deep and consistent thinkers, but they are highly sensitive to new impressions: so they notice things like fanciful advertising campaigns, eccentric new personalities, peculiar rather than essential pieces of news, far more than grown-ups do. They do not think much about such things, but—since they have not yet become blasé and have no very intense inner life—they do experience them. Allusions to such things therefore can clarify a difficult discussion. At the moment this is being written, for instance, it would be wise for anyone trying to explain the ancient Greek "tyrants," those ambitious independent despots, to begin by talking of Marshal Tito. Although the parallel is not really close, it is helpful.

One of the most important qualities of a good teacher is humor. Many are the purposes it serves. The most obvious one is that it keeps the pupils alive and attentive because they are never quite sure what is coming next. Another is that it does in fact help to give a true picture of many important subjects. Suppose you are discussing English literature of the early nineteenth century. If you confine yourself to talking about Wordsworth's lyrical simplicity, and Shelley pinnacled dim in the intense inane, you will be giving an incomplete picture of the group; whereas if you also d-d-describe Ch-Charles Lamb as both f-funny and ch-charming, and bring out the weird boyish comedy of some of Wordsworth's other poems, and read some of Byron's rougher letters, you will then establish the idea that these men were rich and varied and human personalities, not "classics" cast in a single mold of solid bronze, and you can proceed all the better to explain both the nobility of their achievement and the sadness of their failures.

Of course some subjects, notably the sciences, do not admit humorous treatment. There the wise teacher will continue to introduce flashes of humor extraneously, because he knows that fifty-five minutes of work plus five minutes' laughter are worth twice as much as sixty minutes of unvaried work.

Some teachers speak of humor as a useful instrument with which to control their classes. This is a dangerous notion. Those who harbor it often make the mistake of using humor as nineteenth-century schoolmasters used the cane, to terrify the refractory and spur the slow. They begin by mocking a particular set of mistakes. Then they make fun of the boys who make these mistakes. Then they develop a bitter wit which thrives on every kind of personal defect, ruthlessly exposed. They will even feel aggrieved if no boy in their class happens to be a fit subject for satire, and will single out a perfectly innocuous youth simply because they cannot teach without having a butt. They are like the Oriental monarchs who always had a few malefactors impaled before their gates, to remind the citizenry that the master's word was law. Perhaps they would enjoy that comparison, for they are usually so petty and insecure that they would like to be maharajahs. I should compare them rather to the magpies of the Western states which will find a sore patch on a horse's back and perch on it, picking out raw flesh and squawking with self-satisfaction, until the horse runs mad down a cliff-side.

Kipling, who suffered a good deal of torture during his childhood, got this treatment first from his guardians (see *Something of Myself*, Chapter ii) and then from the master whom he immortalized as "King" (note the regal pseudonym) in *Stalky & Co*. What "King" did to him certainly kept him mentally alert; and he says he enjoyed it and profited from it; but it helped to increase that timidity and hypersensitivity which spoilt much of his adult life, and it did something to produce his very odd belief in the pulverizing force of ridicule as a political weapon (see, for instance, "Little Foxes," "As Easy as A.B.C.," and "The Village That Voted the Earth was Flat"), his absolute trust in authority, and his almost delighted contempt for lesser breeds without the Law. If he had only had a teacher like Kim's Lama, he would have been wiser and much happier. But part of his spirit was sacrificed to a schoolmaster who, perhaps, as some schoolmasters also do, detected and resented the superior intellectual brilliance of the grubby boy with the big glasses, and tried to make himself feel great by making young Rudyard Kipling feel small.

No, humor must not be used to tyrannize a class. It seldom is so used. Usually irony and sarcasm are used, because they imply intellectual domination; but not humor. The real purpose of humor in teaching is deeper and more worthy. It is to link the pupils and the teacher, and to link them through enjoyment. A very wise old teacher once said: "I consider a day's teaching is wasted if we do not all have one hearty laugh." He meant that when people laugh together, they cease to be young and old, master and pupils, workers and driver, jailer and prisoners, they become a single group of human beings enjoying its existence.

Jules Romains, the eminent French novelist and dramatist, began his career by working out a theory which he later put into several excellent plays and stories. This is the idea that collections of people remain individuals until a single event or purpose or emotion molds them into groups, and that then the group lives, feels, and thinks in a way of its own, superior in energy and intensity to the activity of any one of its members. Sometimes, no doubt, a collective emotion is silly or degrading, as in a riot or a panic. But sometimes, Romains believes, it can be a truly ennobling experience: it is our duty to understand such experiences fully when they come. To be a member of a meeting which is moved by an energetic speaker to take a generous resolution; to applaud with a crowd of friends when your own team, making a huge effort, wins; to share the emotion of actors and audience at the production of a good new play; to walk through a city and feel yourself part of its beating and driving life—these are worthy emotions, which help us out of our own pettiness.

Romains called this theory Unanimism. Obviously it has its dangers. It leads very easily to the annulment of the individual, to the denial of intelligence, to "thinking with the blood" and believing that the majority is always right. Because it is easy to misapply, and because he knows that no eminent artist has ever been tied to one single theory, Romains has not concentrated on preaching and exploiting the doctrine. But it runs through most of his best work, and has inspired several younger writers. Now, Romains was for some time a teacher in French high schools. One of the most winning figures in his *Men of Good Will* is the schoolmaster Clanricard, while several others are in fact teachers though they are ostensibly priests, doctors, and authors. Although he got his first glimpse of Unanimism in a busy Paris street, I am sure that he confirmed it from his experiences as a pupil and as a teacher. For one of the greatest pleasures in teaching comes from those hours when you feel that every word you say is being heard, not by a collection of bored and dutiful individuals, but instead by a group which you create and which in turn creates you; that, instead of repeating facts learnt by rote, to be telephoned through the drowsy air to half-deaf ears and garbled down in notebooks, you are both stirring minds to ask questions and answering them; that you are being driven by the energy of the young on the search for truth, and drawing therefrom the power to lead the search; and, in fact, that you and your words and the class which listens and thinks are all part of the ceaseless activity of human Reason.

Your pupils will feel this too. If the feeling exists at all, it will be shared. To create it, or to help it to come into being, is one of the teacher's main tasks. It cannot exist unless there is a rapport, a give-and-take, something like a unanimist relationship between the pupils and the teacher. One of the means of establishing that rapport is humor. When a class and its teacher all laugh together, they cease for a time to be separated by individuality, authority, and age. They become a unit, feeling pleasure and enjoying the shared experience. If that community can be prolonged or reestablished, and applied to the job of thinking, the teacher will have succeeded.

This can also be put in terms of traditional psychology. There are two powerful instincts which exist in all human beings, and which can be used in teaching. These are *gregariousness* and *the love of play*. Give fifty men four hours to cross a hill and walk down the valley beyond to the nearest town. If they try it separately, many will come in late, and nearly all will be tired. If they march in groups, they will be far less tired and come in sooner. If they do it in two teams competing with each other, or as a hiking party singing songs in rhythm, they will scarcely be tired at all, they will keep together, and they will enjoy the experience. In just the same way, if you can get a class of thirty youngsters to feel they are all pulling together, and if you can give them some reason to enjoy it, they will do nine times better work than thirty individuals working under compulsion. And one of the best appeals to both gregariousness and the play-instinct is a good joke.

We said that one function of the teacher was to make a bridge between youth and maturity. If he has a sense of humor, he can build the bridge. The young think their elders are dull. The elders think the young are silly. This is the basis of that mutual misunderstanding of the ages, on which scarcely anything can get done without compulsion. Yet a clever teacher, who can use his sense of humor in such a way as to show the young that not everyone over twenty-five is dead, will at the same time learn enough about his pupils to see that their silliness is only awkwardness, easy to penetrate and dissolve. Both sides will understand each other better, and work together. Togetherness is the essence of teaching. . . .

QUESTIONS FOR DISCUSSION

1) One difference between the creative teacher and the non-creative teacher, according to Highet, is that the creative teacher welcomes the resistance of his students. Certain satisfactions compensate for the tensions of challenge and resistance. What are those satisfactions?

2) We tend to believe that the smaller a class is, the more creative its teacher can be. Highet believes that a class of a reasonable size is a necessity for creative teaching. Explain why.

3) One might think that the creative teacher would avoid stereotyping, trying, rather, to deal with his students as individuals. But, to Highet, stereotyping is essential for good teaching, if done creatively. Explain what Highet means by creative stereotyping. Does your experience as a student support Highet's belief? Explain.

4) Explain the function of humor in Highet's method of teaching.

5) Highet says that the teacher must try to be a bridge between maturity and youth, "to know what it is to be a youth again, or a boy, without ceasing to be a man." Comment on Highet's statement as it relates to teaching and as it relates to creativity in general.

from
TEACHER

Sylvia Ashton-Warner

THE GOLDEN SECTION

"Many centuries ago Plato and Pythagoras had already found in *number* the clue to the *nature* of the universe and to the mystery of beauty."

But in school it works out to be of more practical importance to realise these two aspects, nature study and number, as differences, rather than as the fundamental unity that they are, even though number has never been anything other than the basis of all forms which nature assumes.

However, the more a subject refers to its source, the more chance it has of being integrated, and although nature study and number are indispensable landmarks in a syllabus, their separation reminds me of the "cutting up of life," to which Mr. Beeby refers; also I wonder if Tolstoy would have done it this way. I personally see it easier to subordinate them both to a title which has in it the meaning of both. And although there are other deeply rooted points from which nature study and number arise as a unity, there is one which has a particular relation to plant growth: the Golden Section.

The Golden Section is the ideal proportion. It is the division of a distance in such a way that the shorter part is to the longer part as the longer part is to the whole. It's one of the laws governing plant life, and although it is something that cannot be explained in an infant room, it can be felt all right and it can be drawn easily and every day. The diminishing spans between twigs on a branch as it tapers to its tip. Or on a fern. Ferns make wonderful counting boards. When we were on long trips when our children were little, we would sometimes give them a big frond to count, and as an occupational toy I can recommend it. Costs nothing. Just pick one from the side of the road. And all the time they were learning fundamental things about natural form.

However, to return to the infant room, all this going outside ("outside," by the way, has turned out to be a pathetically strong word in the Organic Vocabulary)—all this going outside to see and handle these things and the returning to draw and write about them is the way to find out about this section. The laws of number, nature and beauty turn out to be much the same thing.

Yet there is no evidence to suspect the validity of much of the number material available to an infant room; for instance the square things and the many pieces that are built on even numbers; but the idea has its duplicate often enough outdoors—in the right-angled leafing arrangements and the pairs of leaves set exactly opposite each other as in the koromiko. Some of the infant-room material has gradations, too; not quite the two-three-five-eight-thirteen combination of the tapering nodules of plants but gradations anyway. It's an idea to write this sequence on the blackboard for bead-threading purposes, as a variation to the even sets of two, then of three and so on. It's more exciting, seeing the size of the bead group growing along the string. But the most absorbing number activity is the drawing of a fern frond by the children; ten on this twig, nine on this, eight on this until the one on its own at the end; numbering them.

Then sometimes in the lower groups you can draw a hand, tracing your own hand on the paper and numbering the fingers, when learning to count to five. Or toes. Or a flower with its petals, real flowers outside, unpicked. They make good sums for upper primers, flowers. And it can all happen in a walk and there's nothing destroyed. And there are scents to go with it and beauty.

Clover is an incomparable activity in threes and it's just out the door. Also it is something you can pick in quantities and bring inside. For upper primers learning to count in threes and for the Little Ones learning to count to three. But counting the impermanent birds is the most concentrated game, involving a self-imposed quiet and watchful eyes, and there's the drawing or painting or clay record to follow.

Things don't always work out as ideally as that though. When it's raining or cold we turn to material and chalk. But on a fine morning we all go for a walk down the stop-bank. We play games in it and some of the girls dance the "Babes in the Wood" ballet and cover two children with leaves. We note the turning colour all around and use the word "autumn."

We count the children we can see and work out the ones that are missing. The boy who is sent back to school for disobedience makes a subtraction sum, and the strays we pick up on our way, the half-past fours, addition. The last time we went we each took a small branch and counted the leaves on it. They ranged from six to seventeen. Then I told the children to count a hundred trees in the willow plantation, touching each tree, and afterwards we went on down to the sand by the river and wrote our numbers with sticks.

The thing about all this is that they like doing it and become easy to teach. But they just as much like the games and weighing and snakes and ladders and dominoes and skittles for the winter. And the seven-year-olds try some formal sums and try to write up to a hundred. There's even a place for how many pennies in a shilling, although maybe that belongs beyond what I call the plastic age of children. At this time, when a mind is setting into its permanent future pattern, it might just as well set into a pattern akin to nature. There's time enough for formality and respectability afterwards. So we go for long, noisy, happy walks along the stop-bank by the river. All sorts of things can happen in a walk, not the least being experience itself. To write about or talk or draw about. Then the Golden Section becomes inseparable from writing and reading and drawing and conversation. Three ducks on the wing we like better than three ducks on a number card with a static three beside them.

I think that we don't like seeds grown in eggshells and nasturtiums and onions in tins and a bulb in a jar in the classroom. We like eggs in eggshells, jam in tins, bulbs in the garden and nasturtiums by the fence. When we want to see the construction of a seedling there are millions outside. I hate charts as much as they do. I like the moving currents of children's interests. Draw the poplars straight after a walk and count them and number them. Then drop the subject for the next. I like the "hot prison of the moment."

We don't waste enough in school. We hoard our old ideas on charts to be used again and again like stale bread. Ideas are never the same again, even those of the masters; even if the only change is in our own mood of reapproach. Yet there's never a shortage of ideas if the stimulus is there. Waste the old paper and waste the old pictures and waste the old ideas. It's tidier and simpler.

Birds in our area: Sparrows, mynah, crow, magpie, thrush, blackbird, fantail, fowls, duck, geese.

Unwilling insects brought into school: Mantis, grasshoppers, caterpillars, beetles, crickets, butterflies.

Uninvited insects in school: Wasps, lice, bees, spiders.

One early autumn we had the monarch butterfly caterpillars on the swan plant and watched or tried to watch the sequences of their development into butterflies, but owing to the help given by some of my Maori warriors the butterflies never made it. Over in the junior room, however, they managed to get through.

I think there may be a lack of sympathy between the infant room and the insect world since the enrollment of the wasps. Last week as Arapata was on his way across the playground to get his typhoid injection, a wasp gave him one instead. He got to the nurse all right but not with the same intention. No one pressed him to receive the needle. Not that morning anyway. And when I put Joe outside the other day for discipline's sake, screams told us that the wasps had completed the discipline, so we brought him inside again. We've had no trouble with him since. All of which has provoked passionate discussions on wasps and their ways. Also some passionate paintings.

The birds have supplied us with movements for expressive dancing. There's a magpie dance and a lark dance, although we have seen no larks. We've been told that there are larks, however, but not the spectacular high-flying, high-singing ones. The falling leaves supply us with endless dance designs, both formal and informal. Also the fin movement of fish. And frogs. We've had some frogs inside in tins of muddy, grassy water for observation, but once more the loving ways of my warriors bring their lives to an early close. Also the frogs of these parts are great jumpers and for some reason prefer the machine drawer or the coal tin to the cool water. Or get themselves mixed up in the clay bucket or go for the books. Sammy Snail is the only visitor who has the sense to keep out of reach, dangling on the rafter. And we have a chrysalis or two. Pussy doesn't get much of a time when she strolls in and I don't think the ginger rooster will ever call again.

Informal visitors to the infant room: Sammy Snail, Ginger Rooster, Pussy, Mangu's dog, a fantail, a monkey.

We had some goldfish to watch for a time. They were kept in the senior room and were a great draw to the infants. But owing to the container leaking they were put in the tub in the laundry to ensure the automatic replacement of water. But one laundry day some soap fell in . . . Amen.

I have gathered over the years a collection of pictures, however, of different subjects, some of them animals, some of them birds, along with the nursery rhymes and seasonal pictures, and mounted them, and I keep them in separate packets. Wet day stuff. And they greatly widen the horizon. There's a packet of about thirty pictures of bears, for instance, to follow up on the Three Bears story. Autumn pictures, horse pictures, bird pictures and cat pictures. But they are used for the observation of nature only when we are short of the real live thing, kicking, crawling, singing or stinging.

I place the Golden Section in the output period between one o'clock and two—either for the whole of the time, as during a walk, or for a number lesson outside to be written about when they come in, or for part of the time. So much depends on mood and weather and attendance. The pictures, though, occur in the intake period between eleven and twelve.

The formal number scheme which is provided for our use is essentially creative and belongs in the morning.

Also one soon collects seasonal songs and poems and stories about animals and birds and weather, *e.g.:*

SPRING

Songs: Buttercups and Daisies; Hark, Hark, the Lark; The North Wind.

Poems: Chick-chick; Violet; Jonquil.

Stories: The Black Cat; The Apple-blossom.

SUMMER

Songs: The Birds in the Trees; Catching Fishes.

Poems: Kees-kees; Lady-bird.

Stories: Miscellaneous; Little Red Hen.

AUTUMN

Songs: The Falling Leaves; Rustle, Rustle; A Little Brown Baby.
Poem: Ten Little Yellow Leaves.
Stories: Miscellaneous; "Janet and John" stories.

WINTER

Songs: The South Wind; Jolly Little Eskimo; Mr. Wind; Pitter-Patter; The Rain Fairy.
Poems: Children, Children; Jack Frost.
Story: The Three Goats.

Flowers in our area: Marigolds, stock, roses, poppies, currants, pansies, geraniums, dahlias, delphiniums.
Trees in our area: Cabbage trees, macrocarpa, hoheria, walnut, most fruit trees, pine.

Experience and record could well be the story of the Golden Section. There can't be any tight compartments of age or time or work coverage. I think that this tracking down of number and nature study to their deep common source may give back in integration what it takes from the expertly planned lesson. At least as much. And I think that if we take care of the Golden Section, its parts, nature study and number, will, in the infant room anyway, take care of themselves.

TONE

"The still centre"
—T. S. Eliot

Tone belongs to order and can be won.
It concerns not only classrooms; it is a condition that is or is not implicit in every group of people working together over something, from infant rooms through education departments to groups as big as countries. For in the running of all these, order is the key. It's the expression on the countenance of a group.
But there are two kinds of order, and which is the one we wish for? Is it the conscious order that ends up as respectability? Or is it the unconscious order that looks like chaos on the top? There is a separate world on each side of this question mark.
When we track tone to its source we find that it inhabits the temperament area. We find that the person with tone is not badly disturbed by passions. Following it further beyond temperament it turns out to be, to a large extent, a particular climate of the soul. As the Czech architect

Honzig says in speaking of the final form of a building, "It is a condition of rest."

Whichever kind of order teachers think about, tone is still qualified by the same three things: the personality of the teacher, the personality of the children, and the method used.

I know a teacher who takes tone with her wherever she goes; whether to the infant department of a big school, to an outsized choir in the municipal or to a Red Cross demonstration in a shop window. Whether you meet her in a drawing room, in an infant room, in the street or backstage, you meet tone too. Also I know a headmaster who doesn't have to try to bring a feeling of peace upon the standards, and I've had two out of six juniors who, although they knew nothing of the conscious cultivation of tone, nevertheless carried it about in their pockets. But none of these people is discomforted with "restless passions that would not be stilled." And they have tone; inside and out.

Happily, however, the structure of a teacher is not the whole of the formula for tone in a classroom. There's the tone of the children and the tone of the district. On the east coast, where our neighbors were Sir Apirana Ngata on one side and Reweti Kohere on the other, no upheaval in the school could shake its tone. Whatever the incident, and we were not without them, the tone remained unscratched. The district itself had tone. The people had sitting among them authentic leaders and all remained well. There was serenity. It flowed down from "The Sir" through the Ngatiporou like the influence of a headmaster through his school.

But here, where there never has been a leader and where the Maoris walk precariously the tightrope between the brown and the white, there is none of the tribal confidence and cohesion of the coast. So there's no order or calm in the district, and if a teacher can't supply the missing quality from his own resources or by his own method the days can turn into outlawry.

But not necessarily, for tone can be won. Even when it is missing in the teacher and missing in the children. There's method left. The thing is to forget about appearances and cultivate the order in the unconscious. Which is simple enough and done with creativity. And although the room will seem disorderly by sight, it is not so by feel. Through the vents of creativity forces can get out and away, leaving the lower levels relatively calm. There's a noisy kind of peace throughout the long creative periods in the morning when every child is engrossed in some medium of construction. True, this infant room is fed by a loud-mouthed and disintegrated pa,* but I don't feel hopeless. You can put every subject into the creative vent so that there will be a flow and a release of forces all day. The noise is terrible, but you've got to pay in some way. I sort out the unseemly habits and train seemly ones. I rehearse the periods in mind before we have them.

---

* A *pa* is a fortified Maori settlement [editors' note].

I try to get reciprocal respect and trust between me and them. I go to any lengths in the pursuit of style in their work and continually check up on the feel of the room. All of which another teacher possessing natural tone doesn't need to do. But in spite of the unrest in the tribe and the lack of cohesion in the pa and the "fire that on my bosom preys," I get a precarious sense of some deep order.

And then, when you come to think about it, you find that of the two kinds of order, the conscious and the unconscious order, only one is real. It's the order in the deep hidden places. And whatever the temperament of the teacher and of the children, it is accessible to anyone. When we trace tone beyond the area of temperament and beyond the climate of the personality to its origin, we find that it is simply this order. The true order in the depths. The "still centre."

Workbook

Teachers say they need their workbooks.

They say, I can't rely on myself in the melee of a lesson to work out sequences on the spot. When the time comes I need everything at my fingertips. I've got to have it all thought out beforehand.

Conception in tranquillity can range from the conscious condensation of material and method up to the level of prayer. All the great teachers of the past have drawn their action from non-action. From Christ upon the high mountain, through Lo Tung over his tea, down to us. And I can never see that these names are too big to be used side by side with today. The intention is the same—teaching. It's not this conception in tranquillity that is the point of departure.

I know that the preparation of a workbook may clarify to a teacher what he is thinking about. I know that the order and method of it reflect inescapably upon the minds of the children. And I suspect from what I see that the very fact of a workbook evokes on the mind of a teacher a reliable peace. And that its notes mean that necessary steppingstone between his conception and his execution. Indeed, I can believe comfortably enough that the assessment of a workbook can be truthfully close to the assessment of a man. It is neither the fact of a workbook nor its phase in teaching that is the point of departure. It's the incorrigible variety in man himself.

For some teachers just don't see a workbook in this way. True, they see it in the same place between conception and execution, but not as a steppingstone. To some teachers the workbook is the middleman intercepting some of the energy and glamour directed upon the canvas. Leonardo da Vinci cut straight into his marble, Rabindranath Tagore wrote his verses neat, and I didn't hear of Jesus making notes. Teachers, all of them in one medium or another, who mistrusted the middleman.

To the extent that a teacher is an artist, and according to Plato there should be no distinction, his inner eye has the native power, unatrophied, to hold the work he means to do. And in the places where he can't see, he has a trust in himself that he will see it, either in time for the occasion or eventually. And he would rather risk a blank in his teaching than expend cash on the middleman. He wants the feel of the glamour of direct engagement. He wants to see in his mind, as he teaches, the idea itself, rather than the page it is written on. He wants to work from conception itself directly upon the children without interference from the image of its record on a book. He wants to work in a way that to him is clear, without conflict and without interception.

It doesn't always, I think, clarify a teacher's thoughts to note them down. To some it is a pinioning. Something to evade. I learned when I was a very small girl that you could leave half your meaning behind in a preparatory sketch. When I was very young I worked straight from my mind upon the clay. Then I knew that what I did was all of what I could do and not just the residue of a trial. And when in teaching I found that I was required to precede all my work with the written notes of a workbook, it was with gross payment to the middleman that I did so.

In an infant room, however, where the activity is wholly expressive, with all subjects allowed their legitimate entry into the area of creativity, the question of a workbook can hardly arise. Wherever there's creativity on a large scale there's life, and I, anyway, can't plot life. I just join in. How are we to know what is going to come from the children on this day or that? How can I tell what the reading and spelling is going to be since each morning they write their own books for the day's use? Does a teacher wish to anticipate the purposes of each new day? In an infant room cultivating the organic expansion, a teacher learns to put the factors of mood and change before the prognostications of a workbook.

As Caldwell Cook says: "Not the professor, but the artist, is your true school master."

Dancing

Dancing I place in the morning output time, considering it as good a medium as any other, since Plato said it was the one complete expression involving the faculties on all levels, spiritual, intellectual and physical. That's what I think too. Not that I deliberately teach it for that reason. It just happened one bright spring morning when I was playing some Schubert to please no one but myself that a child stood up from his work and began composing a dance, then another, then another, and there it all was. And here it all still is.

Although most of the interpretations come from them, I indulge myself by providing them with a further selection of movements to use as they choose, to supplement their own movements. But I haven't noticed much of it being used voluntarily in their interpretation of new music. The old story of imposition again.

I never use other than classical music. Not only for my own sake but because it was a classic that brought them to their feet in the first place. So far I have used Schubert, Beethoven, Tchaikovsky, Chopin, Brahms and Grieg. But I'm only feeling my way, since my only source of dancing knowledge is from my own dreaming.

My aim is that a child may be able to create dancing as freely as he draws or writes autobiography or plays. But I haven't got there yet.* Although we place dancing in the output period, we also use it to break any strain of work during the day.

THE UNLIVED LIFE

It's all so merciful on a teacher, this appearance of the subjects of an infant room in the creative vent. For one thing, the drive is no longer the teacher's but the children's own. And for another, the teacher is at last with the stream and not against it: the stream of children's inexorable creativeness. As Dr. Jung says, psychic life is a world power that exceeds by many times all the powers of the earth; as Dr. Burrow says, the secret of our collective ills is to be traced to the suppression of creative ability; and as Erich Fromm says, destructiveness is the outcome of the unlived life.

So it is of more than professional moment that all of the work of young children should be through the creative vent. It is more than a teaching matter or a dominion one. It's an international matter. So often I have said in the past, when a war is over the statesmen should not go into conference with one another but should turn their attention to the infant rooms, since it is from there that comes peace or war. And that's how I see organic teaching. It helps to set the creative pattern in a mind while it is yet malleable, and in this role is a humble contribution to peace.

The expansion of a child's mind can be a beautiful growth. And in beauty are included the qualities of equilibrium, harmony and rest. There's no more comely word in the language than "rest." All the movement in life, and out of it too, is towards a condition of rest. Even the simple movement of a child "coming up."

I can't disassociate the activity in an infant room from peace and war. So often I have seen the destructive vent, beneath an onslaught of creativity, dry up under my eyes. Especially with the warlike Maori five-year-olds who pass through my hands in hundreds, arriving with no other thought in their heads other than to take, break, fight and be first. With no opportunity for creativity they may well develop, as they did in the past, with

---

* By the time I wrote *Spinster* I had got there.

fighting as their ideal of life. Yet all this can be expelled through the creative vent, and the more violent the boy the more I see that he creates, and when he kicks the others with his big boots, treads on fingers on the mat, hits another over the head with a piece of wood or throws a stone, I put clay in his hands, or chalk. He can create bombs if he likes or draw my house in flame, but it is the creative vent that is widening all the time and the destructive one atrophying, however much it may look to the contrary. And anyway I have always been more afraid of the weapon unspoken than of the one on a blackboard.

With all this in mind therefore I try to bring as many facets of teaching into the creative vent as possible, with emphasis on reading and writing. And that's just what organic teaching is; all subjects in the creative vent. It's just as easy for a teacher, who gives a child a brush and lets him paint, to give him a pencil and let him write, and to let him pass his story to the next one to read. Simplicity is so safe. There's no occasion whatever for the early imposition of a dead reading, a dead vocabulary. I'm so afraid of it. It's like a frame over a young tree making it grow in an unnatural shape. It makes me think of that curtailment of a child's expansion of which Erich Fromm speaks, of that unlived life of which destructiveness is the outcome. "And instead of the wholeness of the expansive tree we have only the twisted and stunted bush." The trouble is that a child from a modern respectable home suffers such a serious frame on his behaviour long before he comes near a teacher. Nevertheless I think that after a year of organic work the static vocabularies can be used without misfortune. They can even, under the heads of external stimulus and respect for the standard of English, become desirable.

But only when built upon the organic foundation. And there's hardly anything new in the conception of progress from the known to the unknown. It's just that when the inorganic reading is imposed first it interferes with integration; and it's upon the integrated personality that everything is built. We've lost the gracious movement from the inside outward. We overlook the footing. I talk sometimes about a bridge from the pa to the European environment, but there is a common bridge for a child of any race and of more moment than any other: the bridge from the inner world outward. And that is what organic teaching is. An indispensable step in integration. Without it we get this one-patterned mind of the New Zealand child, accruing from so much American influence of the mass-mind type. I think that we already have so much pressure towards sameness through radio, film and comic outside the school, that we can't afford to do a thing inside that is not toward individual development, and from this stance I can't see that we can indulge in the one imposed reading for all until the particular variety of a mind is set. And a cross-section of children from different places in New Zealand provides me with an automatic check on the progress of the one-patterned mind. (I own seventy fancy-dress costumes which I lend.) All the children want the same costumes. If you made dozens of cowboy and cowgirl costumes, hundreds of Superman and thousands of Rocket Man costumes and hired them at half a guinea a go, you'd get every penny of it and would make a fortune vast enough to retire on and spend the rest of your life in the garden. As for my classics—Bo-Peep, the Chinese Mandarin, Peter Pan and the Witch and so on—they so gather the dust that they have had to be folded and put away. It's this sameness in children that can be so boring. So is death boring.

To write peaceful reading books and put them in an infant room is not the way to peace. They don't even scratch the surface. No child ever asked for a Janet or a John costume. There is only one answer to destructiveness and that is creativity. And it never was and never will be any different. And when I say so I am in august company.

The noticeable thing in New Zealand society is the body of people with their inner resources atrophied. Seldom have they had to reach inward to grasp the thing that they wanted. Everything, from material requirements to ideas, is available ready-made. From mechanical gadgets in the shops to sensation in the films they can buy almost anything they fancy. They can buy life itself from the film and radio—canned life.

And even if they tried to reach inward for something that maybe they couldn't find manufactured, they would no longer find anything there. They've dried up. From babyhood they have had shiny toys put in their hands, and in the kindergartens and infant rooms bright pictures and gay material. Why conceive anything of their own? There has not been the need. The capacity to do so has been atrophied and now there is nothing there. The vast expanses of the mind that could have been alive with creative activity are now no more than empty vaults that must, for comfort's sake, be filled with non-stop radio, and their conversation consists of a list of platitudes and clichés.

I can't quite understand why.

From what I see of modern education the intention is just the opposite: to let children grow up in their own personal way into creative and interesting people. Is it the standard textbooks? Is it the consolidation? Is it the quality of the teachers? Is it the access to film and radio and the quality of those luxuries? Or is it the access to low-grade reading material infused through all of these things? I don't know where the intention fails but we end up with the same pattern of a person in nine hundred ninety-nine instances out of a thousand.

I said to a friend of mine, a professor, recently, "What kind of children arrive at the University to you?" He said, "They're all exactly the same." "But," I said, "how can it be like that? The whole plan of primary education at least is for diversity." "Well," he answered, "they come to me like samples from a mill. Not one can think for himself. I beg them not to serve back to me exactly what I have given to them. I challenge them sometimes with wrong statements to provoke at least some disagreement but even that won't work." "But," I said, "you must confess to about three per cent originality." "One in a thousand," he replied. "One in a thousand."

On the five-year-old level the mind is not yet patterned and it is an exciting thought. True, I often get the over-disciplined European five, crushed beyond recognition as an identity, by respectable parents, but never Maoris; as a rule a five-year-old child is not boring. In an infant room it is still possible to meet an interesting, unpatterned person. "In the infant room," I told this professor, "we still have identity. It's somewhere between my infant-room level and your university level that the story breaks. But I don't think it is the plan of education itself."

I think that the educational story from the infant room to the university is like the writing of a novel. You can't be sure of your beginning until you have checked it with your ending. What might come of infant teachers visiting the university and professors visiting the infant room? I had two other professors in my infant room last year and they proved themselves to be not only delightfully in tune but sensitively helpful.

Yet what I believe and what I practise are not wholly the same thing. For instance, although I have reason to think that a child's occupation until seven should not be other than creative in the many mediums, nevertheless I find myself teaching some things.

With all this in mind, therefore, the intent of the infant room is the nurturing of the organic idea,

the preservation of the inner resources,

the exercise of the inner eye and

the protraction of the true personality.

I like unpredictability and variation; I like drama and I like gaiety; I like peace in the world and I like interesting people, and all this means that I like life in its organic shape and that's just what you get in an infant room where the creative vent widens. For this is where style is born in both writing and art, for art is the way you do a thing and an education based on art at once flashes out style.

The word "jalopy" made its fascinating appearance the other day. Brian wrote, "I went to town. I came back on a jalopy bus." This word stirred us. The others cross-questioned him on the character of such a bus. It turned out to mean "rackety" and although the word was picked up at once nevertheless they still ask for it to go up on the spelling list. We haven't had "jalopy" for spelling lately, Brian says. He loves spelling it, which is what I mean when I say that the drive is the children's own. It's all so merciful on a teacher.

Inescapably war and peace wait in an infant room; wait and vie.

True the toy shops are full of guns, boys' hands hold tanks and war planes while the blackboards, clay boards and easels burst with war play. But I'm unalarmed. My concern is the rearing of the creative disposition, for creativity in this crèche of living where people can still be changed must in the end defy, if not defeat, the capacity for destruction. Every happening in the infant room is either creative or destructive; every drawing, every shaping, every sentence and every dance goes one way or the other. For, as Erich Fromm says, "life has an inner dynamism of its own; it tends to grow, to be expressed, to be lived. The amount of destructiveness in a child is proportionate to the amount to which the expansiveness of his life has been curtailed. Destructiveness is the outcome of the unlived life."

I believe in this as passionately as the artist in his brush and the roadman in his shovel. For every work, and first of all that of a teacher, must have its form, its design. And the design of my work is that creativity in this time of life when character can be influenced forever is the solution to the problem of war. To me it has the validity of a law of physics and all the unstatable, irrepressible emotion of beauty.

QUESTIONS FOR DISCUSSION

1) Miss Ashton-Warner is here describing her teaching experiences with Maori children in rural New Zealand. What are her aims in each day's walks?

2) Miss Ashton-Warner quotes approvingly the statement that "Not the professor, but the artist, is your true school master." Do you agree? Explain.

3) What are the three sources of "tone" in the classroom? What type of order does the author consider to be "real"?

4) Miss Ashton-Warner says that "I like the 'hot prison of the moment.'" What does she mean by this? How does it relate to her teaching?

5) "Destructiveness is the outcome of the unlived life." Miss Ashton-Warner believes that creativity is the only force that can combat destructiveness. Does she offer convincing evidence to support this belief? Explain.

6) What evidence do you see in the very style in which this essay is written that would lead you to believe that Miss Ashton-Warner is indeed a "creative" person?

OF THIS TIME,
OF THAT PLACE

Lionel Trilling

It was a fine September day. By noon it would be summer again, but now it was true autumn with a touch of chill in the air. As Joseph Howe stood on the porch of the house in which he lodged, ready to leave for his first class of the year, he thought with pleasure of the long indoor days that were coming. It was a moment when he could feel glad of his profession.

On the lawn the peach tree was still in fruit and young Hilda Aiken was taking a picture of it. She held the camera tight against her chest. She wanted the sun behind her, but she did not want her own long morning shadow in the foreground. She raised the camera, but that did not help, and she lowered it, but that made things worse. She twisted her body to the left, then to the right. In the end she had to step out of the direct line of the sun. At last she snapped the shutter and wound the film with intense care.

Howe, watching her from the porch, waited for her to finish and called good morning. She turned, startled, and almost sullenly lowered her glance. In the year Howe had lived at the Aikens', Hilda had accepted him as one of her family, but since his absence of the summer she had grown shy. Then suddenly she lifted her head and smiled at him, and the humorous smile confirmed his pleasure in the day. She picked up her bookbag and set off for school.

The handsome houses on the streets to the college were not yet fully awake, but they looked very friendly. Howe went by the Bradby house where he would be a guest this evening at the first dinner party of the year. When he had gone the length of the picket fence, the whitest in town, he turned back. Along the path there was a fine row of asters and he went through the gate and picked one for his buttonhole. The Bradbys would be pleased if they happened to see him invading their lawn and the knowledge of this made him even more comfortable.

He reached the campus as the hour was striking. The students were hurrying to their classes. He himself was in no hurry. He stopped at his dim cubicle of an office and lit a cigarette. The prospect of facing his class had suddenly presented itself to him and his hands were cold; the lawful seizure of power he was about to make seemed momentous. Waiting did not help. He put out his cigarette, picked up a pad of theme paper, and went to his classroom.

As he entered, the rattle of voices ceased, and the twenty-odd freshmen settled themselves and looked at him appraisingly. Their faces seemed gross, his heart sank at their massed impassivity, but he spoke briskly.

"My name is Howe," he said, and turned and wrote it on the blackboard. The carelessness of the scrawl confirmed his authority. He went on, "My office is 412 Slemp Hall, and my office-hours are Monday, Wednesday and Friday from eleven-thirty to twelve-thirty."

He wrote, "M., W., F., 11:30–12:30." He said, "I'll be very glad to see any of you at that time. Or if you can't come then, you can arrange with me for some other time."

He turned again to the blackboard and spoke over his shoulder. "The text for the course is Jarman's *Modern Plays,* revised edition. The Co-op has it in stock." He wrote the name, underlined "revised edition" and waited for it to be taken down in the new notebooks.

When the bent heads were raised again he began his speech of prospectus. "It is hard to explain—" he said, and paused as they composed themselves. "It is hard to explain what a course like this is intended to do. We are going to try to learn something about modern literature and something about prose composition."

As he spoke, his hands warmed and he was able to look directly at the class. Last year on the first day the faces had seemed just as cloddish, but as the term wore on they became gradually alive and quite likable. It did not seem possible that the same thing could happen again.

"I shall not lecture in this course," he continued. "Our work will be carried on by discussion and we will try to learn by an exchange of opinion. But you will soon recognize that my opinion is worth more than anyone else's here."

He remained grave as he said it, but two boys understood and laughed. The rest took permission from them and laughed too. All Howe's private ironies protested the vulgarity of the joke, but the laughter made him feel benign and powerful.

When the little speech was finished, Howe picked up the pad of paper he had brought. He announced that they would write an extemporaneous theme. Its subject was traditional, "Who I am and why I came to Dwight College." By now the class was more at ease and it gave a ritualistic groan of protest. Then there was a stir as fountain pens were brought out and the writing-arms of the chairs were cleared, and the paper was passed about. At last, all the heads bent to work, and the room became still.

Howe sat idly at his desk. The sun shone through the tall clumsy windows. The cool of the morning was already passing. There was a scent of autumn and of varnish and the stillness of the room was deep and oddly touching. Now and then a student's head was raised and scratched in the old, elaborate students' pantomime that calls the teacher to witness honest intellectual effort.

Suddenly a tall boy stood within the frame of the open door. "Is this," he said, and thrust a large nose into a college catalogue, "is this the meeting place of English 1A? The section instructed by Dr. Joseph Howe?"

He stood on the very sill of the door, as if refusing to enter until he was perfectly sure of all his rights. The class looked up from work, found him absurd and gave a low mocking cheer.

The teacher and the new student, with equal pointedness, ignored the disturbance. Howe nodded to the boy, who pushed his head forward and then jerked it back in a wide elaborate arc to clear his brow of a heavy lock of hair. He advanced into the room and halted before Howe, almost at attention. In a loud, clear voice he announced, "I am Tertan, Ferdinand R., reporting at the direction of Head of Department Vincent."

The heraldic formality of this statement brought forth another cheer. Howe looked at the class with a sternness he could not really feel, for there was indeed something ridiculous about this boy. Under his displeased regard the rows of heads dropped to work again. Then he touched Tertan's elbow, led him up to the desk and stood so as to shield their conversation from the class.

"We are writing an extemporaneous theme," he said. "The subject is, 'Who I am and why I came to Dwight College.'"

He stripped a few sheets from the pad and offered them to the boy. Tertan hesitated and then took the paper, but he held it only tentatively. As if with the effort of making something clear, he gulped, and a slow smile fixed itself on his face. It was at once knowing and shy.

"Professor," he said, "to be perfectly fair to my classmates"—he made a large gesture over the room—"and to you"—he inclined his head to Howe—"this would not be for me an extemporaneous subject."

Howe tried to understand. "You mean you've already thought about it—you've heard we always give the same subject? That doesn't matter."

Again the boy ducked his head and gulped. It was the gesture of one who wishes to make a difficult explanation with perfect candor. "Sir," he said, and made the distinction with great care, "the topic I did not expect, but I have given much ratiocination to the subject."

Howe smiled and said, "I don't think that's an unfair advantage. Just go ahead and write."

Tertan narrowed his eyes and glanced sidewise at Howe. His strange mouth smiled. Then in quizzical acceptance, he ducked his head, threw back the heavy, dank lock, dropped into a seat with a great loose noise and began to write rapidly.

The room fell silent again and Howe resumed his idleness. When the bell rang, the students who had groaned when the task had been set now groaned again because they had not finished. Howe took up the papers, and held the class while he made the first assignment. When he dismissed it, Tertan bore down on him, his slack mouth held ready for speech.

"Some professors," he said, "are pedants. They are Dryasdusts. However, some professors are free souls and creative spirits. Kant, Hegel and Nietzsche were all professors." With this pronouncement he paused. "It is my opinion," he continued, "that you occupy the second category."

Howe looked at the boy in surprise and said with good-natured irony, "With Kant, Hegel and Nietzsche?"

Not only Tertan's hand and head but his whole awkward body waved away the stupidity. "It is the kind and not the quantity of the kind," he said sternly.

Rebuked, Howe said as simply and seriously as he could, "It would be nice to think so." He added, "Of course I am not a professor."

This was clearly a disappointment but Tertan met it. "In the French sense," he said with composure. "Generically, a teacher."

Suddenly he bowed. It was such a bow, Howe fancied, as a stage-director might teach an actor playing a medieval student who takes leave of Abelard—stiff, solemn, with elbows close to the body and feet together. Then, quite as suddenly, he turned and left.

A queer fish, and as soon as Howe reached his office, he sifted through the batch of themes and drew out Tertan's. The boy had filled many sheets with his unformed headlong scrawl. "Who am I?" he had begun. "Here, in a mundane, not to say commercialized academe, is asked the question which from time long immemorably out of mind has accreted doubts and thoughts in the psyche of man to pester him as a nuisance. Whether in St. Augustine (or Austin as sometimes called) or Miss Bashkirtsieff or Frederic Amiel or Empedocles, or in less lights of the intellect than these, this posed question has been ineluctable."

Howe took out his pencil. He circled "academe" and wrote "vocab." in the margin. He underlined "time long immemorably out of mind" and wrote "Diction!" But this seemed inadequate for what was wrong. He put down his pencil and read ahead to discover the principle of error in the theme. "Today as ever, in spite of gloomy prophets of the dismal science (economics) the question is uninvalidated. Out of the starry depths of heaven hurtles this spear of query demanding to be caught on the shield of the mind ere it pierces the skull and the limbs be unstrung."

Baffled but quite caught, Howe read on. "Materialism, by which is meant the philosophic concept and not the moral idea, provides no aegis against the question which lies beyond the tangible (metaphysics). Existence without alloy is the question presented. Environment and heredity relegated aside, the rags and old clothes of practical life discarded, the name and the instrumentality of livelihood do not, as the prophets of the dismal science insist on in this connection, give solution to the interrogation which not from the professor merely but veritably from the cosmos is given. I think, therefore I am (cogito etc.) but who am I? Tertan I am, but what is Tertan? Of this time, of that place, of some parentage, what does it matter?"

Existence without alloy: the phrase established itself. Howe put aside

Tertan's paper and at random picked up another. "I am Arthur J. Case-beer, Jr.," he read. "My father is Arthur J. Casebeer and my grandfather was Arthur J. Casebeer before him. My mother is Nina Wimble Casebeer. Both of them are college graduates and my father is in insurance. I was born in St. Louis eighteen years ago and we still make our residence there."

Arthur J. Casebeer, who knew who he was, was less interesting than Tertan, but more coherent. Howe picked up Tertan's paper again. It was clear that none of the routine marginal comments, no "sent. str." or "punct." or "vocab." could cope with this torrential rhetoric. He read ahead, contenting himself with underscoring the errors against the time when he should have the necessary "conference" with Tertan.

It was a busy and official day of cards and sheets, arrangements and small decisions, and it gave Howe pleasure. Even when it was time to at-tend the first of the weekly Convocations he felt the charm of the beginning of things when intention is still innocent and uncorrupted by effort. He sat among the young instructors on the platform, and joined in their humorous complaints at having to assist at the ceremony, but actually he got a clear satisfaction from the ritual of prayer and prosy speech, and even from wearing his academic gown. And when the Convocation was over the pleasure continued as he crossed the campus, exchanging greetings with men he had not seen since the spring. They were people who did not yet, and perhaps never would, mean much to him, but in a year they had grown amiably to be part of his life. They were his fellow-townsmen.

The day had cooled again at sunset, and there was a bright chill in the September twilight. Howe carried his voluminous gown over his arm, he swung his doctoral hood by its purple neckpiece, and on his head he wore his mortarboard with its heavy gold tassel bobbing just over his eye. These were the weighty and absurd symbols of his new profession and they pleased him. At twenty-six Joseph Howe had discovered that he was neither so well off nor so bohemian as he had once thought. A small income, ade-quate when supplemented by a sizable cash legacy, was genteel poverty when the cash was all spent. And the literary life—the room at the La-fayette, or the small apartment without a lease, the long summers on the Cape, the long afternoons and the social evenings—began to weary him. His writing filled his mornings and should perhaps have filled his life, yet it did not. To the amusement of his friends, and with a certain sense that he was betraying his own freedom, he had used the last of his legacy for a year at Harvard. The small but respectable reputation of his two volumes of verse had proved useful—he continued at Harvard on a fellowship and when he emerged as Doctor Howe he received an excellent appointment, with prospects, at Dwight.

He had his moments of fear when all that had ever been said of the dangers of the academic life had occurred to him. But after a year in which he had tested every possibility of corruption and seduction he was ready to rest easy. His third volume of verse, most of it written in his first years of teaching, was not only ampler but, he thought, better than its predecessors.

There was a clear hour before the Bradby dinner party, and Howe looked forward to it. But he was not to enjoy it, for lying with his mail on the hall table was a copy of this quarter's issue of *Life and Letters,* to which his landlord subscribed. Its severe cover announced that its editor, Frederic Woolley, had this month contributed an essay called "Two Poets," and Howe, picking it up, curious to see who the two poets might be, felt his own name start out at him with cabalistic power—Joseph Howe. As he continued to turn the pages his hand trembled.

Standing in the dark hall, holding the neat little magazine, Howe knew that his literary contempt for Frederic Woolley meant nothing, for he suddenly understood how he respected Woolley in the way of the world. He knew this by the trembling of his hand. And of the little world as well as the great, for although the literary groups of New York might dismiss Woolley, his name carried high authority in the academic world. At Dwight it was even a revered name, for it had been here at the college that Frederic Woolley had made the distinguished scholarly career from which he had gone on to literary journalism. In middle life he had been induced to take the editorship of *Life and Letters,* a literary monthly not widely read but heavily endowed, and in its pages he had carried on the defense of what he sometimes called the older values. He was not without wit, he had great knowledge and considerable taste, and even in the full movement of the "new" literature he had won a certain respect for his refusal to accept it. In France, even in England, he would have been connected with a more robust tradition of conservatism, but America gave him an audience not much better than genteel. It was known in the college that to the subsidy of *Life and Letters* the Bradbys contributed a great part.

As Howe read, he saw that he was involved in nothing less than an event. When the Fifth Series of *Studies in Order and Value* came to be collected, this latest of Frederic Woolley's essays would not be merely another step in the old direction. Clearly and unmistakably, it was a turning point. All his literary life Woolley had been concerned with the relation of literature to morality, religion, and the private and delicate pieties, and he had been unalterably opposed to all that he had called "inhuman humanitarianism." But here, suddenly, dramatically late, he had made an about-face, turning to the public life and to the humanitarian politics he had so long despised. This was the kind of incident the histories of literature make much of. Frederic Woolley was opening for himself a new career and winning a kind of new youth. He contrasted the two poets, Thomas Wormser, who was admirable, Joseph Howe, who was almost dangerous. He spoke of the "precious subjectivism" of Howe's verse. "In times like ours," he wrote, "with millions facing penury and want, one feels that the qualities of the *tour d'ivoire* are well-nigh inhuman, nearly insulting. The *tour d'ivoire* becomes the *tour d'ivresse,* and it is not self-intoxicated poets that our people need." The essay said more: "The problem is one of meaning.

I am not ignorant that the creed of the esoteric poets declares that a poem does not and should not *mean* anything, that it *is* something. But poetry is what the poet makes it, and if he is a true poet he makes what his society needs. And what is needed now is the tradition in which Mr. Wormser writes, the true tradition of poetry. The Howes do no harm, but they do no good when positive good is demanded of all responsible men. Or do the Howes indeed do no harm? Perhaps Plato would have said they do, that in some ways theirs is the Phrygian music that turns men's minds from the struggle. Certainly it is true that Thomas Wormser writes in the lucid Dorian mode which sends men into battle with evil."

It was easy to understand why Woolley had chosen to praise Thomas Wormser. The long, lilting lines of *Corn Under Willows* hymned, as Woolley put it, the struggle for wheat in the Iowa fields, and expressed the real lives of real people. But why out of the dozen more notable examples he had chosen Howe's little volume as the example of "precious subjectivism" was hard to guess. In a way it was funny, this multiplication of himself into "the Howes." And yet this becoming the multiform political symbol by whose creation Frederic Woolley gave the sign of a sudden new life, this use of him as a sacrifice whose blood was necessary for the rites of rejuvenation, made him feel oddly unclean.

Nor could Howe get rid of a certain practical resentment. As a poet he had a special and respectable place in the college life. But it might be another thing to be marked as the poet of a wilful and selfish obscurity.

As he walked to the Bradbys', Howe was a little tense and defensive. It seemed to him that all the world knew of the "attack" and agreed with it. And, indeed, the Bradbys had read the essay but Professor Bradby, a kind and pretentious man, said "I see my old friend knocked you about a bit, my boy," and his wife Eugenia looked at Howe with her childlike blue eyes and said, "I shall *scold* Frederic for the untrue things he wrote about you. You aren't the least obscure." They beamed at him. In their genial snobbery they seemed to feel that he had distinguished himself. He was the leader of Howeism. He enjoyed the dinner party as much as he had thought he would.

And in the following days, as he was more preoccupied with his duties, the incident was forgotten. His classes had ceased to be mere groups. Student after student detached himself from the mass and required or claimed a place in Howe's awareness. Of them all it was Tertan who first and most violently signaled his separate existence. A week after classes had begun Howe saw his silhouette on the frosted glass of his office door. It was motionless for a long time, perhaps stopped by the problem of whether or not to knock before entering. Howe called, "Come in!" and Tertan entered with his shambling stride.

He stood beside the desk, silent and at attention. When Howe asked him to sit down, he responded with a gesture of head and hand, as if to say that such amenities were beside the point. Nevertheless, he did take the chair. He put his ragged, crammed briefcase between his legs. His face, which Howe now observed fully for the first time, was confusing, for it was made up of florid curves, the nose arched in the bone and voluted in the nostril, the mouth loose and soft and rather moist. Yet the face was so thin and narrow as to seem the very type of asceticism. Lashes of unusual length veiled the eyes and, indeed, it seemed as if there were a veil over the whole countenance. Before the words actually came, the face screwed itself into an attitude of preparation for them.

"You can confer with me now?" Tertan said.

"Yes, I'd be glad to. There are several things in your two themes I want to talk to you about." Howe reached for the packet of themes on his desk and sought for Tertan's. But the boy was waving them away.

"These are done perforce," he said. "Under the pressure of your requirement. They are not significant; mere duties." Again his great hand flapped vaguely to dismiss his themes. He leaned forward and gazed at his teacher.

"You are," he said, "a man of letters? You are a poet?" It was more a declaration than question.

"I should like to think so," Howe said.

At first Tertan accepted the answer with a show of appreciation, as though the understatement made a secret between himself and Howe. Then he chose to misunderstand. With his shrewd and disconcerting control of expression, he presented to Howe a puzzled grimace. "What does that mean?" he said.

Howe retracted the irony. "Yes. I am a poet." It sounded strange to say.

"That," Tertan said, "is a wonder." He corrected himself with his ducking head. "I mean that is wonderful."

Suddenly, he dived at the miserable briefcase between his legs, put it on his knees, and began to fumble with the catch, all intent on the difficulty it presented. Howe noted that his suit was worn thin, his shirt almost unclean. He became aware, even, of a vague and musty odor of garments worn too long in unaired rooms. Tertan conquered the lock and began to concentrate upon a search into the interior. At last he held in his hand what he was after, a torn and crumpled copy of *Life and Letters*.

"I learned it from here," he said, holding it out.

Howe looked at him sharply, his hackles a little up. But the boy's face was not only perfectly innocent, it even shone with a conscious admiration. Apparently nothing of the import of the essay had touched him except the wonderful fact that his teacher was a "man of letters." Yet this seemed too stupid, and Howe, to test it, said, "The man who wrote that doesn't think it's wonderful."

Tertan made a moist hissing sound as he cleared his mouth of saliva. His head, oddly loose on his neck, wove a pattern of contempt in the air.

"A critic," he said, "who admits *prima facie* that he does not understand." Then he said grandly, "It is the inevitable fate."

It was absurd, yet Howe was not only aware of the absurdity but of a tension suddenly and wonderfully relaxed. Now that the "attack" was on the table between himself and this strange boy, and subject to the boy's funny and absolutely certain contempt, the hidden force of his feeling was revealed to him in the very moment that it vanished. All unsuspected, there had been a film over the world, a transparent but discoloring haze of danger. But he had no time to stop over the brightened aspect of things. Tertan was going on. "I also am a man of letters. Putative."

"You have written a good deal?" Howe meant to be no more than polite, and he was surprised at the tenderness he heard in his words.

Solemnly the boy nodded, threw back the dank lock, and sucked in a deep, anticipatory breath. "First, a work of homiletics, which is a defense of the principles of religious optimism against the pessimism of Schopenhauer and the humanism of Nietzsche."

"Humanism? Why do you call it humanism?"

"It is my nomenclature for making a deity of man," Tertan replied negligently. "Then three fictional works, novels. And numerous essays in science, combating materialism. Is it your duty to read these if I bring them to you?"

Howe answered simply, "No, it isn't exactly my duty, but I shall be happy to read them."

Tertan stood up and remained silent. He rested his bag on the chair. With a certain compunction—for it did not seem entirely proper that, of two men of letters, one should have the right to blue-pencil the other, to grade him or to question the quality of his "sentence structure"—Howe reached for Tertan's papers. But before he could take them up, the boy suddenly made his bow-to-Abelard, the stiff inclination of the body with the hands seeming to emerge from the scholar's gown. Then he was gone.

But after his departure something was still left of him. The timbre of his curious sentences, the downright finality of so quaint a phrase as "It is the inevitable fate" still rang in the air. Howe gave the warmth of his feeling to the new visitor who stood at the door announcing himself with a genteel clearing of the throat.

"Doctor Howe, I believe?" the student said. A large hand advanced into the room and grasped Howe's hand. "Blackburn, sir, Theodore Blackburn, vice-president of the Student Council. A great pleasure, sir."

Out of a pair of ruddy cheeks a pair of small eyes twinkled goodnaturedly. The large face, the large body were not so much fat as beefy and suggested something "typical"—monk, politician, or innkeeper.

Blackburn took the seat beside Howe's desk. "I may have seemed to introduce myself in my public capacity, sir," he said. "But it is really as an individual that I came to see you. That is to say, as one of your students to be."

He spoke with an English intonation and he went on, "I was once an English major, sir."

For a moment Howe was startled, for the roast-beef look of the boy and the manner of his speech gave a second's credibility to one sense of his statement. Then the collegiate meaning of the phrase asserted itself, but some perversity made Howe say what was not really in good taste even with so forward a student, "Indeed? What regiment?"

Blackburn stared and then gave a little pouf-pouf of laughter. He waved the misapprehension away. "*Very* good, sir. It certainly is an ambiguous term." He chuckled in appreciation of Howe's joke, then cleared his throat to put it aside. "I look forward to taking your course in the romantic poets, sir," he said earnestly. "To me the romantic poets are the very crown of English literature."

Howe made a dry sound, and the boy, catching some meaning in it, said, "Little as I know them, of course. But even Shakespeare who is so dear to us of the Anglo-Saxon tradition is in a sense but the preparation for Shelley, Keats and Byron. And Wadsworth."

Almost sorry for him, Howe dropped his eyes. With some embarrassment, for the boy was not actually his student, he said softly "Wordsworth."

"Sir?"

"Wordsworth, not Wadsworth. You said Wadsworth."

"Did I, sir?" Gravely he shook his head to rebuke himself for the error. "Wordsworth, of course—slip of the tongue." Then, quite in command again, he went on. "I have a favor to ask of you, Doctor Howe. You see, I began my college course as an English major,"—he smiled—"as I said."

"Yes?"

"But after my first year I shifted. I shifted to the social sciences. Sociology and government—I find them stimulating and very *real.*" He paused, out of respect for reality. "But now I find that perhaps I have neglected the other side."

"The other side?" Howe said.

"Imagination, fancy, culture. A well-rounded man." He trailed off as if there were perfect understanding between them. "And so, sir, I have decided to end my senior year with your course in the romantic poets."

His voice was filled with an indulgence which Howe ignored as he said flatly and gravely, "But that course isn't given until the spring term."

"Yes, sir, and that is where the favor comes in. Would you let me take your romantic prose course? I can't take it for credit, sir, my program is full, but just for background it seems to me that I ought to take it. I do hope," he concluded in a manly way, "that you will consent."

"Well, it's no great favor, Mr. Blackburn. You can come if you wish, though there's not much point in it if you don't do the reading."

The bell rang for the hour and Howe got up.

"May I begin with this class, sir?" Blackburn's smile was candid and boyish.

Howe nodded carelessly and together, silently, they walked to the classroom down the hall. When they reached the door Howe stood back to let his student enter, but Blackburn moved adroitly behind him and grasped him by the arm to urge him over the threshold. They entered together with Blackburn's hand firmly on Howe's biceps, the student inducting the teacher into his own room. Howe felt a surge of temper rise in him and almost violently he disengaged his arm and walked to the desk, while Blackburn found a seat in the front row and smiled at him.

II

The question was, At whose door must the tragedy be laid?

All night the snow had fallen heavily and only now was abating in sparse little flurries. The windows were valanced high with white. It was very quiet; something of the quiet of the world had reached the class, and Howe found that everyone was glad to talk or listen. In the room there was a comfortable sense of pleasure in being human.

Casebeer believed that the blame for the tragedy rested with heredity. Picking up the book he read, "The sins of the fathers are visited on their children." This opinion was received with general favor. Nevertheless, Johnson ventured to say that the fault was all Pastor Manders' because the Pastor had made Mrs. Alving go back to her husband and was always hiding the truth. To this Hibbard objected with logic enough, "Well then, it was really all her husband's fault. He *did* all the bad things." De Witt, his face bright with an impatient idea, said that the fault was all society's. "By society I don't mean upper-crust society," he said. He looked around a little defiantly, taking in any members of the class who might be members of upper-crust society. "Not in that sense. I mean the social unit."

Howe nodded and said, "Yes, of course."

"If the society of the time had progressed far enough in science," De Witt went on, "then there would be no problem for Mr. Ibsen to write about. Captain Alving plays around a little, gives way to perfectly natural biological urges, and he gets a social disease, a venereal disease. If the disease is cured, no problem. Invent salvarsan and the disease is cured. The problem of heredity disappears and li'l Oswald just doesn't get paresis. No paresis, no problem—no problem, no play."

This was carrying the ark into battle, and the class looked at De Witt with respectful curiosity. It was his usual way and on the whole they were sympathetic with his struggle to prove to Howe that science was better than literature. Still, there was something in his reckless manner that alienated them a little.

"Or take birth-control, for instance," De Witt went on. "If Mrs. Alving had some knowledge of contraception, she wouldn't have had to have li'l Oswald at all. No li'l Oswald, no play."

The class was suddenly quieter. In the back row Stettenhover swung his great football shoulders in a righteous sulking gesture, first to the right, then to the left. He puckered his mouth ostentatiously. Intellect was always ending up by talking dirty.

Tertan's hand went up, and Howe said, "Mr. Tertan." The boy shambled to his feet and began his long characteristic gulp. Howe made a motion with his fingers, as small as possible, and Tertan ducked his head and smiled in apology. He sat down. The class laughed. With more than half the term gone, Tertan had not been able to remember that one did not rise to speak. He seemed unable to carry on the life of the intellect without this mark of respect for it. To Howe the boy's habit of rising seemed to accord with the formal shabbiness of his dress. He never wore the casual sweaters and jackets of his classmates. Into the free and comfortable air of the college classroom he brought the stuffy sordid strictness of some crowded, metropolitan high school.

"Speaking from one sense," Tertan began slowly, "there is no blame ascribable. From the sense of determinism, who can say where the blame lies? The preordained is the preordained and it cannot be said without rebellion against the universe, a palpable absurdity."

In the back row Stettenhover slumped suddenly in his seat, his heels held out before him, making a loud, dry, disgusted sound. His body sank until his neck rested on the back of his chair. He folded his hands across his belly and looked significantly out of the window, exasperated not only with Tertan, but with Howe, with the class, with the whole system designed to encourage this kind of thing. There was a certain insolence in the movement and Howe flushed. As Tertan continued to speak, Howe stalked casually toward the window and placed himself in the line of Stettenhover's vision. He stared at the great fellow, who pretended not to see him. There was so much power in the big body, so much contempt in the Greek-athlete face under the crisp Greek-athlete curls, that Howe felt almost physical fear. But at last Stettenhover admitted him to focus and under his disapproving gaze sat up with slow indifference. His eyebrows raised high in resignation, he began to examine his hands. Howe relaxed and turned his attention back to Tertan.

"Flux of existence," Tertan was saying, "produces all things, so that judgment wavers. Beyond the phenomena, what? But phenomena are adumbrated and to them we are limited."

Howe saw it for a moment as perhaps it existed in the boy's mind— the world of shadows which are cast by a great light upon a hidden reality as in the old myth of the Cave. But the little brush with Stettenhover had tired him, and he said irritably, "But come to the point, Mr. Tertan."

He said it so sharply that some of the class looked at him curiously. For three months he had gently carried Tertan through his verbosities, to the vaguely respectful surprise of the other students, who seemed to conceive that there existed between this strange classmate and their teacher some special understanding from which they were content to be excluded. Tertan looked at him mildly, and at once came brilliantly to the point. "This is the summation of the play," he said and took up his book and read, " 'Your poor father never found any outlet for the overmastering joy of life that was in him. And I brought no holiday into his home, either. Everything seemed to turn upon duty and I am afraid I made your poor father's home unbearable to him, Oswald.' Spoken by Mrs. Alving."

Yes that was surely the "summation" of the play and Tertan had hit it, as he hit, deviously and eventually, the literary point of almost everything. But now, as always, he was wrapping it away from sight. "For most mortals," he said, "there are only joys of biological urgings, gross and crass, such as the sensuous Captain Alving. For certain few there are the transmutations beyond these to a contemplation of the utter whole."

Oh, the boy was mad. And suddenly the word, used in hyperbole, intended almost for the expression of exasperated admiration, became literal. Now that the word was used, it became simply apparent to Howe that Tertan was mad.

It was a monstrous word and stood like a bestial thing in the room. Yet it so completely comprehended everything that had puzzled Howe, it so arranged and explained what for three months had been perplexing him that almost at once its horror became domesticated. With this word Howe was able to understand why he had never been able to communicate to Tertan the value of a single criticism or correction of his wild, verbose themes. Their conferences had been frequent and long but had done nothing to reduce to order the splendid confusion of the boy's ideas. Yet, impossible though its expression was, Tertan's incandescent mind could always strike for a moment into some dark corner of thought.

And now it was suddenly apparent that it was not a faulty rhetoric that Howe had to contend with. With his new knowledge he looked at Tertan's face and wondered how he could have so long deceived himself. Tertan was still talking, and the class had lapsed into a kind of patient unconsciousness, a coma of respect for words which, for all that most of them knew, might be profound. Almost with a suffusion of shame, Howe believed that in some dim way the class had long ago had some intimation of Tertan's madness. He reached out as decisively as he could to seize the thread of Tertan's discourse before it should be entangled further.

"Mr. Tertan says that the blame must be put upon whoever kills the joy of living in another. We have been assuming that Captain Alving was a wholly bad man, but what if we assume that he became bad only because Mrs. Alving, when they were first married, acted toward him in the prudish way she says she did?"

It was a ticklish idea to advance to freshmen and perhaps not profitable. Not all of them were following.

"That would put the blame on Mrs. Alving herself, whom most of you admire. And she herself seems to think so." He glanced at his watch. The hour was nearly over. "What do you think, Mr. De Witt?"

De Witt rose to the idea; he wanted to know if society couldn't be blamed for educating Mrs. Alving's temperament in the wrong way. Casebeer was puzzled, Stettenhover continued to look at his hands until the bell rang.

Tertan, his brows louring in thought, was making as always for a private word. Howe gathered his books and papers to leave quickly. At this moment of his discovery and with the knowledge still raw, he could not engage himself with Tertan. Tertan sucked in his breath to prepare for speech and Howe made ready for the pain and confusion. But at that moment Casebeer detached himelf from the group with which he had been conferring and which he seemed to represent. His constituency remained at a tactful distance. The mission involved the time of an assigned essay. Casebeer's presentation of the plea—it was based on the freshmen's heavy duties at the fraternities during Carnival Week—cut across Tertan's preparations for speech. "And so some of us fellows thought," Casebeer concluded with heavy solemnity, "that we could do a better job, give our minds to it more, if we had more time."

Tertan regarded Casebeer with mingled curiosity and revulsion. Howe not only said that he would postpone the assignment but went on to talk about the Carnival, and even drew the waiting constituency into the conversation. He was conscious of Tertan's stern and astonished stare, then of his sudden departure.

Now that the fact was clear, Howe knew that he must act on it. His course was simple enough. He must lay the case before the Dean. Yet he hesitated. His feeling for Tertan must now, certainly, be in some way invalidated. Yet could he, because of a word, hurry to assign to official and reasonable solicitude what had been, until this moment, so various and warm? He could at least delay and, by moving slowly, lend a poor grace to the necessary, ugly act of making his report.

It was with some notion of keeping the matter in his own hands that he went to the Dean's office to look up Tertan's records. In the outer office the Dean's secretary greeted him brightly, and at his request brought him the manila folder with the small identifying photograph pasted in the corner. She laughed. "He was looking for the birdie in the wrong place," she said.

Howe leaned over her shoulder to look at the picture. It was as bad as all the Dean's-office photographs were, but it differed from all that Howe had ever seen. Tertan, instead of looking into the camera, as no doubt he had been bidden, had, at the moment of exposure, turned his eyes upward. His mouth, as though conscious of the trick played on the photographer, had the sly superior look that Howe knew.

The secretary was fascinated by the picture. "What a funny boy," she said. "He looks like Tartuffe!"

And so he did, with the absurd piety of the eyes and the conscious slyness of the mouth and the whole face bloated by the bad lens.

"Is he *like* that?" the secretary said.

"Like Tartuffe? No."

From the photograph there was little enough comfort to be had. The records themselves gave no clue to madness, though they suggested sadness enough. Howe read of a father, Stanislaus Tertan, born in Budapest and trained in engineering in Berlin, once employed by the Hercules Chemical Corporation—this was one of the factories that dominated the south end of the town—but now without employment. He read of a mother Erminie (Youngfellow) Tertan, born in Manchester, educated at a Normal School at Leeds, now housewife by profession. The family lived on Greenbriar Street which Howe knew as a row of once elegant homes near what was now the factory district. The old mansion had long ago been divided into small and primitive apartments. Of Ferdinand himself there was little to learn. He lived with his parents, had attended a Detroit high school and had transferred to the local school in his last year. His rating for intelligence, as expressed in numbers, was high, his scholastic record was remarkable, he held a college scholarship for his tuition.

Howe laid the folder on the secretary's desk. "Did you find what you wanted to know?" she asked.

The phrases from Tertan's momentous first theme came back to him. "Tertan I am, but what is Tertan? Of this time, of that place, of some parentage, what does it matter?"

"No, I didn't find it," he said.

Now that he had consulted the sad, half-meaningless record he knew all the more firmly that he must not give the matter out of his own hands. He must not release Tertan to authority. Not that he anticipated from the Dean anything but the greatest kindness for Tertan. The Dean would have the experience and skill which he himself could not have. One way or another the Dean could answer the question, "What is Tertan?" Yet this was precisely what he feared. He alone could keep alive—not forever but for a somehow important time—the question, "What is Tertan?" He alone could keep it still a question. Some sure instinct told him that he must not surrender the question to a clean official desk in a clear official light to be dealt with, settled and closed.

He heard himself saying, "Is the Dean busy at the moment? I'd like to see him."

His request came thus unbidden, even forbidden, and it was one of the surprising and startling incidents of his life. Later when he reviewed the events, so disconnected in themselves, or so merely odd, of the story that unfolded for him that year, it was over this moment, on its face the least notable, that he paused longest. It was frequently to be with fear and never without a certainty of its meaning in his own knowledge of himself that he would recall this simple, routine request, and the feeling of shame and freedom it gave him as he sent everything down the official chute. In the end, of course, no matter what he did to "protect" Tertan, he would have had to make the same request and lay the matter on the Dean's clean desk. But it would always be a landmark of his life that, at the very moment when he was rejecting the official way, he had been, without will or intention, so gladly drawn to it.

After the storm's last delicate flurry, the sun had come out. Reflected by the new snow, it filled the office with a golden light which was almost musical in the way it made all the commonplace objects of efficiency shine with a sudden sad and noble significance. And the light, now that he noticed it, made the utterance of his perverse and unwanted request even more momentous.

The secretary consulted the engagement pad. "He'll be free any minute. Don't you want to wait in the parlor?"

She threw open the door of the large and pleasant room in which the Dean held his Committee meetings, and in which his visitors waited. It was designed with a homely elegance on the masculine side of the eighteenth-century manner. There was a small coal fire in the grate and the handsome mahogany table was strewn with books and magazines. The large windows gave on the snowy lawn, and there was such a fine width of window that the white casements and walls seemed at this moment but a continuation of the snow, the snow but an extension of casement and walls. The outdoors seemed taken in and made safe, the indoors seemed luxuriously freshened and expanded.

Howe sat down by the fire and lighted a cigarette. The room had its intended effect upon him. He felt comfortable and relaxed, yet nicely organized, some young diplomatic agent of the eighteenth century, the newly fledged Swift carrying out Sir William Temple's business. The rawness of Tertan's case quite vanished. He crossed his legs and reached for a magazine.

It was that famous issue of *Life and Letters* that his idle hand had found and his blood raced as he sifted through it, and the shape of his own name, Joseph Howe, sprang out at him, still cabalistic in its power. He tossed the magazine back on the table as the door of the Dean's office opened and the Dean ushered out Theodore Blackburn.

"Ah, Joseph!" the Dean said.

Blackburn said, "Good morning, Doctor." Howe winced at the title and caught the flicker of amusement over the Dean's face. The Dean stood with his hand high on the door-jamb and Blackburn, still in the doorway, remained standing almost under the long arm.

Howe nodded briefly to Blackburn, snubbing his eager deference. "Can you give me a few minutes?" he said to the Dean.

"All the time you want. Come in." Before the two men could enter the office, Blackburn claimed their attention with a long full "er." As they turned to him, Blackburn said, "Can *you* give *me* a few minutes, Doctor Howe?" His eyes sparkled at the little audacity he had committed, the slightly impudent play with hierarchy. Of the three of them Blackburn kept himself the lowest, but he reminded Howe of his subaltern relation to the Dean.

"I mean, of course," Blackburn went on easily, "when you've finished with the Dean."

"I'll be in my office shortly," Howe said, turned his back on the ready "Thank you, sir," and followed the Dean into the inner room.

"Energetic boy," said the Dean. "A bit beyond himself but very energetic. Sit down."

The Dean lighted a cigarette, leaned back in his chair, sat easy and silent for a moment, giving Howe no signal to go ahead with business. He was a young Dean, not much beyond forty, a tall handsome man with sad, ambitious eyes. He had been a Rhodes scholar. His friends looked for great things from him, and it was generally said that he had notions of education which he was not yet ready to try to put into practice.

His relaxed silence was meant as a compliment to Howe. He smiled and said, "What's the business, Joseph?"

"Do you know Tertan—Ferdinand Tertan, a freshman?"

The Dean's cigarette was in his mouth and his hands were clasped behind his head. He did not seem to search his memory for the name. He said, "What about him?"

Clearly the Dean knew something, and he was waiting for Howe to tell him more. Howe moved only tentatively. Now that he was doing what he had resolved not to do, he felt more guilty at having been so long deceived by Tertan and more need to be loyal to his error.

"He's a strange fellow," he ventured. He said stubbornly, "In a strange way he's very brilliant." He concluded, "But very strange."

The springs of the Dean's swivel chair creaked as he came out of his sprawl and leaned forward to Howe. "Do you mean he's so strange that it's something you could give a name to?"

Howe looked at him stupidly. "What do you mean?" he said.

"What's his trouble?" the Dean said more neutrally.

"He's very brilliant, in a way. I looked him up and he has a top intelligence rating. But somehow, and it's hard to explain just how, what he says is always on the edge of sense and doesn't quite make it."

The Dean looked at him and Howe flushed up. The Dean had surely read Woolley on the subject of "the Howes" and the *tour d'ivresse*. Was that quick glance ironical?

The Dean picked up some papers from his desk, and Howe could see that they were in Tertan's impatient scrawl. Perhaps the little gleam in the Dean's glance had come only from putting facts together.

"He sent me this yesterday," the Dean said. "After an interview I had with him. I haven't been able to do more than glance at it. When you said what you did, I realized there was something wrong."

Twisting his mouth, the Dean looked over the letter. "You seem to be involved," he said without looking up. "By the way, what did you give him at mid-term?"

Flushing, setting his shoulders, Howe said firmly, "I gave him A-minus."

The Dean chuckled. "Might be a good idea if some of our nicer boys went crazy—just a little." He said, "Well," to conclude the matter and handed the papers to Howe. "See if this is the same thing you've been finding. Then we can go into the matter again."

Before the fire in the parlor, in the chair that Howe had been occupying, sat Blackburn. He sprang to his feet as Howe entered.

"I said my office, Mr. Blackburn." Howe's voice was sharp. Then he was almost sorry for the rebuke, so clearly and naively did Blackburn seem to relish his stay in the parlor, close to authority.

"I'm in a bit of a hurry, sir," he said, "and I did want to be sure to speak to you, sir."

He was really absurd, yet fifteen years from now he would have grown up to himself, to the assurance and mature beefiness. In banks, in consular offices, in brokerage firms, on the bench, more seriously affable, a little sterner, he would make use of his ability to be administered by his job. It was almost reassuring. Now he was exercising his too-great skill on Howe. "I owe you an apology sir," he said.

Howe knew that he did, but he showed surprise.

"I mean, Doctor, after your having been so kind about letting me attend your class, I stopped coming." He smiled in deprecation. "Extracurricular activities take up so much of my time. I'm afraid I undertook more than I could perform."

Howe had noticed the absence and had been a little irritated by it after Blackburn's elaborate plea. It was an absence that might be interpreted as a comment on the teacher. But there was only one way for him to answer. "You've no need to apologize," he said. "It's wholly your affair."

Blackburn beamed. "I'm so glad you feel that way about it, sir. I was worried you might think I had stayed away because I was influenced by—" he stopped and lowered his eyes.

Astonished, Howe said, "Influenced by what?"

"Well, by—" Blackburn hesitated and for answer pointed to the table on which lay the copy of *Life and Letters*. Without looking at it, he knew where to direct his hand. "By the unfavorable publicity, sir." He hurried on. "And that brings me to another point, sir. I am secretary of Quill and Scroll, sir, the student literary society, and I wonder if you would address us. You could read your own poetry, sir, and defend your own point of view. It would be very interesting."

It was truly amazing. Howe looked long and cruelly into Blackburn's face, trying to catch the secret of the mind that could have conceived this way of manipulating him, this way so daring and inept—but not entirely inept—with its malice so without malignity. The face did not yield its secret. Howe smiled broadly and said, "Of course I don't think you were influenced by the unfavorable publicity."

"I'm still going to take—regularly, for credit—your romantic poets course next term," Blackburn said.

"Don't worry, my dear fellow, don't worry about it."

Howe started to leave and Blackburn stopped him with, "But about Quill, sir?"

"Suppose we wait until next term? I'll be less busy then."

And Blackburn said, "Very good, sir, and thank you."

In his office the little encounter seemed less funny to Howe, was even in some indeterminate way disturbing. He made an effort to put it from his mind by turning to what was sure to disturb him more, the Tertan letter read in the new interpretation. He found what he had always found, the same florid leaps beyond fact and meaning, the same headlong certainty. But as his eye passed over the familiar scrawl it caught his own name, and for the second time that hour he felt the race of his blood.

"The Paraclete," Tertan had written to the Dean, "from a Greek word meaning to stand in place of, but going beyond the primitive idea to mean traditionally the helper, the one who comforts and assists, cannot without fundamental loss be jettisoned. Even if taken no longer in the supernatural sense, the concept remains deeply in the human consciousness inevitably. Humanitarianism is no reply, for not every man stands in the place of every other man for this other comrade's comfort. But certain are chosen out of the human race to be the consoler of some other. Of these, for example, is Joseph Barker Howe, Ph.D. Of intellects not the first yet of true intellect and lambent instructions, given to that which is intuitive and irrational, not to what is logical in the strict word, what is judged by him is of the heart and not the head. Here is one chosen, in that he chooses himself to stand in the place of another for comfort and consolation. To him more than another I give my gratitude, with all respect to our Dean who reads this, a noble man, but merely dedicated, not consecrated. But not in the aspect of the Paraclete only is Dr. Joseph Barker Howe established, for he must be the Paraclete to another aspect of himself, that which is driven and persecuted by the lack of understanding in the world at large, so that he in himself embodies the full history of man's tribulations and, overflowing upon others, notably the present writer, is the ultimate end."

This was love. There was no escape from it. Try as Howe might to remember that Tertan was mad and all his emotions invalidated, he could not destroy the effect upon him of his student's stern, affectionate regard. He had betrayed not only a power of mind but a power of love. And, however firmly he held before his attention the fact of Tertan's madness, he could do nothing to banish the physical sensation of gratitude he felt. He had never thought of himself as "driven and persecuted" and he did not now. But still he could not make meaningless his sensation of gratitude. The pitiable Tertan sternly pitied him, and comfort came from Tertan's never-to-be-comforted mind.

III

In an academic community, even an efficient one, official matters move slowly. The term drew to a close with no action in the case of Tertan, and Joseph Howe had to confront a curious problem. How should he grade his strange student, Tertan?

Tertan's final examination had been no different from all his other writing, and what did one "give" such a student? De Witt must have his A, that was clear. Johnson would get a B. With Casebeer it was a question of a B-minus or a C-plus, and Stettenhover, who had been crammed by the team tutor to fill half a blue-book with his thin feminine scrawl would have his C-minus which he would accept with mingled indifference and resentment. But with Tertan it was not so easy.

The boy was still in the college process and his name could not be omitted from the grade sheet. Yet what should a mind under suspicion of madness be graded? Until the medical verdict was given, it was for Howe to continue as Tertan's teacher and to keep his judgment pedagogical. Impossible to give him an F: he had not failed. B was for Johnson's stolid mediocrity. He could not be put on the edge of passing with Stettenhover, for he exactly did not pass. In energy and richness of intellect he was perhaps even De Witt's superior, and Howe toyed grimly with the notion of giving him an A, but that would lower the value of the A De Witt had won with his beautiful and clear, if still arrogant, mind. There was a notation which the Registrar recognized—Inc., for Incomplete, and in the horrible comedy of the situation, Howe considered that. But really only a mark of M for Mad would serve.

In his perplexity, Howe sought the Dean, but the Dean was out of town. In the end, he decided to maintain the A-minus he had given Tertan at mid-term. After all, there had been no falling away from that quality. He entered it on the grade sheet with something like bravado.

Academic time moves quickly. A college year is not really a year, lacking as it does three months. And it is endlessly divided into units which, at their beginning, appear larger than they are—terms, half-terms, months, weeks. And the ultimate unit, the hour, is not really an hour, lacking as it does ten minutes. And so the new term advanced rapidly, and one day the fields about the town were all brown, cleared of even the few thin patches of snow which had lingered so long.

Howe, as he lectured on the romantic poets, became conscious of Blackburn emanating wrath. Blackburn did it well, did it with enormous dignity. He did not stir in his seat, he kept his eyes fixed on Howe in perfect attention, but he abstained from using his notebook, there was no mistaking what he proposed to himself as an attitude. His elbow on the writing-wing of the chair, his chin on the curled fingers of his hand, he was the embodiment of intellectual indignation. He was thinking his own thoughts, would give no public offense, yet would claim his due, was not to be intimidated. Howe knew that he would present himself at the end of the hour.

Blackburn entered the office without invitation. He did not smile; there was no cajolery about him. Without invitation he sat down beside Howe's desk. He did not speak until he had taken the blue-book from his pocket. He said, "What does this mean, sir?"

It was a sound and conservative student tactic. Said in the usual way it meant, "How could you have so misunderstood me?" or "What does this mean for my future in the course?" But there were none of the humbler tones in Blackburn's way of saying it.

Howe made the established reply, "I think that's for you to tell me."

Blackburn continued icy. "I'm sure I can't, sir."

There was a silence between them. Both dropped their eyes to the blue-book on the desk. On its cover Howe had penciled: "F. This is very poor work."

Howe picked up the blue-book. There was always the possibility of injustice. The teacher may be bored by the mass of papers and not wholly attentive. A phrase, even the student's handwriting, may irritate him unreasonably. "Well," said Howe, "Let's go through it."

He opened the first page. "Now here: you write, 'In *The Ancient Mariner,* Coleridge lives in and transports us to a honey-sweet world where all is rich and strange, a world of charm to which we can escape from the humdrum existence of our daily lives, the world of romance. Here, in this warm and honey-sweet land of charming dreams we can relax and enjoy ourselves.' "

Howe lowered the paper and waited with a neutral look for Blackburn to speak. Blackburn returned the look boldly, did not speak, sat stolid and lofty. At last Howe said, speaking gently, "Did you mean that, or were you just at a loss for something to say?"

"You imply that I was just 'bluffing'?" The quotation marks hung palpable in the air about the word.

"I'd like to know. I'd prefer believing that you were bluffing to believing that you really thought this."

Blackburn's eyebrows went up. From the height of a great and firm-based idea he looked at his teacher. He clasped the crags for a moment and then pounced, craftily, suavely. "Do you mean, Doctor Howe, that there aren't two opinions possible?"

It was superbly done in its air of putting all of Howe's intellectual life into the balance. Howe remained patient and simple. "Yes, many opinions are possible, but not this one. Whatever anyone believes of *The Ancient Mariner,* no one can in reason believe that it represents a—a honey-sweet world in which we can relax."

"But that is what I *feel,* sir."

This was well-done, too. Howe said, "Look, Mr. Blackburn. Do you really relax with hunger and thirst, the heat and the sea-serpents, the dead men with staring eyes, Life in Death and the skeletons? Come now, Mr. Blackburn."

Blackburn made no answer, and Howe pressed forward. "Now, you say of Wordsworth, 'Of peasant stock himself, he turned from the effete life of the salons and found in the peasant the hope of a flaming revolution which would sweep away all the old ideas. This is the subject of his best poems.' "

Beaming at his teacher with youthful eagerness, Blackburn said, "Yes, sir, a rebel, a bringer of light to suffering mankind. I see him as a kind of Prothemeus."

"A kind of what?"

"Prothemeus, sir."

"Think, Mr. Blackburn. We were talking about him only today and I mentioned his name a dozen times. You don't mean Prothemeus. You mean—" Howe waited, but there was no response.

"You mean Prometheus."

Blackburn gave no assent, and Howe took the reins. "You've done a bad job here, Mr. Blackburn, about as bad as could be done." He saw Blackburn stiffen and his genial face harden again. "It shows either a lack of preparation or a complete lack of understanding." He saw Blackburn's face begin to go to pieces and he stopped.

"Oh, sir," Blackburn burst out, "I've never had a mark like this before, never anything below a B, never. A thing like this has never happened to me before."

It must be true, it was a statement too easily verified. Could it be that other instructors accepted such flaunting nonsense? Howe wanted to end the interview. "I'll set it down to lack of preparation," he said. "I know you're busy. That's not an excuse, but it's an explanation. Now, suppose you really prepare, and then take another quiz in two weeks. We'll forget this one and count the other."

Blackburn squirmed with pleasure and gratitude. "Thank you, sir. You're really very kind, very kind."

Howe rose to conclude the visit. "All right, then—in two weeks."

It was that day that the Dean imparted to Howe the conclusion of the case of Tertan. It was simple and a little anti-climactic. A physician had been called in, and had said the word, given the name.

"A classic case, he called it," the Dean said. "Not a doubt in the world," he said. His eyes were full of miserable pity, and he clutched at a word. "A classic case, a classic case." To his aid and to Howe's there came the Parthenon and the form of the Greek drama, the Aristotelian logic, Racine and the Well-Tempered Clavichord, the blueness of the Aegean and its clear sky. Classic—that is to say, without a doubt, perfect in its way, a veritable model, and, as the Dean had been told, sure to take a perfectly predictable and inevitable course to a foreknown conclusion.

It was not only pity that stood in the Dean's eyes. For a moment there was fear too. "Terrible," he said, "it is simply terrible."

Then he went on briskly. "Naturally, we've told the boy nothing. And, naturally, we won't. His tuition's paid by his scholarship, and we'll continue him on the rolls until the end of the year. That will be kindest. After that the matter will be out of our control. We'll see, of course, that he gets into the proper hands. I'm told there will be no change, he'll go on like this, be as good as this, for four to six months. And so we'll just go along as usual."

So Tertan continued to sit in Section 5 of English 1A, to his classmates still a figure of curiously dignified fun, symbol to most of them of the respectable but absurd intellectual life. But to his teacher he was now very different. He had not changed—he was still the greyhound casting for the scent of ideas, and Howe could see that he was still the same Tertan, but he could not feel it. What he felt as he looked at the boy sitting in his accustomed place was the hard blank of a fact. The fact itself was formidable and depressing. But what Howe was chiefly aware of was that he had permitted the metamorphosis of Tertan from person to fact.

As much as possible he avoided seeing Tertan's upraised hand and eager eye. But the fact did not know of its mere factuality, it continued its existence as if it were Tertan, hand up and eye questioning, and one day it appeared in Howe's office with a document.

"Even the spirit who lives egregiously, above the herd, must have its relations with the fellowman," Tertan declared. He laid the document on Howe's desk. It was headed "Quill and Scroll Society of Dwight College. Application for Membership."

"In most ways these are crass minds," Tertan said, touching the paper. "Yet as a whole, bound together in their common love of letters, they transcend their intellectual lacks since it is not a paradox that the whole is greater than the sum of its parts."

"When are the elections?" Howe asked.

"They take place tomorrow."

"I certainly hope you will be successful."

"Thank you. Would you wish to implement that hope?" A rather dirty finger pointed to the bottom of the sheet. "A faculty recommender is necessary," Tertan said stiffly, and waited.

"And you wish me to recommend you?"

"It would be an honor."

"You may use my name."

Tertan's finger pointed again. "It must be a written sponsorship, signed by the sponsor." There was a large blank space on the form under the heading, "Opinion of Faculty Sponsor."

This was almost another thing and Howe hesitated. Yet there was nothing else to do and he took out his fountain pen. He wrote, "Mr. Ferdinand Tertan is marked by his intense devotion to letters and by his exceptional love of all things of the mind." To this he signed his name, which looked bold and assertive on the white page. It disturbed him, the strange affirming power of a name. With a business-like air, Tertan whipped up the paper, folding it with decision, and put it into his pocket. He bowed and took his departure, leaving Howe with the sense of having done something oddly momentous.

And so much now seemed odd and momentous to Howe that should not have seemed so. It was odd and momentous, he felt, when he sat with Blackburn's second quiz before him, and wrote in an excessively firm hand the grade of C-minus. The paper was a clear, an indisputable failure. He was carefully and consciously committing a cowardice. Blackburn had told the truth when he had pleaded his past record. Howe had consulted it in the Dean's office. It showed no grade lower than a B-minus. A canvass of some of Blackburn's previous instructors had brought vague attestations to the adequate powers of a student imperfectly remembered, and sometimes surprise that his abilities could be questioned at all.

As he wrote the grade, Howe told himself that his cowardice sprang from an unwillingness to have more dealings with a student he disliked. He knew it was simpler than that. He knew he feared Blackburn: that was the absurd truth. And cowardice did not solve the matter after all. Blackburn, flushed with a first success, attacked at once. The minimal passing grade had not assuaged his feelings and he sat at Howe's desk and again the bluebook lay between them. Blackburn said nothing. With an enormous impudence, he was waiting for Howe to speak and explain himself.

At last Howe said sharply and rudely, "Well?" His throat was tense and the blood was hammering in his head. His mouth was tight with anger at himself for his disturbance.

Blackburn's glance was almost baleful. "This is impossible, sir."

"But there it is," Howe answered.

"Sir?" Blackburn had not caught the meaning but his tone was still haughty.

Impatiently Howe said, "There it is, plain as day. Are you here to complain again?"

"Indeed I am, sir." There was surprise in Blackburn's voice that Howe should ask that question.

"I shouldn't complain if I were you. You did a thoroughly bad job on your first quiz. This one is a little, only a very little, better." This was not true. If anything, it was worse.

"That might be a matter of opinion, sir."

"It is a matter of opinion. Of my opinion."

"Another opinion might be different, sir."

"You really believe that?" Howe said.

"Yes." The omission of the "sir" was monumental.

"Whose, for example?"

"The Dean's, for example." Then the fleshy jaw came forward a little "Or a certain literary critic's, for example."

It was colossal and almost too much for Blackburn himself to handle. The solidity of his face almost crumpled under it. But he withstood his own audacity and went on. "And the Dean's opinion might be guided by the knowledge that the person who gave me this mark is the man whom a famous critic, the most eminent judge of literature in this country, called a drunken man. The Dean might think twice about whether such a man is fit to teach Dwight students."

Howe said in quiet admonition, "Blackburn, you're mad," meaning no more than to check the boy's extravagance.

But Blackburn paid no heed. He had another shot in the locker. "And the Dean might be guided by the information, of which I have evidence, documentary evidence,"—he slapped his breast pocket twice—"that this same person personally recommended to the college literary society, the oldest in the country, that he personally recommended a student who is crazy, who threw the meeting into an uproar—a psychiatric case. The Dean might take that into account."

Howe was never to learn the details of that "uproar." He had always to content himself with the dim but passionate picture which at that moment sprang into his mind, of Tertan standing on some abstract height and madly denouncing the multitude of Quill and Scroll who howled him down.

He sat quiet a moment and looked at Blackburn. The ferocity had entirely gone from the student's face. He sat regarding his teacher almost benevolently. He had played a good card and now, scarcely at all unfriendly, he was waiting to see the effect. Howe took up the blue-book and negligently sifted through it. He read a page, closed the book, struck out the C-minus and wrote an F.

"Now you may take the paper to the Dean," he said. "You may tell him that after reconsidering it, I lowered the grade."

The gasp was audible. "Oh, sir!" Blackburn cried. "Please!" His face was agonized. "It means my graduation, my livelihood, my future. Don't do this to me."

"It's done already."

Blackburn stood up, "I spoke rashly, sir, hastily. I had no intention, no real intention, of seeing the Dean. It rests with you—entirely, entirely. I *hope* you will restore the first mark."

"Take the matter to the Dean or not, just as you choose. The grade is what you deserve and it stands."

Blackburn's head dropped. "And will I be failed at mid-term, sir?"

"Of course."

From deep out of Blackburn's great chest rose a cry of anguish. "Oh, sir, if you want me to go down on my knees to you, I will, I will."

Howe looked at him in amazement.

"I will, I will. On my knees, sir. This mustn't, mustn't happen."

He spoke so literally, meaning so very truly that his knees and exactly his knees were involved and seeming to think that he was offering something of tangible value to his teacher, that Howe, whose head had become icy clear in the nonsensical drama, thought, "The boy is mad," and began to speculate fantastically whether something in himself attracted or developed aberration. He could see himself standing absurdly before the Dean and saying, "I've found another. This time it's the vice-president of the Council, the manager of the debating team and secretary of Quill and Scroll."

One more such discovery, he thought, and he himself would be discovered! And there, suddenly, Blackburn was on his knees with a thump, his huge thighs straining his trousers, his hand outstretched in a great gesture of supplication.

With a cry, Howe shoved back his swivel chair and it rolled away on its casters half across the little room. Blackburn knelt for a moment to nothing at all, then got to his feet.

Howe rose abruptly. He said, "Blackburn, you will stop acting like an idiot. Dust your knees off, take your paper and get out. You've behaved like a fool and a malicious person. You have half a term to do a decent job. Keep your silly mouth shut and try to do it. Now get out."

Blackburn's head was low. He raised it and there was a pious light in his eyes. "Will you shake hands, sir?" he said. He thrust out his hand.

"I will not," Howe said.

Head and hand sank together. Blackburn picked up his blue-book and walked to the door. He turned and said, "Thank you, sir." His back, as he departed, was heavy with tragedy and stateliness.

IV

After years of bad luck with the weather, the College had a perfect day for Commencement. It was wonderfully bright, the air so transparent, the wind so brisk that no one could resist talking about it.

As Howe set out for the campus he heard Hilda calling from the back yard. She called, "Professor, professor," and came running to him.

Howe said, "What's this 'professor' business?"

"Mother told me," Hilda said. "You've been promoted. And I want to take your picture."

"Next year," said Howe. "I won't be a professor until next year. And you know better than to call anybody 'professor.' "

"It was just in fun," Hilda said. She seemed disappointed.

"But you can take my picture if you want. I won't look much different next year." Still, it was frightening. It might mean that he was to stay in this town all his life.

Hilda brightened. "Can I take it in this?" she said, and touched the gown he carried over his arm.

Howe laughed. "Yes, you can take it in this."

"I'll get my things and meet you in front of Otis," Hilda said. "I have the background all picked out."

On the campus the Commencement crowd was already large. It stood about in eager, nervous little family groups. As he crossed, Howe was greeted by a student, capped and gowned, glad of the chance to make an event for his parents by introducing one of his teachers. It was while Howe stood there chatting that he saw Tertan.

He had never seen anyone quite so alone, as though a circle had been woven about him to separate him from the gay crowd on the campus. Not that Tertan was not gay, he was the gayest of all. Three weeks had passed since Howe had last seen him, the weeks of examination, the lazy week before Commencement, and this was now a different Tertan. On his head he wore a panama hat, broad-brimmed and fine, of the shape associated with South American planters. He wore a suit of raw silk, luxurious, but yellowed with age and much too tight, and he sported a whangee cane. He walked sedately, the hat tilted at a devastating angle, the stick coming up and down in time to his measured tread. He had, Howe guessed, outfitted himself to greet the day in the clothes of that ruined father whose existence was on record in the Dean's office. Gravely and arrogantly he surveyed the scene—in it, his whole bearing seemed to say, but not of it. With his haughty step, with his flashing eye, Tertan was coming nearer. Howe did not wish to be seen. He shifted his position slightly. When he looked again, Tertan was not in sight.

The chapel clock struck the quarter hour. Howe detached himself from his chat and hurried to Otis Hall at the far end of the campus. Hilda had not yet come. He went up into the high portico and, using the glass of the door for a mirror, put on his gown, adjusted the hood on his shoulders and set the mortarboard on his head. When he came down the steps, Hilda had arrived.

Nothing could have told him more forcibly that a year had passed than the development of Hilda's photographic possessions from the box camera of the previous fall. By a strap about her neck was hung a leather case, so thick and strong, so carefully stitched and so molded to its contents that it could only hold a costly camera. The appearance was deceptive, Howe knew, for he had been present at the Aiken's pre-Christmas conference about its purchase. It was only a fairly good domestic camera. Still, it looked very impressive. Hilda carried another leather case from which she drew a collapsible tripod. Decisively she extended each of its gleaming legs and set it up on the path. She removed the camera from its case and fixed it to the tripod. In its compact efficiency the camera almost had a life of its own, but Hilda treated it with easy familiarity, looked into its eye, glanced casually at its gauges. Then from a pocket she took still another leather case and drew from it a small instrument through which she looked first at Howe, who began to feel inanimate and lost, and then at the sky. She made some adjustment on the instrument, then some adjustment on the camera. She swept the scene with her eye, found a spot and pointed the camera in its direction. She walked to the spot, stood on it and beckoned to Howe. With each new leather case, with each new instrument, and with each new adjustment she had grown in ease and now she said, "Joe, will you stand here?"

Obediently Howe stood where he was bidden. She had yet another instrument. She took out a tape-measure on a mechanical spool. Kneeling down before Howe, she put the little metal ring of the tape under the tip of his shoe. At her request, Howe pressed it with his toe. When she had measured her distance, she nodded to Howe who released the tape. At a touch, it sprang back into the spool. "You have to be careful if you're going to get what you want," Hilda said. "I don't believe in all this snap-snap-snapping," she remarked loftily. Howe nodded in agreement, although he was beginning to think Hilda's care excessive.

Now at last the moment had come. Hilda squinted into the camera, moved the tripod slightly. She stood to the side, holding the plunger of the shutter-cable. "Ready," she said. "Will you relax, Joseph, please?" Howe realized that he was standing frozen. Hilda stood poised and precise as a setter, one hand holding the little cable, the other extended with curled dainty fingers like a dancer's, as if expressing to her subject the precarious delicacy of the moment. She pressed the plunger and there was the click. At once she stirred to action, got behind the camera, turned a new exposure. "Thank you," she said. "Would you stand under that tree and let me do a character study with light and shade?"

The childish absurdity of the remark restored Howe's ease. He went to the little tree. The pattern the leaves made on his gown was what Hilda was after. He had just taken a satisfactory position when he heard in the unmistakable voice, "Ah, Doctor! Having your picture taken?"

Howe gave up the pose and turned to Blackburn who stood on the walk, his hands behind his back, a little too large for his bachelor's gown. Annoyed that Blackburn should see him posing for a character study in light and shade, Howe said irritably, "Yes, having my picture taken."

Blackburn beamed at Hilda. "And the little photographer?" he said. Hilda fixed her eyes on the ground and stood closer to her brilliant and aggressive camera. Blackburn, teetering on his heels, his hands behind his back, wholly prelatical and benignly patient, was not abashed at the silence. At last Howe said, "If you'll excuse us, Mr. Blackburn, we'll go on with the picture."

"Go right ahead, sir. I'm running along." But he only came closer.

"Doctor Howe," he said fervently, "I want to tell you how glad I am that I was able to satisfy your standards at last."

Howe was surprised at the hard, insulting brightness of his own voice, and even Hilda looked up curiously as he said, "Nothing you have ever done has satisfied me, and nothing you could ever do would satisfy me, Blackburn."

With a glance at Hilda, Blackburn made a gesture as if to hush Howe —as though all his former bold malice had taken for granted a kind of understanding between himself and his teacher, a secret which must not be betrayed to a third person. "I only meant, sir," he said, "that I was able to pass your course after all."

Howe said, "You didn't pass my course. I passed you out of my course. I passed you without even reading your paper. I wanted to be sure the college would be rid of you. And when all the grades were in and I did read your paper, I saw I was right not to have read it first."

Blackburn presented a stricken face. "It was very bad, sir?"

But Howe had turned away. The paper had been fantastic. The paper had been, if he wished to see it so, mad. It was at this moment that the Dean came up behind Howe and caught his arm. "Hello, Joseph," he said. "We'd better be getting along, it's almost late."

He was not a familiar man, but when he saw Blackburn, who approached to greet him, he took Blackburn's arm, too. "Hello, Theodore," he said. Leaning forward on Howe's arm and on Blackburn's he said, "Hello, Hilda dear." Hilda replied quietly, "Hello, Uncle George."

Still clinging to their arms, still linking Howe and Blackburn, the Dean said, "Another year gone, Joe, and we've turned out another crop. After you've been here a few years, you'll find it reasonably upsetting— you wonder how there can be so many graduating classes while you stay the same. But of course you don't stay the same." Then he said, "Well," sharply, to dismiss the thought. He pulled Blackburn's arm and swung him around to Howe. "Have you heard about Teddy Blackburn?" he asked. "He has a job already, before graduation—the first man of his class to be placed." Expectant of congratulations, Blackburn beamed at Howe. Howe remained silent.

"Isn't that good?" the Dean said. Still Howe did not answer and the Dean, puzzled and put out, turned to Hilda. "That's a very fine-looking camera, Hilda." She touched it with affectionate pride.

"Instruments of precision," said a voice. "Instruments of precision." Of the three with joined arms, Howe was the nearest to Tertan, whose gaze took in all the scene except the smile and the nod which Howe gave him. The boy leaned on his cane. The broad-brimmed hat, canting jauntily over his eye, confused the image of his face that Howe had established, suppressed the rigid lines of the ascetic and brought out the baroque curves. It made an effect of perverse majesty.

"Instruments of precision," said Tertan for the last time, addressing no one, making a casual comment to the universe. And it occurred to Howe that Tertan might not be referring to Hilda's equipment. The sense of the thrice-woven circle of the boy's loneliness smote him fiercely. Tertan stood in majestic jauntiness, superior to all the scene, but his isolation made Howe ache with a pity of which Tertan was more the cause than the object, so general and indiscriminate was it.

Whether in his sorrow he made some unintended movement toward Tertan which the Dean checked, or whether the suddenly tightened grip on his arm was the Dean's own sorrow and fear, he did not know. Tertan watched them in the incurious way people watch a photograph being taken, and suddenly the thought that, to the boy, it must seem that the three were posing for a picture together made Howe detach himself almost rudely from the Dean's grasp.

"I promised Hilda another picture," he announced—needlessly, for Tertan was no longer there, he had vanished in the last sudden flux of visitors who, now that the band had struck up, were rushing nervously to find seats.

"You'd better hurry," the Dean said. "I'll go along, it's getting late for me." He departed and Blackburn walked stately by his side.

Howe again took his position under the little tree which cast its shadow over his face and gown. "Just hurry, Hilda, won't you?" he said. Hilda held the cable at arm's length, her other arm crooked and her fingers crisped. She rose on her toes and said "Ready," and pressed the release. "Thank you," she said gravely and began to dismantle her camera as he hurried off to join the procession.

QUESTIONS FOR DISCUSSION

1) Is Joseph Howe a "creative" teacher? Was his "solution" to the problem of Tertan a "creative" one? Explain.

2) Is Tertan "mad"? Is he "creative"? Or both? Explain.

3) "Instruments of precision," Tertan observes at the end of the story, perhaps referring to Hilda's camera equipment, perhaps to Howe, Blackburn, and the Dean, or perhaps "to the universe." What is the importance of this statement to our understanding of Tertan, of Howe, and of the story as a whole?

4) Lionel Trilling is also the author of another article in this book, the essay "Art and Neurosis" (p. 94), in which he argues that neurosis is not the *source* of artistic accomplishment, though it may *accompany* it. To what extent are the ideas expressed in "Art and Neurosis" also implied in this short story?

Are there any apparent contradictions between Trilling's attitudes in the essay and those occurring in the story? Explain.

5) This story seems to ask the general question: Which of us is sane? You have already answered the question as to whether Tertan is "mad." But is Blackburn? Howe? Hilda? Or is it "society" itself which is sick? Try to answer each of these questions, in terms of the story, and then explain how your answers relate to your own general feelings about "madness," "education," "literature," "art"—and especially "creativity."

V. SOCIAL SCIENCES

From Plato and Aristotle to Galbraith and Durkheim, Western Civilization has produced a great store of social analysis—analysis of social problems, of our failures to achieve our social ends. We may be short of workable answers to our problems—be they war, poverty, or prejudice—but we have no lack of explanations as to why these problems are with us. Essentially there is but one social problem—that of finding a balance between individual fulfillment and social regulation. Man created society because he needed the support of social institutions, yet he was creating something with which he must forever exist in tension. The achievement of the social analysts and scientists can be measured not only by their recognition of the basic conflict between the individual and society, but by their development of effective methods for exploring and recording all of man's social problems. It is clear that the disciplines of history, sociology, and anthropology are creations, no less than paintings and poems.

THE HISTORIAN AND HIS FACTS

Edward Hallett Carr

What is history? Lest anyone think the question meaningless or superfluous, I will take as my text two passages relating respectively to the first and second incarnations of *The Cambridge Modern History*. Here is Acton in his report of October 1896 to the Syndics of the Cambridge University Press on the work which he had undertaken to edit:

> *It is a unique opportunity of recording, in the way most useful to the greatest number, the fullness of the knowledge which the nineteenth century is about to bequeath. . . . By the judicious division of labor we should be able to do it, and to bring home to every man the last document, and the ripest conclusions of international research.*
>
> *Ultimate history we cannot have in this generation; but we can dispose of conventional history, and show the point we have reached on the road from one to the other, now that all information is within reach, and every problem has become capable of solution.*[1]

And almost exactly sixty years later Professor Sir George Clark, in his general introduction to the second *Cambridge Modern History*, commented on this belief of Acton and his collaborators that it would one day be possible to produce "ultimate history," and went on:

> *Historians of a later generation do not look forward to any such prospect. They expect their work to be superseded again and again. They consider that knowledge of the past has come down through one or more human minds, has been "processed" by them, and therefore cannot consist of elemental and impersonal atoms which nothing can alter. . . . The exploration seems to be endless, and some impatient scholars take refuge in scepticism, or at least in the doctrine that, since all historical judgments*

---

[1] *The Cambridge Modern History: Its Origin, Authorship and Production* (Cambridge University Press, 1907), pp. 10–12.

> *involve persons and points of view, one is as good as
> another and there is no "objective" historical truth.*[2]

Where the pundits contradict each other so flagrantly the field is open to enquiry. I hope that I am sufficiently up-to-date to recognize that anything written in the 1890's must be nonsense. But I am not yet advanced enough to be committed to the view that anything written in the 1950's necessarily makes sense. Indeed, it may already have occurred to you that this enquiry is liable to stray into something even broader than the nature of history. The clash between Acton and Sir George Clark is a reflection of the change in our total outlook on society over the interval between these two pronouncements. Acton speaks out of the positive belief, the clear-eyed self-confidence of the later Victorian age; Sir George Clark echoes the bewilderment and distracted scepticism of the beat generation. When we attempt to answer the question, What is history?, our answer, consciously or unconsciously, reflects our own position in time, and forms part of our answer to the broader question, what view we take of the society in which we live. I have no fear that my subject may, on closer inspection, seem trivial. I am afraid only that I may seem presumptuous to have broached a question so vast and so important.

The nineteenth century was a great age for facts. "What I want," said Mr. Gradgrind in *Hard Times,* "is Facts. . . . Facts alone are wanted in life." Nineteenth-century historians on the whole agreed with him. When Ranke in the 1830's, in legitimate protest against moralizing history, remarked that the task of the historian was "simply to show how it really was [*wie es eigentlich gewesen*]" this not very profound aphorism had an astonishing success. Three generations of German, British, and even French historians marched into battle intoning the magic words, *"Wie es eigentlich gewesen"* like an incantation—designed, like most incantations, to save them from the tiresome obligation to think for themselves. The Positivists, anxious to stake out their claim for history as a science, contributed the weight of their influence to this cult of facts. First ascertain the facts, said the positivists, then draw your conclusions from them. In Great Britain, this view of history fitted in perfectly with the empiricist tradition which was the dominant strain in British philosophy from Locke to Bertrand Russell. The empirical theory of knowledge presupposes a complete separation between subject and object. Facts, like sense-impressions, impinge on the observer from outside, and are independent of his consciousness. The process of reception is passive: having received the data, he then acts on them. *The Shorter Oxford English Dictionary,* a useful but tendentious work of the empirical school, clearly marks the separateness of the two processes by defining a fact as "a datum of experience as distinct from

[2] *The New Cambridge Modern History,* I (Cambridge University Press, 1957), pp. xxiv–xxv.

conclusions." This is what may be called the common-sense view of history. History consists of a corpus of ascertained facts. The facts are available to the historian in documents, inscriptions, and so on, like fish on the fish-monger's slab. The historian collects them, takes them home, and cooks and serves them in whatever style appeals to him. Acton, whose culinary tastes were austere, wanted them served plain. In his letter of instructions to contributors to the first *Cambridge Modern History* he announced the requirement "that our Waterloo must be one that satisfies French and English, German and Dutch alike; that nobody can tell, without examining the list of authors where the Bishop of Oxford laid down the pen, and whether Fairbairn or Gasquet, Liebermann or Harrison took it up."[3] Even Sir George Clark, critical as he was of Acton's attitude, himself contrasted the "hard core of facts" in history with the "surrounding pulp of disputable interpretation"[4]—forgetting perhaps that the pulpy part of the fruit is more rewarding than the hard core. First get your facts straight, then plunge at your peril into the shifting sands of interpretation—that is the ultimate wisdom of the empirical, common-sense school of history. It re-calls the favorite dictum of the great liberal journalist C. P. Scott: "Facts are sacred, opinion is free."

Now this clearly will not do. I shall not embark on a philosophical discussion of the nature of our knowledge of the past. Let us assume for present purposes that the fact that Caesar crossed the Rubicon and the fact that there is a table in the middle of the room are facts of the same or of a comparable order, that both these facts enter our consciousness in the same or in a comparable manner, and that both have the same objective character in relation to the person who knows them. But, even on this bold and not very plausible assumption, our argument at once runs into the difficulty that not all facts about the past are historical facts, or are treated as such by the historian. What is the criterion which distinguishes the facts of history from other facts about the past?

What is a historical fact? This is a crucial question into which we must look a little more closely. According to the common-sense view, there are certain basic facts which are the same for all historians and which form, so to speak, the backbone of history—the fact, for example, that the Battle of Hastings was fought in 1066. But this view calls for two observa-tions. In the first place, it is not with facts like these that the historian is primarily concerned. It is no doubt important to know that the great battle was fought in 1066 and not in 1065 or 1067, and that it was fought at Hastings and not at Eastbourne or Brighton. The historian must not get these things wrong. But when points of this kind are raised, I am reminded of Housman's remark that "accuracy is a duty, not a virtue."[5] To praise a

---

[3] Acton: *Lectures on Modern History* (London: Macmillan & Co., 1906), p. 318.
[4] Quoted in *The Listener* (June 19, 1952), p. 992.
[5] M. Manilius: *Astronomicon: Liber Primus,* 2nd ed. (Cambridge University Press, 1937), p. 87.

historian for his accuracy is like praising an architect for using well-seasoned timber or properly mixed concrete in his building. It is a necessary condition of his work, but not his essential function. It is precisely for matters of this kind that the historian is entitled to rely on what have been called the "auxiliary sciences" of history—archaeology, epigraphy, numismatics, chronology, and so forth. The historian is not required to have the special skills which enable the expert to determine the origin and period of a fragment of pottery or marble, or decipher an obscure inscription, or to make the elaborate astronomical calculations necessary to establish a precise date. These so-called basic facts which are the same for all historians commonly belong to the category of the raw materials of the historian rather than of history itself. The second observation is that the necessity to establish these basic facts rests not on any quality in the facts themselves, but on an *a priori* decision of the historian. In spite of C. P. Scott's motto, every journalist knows today that the most effective way to influence opinion is by the selection and arrangement of the appropriate facts. It used to be said that facts speak for themselves. This is, of course, untrue. The facts speak only when the historian calls on them: It is he who decides to which facts to give the floor, and in what order or context. It was, I think, one of Pirandello's characters who said that a fact is like a sack—it won't stand up till you've put something in it. The only reason why we are interested to know that the battle was fought at Hastings in 1066 is that historians regard it as a major historical event. It is the historian who has decided for his own reasons that Caesar's crossing of that petty stream, the Rubicon, is a fact of history, whereas the crossing of the Rubicon by millions of other people before or since interests nobody at all. The fact that you arrived in this building half an hour ago on foot, or on a bicycle, or in a car, is just as much a fact about the past as the fact that Caesar crossed the Rubicon. But it will probably be ignored by historians. Professor Talcott Parsons once called science "a selective system of cognitive orientations to reality."[6] It might perhaps have been put more simply. But history is, among other things, that. The historian is necessarily selective. The belief in a hard core of historical facts existing objectively and independently of the interpretation of the historian is a preposterous fallacy, but one which it is very hard to eradicate.

Let us take a look at the process by which a mere fact about the past is transformed into a fact of history. At Stalybridge Wakes in 1850, a vendor of gingerbread, as the result of some petty dispute, was deliberately kicked to death by an angry mob. Is this a fact of history? A year ago I should unhesitatingly have said "no." It was recorded by an eyewitness in some little-known memoirs;[7] but I had never seen it judged worthy of

[6] Talcott Parsons and Edward A. Shils: *Toward a General Theory of Action,* 3rd ed. (Cambridge, Mass.: Harvard University Press, 1954), p. 167.
[7] Lord George Sanger: *Seventy Years a Showman* (London: J. M. Dent & Sons, 1926), pp. 188–9.

mention by any historian. A year ago Dr. Kitson Clark cited it in his Ford lectures in Oxford.[8] Does this make it into a historical fact? Not, I think, yet. Its present status, I suggest, is that it has been proposed for membership of the select club of historical facts. It now awaits a seconder and sponsors. It may be that in the course of the next few years we shall see this fact appearing first in footnotes, then in the text, of articles and books about nineteenth-century England, and that in twenty or thirty years' time it may be a well established historical fact. Alternatively, nobody may take it up, in which case it will relapse into the limbo of unhistorical facts about the past from which Dr. Kitson Clark has gallantly attempted to rescue it. What will decide which of these two things will happen? It will depend, I think, on whether the thesis or interpretation in support of which Dr. Kitson Clark cited this incident is accepted by other historians as valid and significant. Its status as a historical fact will turn on a question of interpretation. This element of interpretation enters into every fact of history.

May I be allowed a personal reminiscence? When I studied ancient history in this university many years ago, I had as a special subject "Greece in the period of the Persian Wars." I collected fifteen or twenty volumes on my shelves and took it for granted that there, recorded in these volumes, I had all the facts relating to my subject. Let us assume—it was very nearly true—that those volumes contained all the facts about it that were then known, or could be known. It never occurred to me to enquire by what accident or process of attrition that minute selection of facts, out of all the myriad facts that must have once been known to somebody, had survived to become *the* facts of history. I suspect that even today one of the fascinations of ancient and mediaeval history is that it gives us the illusion of having all the facts at our disposal within a manageable compass: the nagging distinction between the facts of history and other facts about the past vanishes because the few known facts are all facts of history. As Bury, who had worked in both periods, said "the records of ancient and mediaeval history are starred with lacunae."[9] History has been called an enormous jig-saw with a lot of missing parts. But the main trouble does not consist of the lacunae. Our picture of Greece in the fifth century B.C. is defective not primarily because so many of the bits have been accidentally lost, but because it is, by and large, the picture formed by a tiny group of people in the city of Athens. We know a lot about what fifth-century Greece looked like to an Athenian citizen; but hardly anything about what it looked like to a Spartan, a Corinthian, or a Theban—not to mention a Persian, or a slave or other non-citizen resident in Athens. Our picture has been preselected and predetermined for us, not so much by accident as by people who were consciously or unconsciously imbued with a partic-ular view and thought the facts which supported that view worth preserv-

---

[8] These will shortly be published under the title *The Making of Victorian England.*
[9] John Bagnell Bury: *Selected Essays* (Cambridge University Press, 1930), p. 52.

ing. In the same way, when I read in a modern history of the Middle Ages that the people of the Middle Ages were deeply concerned with religion, I wonder how we know this, and whether it is true. What we know as the facts of mediaeval history have almost all been selected for us by generations of chroniclers who were professionally occupied in the theory and practice of religion, and who therefore thought it supremely important, and recorded everything relating to it, and not much else. The picture of the Russian peasant as devoutly religious was destroyed by the revolution of 1917. The picture of mediaeval man as devoutly religious, whether true or not, is indestructible, because nearly all the known facts about him were preselected for us by people who believed it, and wanted others to believe it, and a mass of other facts, in which we might possibly have found evidence to the contrary, has been lost beyond recall. The dead hand of vanished generations of historians, scribes, and chroniclers has determined beyond the possibility of appeal the pattern of the past. "The history we read," writes Professor Barraclough, himself trained as a mediaevalist, "though based on facts, is, strictly speaking, not factual at all, but a series of accepted judgments."[10]

But let us turn to the different, but equally grave, plight of the modern historian. The ancient or mediaeval historian may be grateful for the vast winnowing process which, over the years, has put at his disposal a manageable corpus of historical facts. As Lytton Strachey said in his mischievous way, "ignorance is the first requisite of the historian, ignorance which simplifies and clarifies, which selects and omits."[11] When I am tempted, as I sometimes am, to envy the extreme competence of colleagues engaged in writing ancient or mediaeval history, I find consolation in the reflection that they are so competent mainly because they are so ignorant of their subject. The modern historian enjoys none of the advantages of this built-in ignorance. He must cultivate this necessary ignorance for himself—the more so the nearer he comes to his own times. He has the dual task of discovering the few significant facts and turning them into facts of history, and of discarding the many insignificant facts as unhistorical. But this is the very converse of the nineteenth-century heresy that history consists of the compilation of a maximum number of irrefutable and objective facts. Anyone who succumbs to this heresy will either have to give up history as a bad job, and take to stamp-collecting or some other form of antiquarianism, or end in a madhouse. It is this heresy, which during the past hundred years has had such devastating effects on the modern historian, producing in Germany, in Great Britain, and in the United States a vast and growing mass of dry-as-dust factual histories, of minutely specialized monographs, of would-be historians knowing more and more about less

---

[10] Geoffrey Barraclough: *History in a Changing World* (London: Basil Blackwell & Mott, 1955), p. 14.
[11] Lytton Strachey: Preface to *Eminent Victorians*.

and less, sunk without trace in an ocean of facts. It was, I suspect, this heresy—rather than the alleged conflict between liberal and Catholic loyalties—which frustrated Acton as a historian. In an early essay he said of his teacher Döllinger: "He would not write with imperfect materials, and to him the materials were always imperfect."[12] Acton was surely here pronouncing an anticipatory verdict on himself, on that strange phenomenon of a historian whom many would regard as the most distinguished occupant the Regius Chair of Modern History in this university has ever had—but who wrote no history. And Acton wrote his own epitaph in the introductory note to the first volume of the *Cambridge Modern History,* published just after his death, when he lamented that the requirements pressing on the historian "threaten to turn him from a man of letters into the compiler of an encyclopedia."[13] Something had gone wrong. What had gone wrong was the belief in this untiring and unending accumulation of hard facts as the foundation of history, the belief that facts speak for themselves and that we cannot have too many facts, a belief at that time so unquestioning that few historians then thought it necessary—and some still think it unnecessary today—to ask themselves the question: What is history?

The nineteenth-century fetishism of facts was completed and justified by a fetishism of documents. The documents were the Ark of the Covenant in the temple of facts. The reverent historian approached them with bowed head and spoke of them in awed tones. If you find it in the documents, it is so. But what, when we get down to it, do these documents—the decrees, the treaties, the rent-rolls, the blue books, the official correspondence, the private letters and diaries—tell us? No document can tell us more than what the author of the document thought—what he thought had happened, what he thought ought to happen or would happen, or perhaps only what he wanted others to think he thought, or even only what he himself thought he thought. None of this means anything until the historian has got to work on it and deciphered it. The facts, whether found in documents or not, have still to be processed by the historian before he can make any use of them: the use he makes of them is, if I may put it that way, the processing process.

Let me illustrate what I am trying to say by an example which I happen to know well. When Gustav Stresemann, the Foreign Minister of the Weimar Republic, died in 1929, he left behind him an enormous mass —300 boxes full—of papers, official, semi-official, and private, nearly all relating to the six years of his tenure of office as Foreign Minister. His

---

[12] Quoted in George P. Gooch: *History and Historians in the Nineteenth Century* (London: Longmans, Green & Company, 1952), p. 385. Later Acton said of Döllinger that "it was given him to form his philosophy of history on the largest induction ever available to man" (*History of Freedom and Other Essays* [London: Macmillan & Co., 1907], p. 435).

[13] *The Cambridge Modern History,* I (1902), p. 4.

friends and relatives naturally thought that a monument should be raised
to the memory of so great a man. His faithful secretary Bernhardt got to
work; and within three years there appeared three massive volumes, of
some 600 pages each, of selected documents from the 300 boxes, with
the impressive title *Stresemann's Vermächtnis*.[14] In the ordinary way the
documents themselves would have moldered away in some cellar or attic
and disappeared for ever; or perhaps in a hundred years or so some curious
scholar would have come upon them and set out to compare them with
Bernhardt's text. What happened was far more dramatic. In 1945 the
documents fell into the hands of the British and the American governments, who photographed the lot and put the photostats at the disposal of
scholars in the Public Record Office in London and in the National
Archives in Washington, so that, if we have sufficient patience and curiosity, we can discover exactly what Bernhardt did. What he did was neither
very unusual nor very shocking. When Stresemann died, his Western policy
seemed to have been crowned with a series of brilliant successes—Locarno,
the admission of Germany to the League of Nations, the Dawes and Young
plans and the American loans, the withdrawal of allied occupation armies
from the Rhineland. This seemed the important and rewarding part of
Stresemann's foreign policy; and it was not unnatural that it should have
been over-represented in Bernhardt's selection of documents. Stresemann's
Eastern policy, on the other hand, his relations with the Soviet Union,
seemed to have led nowhere in particular; and, since masses of documents
about negotiations which yielded only trivial results were not very interesting and added nothing to Stresemann's reputation, the process of
selection could be more rigorous. Stresemann in fact devoted a far more
constant and anxious attention to relations with the Soviet Union, and
they played a far larger part in his foreign policy as a whole, than the
reader of the Bernhardt selection would surmise. But the Bernhardt volumes compare favorably, I suspect, with many published collections of
documents on which the ordinary historian implicitly relies.

This is not the end of my story. Shortly after the publication of Bernhardt's volumes, Hitler came into power. Stresemann's name was consigned
to oblivion in Germany, and the volumes disappeared from circulation:
many, perhaps most, of the copies must have been destroyed. Today
Stresemann's Vermächtnis is a rather rare book. But in the West Stresemann's reputation stood high. In 1935 an English publisher brought out
an abbreviated translation of Bernhardt's work—a selection from Bernhardt's selection; perhaps one third of the original was omitted. Sutton,
a well-known translator from the German, did his job competently and
well. The English version, he explained in the preface, was "slightly condensed, but only by the omission of a certain amount of what, it was felt,

[14] *Stresemann's Legacy.*

was more ephemeral matter . . . of little interest to English readers or students."[15] This again is natural enough. But the result is that Stresemann's Eastern policy, already under-represented in Bernhardt, recedes still further from view, and the Soviet Union appears in Sutton's volumes merely as an occasional and rather unwelcome intruder in Stresemann's predominantly Western foreign policy. Yet it is safe to say that, for all except a few specialists, Sutton and not Bernhardt—and still less the documents themselves—represents for the Western world the authentic voice of Stresemann. Had the documents perished in 1945 in the bombing, and had the remaining Bernhardt volumes disappeared, the authenticity and authority of Sutton would never have been questioned. Many printed collections of documents gratefully accepted by historians in default of the originals rest on no securer basis than this.

But I want to carry the story one step further. Let us forget about Bernhardt and Sutton, and be thankful that we can, if we choose, consult the authentic papers of a leading participant in some important events of recent European history. What do the papers tell us? Among other things they contain records of some hundreds of Stresemann's conversations with the Soviet ambassador in Berlin and of a score or so with Chicherin.[16] These records have one feature in common. They depict Stresemann as having the lion's share of the conversations and reveal his arguments as invariably well put and cogent, while those of his partner are for the most part scanty, confused, and unconvincing. This is a familiar characteristic of all records of diplomatic conversations. The documents do not tell us what happened, but only what Stresemann thought had happened. It was not Sutton or Bernhardt, but Stresemann himself, who started the process of selection. And, if we had, say, Chicherin's records of these same conversations, we should still learn from them only what Chicherin thought, and what really happened would still have to be reconstructed in the mind of the historian. Of course, facts and documents are essential to the historian. But do not make a fetish of them. They do not by themselves constitute history; they provide in themselves no ready-made answer to this tiresome question: What is history?

At this point I should like to say a few words on the question of why nineteenth-century historians were generally indifferent to the philosophy of history. The term was invented by Voltaire, and has since been used in different senses; but I shall take it to mean, if I use it at all, our answer to the question: What is history? The nineteenth century was, for the intellectuals of Western Europe, a comfortable period exuding confidence and optimism. The facts were on the whole satisfactory; and the

---

[15] *Gustav Stresemann: His Diaries, Letters, and Papers* (London: Macmillan & Co.; 1935), I.
[16] Soviet foreign minister, 1918–1928 [Editor's note].

inclination to ask and answer awkward questions about them was correspondingly weak. Ranke piously believed that divine providence would take care of the meaning of history if he took care of the facts; and Burckhardt with a more modern touch of cynicism observed that "we are not initiated into the purposes of the eternal wisdom." Professor Butterfield as late as 1931 noted with apparent satisfaction that "historians have reflected little upon the nature of things and even the nature of their own subject."[17] But my predecessor in these lectures, Dr. A. L. Rowse, more justly critical, wrote of Sir Winston Churchill's *The World Crisis*—his book about the First World War—that, while it matched Trotsky's *History of the Russian Revolution* in personality, vividness, and vitality, it was inferior in one respect: it had "no philosophy of history behind it."[18] British historians refused to be drawn, not because they believed that history had no meaning, but because they believed that its meaning was implicit and self-evident. The liberal nineteenth-century view of history had a close affinity with the economic doctrine of *laissez-faire*—also the product of a serene and self-confident outlook on the world. Let everyone get on with his particular job, and the hidden hand would take care of the universal harmony. The facts of history were themselves a demonstration of the supreme fact of a beneficent and apparently infinite progress towards higher things. This was the age of innocence, and historians walked in the Garden of Eden, without a scrap of philosophy to cover them, naked and unashamed before the god of history. Since then, we have known Sin and experienced a Fall; and those historians who today pretend to dispense with a philosophy of history are merely trying, vainly and self-consciously, like members of a nudist colony, to recreate the Garden of Eden in their garden suburb. Today the awkward question can no longer be evaded. . . .

During the past fifty years a good deal of serious work has been done on the question: What is history? It was from Germany, the country which was to do so much to upset the comfortable reign of nineteenth-century liberalism, that the first challenge came in the 1880's and 1890's to the doctrine of the primacy and autonomy of facts in history. The philosophers who made the challenge are now little more than names: Dilthey is the only one of them who has recently received some belated recognition in Great Britain. Before the turn of the century, prosperity and confidence were still too great in this country for any attention to be paid to heretics who attacked the cult of facts. But early in the new century, the torch passed to Italy, where Croce began to propound a philosophy of history which obviously owed much to German masters. All history is

[17] Herbert Butterfield: *The Whig Interpretation of History* (London: George Bell & Sons, 1931), p. 67.
[18] Alfred L. Rowse: *The End of an Epoch* (London: Macmillan & Co., 1947), pp. 282-3.

"contemporary history," declared Croce,[19] meaning that history consists essentially in seeing the past through the eyes of the present and in the light of its problems, and that the main work of the historian is not to record, but to evaluate; for, if he does not evaluate, how can he know what is worth recording? In 1910 the American philosopher, Carl Becker, argued in deliberately provocative language that "the facts of history do not exist for any historian till he creates them."[20] These challenges were for the moment little noticed. It was only after 1920 that Croce began to have a considerable vogue in France and Great Britain. This was not perhaps because Croce was a subtler thinker or a better stylist than his German predecessors, but because, after the First World War, the facts seemed to smile on us less propitiously than in the years before 1914, and we were therefore more accessible to a philosophy which sought to diminish their prestige. Croce was an important influence on the Oxford philosopher and historian Collingwood, the only British thinker in the present century who has made a serious contribution to the philosophy of history. He did not live to write the systematic treatise he had planned; but his published and unpublished papers on the subject were collected after his death in a volume entitled *The Idea of History,* which appeared in 1945.

The views of Collingwood can be summarized as follows. The philosophy of history is concerned neither with "the past by itself" nor with "the historian's thought about it by itself," but with "the two things in their mutual relations." (This dictum reflects the two current meanings of the word "history"—the enquiry conducted by the historian and the series of past events into which he enquires.) "The past which a historian studies is not a dead past, but a past which in some sense is still living in the present." But a past act is dead, *i.e.* meaningless to the historian, unless he can understand the thought that lay behind it. Hence "all history is the history of thought," and "history is the re-enactment in the historian's mind of the thought whose history he is studying." The reconstitution of the past in the historian's mind is dependent on empirical evidence. But it is not in itself an empirical process, and cannot consist in a mere recital of facts. On the contrary, the process of reconstitution governs the selection and interpretation of the facts: this, indeed, is what makes them historical facts. "History," says Professor Oakeshott, who on this point stands near to Collingwood, "is the historian's experience. It is 'made' by nobody save the historian: to write history is the only way of making it."[21]

---

[19] The context of this celebrated aphorism is as follows: "The practical requirements which underlie every historical judgment give to all history the character of 'contemporary history,' because, however remote in time events thus recounted may seem to be, the history in reality refers to present needs and present situations wherein those events vibrate" (Benedetto Croce: *History as the Story of Liberty* [London: George Allen & Unwin, 1941], p. 19).

[20] *Atlantic Monthly* (October 1928), p. 528.

[21] Michael Oakeshott: *Experience and Its Modes* (Cambridge University Press, 1933), p. 99.

This searching critique, though it may call for some serious reservations, brings to light certain neglected truths.

In the first place, the facts of history never come to us "pure," since they do not and cannot exist in a pure form: they are always refracted through the mind of the recorder. It follows that when we take up a work of history, our first concern should be not with the facts which it contains but with the historian who wrote it. Let me take as an example the great historian in whose honor and in whose name these lectures were founded. Trevelyan, as he tells us in his autobiography, was "brought up at home on a somewhat exuberantly Whig tradition"[22]; and he would not, I hope, disclaim the title if I described him as the last and not the least of the great English liberal historians of the Whig tradition. It is not for nothing that he traces back his family tree, through the great Whig historian George Otto Trevelyan, to Macaulay, incomparably the greatest of the Whig historians. Dr. Trevelyan's finest and maturest work *England under Queen Anne* was written against that background, and will yield its full meaning and significance to the reader only when read against that background. The author, indeed, leaves the reader with no excuse for failing to do so. For if, following the technique of connoisseurs of detective novels, you read the end first, you will find on the last few pages of the third volume the best summary known to me of what is nowadays called the Whig interpretation of history; and you will see that what Trevelyan is trying to do is to investigate the origin and development of the Whig tradition, and to roof it fairly and squarely in the years after the death of its founder, William III. Though this is not, perhaps, the only conceivable interpretation of the events of Queen Anne's reign, it is a valid and, in Trevelyan's hands, a fruitful interpretation. But, in order to appreciate it at its full value, you have to understand what the historian is doing. For if, as Collingwood says, the historian must re-enact in thought what has gone on in the mind of his *dramatis personae,* so the reader in his turn must re-enact what goes on in the mind of the historian. Study the historian before you begin to study the facts. This is, after all, not very abstruse. It is what is already done by the intelligent undergraduate who, when recommended to read a work by that great scholar Jones of St. Jude's, goes round to a friend at St. Jude's to ask what sort of chap Jones is, and what bees he has in his bonnet. When you read a work of history, always listen out for the buzzing. If you can detect none, either you are tone deaf or your historian is a dull dog. The facts are really not at all like fish on the fishmonger's slab. They are like fish swimming about in a vast and sometimes inaccessible ocean; and what the historian catches will depend partly on chance, but mainly on what part of the ocean he chooses to fish in and what tackle he chooses to use—these two factors being, of

---

[22] G. M. Trevelyan: *An Autobiography* (London: Longmans, Green & Company, 1949), p. 11.

course, determined by the kind of fish he wants to catch. By and large, the historian will get the kind of facts he wants. History means interpretation. Indeed, if, standing Sir George Clark on his head, I were to call history "a hard core of interpretation surrounded by a pulp of disputable facts," my statement would, no doubt, be one-sided and misleading, but no more so, I venture to think, than the original dictum.

The second point is the more familiar one of the historian's need of imaginative understanding for the minds of the people with whom he is dealing, for the thought behind their acts: I say "imaginative understanding," not "sympathy," lest sympathy should be supposed to imply agreement. The nineteenth century was weak in mediaeval history, because it was too much repelled by the superstitious beliefs of the Middle Ages and by the barbarities which they inspired, to have any imaginative understanding of mediaeval people. Or take Burckhardt's censorious remark about the Thirty Years' War: "It is scandalous for a creed, no matter whether it is Catholic or Protestant, to place its salvation above the integrity of the nation."[23] It was extremely difficult for a nineteenth-century liberal historian, brought up to believe that it is right and praiseworthy to kill in defense of one's country, but wicked and wrongheaded to kill in defense of one's religion, to enter into the state of mind of those who fought the Thirty Years' War. This difficulty is particularly acute in the field in which I am now working. Much of what has been written in English-speaking countries in the last ten years about the Soviet Union, and in the Soviet Union about the English-speaking countries, has been vitiated by this inability to achieve even the most elementary measure of imaginative understanding of what goes on in the mind of the other party, so that the words and actions of the other are always made to appear malign, senseless, or hypocritical. History cannot be written unless the historian can achieve some kind of contact with the mind of those about whom he is writing.

The third point is that we can view the past, and achieve our understanding of the past, only through the eyes of the present. The historian is of his own age, and is bound to it by the conditions of human existence. The very words which he uses—words like democracy, empire, war, revolution—have current connotations from which he cannot divorce them. Ancient historians have taken to using words like *polis* and *plebs* in the original, just in order to show that they have not fallen into this trap. This does not help them. They, too, live in the present, and cannot cheat themselves into the past by using unfamiliar or obsolete words, any more than they would become better Greek or Roman historians if they delivered their lectures in a *chlamys* or a *toga*. The names by which successive French historians have described the Parisian crowds which played so prominent a role in the French revolution—*les sans-culottes, le peuple, la canaille, les bras-nus*—are all, for those who know the rules of the game, mani-

---

[23] Jacob Burckhardt: *Judgments on History and Historians* (London: S. J. Reginald Saunders & Company, 1958), p. 179.

festos of a political affiliation and of a particular interpretation. Yet the historian is obliged to choose: the use of language forbids him to be neutral. Nor is it a matter of words alone. Over the past hundred years the changed balance of power in Europe has reversed the attitude of British historians to Frederick the Great. The changed balance of power within the Christian churches between Catholicism and Protestantism has profoundly altered their attitude to such figures as Loyola, Luther, and Cromwell. It requires only a superficial knowledge of the work of French historians of the last forty years on the French revolution to recognize how deeply it has been affected by the Russian revolution of 1917. The historian belongs not to the past but to the present. Professor Trevor-Roper tells us that the historian "ought to love the past."[24] This is a dubious injunction. To love the past may easily be an expression of the nostalgic romanticism of old men and old societies, a symptom of loss of faith and interest in the present or future.[25] *Cliché* for *cliché,* I should prefer the one about freeing oneself from "the dead hand of the past." The function of the historian is neither to love the past nor to emancipate himself from the past, but to master and understand it as the key to the understanding of the present.

If, however, these are some of the sights of what I may call the Collingwood view of history, it is time to consider some of the dangers. The emphasis on the role of the historian in the making of history tends, if pressed to its logical conclusion, to rule out any objective history at all: history is what the historian makes. Collingwood seems indeed, at one moment, in an unpublished note quoted by his editor, to have reached this conclusion:

> *St. Augustine looked at history from the point of view of the early Christian; Tillemont, from that of a seventeenth-century Frenchman; Gibbon, from that of an eighteenth-century Englishman; Mommsen, from that of a nineteenth-century German. There is no point in asking which was the right point of view. Each was the only one possible for the man who adopted it.*[26]

This amounts to total scepticism, like Froude's remark that history is "a child's box of letters with which we can spell any word we please."[27] Collingwood, in his reaction against "scissors-and-paste history," against the

---

[24] Introduction to Burckhardt: *Judgments on History and Historians,* p. 17.
[25] Compare Nietzsche's view of history: "To old age belongs the old man's business of looking back and casting up his accounts, of seeking consolation in the memories of the past, in historical culture" (*Thoughts Out of Season* [London: Macmillan & Co., 1909], II, pp. 65–6).
[26] Robin G. Collingwood: *The Idea of History* (London: Oxford University Press, 1946), p. xii.
[27] James Anthony Froude: *Short Studies on Great Subjects* (1894), I, p. 21.

view of history as a mere compilation of facts, comes perilously near to treating history as something spun out of the human brain, and leads back to the conclusion referred to by Sir George Clark in the passage which I quoted earlier, that "there is no 'objective' historical truth." In place of the theory that history has no meaning, we are offered here the theory of an infinity of meanings, none any more right than any other—which comes to much the same thing. The second theory is surely as untenable as the first. It does not follow that, because a mountain appears to take on different shapes from different angles of vision, it has objectively either no shape at all or an infinity of shapes. It does not follow that, because interpretation plays a necessary part in establishing the facts of history, and because no existing interpretation is wholly objective, one interpretation is as good as another, and the facts of history are in principle not amenable to objective interpretation. I shall have to consider at a later stage what exactly is meant by objectivity in history.

But a still greater danger lurks in the Collingwood hypothesis. If the historian necessarily looks at his period of history through the eyes of his own time, and studies the problems of the past as a key to those of the present, will he not fall into a purely pragmatic view of the facts, and maintain that the criterion of a right interpretation is its suitability to some present purpose? On this hypothesis, the facts of history are nothing, interpretation is everything. Nietzsche had already enunciated the principle: "The falseness of an opinion is not for us any objection to it. . . . The question is how far it is life-furthering, life-preserving, species-preserving, perhaps species-creating."[28] The American pragmatists moved, less explicitly and less wholeheartedly, along the same line. Knowledge is knowledge for some purpose. The validity of the knowledge depends on the validity of the purpose. But, even where no such theory has been professed, the practice has often been no less disquieting. In my own field of study, I have seen too many examples of extravagant interpretation riding roughshod over facts, not to be impressed with the reality of this danger. It is not surprising that perusal of some of the more extreme products of Soviet and anti-Soviet schools of historiography should sometimes breed a certain nostalgia for that illusory nineteenth-century heaven of purely factual history.

How then, in the middle of the twentieth century, are we to define the obligation of the historian to his facts? I trust that I have spent a sufficient number of hours in recent years chasing and perusing documents, and stuffing my historical narrative with properly footnoted facts, to escape the imputation of treating facts and documents too cavalierly. The duty of the historian to respect his facts is not exhausted by the obligation to see that his facts are accurate. He must seek to bring into the picture all known

---

[28] Nietzsche: *Beyond Good and Evil,* Ch. i.

or knowable facts relevant, in one sense or another, to the theme on which he is engaged and to the interpretation proposed. If he seeks to depict the Victorian Englishman as a moral and rational being, he must not forget what happened at Stalybridge Wakes in 1850. But this, in turn, does not mean that he can eliminate interpretation, which is the life-blood of history. Laymen—that is to say, non-academic friends or friends from other academic disciplines—sometimes ask me how the historian goes to work when he writes history. The commonest assumption appears to be that the historian divides his work into two sharply distinguishable phases or periods. First, he spends a long preliminary period reading his source and filling his notebooks with facts: then, when this is over, he puts away his sources, takes out his notebooks, and writes his book from beginning to end. This is to me an unconvincing and unplausible picture. For myself, as soon as I have got going on a few of what I take to be the capital sources, the itch becomes too strong and I begin to write—not necessarily at the beginning, but somewhere, anywhere. Thereafter, reading and writing go on simultaneously. The writing is added to, subtracted from, re-shaped, cancelled, as I go on reading. The reading is guided and directed and made fruitful by the writing: the more I write, the more I know what I am looking for, the better I understand the significance and relevance of what I find. Some historians probably do all this preliminary writing in their head without using pen, paper, or typewriter, just as some people play chess in their heads without recourse to board and chess-men: this is a talent which I envy, but cannot emulate. But I am convinced that, for any historian worth the name, the two processes of what economists call "input" and "output" go on simultaneously and are, in practice, parts of a single process. If you try to separate them, or to give one priority over the other, you fall into one of two heresies. Either you write scissors-and-paste history without meaning or significance; or you write propaganda or historical fiction, and merely use facts of the past to embroider a kind of writing which has nothing to do with history.

Our examination of the relation of the historian to the facts of history finds us, therefore, in an apparently precarious situation, navigating delicately between the Scylla of an untenable theory of history as an objective compilation of facts, of the unqualified primacy of fact over interpretation, and the Charybdis of an equally untenable theory of history as the subjective product of the mind of the historian who establishes the facts of history and masters them through the process of interpretation, between a view of history having the center of gravity in the past and the view having the center of gravity in the present. But our situation is less precarious than it seems. We shall encounter the same dichotomy of fact and interpretation again in these lectures in other guises—the particular and the general, the empirical and the theoretical, the objective and the subjective. The predicament of the historian is a reflection of the nature of man. Man, except perhaps in earliest infancy and in extreme old age, is not totally involved in his environment and unconditionally subject to it. On the other hand, he is never totally independent of it and its unconditional master. The relation of man to his environment is the relation of the historian to his theme. The historian is neither the humble slave, nor the tyrannical master, of his facts. The relation between the historian and his facts is one of equality, of give-and-take. As any working historian knows, if he stops to reflect what he is doing as he thinks and writes, the historian is engaged in a continuous process of molding his facts to his interpretation and his interpretation to his facts. It is impossible to assign primacy to one over the other.

The historian starts with the provisional selection of facts and a provisional interpretation in the light of which that selection has been made— by others as well as by himself. As he works, both the interpretation and the selection and ordering of facts undergo subtle and perhaps partly unconscious changes through the reciprocal action of one or the other. And this reciprocal action also involves reciprocity between present and past, since the historian is part of the present and the facts belong to the past. The historian and the facts of history are necessary to one another. The historian without his facts is rootless and futile; the facts without their historian are dead and meaningless. My first answer therefore to the question, What is history?, is that it is a continuous process of interaction between the historian and his facts, an unending dialogue between the present and the past.

QUESTIONS FOR DISCUSSION

1) History is a term like Democracy: everyone thinks he fully understands its meaning. This is a very disturbing fact to the historian Edward Hallett Carr. In his essay "The Historian and His Facts," Carr notes that most readers of history do not realize that all history is written from the historian's point of view and that no historical fact should be accepted at face value. According to Carr, what precisely is the relationship between the facts of experienced history and the facts of recorded history? What transforms a "mere fact about the past" into a "fact about history"?

2) According to Carr, what was the view of history in the nineteenth century? What philosophical disposition caused this view of history? Why did the view change in the twentieth century?

3) How do the events relating to the state papers of Gustav Stresemann illustrate Carr's belief about historical facts?

4) Explain the notion that all history is contemporary history. To what degree is the writing of history creative rather than mechanical?

from

BALOMA: THE SPIRITS OF THE DEAD IN THE TROBRIAND ISLANDS

Bronislaw Malinowski

All these data bearing upon the relations between the *baloma* and the living, are, in a way, a digression from the story of the afterlife of the *baloma* in Tuma, and to this let us now return.

We left the *baloma* settled to his new life in the nether world, more or less comforted concerning those left behind; having, very likely, married again and formed new ties and connections. If the man died young, his *baloma* is also young, but with time he will age, and finally his life in Tuma will also come to an end. If the man was old at his death, his *baloma* is old, and after a period his life in Tuma will also cease. In all cases the end of the life of the *baloma* in Tuma brings with it a very important crisis in the cycle of his existence. This is the reason why I have avoided the use of the term death in describing the end of the *baloma*.

I shall give a simple version of these events and discuss the details subsequently. When the *baloma* has grown old, his teeth fall out, his skin gets loose and wrinkled; he goes to the beach and bathes in the salt water; then he throws off his skin just as a snake would do, and becomes a young child again; really an embryo, a *waiwaia*—a term applied to children *in utero* and immediately after birth. A *baloma* woman sees this *waiwaia;* she takes it up, and puts it in a basket or a plaited and folded coconut leaf (*puatai*). She carries the small being to Kiriwina, and places it in the womb of some woman, inserting it *per vaginam*. Then that woman becomes pregnant (*nasusuma*).

This is the story as I obtained it from the first informant who mentioned the subject to me. It implies two important psychological facts: the belief in reincarnation, and the ignorance of the physiological causes of pregnancy. I shall now discuss both these subjects in the light of the details obtained on further inquiry.

First of all, everybody in Kiriwina knows, and has not the slightest doubt about, the following propositions. The real cause of pregnancy is always a *baloma,* who is inserted into or enters the body of a woman, and without whose existence a woman could not become pregnant; all babies are made or come into existence (*ibubulisi*) in Tuma. These tenets form the main stratum of what can be termed popular or universal belief. If you question any man, woman, or even an intelligent child, you will obtain from him or her this information. But any further details are much less universally known; one obtains a fact here and a detail there, and some of them contradict the others, and none of them seems to loom particularly clear in the native mind, though here and there it is obvious that some of these beliefs influence behavior, and are connected with some customs.

First, as to the nature of these "spirit children," *waiwaia*. It must be kept in mind that, as is usual in dogmatic assertions, the natives take very much for granted, do not trouble to give clear definitions or to imagine details very concretely and vividly. The most natural assumption—namely, that, of the "spirit child" being a small undeveloped child, an embryo—is the most frequently met with. The term *waiwaia*, which means embryo, child in the womb, and also infant immediately after birth, is also applied to the non-incarnated spirit children. Again, in a discussion on this subject, in which several men took part, some asserted that the man, after his transformation in Tuma, becomes just some sort of "blood," *buia'i*. In what manner he could be subsequently transported in such liquid form was not certain. But the term *buia'i* seems to have a slightly wider connotation than fluid blood merely, and it may mean something like flesh in this case.

Another cycle of beliefs and ideas about reincarnation implies a pronounced association between the sea and the spirit children. Thus I was told by several informants that after his transformation into a *waiwaia*, the spirit goes into the sea. The first version obtained (quoted above) implied that the spirit, after having washed on the seabeach and become rejuvenated, is taken up immediately by a female *baloma* and carried to Kiriwina. Other accounts state that the spirit, after being transformed, goes into the sea and dwells there for a time. There are several corollaries to this version. Thus in all the coastal villages on the western shore (where this information was collected) mature unmarried girls observe certain precautions when bathing. The spirit children are supposed to be concealed in the *popewo*, the floating sea scum; also in some stones called *dukupi*. They come along on large tree trunks (*kaibilabala*), and they may be attached to dead leaves (*libulibu*) floating on the surface. Thus when at certain times the wind and tide blow plenty of this stuff towards the shore, the girls are afraid of bathing in the sea, especially at high tide. Again, if a married woman wants to conceive, she may hit the *dukupi* stones in order to induce a concealed *waiwaia* to enter her womb. But this is not a ceremonial action.

In the inland villages the association between conception and bathing is also known. To receive the *waiwaia* whilst in the water seems to be the most usual way of becoming pregnant. Often whilst bathing a woman will feel that something has touched her, or even hurt her. She will say, "A fish has bitten me." In fact, it was the *waiwaia* entering or being inserted into her.

Another rather important connection between the belief of the *wai-*

waia dwelling in the sea and conception is expressed in the only important ceremony connected with pregnancy. About four to five months after the first symptoms of pregnancy the woman begins to observe certain taboos, and at the same time a large and long *dobe* (grass petticoat) is made (called *saikeulo*), which she will wear after the birth of the child. This is made by certain female relatives, who also perform magic over it, in order to benefit the child. On the same day the woman is taken to the sea, where relatives of the same class as those that made the *saikeulo* bathe her in the salt water. A *sagali* (ceremonial distribution of food) follows the proceedings.

The usual explanation of the *u'ula* (reason) for this ceremony is that it makes the "skin of the woman white," and that it makes the birth of the baby easier. But in the coastal village of Kavataria a very definite statement was volunteered, to the effect that the *kokuwa* ceremony is connected with incarnation of the spirit children. The view taken by one of my informants was that during the first stage of pregnancy the *waiwaia* has not really entered the woman's body, but that there is merely a kind of preparation made for its reception. Then, during the ceremonial bathing, the spirit child enters the body of the woman. Whether this volunteered interpretation was only his opinion or whether it is a universal belief in the coastal villages, is not known to me, but I am inclined to believe that it does represent an aspect of the coastal natives' belief. But it must be emphatically stated that this interpretation was absolutely pooh-poohed by my informants of the inland villages, who also pointed out the contradiction that this ceremony is performed later on, during pregnancy, and that the *waiwaia* has been established long ago in the mother's womb. It is characteristic that any inconsistency is noted in a view which is not the informant's own standpoint, while similar contradictions are most blandly overlooked in his own theories. The natives are, remarkably enough, not a whit more consistent on this point or intellectually honest than civilized people.

Besides the belief in reincarnation by action of the sea, the view that the *waiwaia* is inserted by a *baloma* is prevalent. These two ideas blend in the version that the *baloma* who inserts the *waiwaia* does it under water. The *baloma* often appears in a dream to the prospective mother, who will tell her husband: "I dreamed that my mother (or maternal aunt, or my elder sister or grandmother) inserted a child into me; my breasts are swelling." As a rule, it is a female *baloma* that appears in the dream and brings the *waiwaia,* though it may be a man, but the *baloma* must always be of the *veiola* (maternal kindred) of the woman. Many know who brought them to their mother. Thus To'uluwa, the chief of Omarakana, was given to his mother (Bomakata) by Buguabuaga, one of her *tabula* ("grandfathers"— in this case her mother's mother's brother). Again, Bwoilagesi, the woman mentioned [previously], who goes to Tuma, had her son, Tukulubakiki, given her by Tomnavabu, her *kadala* (mother's brother). Tukulubakiki's wife, Kuwo'igu, knows that her mother came to her, and gave her the baby, a girl now about twelve months old. Such knowledge is possible only in the cases when the *baloma* actually appears in a dream to the woman and tells her that he will insert a *waiwaia* into her. Of course, such annunciations are not absolutely in the program; indeed, the majority of people do not know who it is to whom they owe their existence.

There is one extremely important feature of the beliefs about reincarnation, and however opinions differ about the other details, this feature is stated and affirmed by all the informants; namely, that the social division, the clan and subclan of the individual, is preserved through all his transformations. The *baloma,* in the nether world, belongs to the same subclan as the man before death; and the reincarnation moves also strictly within the boundaries of the subclan. The *waiwaia* is conveyed by a *baloma* belonging to the same subclan as the woman, as just stated, the carrier is even as a rule some near *veiola.* And it was considered absolutely impossible that any exception to this rule could happen, or that an individual could change his or her subclan in the cycle of reincarnation.

So much about the belief in reincarnation. Though it is a universal and popular belief, *i.e.,* though it is known to everybody, it does not play an important role in social life. The last mentioned detail only about the persistence of kinship ties throughout the cycle is decidedly a belief illustrating the strength of the social division, the finality of belonging to a social group. Conversely, this belief must strengthen those ties.

It might seem quite safe to say that the belief in reincarnation, and the views about a spirit child being inserted into, or entering the womb of the mother, exclude any knowledge of the physiological process of impregnation. But any drawing of conclusions, or arguing by the law of logical contradiction, is absolutely futile in the realm of belief, whether savage or civilized. Two beliefs, quite contradictory to each other on logical grounds, may coexist, while a perfectly obvious inference from a very firm tenet may be simply ignored. Thus the only safe way for an ethnological inquirer is to investigate every detail of native belief, and to mistrust any conclusion obtained through inference only.

The broad assertion that the natives are entirely ignorant of the existence of physiological impregnation may be laid down quite safely and correctly. But though the subject is undoubtedly difficult, it is absolutely necessary to go into details in order to avoid serious mistakes.

One distinction must be made at the outset: the distinction between impregnation, that is the idea of the father having a share in building up the body of the child on the one hand, and the purely physical action of sexual intercourse on the other. Concerning the latter, the view held by the natives may be formulated thus: it is necessary for the woman to have gone through sexual life before she can bear a child.

I was forced to make the above distinction under the stress of the information I was gathering, in order to explain certain contradictions which cropped up in the course of inquiries. And it must be therefore accepted as a "natural" distinction, as one which corresponds to and expresses the native point of view. In fact, it was impossible to foresee how the natives would look upon these matters, and from which side they would approach the correct knowledge of facts. Nevertheless, the distinction once made, its theoretical importance is obvious. It is clear that only the knowledge of the first fact (that of the father's share in impregnation) would have any influence in shaping native ideas about kinship. As long as the father does nothing to form the body of the child (in the ideas of a people), there can be no question of consanguinity in the agnatic line. A mere mechanical share in opening up the child's way into the womb, and out of it, is of no fundamental importance. The state of knowledge in Kiriwina is just at the point where there is a vague idea as to some *nexus* between sexual connection and pregnancy, whereas there is no idea whatever concerning the man's contribution towards the new life which is being formed in the mother's body. . . .

Besides the concrete data about native beliefs which have been given above, there is another set of facts of no less importance which must be discussed before the present subject can be considered exhausted. I mean the general sociological laws that have to be grasped and framed in the field, in order that the material, which observation brings in a chaotic and unintelligible form, may be understood by the observer and recorded in a scientifically useful form. I have found the lack of philosophical clearness on matters connected with ethnographical and sociological field work a great setback in my first attempts to observe and describe native institutions, and I consider it quite essential to state the difficulties I encountered in my work and the manner in which I tried to cope with them.

Thus one of the main rules with which I set out on my field work was "to gather pure facts, to keep the facts and interpretations apart." This rule is quite correct if under "interpretations" be understood all hypothetical speculations about origins, etc., and all hasty generalizations. But there is a form of interpretation of facts without which no scientific observation can possibly be carried on—I mean the interpretation which sees in the endless diversity of facts general laws; which severs the essential from the irrelevant; which classifies and orders phenomena, and puts them into mutual relationship. Without such interpretation all scientific work in the field must degenerate into pure "collectioneering" of data; at its best it may give odds and ends without inner connection. But it never will be able to lay bare the sociological structure of a people, or to give an organic account of their beliefs, or to render the picture of the world from the native perspective. The often fragmentary, incoherent, non-organic nature of much of the present ethnological material is due to the cult of "pure fact."

As if it were possible to wrap up in a blanket a certain number of "facts as you find them" and bring them all back for the home student to generalize upon and to build up his theoretical constructions upon.

But the fact is that such a proceeding is quite impossible. Even if you spoil a district of all its material objects, and bring them home without much bothering about a careful description of their use—a method which has been carried out systematically in certain non-British possessions in the Pacific—such a museum collection will have little scientific value, simply because the ordering, the classifying, and interpreting should be done in the field with reference to the organic whole of native social life. What is impossible with the most "crystallized" phenomena—the material objects—is still less possible with those which float on the surface of native behavior, or lie in the depths of the native mind, or are only partially consolidated into native institutions and ceremonies. In the field one has to face a chaos of facts, some of which are so small that they seem insignificant; others loom so large that they are hard to encompass with one synthetic glance. But in this crude form they are not scientific facts at all; they are absolutely elusive, and can be fixed only by interpretation, by seeing them *subspecie aeternitatis,* by grasping what is essential in them and fixing this. *Only laws and generalizations are scientific facts,* and field work consists only and exclusively in the interpretation of the chaotic social reality, in subordinating it to general rules.

All statistics, every plan of a village or of grounds, every genealogy, every description of a ceremony—in fact, every ethnological document—is in itself a generalization, at times quite a difficult one, because in every case one has first to discover and formulate the rules: what to count and how to count; every plan must be drawn to express certain economic or sociological arrangements; every genealogy has to express kinship connections between people, and it is only valuable if all the relevant data about the people are collected as well. In every ceremony the accidental has to be sifted from the essential, the minor elements from the essential features, those that vary with every performance from those that are customary. All this may appear almost a truism, yet the unfortunate stress on keeping to "pure fact only" is constantly being used as the guiding principle in all instructions for field work.

Returning from this digression to the main subject, I want to adduce some general sociological rules which I had to formulate in order to deal with certain difficulties and discrepancies in the information, and in order to do justice to the complexity of facts, at the same time simplifying them in order to present a clear outline. What will be said in this place applies to Kiriwina, but not necessarily to any other or wider area. And, again, only those sociological generalizations will be discussed here which bear directly on belief, or even, more specially, on the beliefs described in this article.

The most important general principle concerning belief that I have been forced to respect and consider in the course of my field studies is this: Any belief or any item of folklore is not a simple piece of information to be picked up from any haphazard source, from any chance informant, and to be laid down as an axiom to be drawn with one single contour. On the contrary, every belief is reflected in all the minds of a given society, and it is expressed in many social phenomena. It is therefore complex, and, in fact, it is present in the social reality in overwhelming variety, very often puzzling, chaotic and elusive. In other words, there is a "social dimension" to a belief, and this must be carefully studied; the belief must be studied as it moves along this social dimension; it must be examined in the light of diverse types of minds and of the diverse institutions in which it can be traced. To ignore this social dimension, to pass over the variety in which any given item of folklore is found in a social group, is unscientific. It is equally unscientific to acknowledge this difficulty and to solve it by simply assuming the variations as non-essential, because that only is non-essential in science which cannot be formulated into general laws.

The manner in which ethnological information about beliefs is usually formulated is somewhat like this: "The natives believe in the existence of seven souls"; or else, "In this tribe we find that the evil spirit kills people in the bush," etc. Yet such statements are undoubtedly false, or at the best incomplete, because no "natives" (in the plural) have ever any belief or any idea; each one has his own ideas and his own beliefs. Moreover, the beliefs and ideas exist not only in the conscious and formulated opinions of the members of a community. They are embodied in social institutions and expressed by native behavior, from both of which they must be, so to speak, extricated. At any rate, it appears clearly that the matter is not as simple as the ethnological usage of "one-dimensional" accounts would imply. The ethnographer gets hold of an informant, and from conversation with him is able to formulate the native's opinion, say, about afterlife. This opinion is written down, the grammatical subject of the sentence put into the plural, and we learn about the "natives believing so-and-so." This is what I call a "one-dimensional" account, as it ignores the social dimensions, along which belief must be studied, just as it ignores its essential complexity and multiplicity.

Of course, very often, though by no means always, this multiplicity may be ignored, and the variations in detail overlooked as unessential, in view of the uniformity which obtains in all essential and main features of a belief. But the matter must be studied, and methodical rules applied to the simplification of the variety, and unification of the multiplicity of facts. Any haphazard proceeding must, obviously, be discarded as unscientific. Yet, as far as I am aware, no attempt has been made by any inquirer in the field, even the most illustrious, to discover and lay down such methodical rules. The following remarks ought, therefore, to be treated indulgently, being only an unaided attempt to suggest certain important connections. They deserve indulgence also on account of being the result of actual ex-

periences and difficulties encountered in the field. If, in the account of beliefs given above, there is a certain lack of uniformity and smoothness; if,
further, the observer's own difficulties are somewhat brought into relief,
this must be excused on the same account. I attempted to show as plainly
as possible the "social dimension" in the domain of belief, not to conceal
the difficulties which result from the variety of native opinions, and also
from the necessity of constantly holding in view both social institutions and
native interpretation, as well as the behavior of the natives; of checking social fact by psychological data, and *vice versa.*

Now let us proceed to lay down the rules which allow us to reduce
the multiplicity of the manifestations of a belief to simpler data. Let us
start with the statement made several times, namely, that the crude data
present almost a chaos of diversity and multiplicity. Examples may be easily found among the material presented in this article, and they will allow
the argument to be clear and concrete. Thus, let us take the beliefs corresponding to the question, "How do the natives imagine the return of the
baloma?" I have actually put this question, adequately formulated, to a
series of informants. The answers were, in the first place, always fragmentary—a native will just tell you one aspect, very often an irrelevant one,
according to what your question has suggested in his mind at the moment.
Nor would an untrained "civilized man" do anything else. Besides being
fragmentary, which could be partially remedied by repeating the question
and using each informant to fill up the gaps, the answers were at times
hopelessly inadequate and contradictory. Inadequate because some informants were unable even to grasp the question, at any rate unable to describe such a complex fact as their own mental attitude, though others were
astonishingly clever, and almost able to understand what the ethnological
inquirer was driving at.

What was I to do? To concoct a kind of "average" opinion? The degree of arbitrariness seemed much too great. Moreover, it was obvious that
the opinions were only a small part of the information available. All the
people, even those who were unable to state what they thought about the
returning *baloma* and how they felt towards them, none the less behaved
in a certain manner towards those *baloma,* conforming to certain customary rules and obeying certain canons of emotional reaction.

Thus, in searching for an answer to the above question—or to any
other question of belief and behavior—I was moved to look for the answer
in the corresponding customs. The distinction between private opinion, information gathered by asking the informants, and public ceremonial practices, had to be laid down as a first principle. As the reader will remember,
a number of dogmatic tenets have been enumerated above, which I have
found expressed in customary traditional acts. Thus the general belief that
the *baloma* return is embodied in the broad fact of the *milamala* itself.
Again, the display of valuables (*ioiova*), the erection of special platforms
(*tokaikaya*), the display of food on the *lalogua*—all this expresses the

presence of the *baloma* in the village, the efforts to please them, to do something for them. The food presents (*silakutuva* and *bubualu'a*) show an even more intimate participation in village life by the *baloma.*

The dreams, which often preceded such offerings, are also customary features, just because they are associated with, and sanctioned by, such customary offerings. They make the communion between the *baloma* and the living, in a way, personal, and certainly more distinct. The reader will be able easily to multiply these examples (connection between belief in Topileta and his fee, and the valuables laid round the body before burial; beliefs embodied in the *ioba,* etc.).

Besides the beliefs expressed in the traditional ceremonies, there are those embodied in magical formulae. These formulae are as definitely fixed by tradition as the customs. If anything, they are more precise as documents than the customs can be, since they do not allow of any variations. Only small fragments of magical formulae have been given above, yet even these serve to exemplify the fact that beliefs can be unmistakably expressed by spells, in which they are embedded. Any formula accompanied by a rite expresses certain concrete, detailed, particular beliefs. Thus, when, in one of the above-named garden rites, the magician puts a tuber on the stone in order to promote the growth of the crops, and the formula which he recites comments on this action and describes it, there are certain beliefs unmistakably documented by it: the belief in the sacredness of the particular grove (here our information is corroborated by the taboos surrounding that grove); the belief in the connection between the tuber put on the sacred stone and the tubers in the garden, etc. There are other, more general, beliefs embodied and expressed in some of the above-mentioned formulae. Thus the general belief in the assistance of ancestral *baloma* is standardized, so to speak, by the spells by which those *baloma* are invoked, and the accompanying rites in which they receive their *ula'ula.*

As mentioned above, some magical spells are based upon certain myths, details of which appear in the formulae. Such myths, and myth in general, must be put side by side with the magical spells as traditional, fixed expressions of belief. As an empirical definition of a myth (again only claiming a validity for the Kiriwinian material) the following criteria can be accepted: it is a tradition explaining essential sociological features (*e.g.,* myths about the division in clans and subclans), referring to persons who performed notable feats, and whose past existence is implicitly believed in. Traces of such existence in various memorial spots are still shown: a dog petrified, some food transformed into stone, a grotto with bones, where the ogre Dokonikan lived, etc. The reality of mythical persons and mythical occurrences stands in vivid contrast to the unreality of ordinary fables, many of which are told.

All beliefs embodied in mythological tradition can be assumed to be almost as invariable as those embodied in magical formulae. In fact, the mythical tradition is extremely well fixed, and accounts given by natives of different places in Kiriwina—natives of Luba and natives of Sinaketa—agreed in all details. Moreover, I obtained an account of certain myths of the Tudava cycle during a short visit to Woodlark Island, which lies some sixty miles to the east of the Trobriands but belongs to the same ethnological group, called by Prof. Seligman the Northern Massim, which agrees in all essential features with the facts obtained in Kiriwina.

Summing up all these considerations, we may say that all beliefs as implied in native customs and tradition must be treated as invariably fixed items. They are believed and acted upon by all, and, as customary actions do not allow of any individual varieties, this class of belief is standardized by its social embodiments. They may be called the dogmas of native belief, or the social ideas of a community, as opposed to individual ideas. One important addition has to be made, however, to complete this statement: only such items of belief can be considered as "social ideas" as are not only embodied in native institutions, but are also explicitly formulated by the natives and acknowledged to exist therein. Thus all the natives will acknowledge the presence of the *baloma* during the *milamala,* their expulsion at the *ioba,* etc. And all the competent ones will give unanimous answers in the interpretation of magical rites, etc. On the other hand, the observer can never safely venture to read his own interpretations into the native customs. Thus, for instance, in the above-mentioned fact, that mourning is always finally discarded immediately after an *ioba,* there seems to be unmistakably expressed the belief that the person waits till the *baloma* of the deceased has gone before giving up the mourning. But the natives do not endorse this interpretation, and therefore it cannot possibly be considered as a social idea, as a standardized belief. The question whether this belief was not originally the reason for the practice belongs to quite a different class of problem, but it is obvious that the two cases must not be confounded; one, where a belief is formulated in a society universally, besides being embodied in institutions; the other, where the belief is ignored, though apparently expressed in an institution.

This allows us to formulate a definition of a "social idea": *It is a tenet of belief embodied in institutions or traditional texts, and formulated by the unanimous opinion of all competent informants.* The word "competent" simply excludes small children and hopelessly unintelligent individuals. Such social ideas can be treated as the "invariants" of native belief.

Besides the social institutions and traditions, both of which embody and standardize belief, there is another important factor, which stands in a somewhat similar relation to belief—I mean the general behavior of the natives towards the object of a belief. Such behavior has been described above as illuminating important aspects of native belief about the *baloma,* the *kosi,* the *mulukuausi,* and as expressing the natives' emotional attitude towards them. This aspect of the question is beyond doubt of extreme importance. To describe the ideas of the natives concerning a ghost or spirit is absolutely insufficient. Such objects of belief arouse pronounced emotional reactions, and one ought to look, in the first place, for the objective facts corresponding to these emotional reactions. The above data concerning this aspect of native belief, insufficient as they are, show clearly that with more experience in method a systematic inquiry could be carried out into the emotional side of belief on lines as strict as ethnological observations admit.

The behavior can be described by putting the natives to certain tests concerning their fear of ghosts, or their respect for spirits, etc. I have to admit that, though realizing the importance of the subject, I did not quite see, whilst in the field, the proper manner to deal with this difficult and new subject. But I now clearly see that, had I been better on the look out for relevant data in this line, I should have been able to present much more convincing and objectively valid data. Thus in the problem of fear my tests were not sufficiently elaborate, and even as they were made, not sufficiently minutely recorded in my notes. Again, though I will remember the tone in which I heard them speaking—rather irreverently—about the *baloma,* I also remember that a few characteristic expressions struck me at the time, which I ought to have noted at once, and did not. Again, watching the behavior of the performers and spectators in a magical ceremony, certain small facts characterizing the general "tone" of the natives' attitude are to be found. Such facts I have observed partly, though, I think, insufficiently (they were only just mentioned in this article when speaking about the *kamkokola* ceremony, as they really do not bear on the subject of spirits or afterlife). The fact is, however, that until this aspect is more generally taken under observation and some comparative material exists, the full development of the method of observation is very difficult.

The emotional attitude expressed in behavior, and characterizing a belief, is not an invariable element: it varies with individuals, and it has no objective "seat" (such as the beliefs embodied in institutions have). Nevertheless, it is expressed by objective facts, which can be almost quantitatively stated, as in measuring the amount of inducement needed and the length of an expedition on which a native will venture alone under fear-inspiring conditions. Now, in each society there are braver and more cowardly individuals, emotional people and callous ones, etc. But divers types of behavior are characteristic for different societies, and it seems enough to state the type, since the variations are well-nigh the same in all societies. Of course, if it be possible to state the variations, so much the better.

To illustrate the matter concretely, by the simplest example, that of fear, I have experimented with this element in another district in Papua— in Mailu, on the south coast—and found that no normal inducement, no offering of even an excessive payment in tobacco, would prevail upon any native to cover at night and alone any distance out of sight and earshot of the village. Even here, however, there were variations, some men and boys being unwilling to run the risk even at dusk, others being ready to go out at night to some inconsiderable distance for a payment of a stick of tobacco. In Kiriwina, as described above, the type of behavior is absolutely different. But here again some people are much more timorous than others. Perhaps these variations could be expressed more exactly, but I am not in the position to do it, and at any rate the type of behavior characterizes the corresponding beliefs, when compared with the Mailu type, for instance.

It seems feasible, therefore, as the first approach to exactness, to treat elements of belief expressed by behavior as types; that is, not to trouble about the individual variation. In fact, the types of behavior seem to vary considerably with the society, whereas the individual differences seem to cover the same range. This does not mean that they ought to be ignored, but that, in the first approach, they may be ignored without making the information incorrect through incompleteness.

Let us pass now to the last class of material which must be studied in order to grasp the beliefs of a certain community—the individual opinions or interpretations of facts. These cannot be considered as invariable, nor are they sufficiently described by indicating their "type." Behavior, referring to the emotional aspect of belief, can be described by showing its type, because the variations move within certain well-described limits, the emotional and instinctive nature of man being as far as one can judge, very uniform, and the individual variations remaining practically the same in any human society. In the domain of the purely intellectual aspect of belief, in the ideas and opinions explaining belief, there is room for the greatest range of variations. Belief, of course, does not obey the laws of logic, and the contradictions, divergencies, and all the general chaos pertaining to belief must be acknowledged as a fundamental fact.

One important simplification in this chaos is obtained by referring the variety of individual opinions to the social structure. In almost every domain of belief there is a class of men whose social position entitles them to a special knowledge of the beliefs in question. In a given community they are generally and officially considered to be the possessors of the orthodox version, and their opinion is considered the correct one. Their opinion, moreover, is to a considerable extent based on a traditional view which they have received from their ancestors.

This state of things is, in Kiriwina, very well exemplified in the tradition of magic and of the connected myths. Although there is as little esoteric lore and tradition, and as little taboo and secrecy, as in any native society which I know from experience or literature, nevertheless there is complete respect for a man's right to his own domain. If you ask in any village any question referring to more detailed magical proceedings in the gardening department, your interlocutor will immediately refer you to the *towosi* (garden magician). And then on further inquiry you learn, as often as not, that your first informant knew all the facts absolutely well and was perhaps able to explain them better than the specialist himself. None the less, native etiquette, and the feeling of what is right, compelled him to refer you to the "proper person." If this proper person be present, you will not be able to induce anyone else to talk on the matter, even if you announce that you do not want to hear the specialist's opinion. And, again, I have several times obtained information from one of my usual instructors and subsequently the "specialist" has told me that it is not correct. When, later, I referred this correction to my original informant, he would, as a rule, withdraw his opinion saying, "Well, if he says so, it must be correct." Special caution ought of course to be exercised when the specialist is naturally inclined to lie, as is often the case with the sorcerers (those who possess the power to kill people by magic).

Again, if the magic and corresponding tradition belong to another village, the same discretion and reserve is observed. You are advised to go to that village for information. When pressed, your native friends may perhaps tell you what they know about the matter, but they will always wind up the report by saying: "You must go there and gather the right knowledge at the right source." In the case of magic formulae, this is absolutely necessary. Thus I had to go to Laba'i in order to get the *kalala*-fishing magic, and to Kuaibola to record the shark-fishing charms. I obtained the canoe-building magic from men of Lu'ebila, and I went to Buai-talu to get the tradition and spell of the *toginivaiu,* the most powerful form of sorcery, though I was unable to procure the *silami* or evil spell and was only partially successful in getting the *vivisa* or healing spell. Even if the knowledge to be obtained is not spells, but mere traditional lore, one is often sorely disappointed. Thus, for instance, the proper seat of the Tudava myth is Laba'i. Before I went there I had gathered all that my informants in Omarakana could tell me and expected to reap an enormous harvest of additional information, but as a matter of fact, it was I who impressed the natives of Laba'i, by quoting details which were hailed by them as quite true, but which had escaped their memory. In fact, no one there was half as good on the Tudava cyclus as my friend Bagido'u of Omarakana. Again, the village of Ialaka is the historic spot where once a tree was erected up to heaven. And this was the origin of thunder. If you ask about the nature of thunder, everybody will tell you straight off: "Go to Ialaka and ask the *tolivalu* (the headman)," although practically everybody is able to tell you all about the origin and nature of thunder, and your pilgrimage to Ialaka, if you undertake it, will prove a great disappointment.

Nevertheless, these facts show that the idea of specialization in traditional lore is strongly developed; that in many items of belief, and in many opinions about belief, the natives recognize a class of specialist. Some of these are associated with a certain locality; in such cases it is always the headman of the village who represents the orthodox doctrine, or else the most intelligent of his *veiola* (maternal kinsmen). In other cases the specialization goes within the village community. In this place we are not concerned with this specialization, in so far as it determines the right to obtain magical formulae, or the correct reciting of certain myths, but only in so

far as it refers to the interpretation of all beliefs connected with such formulae or myths. Because, besides the traditional text, the "specialists" are
always in possession of the traditional interpretations or commentaries. It
is characteristic that, when talking with such specialists, you always get
clearer answers and opinions. You clearly see that the man does not speculate or give you his own views, but that he is fully aware of being asked
about the orthodox view, about the traditional interpretation. Thus when I
asked certain informants about the meaning of the *"si buala baloma,"* the
miniature hut made of dry twigs during one of the garden rites, they tried
to give me a kind of explanation, which I saw at once, was their own private
view of the matter. When I asked Bagido'u, the *towosi* (garden magician)
himself, he simply waved away all explanations and said, "This is merely
an old traditional thing, no one knows its meaning."

Thus in the diversity of opinions there is one important line of de-
marcation to be drawn: that between the opinions of competent specialists
and the views of the profane public. The opinions of the specialists have
a traditional basis: they are clearly and categorically formulated and, in
the eyes of the native, they represent the orthodox version of the belief.
And, since on each subject there is a small group of people, in the last
instance one man, to be considered, it is easy to see that the most important interpretation of belief does not present any great difficulties in handling.

But in the first place, this most important interpretation does not
represent all the views, it cannot be taken even as typical, at times. Thus
for instance, in sorcery (evil, homicidal magic), it is of absolute importance
to distinguish between the views of the specialist and those of the outsider, because both represent equally important and naturally different
aspects of the same problem. Again, there are certain classes of belief
where one would in vain look for departmental specialists. Thus about the
nature of the *baloma* and their relation to the *kosi,* there were some statements more trustworthy and detailed than others, but there was no one
who would be a naturally and generally acknowledged authority.

In all matters where there are no specialists, and again in matters in
which the opinion of non-specialists is of intrinsic interest, it is necessary
to have certain rules for fixing the fluctuating opinion of the community.
Here I see only one clear and important distinction: namely, between
what can be called public opinion, or more correctly—since public opinion has a specific meaning—the general opinion of a given community on
the one hand, and the private speculations of individuals on the other. This
distinction is, as far as I can see, sufficient.

If you examine the "broad masses" of the community, the women
and children included (a proceeding which is easy enough when you speak
the language well and have lived for months in the same village, but which
otherwise is impossible), you will find that, whenever they grasp your

question, their answers will not vary: they will never venture into private speculations. I have had most valuable information on several points from boys and even girls of seven to twelve years of age. Very often, on my long afternoon walks, I was accompanied by the children of the village and then, without the constraint of being obliged to sit and be attentive, they would talk and explain things with a surprising lucidity and knowledge of tribal matters. In fact, I was often able to unravel sociological difficulties with the help of children, which old men could not explain to me. The mental volubility, lack of the slightest suspicion and sophistication, and, possibly a certain amount of training received in the Mission School, made of them incomparable informants in many matters. As to the danger of their views being modified by missionary teaching, well, I can only say that I was amazed at the absolute impermeability of the native mind to those things. The very small amount of our creed and ideas they acquire remains in a watertight compartment of their mind. Thus the general tribal opinion in which practically no variety is to be found can be ascertained even from the humblest informants.

When dealing with intelligent grown-up informants, things are quite different. And as they are the class with whom an ethnographer has to do most of his work, the variety of their opinion comes very much to the fore, unless the inquirer is satisfied in taking one version of each subject and sticking to it through thick and thin. Such opinions of intelligent, mentally enterprising informants, as far as I can see, cannot be reduced or simplified according to any principles: they are important documents, illustrating the mental faculties of a community. Further on, they very often represent certain typical ways of conceiving a belief, or of solving a difficulty. But it must be clearly borne in mind that such opinions are sociologically quite different from what we called above dogmas or social ideas. They are also different from generally accepted or popular ideas. They form a class of interpretation of belief, which closely corresponds to our free speculation on belief. They are characterized by their variety, by not being expressed in customary or traditional formulae, by being neither the orthodox expert opinion, nor the popular view.

These theoretical considerations about the sociology of belief may be summarized in the following table, in which the various groups of belief are classified in a manner which seems to express their natural affinities and distinctions, as far, at least, as the Kiriwinian material requires:—

1. *Social ideas or dogmas.*—Beliefs embodied in institutions, in customs, in magico-religious formulae and rites and in myths. Essentially connected with and characterized by emotional elements, expressed in behavior.
2. *Theology or interpretation of the dogmas.*—
   (*a*) Orthodox explanations, consisting of opinions of specialists.

> (b) Popular, general views, formulated by the majority of the members of a community.
>
> (c) Individual speculations.

Examples for each group can be easily found in this article, where the degree and quality of social depth, the "social dimension" of every item of belief, has been given, at least approximately. It must be remembered that this theoretical scheme, though dimly recognized at the beginning, has been only imperfectly applied, because the technique of its applicability in field work had to be elaborated bit by bit, through actual experience. It is, therefore, with reference to my Kiriwinian material, rather a conclusion *ex post facto* than a basis of method adopted at the outset and systematically carried out throughout the work.

Examples of dogma or social ideas are to be found in all the beliefs, which have been described as embodied in the customs of the *milamala* and in the magical rites and formulae. Also in corresponding myths, as well as in the mythological tradition, referring to afterlife. The emotional aspect has been treated, as far as my knowledge allows, in describing the behavior of the natives towards magical performances during the *milamala*, their behavior towards the *baloma,* the *kosi,* and the *mulukuausi.*

Of the theological views, several orthodox interpretations have been given in the explanations by a magician of his magic. As popular views (barring such as are dogmas at the same time) I may note the belief concerning spiritism: everybody, even the children, knew well that certain people went to Tuma and brought back songs and messages to the living. This, however, was in no way a dogma, since it was even open to scepticism on the part of some exceptionally sophisticated informants, and since it was connected with no customary institution.

The speculations about the nature of the *baloma* are the best example illustrating the purely individual class of theology, consisting of private opinions.

I wish to remind the reader that local differences, that is the variation of belief according to district, have not been considered at all in this theoretical section. Such differences belong to the domain of anthropogeography rather than sociology. Moreover, they affect only to a very small extent the data presented in this paper, as practically all of my material has been collected within a small district, where local variations hardly exist at all. Only as regards the reincarnation, local differences may account for some divergencies in belief.

From such district variations the above-mentioned localized specialization in certain departments (thunder in Ialaka, shark in Kuaibuola, etc.) must be carefully distinguished, because this is a factor connected with the structure of society and not merely an example of the broad anthropological fact, that everything changes as we move over the surface of the earth.

All these theoretical remarks, it is plain, are the outcome of experience in the field, and it was considered well to print them here in connection with the data already given, because they are also ethnological facts, only of a much more general nature. This, however, makes them, if anything, more important than the details of custom and belief. Only the two aspects, the general law and the detailed documentation, make information really complete, as far as it goes.

QUESTIONS FOR DISCUSSION

1) Like the other social sciences, anthropology seeks to study and interpret the special characteristics of a society. This article is particularly interesting in that it not only discusses the Kiriwinians and their beliefs, but discusses "the general sociological laws that have to be grasped and framed in the field" for the study of such groups. Give a brief description of Malinowski's techniques of study in the field, as you can infer them from this article.

2) Discuss Malinowski's feelings about what constitutes "facts" and "interpretations" (or "generalizations"). Is one more important than the other? How do they operate together, according to Malinowski? Are Malinowski's views on "facts" and "interpretations" similar to those expressed by Carr in the preceding essay? Explain.

3) Malinowski was faced in his work with "crude data" which presented "almost a chaos of diversity and multiplicity." In his attempts to understand this material, to order and record it, how different or similar was he to, say, a writer or a painter, creatively ordering his materials?

WHAT IS A SOCIAL FACT?

Émile Durkheim

Before inquiring into the method suited to the study of social facts, it is important to know which facts are commonly called "social." This information is all the more necessary since the designation "social" is used with little precision. It is currently employed for practically all phenomena generally diffused within society, however small their social interest. But on that basis, there are, as it were, no human events that may not be called social. Each individual drinks, sleeps, eats, reasons; and it is to society's interest that these functions be exercised in an orderly manner. If, then, all these facts are counted as "social" facts, sociology would have no subject matter exclusively its own, and its domain would be confused with that of biology and psychology.

But in reality there is in every society a certain group of phenomena which may be differentiated from those studied by the other natural sciences. When I fulfil my obligations as brother, husband, or citizen, when I execute my contracts, I perform duties which are defined, externally to myself and my acts, in law and in custom. Even if they conform to my own sentiments and I feel their reality subjectively, such reality is still objective, for I did not create them; I merely inherited them through my education. How many times it happens, moreover, that we are ignorant of the details of the obligations incumbent upon us, and that in order to acquaint ourselves with them we must consult the law and its authorized interpreters! Similarly, the church-member finds the beliefs and practices of his religious life ready-made at birth; their existence prior to his own implies their existence outside of himself. The system of signs I use to express my thought, the system of currency I employ to pay my debts, the instruments of credit I utilize in my commercial relations, the practices followed in my profession, etc., function independently of my own use of them. And these statements can be repeated for each member of society. Here, then, are ways of acting, thinking, and feeling that present the noteworthy property of existing outside the individual consciousness.

These types of conduct or thought are not only external to the individual but are, moreover, endowed with coercive power by virtue of which they impose themselves upon him, independent of his individual will. Of course, when I fully consent and conform to them, this constraint is felt only slightly, if at all, and is therefore unnecessary. But it is, nonetheless, an intrinsic characteristic of these facts, the proof thereof being that it asserts itself as soon as I attempt to resist it. If I attempt to violate the law, it reacts against me so as to prevent my act before its accomplishment, or to nullify my violation by restoring the damage, if it is accomplished and reparable, or to make me expiate it if it cannot be compensated for otherwise.

In the case of purely moral maxims, the public conscience exercises a check on every act which offends it by means of the surveillance it exercises over the conduct of citizens, and the appropriate penalties at its disposal. In many cases the constraint is less violent, but nevertheless it always exists. If I do not submit to the conventions of society, if in my dress I do not conform to the customs observed in my country and in my class, the ridicule I provoke, the social isolation in which I am kept, produce, although in an attenuated form, the same effects as a punishment in the strict sense of the word. The constraint is nonetheless efficacious for being indirect. I am not obliged to speak French with my fellow-countrymen nor to use the legal currency, but I cannot possibly do otherwise. If I tried to escape this necessity, my attempt would fail miserably. As an industrialist, I am free to apply the technical methods of former centuries; but by doing so, I should invite certain ruin. Even when I free myself from these rules and violate them successfully, I am always compelled to struggle with them. When finally overcome, they make their constraining power sufficiently felt by the resistance they offer. The enterprises of all innovators, including successful ones, come up against resistance of this kind.

Here, then, is a category of facts with very distinctive characteristics: it consists of ways of acting, thinking, and feeling, external to the individual, and endowed with a power of coercion, by reason of which they control him. These ways of thinking could not be confused with biological phenomena, since they consist of representations and of actions; nor with psychological phenomena, which exist only in the individual consciousness and through it. They constitute, thus, a new variety of phenomena; and it is to them exclusively that the term "social" ought to be applied. And this term fits them quite well, for it is clear that, since their source is not in the individual, their substratum can be no other than society, either the political society as a whole or some one of the partial groups it includes, such as religious denominations, political, literary, and occupational associations, etc. On the other hand, this term "social" applies to them exclusively, for it has a distinct meaning only if it designates exclusively the phenomena which are not included in any of the categories of facts that have already been established and classified. These ways of thinking and acting therefore constitute the proper domain of sociology. It is true that, when we define them with this word "constraint," we risk shocking the zealous partisans of absolute individualism. For those who profess the complete autonomy of the individual, man's dignity is diminished whenever he is made to feel that he is not completely self-determinant. It is generally accepted today, however, that most of our ideas and our tendencies are not developed by ourselves but come to us from without. How can they become a part of us except by imposing themselves upon us? This is the whole meaning of our definition. And it is generally accepted, moreover, that social constraint is not necessarily incompatible with the individual personality.

Since the examples that we have just cited (legal and moral regulations, religious faiths, financial systems, etc.) all consist of established beliefs and practices, one might be led to believe that social facts exist only where there is some social organization. But there are other facts without such crystallized form which have the same objectivity and the same ascendency over the individual. These are called "social currents." Thus the great movements of enthusiasm, indignation, and pity in a crowd do not originate in any one of the particular individual consciousnesses. They come to each one of us from without and can carry us away in spite of ourselves. Of course, it may happen that, in abandoning myself to them unreservedly, I do not feel the pressure they exert upon me. But it is revealed as soon as I try to resist them. Let an individual attempt to oppose one of these collective manifestations, and the emotions that he denies will turn against him. Now, if this power of external coercion asserts itself so clearly in cases of resistance, it must exist also in the first-mentioned cases, although we are unconscious of it. We are then victims of the illusion of having ourselves created that which actually forced itself from without. If the complacency with which we permit ourselves to be carried along conceals the pressure undergone, nevertheless it does not abolish it. Thus, air is no less heavy because we do not detect its weight. So, even if we ourselves have spontaneously contributed to the production of the common emotion, the impression we have received differs markedly from that which we would have experienced if we had been alone. Also, once the crowd has dispersed, that is, once these social influences have ceased to act upon us and we are alone again, the emotions which have passed through the mind appear strange to us, and we no longer recognize them as ours. We realize that these feelings have been impressed upon us to a much greater extent than they were created by us. It may even happen that they horrify us, so much were they contrary to our nature. Thus, a group of individuals, most of whom are perfectly inoffensive, may, when gathered in a crowd, be drawn into acts of atrocity. And what we say of these transitory outbursts applies similarly to those more permanent currents of opinion on religious, political, literary, or artistic matters which are constantly being formed around us, whether in society as a whole or in more limited circles.

To confirm this definition of the social fact by a characteristic illustration from common experience, one need only observe the manner in which children are brought up. Considering the facts as they are and as they have always been, it becomes immediately evident that all education is a continuous effort to impose on the child ways of seeing, feeling, and acting which he could not have arrived at spontaneously. From the very first hours of his life, we compel him to eat, drink, and sleep at regular hours; we constrain him to cleanliness, calmness, and obedience; later we exert pressure upon him in order that he may learn proper consideration for others, respect for customs and conventions, the need for work, etc. If, in time, this constraint ceases to be felt, it is because it gradually gives rise to habits and to internal tendencies that render constraint unnecessary; but nevertheless it is not abolished, for it is still the source from which these habits were derived. It is true that, according to Spencer, a rational education ought to reject such methods, allowing the child to act in complete liberty; but as this pedagogic theory has never been applied by any known people, it must be accepted only as an expression of personal opinion, not as a fact which can contradict the aforementioned observations. What makes these facts particularly instructive is that the aim of education is, precisely, the socialization of the human being; the process of education, therefore, gives us in a nutshell the historical fashion in which the social being is constituted. This unremitting pressure to which the child is subjected is the very pressure of the social milieu which tends to fashion him in its own image, and of which parents and teachers are merely the representatives and intermediaries.

It follows that sociological phenomena cannot be defined by their universality. A thought which we find in every individual consciousness, a movement repeated by all individuals, is not thereby a social fact. If sociologists have been satisfied with defining them by this characteristic, it is because they confused them with what one might call their reincarnation in the individual. It is, however, the collective aspects of the beliefs, tendencies, and practices of a group that characterize truly social phenomena. As for the forms that the collective states assume when refracted in the individual, these are things of another sort. This duality is clearly demonstrated by the fact that these two orders of phenomena are frequently found dissociated from one another. Indeed, certain of these social manners of acting and thinking acquire, by reason of their repetition, a certain rigidity which on its own account crystallizes them, so to speak, and isolates them from the particular events which reflect them. They thus acquire a body, a tangible form, and constitute a reality in their own right, quite distinct from the individual facts which produce it. Collective habits are inherent not only in the successive acts which they determine but, by a privilege of which we find no example in the biological realm, they are given permanent expression in a formula which is repeated from mouth to mouth, transmitted by education, and fixed even in writing. Such is the origin and nature of legal and moral rules, popular aphorisms and proverbs, articles of faith wherein religious or political groups condense their beliefs, standards of taste established by literary schools, etc. None of these can be found entirely reproduced in the applications made of them by individuals since they can exist even without being actually applied.

No doubt, this dissociation does not always manifest itself with equal distinctness, but its obvious existence in the important and numerous cases just cited is sufficient to prove that the social fact is a thing distinct from its individual manifestations. Moreover, even when this dissociation is not immediately apparent, it may often be disclosed by certain devices of method. Such dissociation is indispensable if one wishes to separate social facts from their alloys in order to observe them in a state of purity. Currents of opinion, with an intensity varying according to the time and place, impel certain groups either to more marriages, for example, or to more suicides, or to a higher or lower birthrate, etc. These currents are plainly social facts. At first sight they seem inseparable from the forms they take in individual cases. But statistics furnish us with the means of isolating them. They are, in fact, represented with considerable exactness by the rates of births, marriages, and suicides, that is, by the number obtained by dividing the average annual total of marriages, births, suicides, by the number of persons whose ages lie within the range in which marriages, births, and suicides occur. Since each of these figures contains all the individual cases indiscriminately, the individual circumstances which may have had a share in the production of the phenomenon are neutralized and, consequently, do not contribute to its determination. The average, then, expresses a certain state of the group mind [l'âme collective].

Such are social phenomena, when disentangled from all foreign matter. As for their individual manifestations, these are indeed, to a certain extent, social, since they partly reproduce a social model. Each of them also depends, and to a large extent, on the organopsychological constitution of the individual and on the particular circumstances in which he is placed. Thus they are not sociological phenomena in the strict sense of the word. They belong to two realms at once; one could call them sociopsychological. They interest the sociologist without constituting the immediate subject matter of sociology. There exist in the interior of organisms similar phenomena, compound in their nature, which form in their turn the subject matter of the "hybrid sciences," such as physiological chemistry, for example.

The objection may be raised that a phenomenon is collective only if it is common to all members of society, or at least to most of them—in other words, if it is truly general. This may be true; but it is general because it is collective (that is, more or less obligatory), and certainly not collective because general. It is a group condition repeated in the individual because imposed on him. It is to be found in each part because it exists in the whole, rather than in the whole because it exists in the parts. This becomes conspicuously evident in those beliefs and practices which are transmitted to us ready-made by previous generations; we receive and adopt them because, being both collective and ancient, they are invested with a particular authority that education has taught us to recognize and respect. It is, of course, true that a vast portion of our social culture is transmitted to us in this way; but even when the social fact is due in part to our direct collaboration, its nature is not different. A collective emotion which bursts forth suddenly and violently in a crowd does not express merely what all the individual sentiments had in common; it is something entirely different, as we have shown. It results from their being together, a product of the actions and reactions which take place between individual consciousnesses; and if each individual consciousness echoes the collective sentiment, it is by virtue of the special energy resident in its collective origin. If all hearts beat in unison, this is not the result of a spontaneous and pre-established harmony but rather because an identical force propels them in the same direction. Each is carried along by all.

We thus arrive at the point where we can formulate and delimit in a precise way the domain of sociology. It comprises only a limited group of phenomena. A social fact is to be recognized by the power of external coercion which it exercises or is capable of exercising over individuals, and the presence of this power may be recognized in its turn either by the existence of some specific sanction or by the resistance offered against every individual effort that tends to violate it. One can, however, define it also by its diffusion. This last criterion is perhaps, in certain cases, easier to apply than the preceding one. In fact, the constraint is easy to ascertain when it expresses itself externally by some direct reaction of society, as is the case in law, morals, beliefs, customs, and even fashions. But when it is only indirect, like the constraint which an economic organization exercises, it cannot always be so easily detected. Generality combined with externality may, then, be easier to establish. Moreover, this second definition is but another form of the first; for if a mode of behavior whose existence is external to individual consciousnesses becomes general, this can only be brought about by its being imposed upon them.

But these several phenomena present the same characteristic by which we defined the others. These "ways of existing" are imposed on the individual precisely in the same fashion as the "ways of acting" of which we have spoken. Indeed, when we wish to know how a society is divided politically, of what these divisions themselves are composed, and how complete is the fusion existing between them, we shall not achieve our purpose by physical inspection and by geographical observations; for these phenomena are social, even when they have some basis in physical nature. It is only by a study of public law that a comprehension of this organization is possible, for it is this law that determines the organization, as it equally determines our domestic and civil relations. This political organization is, then, no less obligatory than the social facts mentioned above. If the population crowds into our cities instead of scattering into the country, this is due to a trend of public opinion, a collective drive that imposes this concentration upon the individuals. We can no more choose the style of our houses than of our clothing—at least, both are equally obligatory. The channels of communication prescribe the direction of internal migrations and commerce, etc., and even their extent. Consequently, at the very most, it should be necessary to add to the list of phenomena which we have enumerated as presenting the distinctive criterion of a social fact only one additional category, "ways of existing"; and, as this enumeration was not meant to be rigorously exhaustive, the addition would not be absolutely necessary.

Such an addition is perhaps not necessary, for these "ways of existing" are only crystallized "ways of acting." The political structure of a society is merely the way in which its component segments have become accustomed to live with one another. If their relations are traditionally intimate, the segments tend to fuse with one another, or, in the contrary case, to retain their identity. The type of habitation imposed upon us is merely the way in which our contemporaries and our ancestors have been accustomed to construct their houses. The methods of communication are merely the channels which the regular currents of commerce and migrations have dug, by flowing in the same direction. To be sure, if the phenomena of a structural character alone presented this permanence, one might believe that they constituted a distinct species. A legal regulation is an arrangement no less permanent than a type of architecture, and yet the regulation is a "physiological" fact. A simple moral maxim is assuredly somewhat more malleable, but it is much more rigid than a simple professional custom or a fashion. There is thus a whole series of degrees without a break in continuity between the facts of the most articulated structure and those free currents of social life which are not yet definitely molded. The differences between them are, therefore, only differences in the degree of consolidation they present. Both are simply life, more or less crystallized. No doubt, it may be of some advantage to reserve the term "morphological" for those social facts which concern the social substratum, but only on condition of not overlooking the fact that they are of the same nature as the others. Our definition will then include the whole relevant range of facts if we say: A social fact is every way of acting, fixed or not, capable of exercising on the individual an external constraint; or again, every way of acting which is general throughout a given society, while at the same time existing in its own right independent of its individual manifestations.

QUESTIONS FOR DISCUSSION

1) What, briefly, is a "social fact," according to Durkheim? What gives such facts their "power of coercion"?

2) How does Durkheim differentiate between sociology and biology, and between sociology and psychology? Why is sociology as "scientific" as biology and psychology?

3) Durkheim says that the "constraint" of social facts—their power over us to make us conform to them—may prove "shocking" to "zealous partisans of absolute individualism." But, Durkheim argues, "social constraint is not necessarily incompatible with the individual personality." Do you agree? Discuss. Is "social constraint" also a factor in creativity? Explain.

4) Compare and contrast the views of Carr (p. 216), Malinowski (p. 233), and Durkheim on "facts."

from

INVISIBLE MAN

Ralph Ellison

It goes a long way back, some twenty years. All my life I had been look-ing for something, and everywhere I turned someone tried to tell me what it was. I accepted their answers too, though they were often in contradic-tion and even self-contradictory. I was naïve. I was looking for myself and asking everyone except myself questions which I, and only I, could answer. It took me a long time and much painful boomeranging of my expectations to achieve a realization everyone else appears to have been born with: That I am nobody but myself. But first I had to discover that I am an invisible man!

And yet I am no freak of nature, nor of history. I was in the cards, other things having been equal (or unequal) eighty-five years ago. I am not ashamed of my grandparents for having been slaves. I am only ashamed of myself for having at one time been ashamed. About eighty-five years ago they were told that they were free, united with others of our country in everything pertaining to the common good, and, in everything social, separate like the fingers of the hand. And they believed it. They exulted in it. They stayed in their place, worked hard, and brought up my father to do the same. But my grandfather is the one. He was an odd old guy, my grandfather, and I am told I take after him. It was he who caused the trouble. On his deathbed he called my father to him and said, "Son, after I'm gone I want you to keep up the good fight. I never told you, but our life is a war and I have been a traitor all my born days, a spy in the enemy's country ever since I give up my gun back in the Reconstruction. Live with your head in the lion's mouth. I want you to overcome 'em with yeses, undermine 'em with grins, agree 'em to death and destruction, let 'em swoller you till they vomit or bust wide open." They thought the old man had gone out of his mind. He had been the meekest of men. The younger children were rushed from the room, the shades drawn and the flame of the lamp turned so low that it sputtered on the wick like the old man's breathing. "Learn it to the younguns," he whispered fiercely; then he died.

But my folks were more alarmed over his last words than over his dying. It was as though he had not died at all, his words caused so much anxiety. I was warned emphatically to forget what he had said and, indeed, this is the first time it has been mentioned outside the family circle. It had a tremendous effect upon me, however. I could never be sure of what he meant. Grandfather had been a quiet old man who never made any trouble, yet on his deathbed he had called himself a traitor and a spy, and he had spoken of his meekness as a dangerous activity. It became a constant puzzle which lay unanswered in the back of my mind. And whenever things went well for me I remembered my grandfather and felt guilty and uncomfortable. It was as though I was carrying out his advice in spite of myself. And to make it worse, everyone loved me for it. I was praised by the most lily-white men of the town. I was considered an example of desirable conduct—just as my grandfather had been. And what puzzled me was that the old man had defined it as *treachery*. When I was praised for my conduct I felt a guilt that in some way I was doing something that was really against the wishes of the white folks, that if they had understood they would have desired me to act just the opposite, that I should have been sulky and mean, and that that really would have been what they wanted, even though they were fooled and thought they wanted me to act as I did. It made me afraid that some day they would look upon me as a traitor and I would be lost. Still I was more afraid to act any other way because they didn't like that at all. The old man's words were like a curse. On my graduation day I delivered an oration in which I showed that humility was the secret, indeed, the very essence of progress. (Not that I believed this—how could I, remembering my grandfather?—I only believed that it worked.) It was a great success. Everyone praised me and I was invited to give the speech at a gathering of the town's leading white citizens. It was a triumph for our whole community.

It was in the main ballroom of the leading hotel. When I got there I discovered that it was on the occasion of a smoker, and I was told that since I was to be there anyway I might as well take part in the battle royal to be fought by some of my schoolmates as part of the entertainment. The battle royal came first.

All of the town's big shots were there in their tuxedoes, wolfing down the buffet foods, drinking beer and whiskey and smoking black cigars. It was a large room with a high ceiling. Chairs were arranged in neat rows around three sides of a portable boxing ring. The fourth side was clear, revealing a gleaming space of polished floor. I had some misgivings over the battle royal, by the way. Not from a distaste for fighting, but because I didn't care too much for the other fellows who were to take part. They were tough guys who seemed to have no grandfather's curse worrying their minds. No one could mistake their toughness. And besides, I suspected that fighting a battle royal might detract from the dignity of my speech. In those pre-invisible days I visualized myself as a potential Booker T. Washington. But the other fellows didn't care too much for me either, and there were nine of them. I felt superior to them in my way, and I didn't like the manner in which we were all crowded together into the servants' elevator. Nor did they like my being there. In fact, as the warmly lighted floors flashed past the elevator we had words over the fact that I, by taking part in the fight, had knocked one of their friends out of a night's work.

We were led out of the elevator through a rococo hall into an ante-room and told to get into our fighting togs. Each of us was issued a pair of boxing gloves and ushered out into the big mirrored hall, which we entered looking cautiously about us and whispering, lest we might accidentally be heard above the noise of the room. It was foggy with cigar smoke. And already the whiskey was taking effect. I was shocked to see some of the most important men of the town quite tipsy. They were all there—bankers, lawyers, judges, doctors, fire chiefs, teachers, merchants. Even one of the more fashionable pastors. Something we could not see was going on up front. A clarinet was vibrating sensuously and the men were standing up and moving eagerly forward. We were a small tight group, clustered to-gether, our bare upper bodies touching and shining with anticipatory sweat; while up front the big shots were becoming increasingly excited over some-thing we still could not see. Suddenly I heard the school superintendent, who had told me to come, yell, "Bring up the shines, gentlemen! Bring up the little shines!"

We were rushed up to the front of the ballroom, where it smelled even more strongly of tobacco and whiskey. Then we were pushed into place. I almost wet my pants. A sea of faces, some hostile, some amused, ringed around us, and in the center, facing us, stood a magnificent blonde —stark naked. There was dead silence. I felt a blast of cold air chill me. I tried to back away, but they were behind me and around me. Some of the boys stood with lowered heads, trembling. I felt a wave of irrational guilt and fear. My teeth chattered, my skin turned to goose flesh, my knees knocked. Yet I was strongly attracted and looked in spite of myself. Had the price of looking been blindness, I would have looked. The hair was yellow like that of a circus kewpie doll, the face heavily powdered and rouged, as though to form an abstract mask, the eyes hollow and smeared a cool blue, the color of a baboon's butt. I felt a desire to spit upon her as my eyes brushed slowly over her body. Her breasts were firm and round as the domes of East Indian temples, and I stood so close as to see the fine skin texture and beads of pearly perspiration glistening like dew around the pink and erected buds of her nipples. I wanted at one and the same time to run from the room, to sink through the floor, or go to her and cover her from my eyes and the eyes of the others with my body; to feel the soft thighs, to caress her and destroy her, to love her and murder her, to hide from her, and yet to stroke where below the small American flag tattooed upon her belly her thighs formed a capital V. I had a notion that of all in the room she saw only me with her impersonal eyes.

And then she began to dance, a slow sensuous movement; the smoke of a hundred cigars clinging to her like the thinnest of veils. She seemed like a fair bird-girl girdled in veils calling to me from the angry surface of some gray and threatening sea. I was transported. Then I became aware of the clarinet playing and the big shots yelling at us. Some threatened us if we looked and others if we did not. On my right I saw one boy faint. And now a man grabbed a silver pitcher from a table and stepped close as he dashed ice water upon him and stood him up and forced two of us to support him as his head hung and moans issued from his thick bluish lips. Another boy began to plead to go home. He was the largest of the group, wearing dark red fighting trunks much too small to conceal the erection which projected from him as though in answer to the insinuating low-registered moaning of the clarinet. He tried to hide himself with his boxing gloves.

And all the while the blonde continued dancing, smiling faintly at the big shots who watched her with fascination, and faintly smiling at our fear. I noticed a certain merchant who followed her hungrily, his lips loose and drooling. He was a large man who wore diamond studs in a shirtfront which swelled with the ample paunch underneath, and each time the blonde swayed her undulating hips he ran his hand through the thin hair of his bald head and, with his arms upheld, his posture clumsy like that of an intoxicated panda, wound his belly in a slow and obscene grind. This creature was completely hypnotized. The music had quickened. As the dancer flung herself about with a detached expression on her face, the men began reaching out to touch her. I could see their beefy fingers sink into the soft flesh. Some of the others tried to stop them and she began to move around the floor in graceful circles, as they gave chase, slipping and sliding over the polished floor. It was mad. Chairs went crashing, drinks were spilt, as they ran laughing and howling after her. They caught her just as she reached a door, raised her from the floor, and tossed her as college boys are tossed at a hazing, and above her red, fixed-smiling lips I saw the terror and disgust in her eyes, almost like my own terror and that which I saw in some of the other boys. As I watched, they tossed her twice and her soft breasts seemed to flatten against the air and her legs flung wildly as she spun. Some of the more sober ones helped her to escape. And I started off the floor, heading for the anteroom with the rest of the boys.

Some were still crying and in hysteria. But as we tried to leave we were stopped and ordered to get into the ring. There was nothing to do but what we were told. All ten of us climbed under the ropes and allowed ourselves to be blindfolded with broad bands of white cloth. One of the men seemed to feel a bit sympathetic and tried to cheer us up as we stood with our backs against the ropes. Some of us tried to grin. "See that boy over there?" one of the men said. "I want you to run across at the bell and give it to him right in the belly. If you don't get him, I'm going to get you. I don't like his looks." Each of us was told the same. The blindfolds were put on. Yet even then I had been going over my speech. In my mind each word was as bright as flame. I felt the cloth pressed into place, and frowned so that it would be loosened when I relaxed.

But now I felt a sudden fit of blind terror. I was unused to darkness. It was as though I had suddenly found myself in a dark room filled with poisonous cottonmouths. I could hear the bleary voices yelling insistently for the battle royal to begin.

"Get going in there!"

"Let me at that big nigger!"

I strained to pick up the school superintendent's voice, as though to squeeze some security out of that slightly more familiar sound.

"Let me at those black sonsabitches!" someone yelled.

"No, Jackson, no!" another voice yelled. "Here, somebody, help me hold Jack."

"I want to get at that ginger-colored nigger. Tear him limb from limb," the first voice yelled.

I stood against the ropes trembling. For in those days I was what they called ginger-colored, and he sounded as though he might crunch me between his teeth like a crisp ginger cookie.

Quite a struggle was going on. Chairs were being kicked about and I could hear voices grunting as with a terrific effort. I wanted to see, to see more desperately than ever before. But the blindfold was as tight as a thick skin-puckering scab and when I raised my gloved hands to push the layers of white aside a voice yelled, "Oh, no you don't, black bastard! Leave that alone!"

"Ring the bell before Jackson kills him a coon!" someone boomed in the sudden silence. And I heard the bell clang and the sound of the feet scuffling forward.

A glove smacked against my head. I pivoted, striking out stiffly as someone went past, and felt the jar ripple along the length of my arm to my shoulder. Then it seemed as though all nine of the boys had turned upon me at once. Blows pounded me from all sides while I struck out as best I could. So many blows landed upon me that I wondered if I were not the only blindfolded fighter in the ring, or if the man called Jackson hadn't succeeded in getting me after all.

Blindfolded, I could no longer control my motions. I had no dignity. I stumbled about like a baby or a drunken man. The smoke had become thicker and with each new blow it seemed to sear and further restrict my lungs. My saliva became like hot bitter glue. A glove connected with my head, filling my mouth with warm blood. It was everywhere. I could not tell if the moisture I felt upon my body was sweat or blood. A blow landed hard against the nape of my neck. I felt myself going over, my head hitting the floor. Streaks of blue light filled the black world behind the blindfold. I lay prone, pretending that I was knocked out, but felt myself seized by hands and yanked to my feet. "Get going, black boy! Mix it up!" My arms were like lead, my head smarting from blows. I managed to feel my way to the ropes and held on, trying to catch my breath. A glove landed in my mid-section and I went over again, feeling as though the smoke had become a knife jabbed into my guts. Pushed this way and that by the legs milling around me, I finally pulled erect and discovered that I could see the black, sweat-washed forms weaving in the smoky-blue atmosphere like drunken dancers weaving to the rapid drum-like thuds of blows.

Everyone fought hysterically. It was complete anarchy. Everybody fought everybody else. No group fought together for long. Two, three, four, fought one, then turned to fight each other, were themselves attacked. Blows landed below the belt and in the kidney, with the gloves open as well as closed, and with my eye partly opened now there was not so much terror. I moved carefully, avoiding blows, although not too many to attract attention, fighting from group to group. The boys groped about like blind, cautious crabs crouching to protect their mid-sections, their heads pulled in short against their shoulders, their arms stretched nervously before them, with their fists testing the smoke-filled air like the knobbed feelers of hyper-sensitive snails. In one corner I glimpsed a boy violently punching the air and heard him scream in pain as he smashed his hand against a ring post. For a second I saw him bent over holding his hand, then going down as a blow caught his unprotected head. I played one group against the other, slipping in and throwing a punch then stepping out of range while pushing the others into the melee to take the blows blindly aimed at me. The smoke was agonizing and there were no rounds, no bells at three minute intervals to relieve our exhaustion. The room spun round me, a swirl of lights, smoke, sweating bodies surrounded by tense white faces. I bled from both nose and mouth, the blood spattering upon my chest.

The men kept yelling, "Slug him, black boy! Knock his guts out!"

"Uppercut him! Kill him! Kill that big boy!"

Taking a fake fall, I saw a boy going down heavily beside me as though we were felled by a single blow, saw a sneaker-clad foot shoot into his groin as the two who had knocked him down stumbled upon him. I rolled out of range, feeling a twinge of nausea.

The harder we fought the more threatening the men became. And yet, I had begun to worry about my speech again. How would it go? Would they recognize my ability? What would they give me?

I was fighting automatically when suddenly I noticed that one after another of the boys was leaving the ring. I was surprised, filled with panic, as though I had been left alone with an unknown danger. Then I understood. The boys had arranged it among themselves. It was the custom for the two men left in the ring to slug it out for the winner's prize. I discovered this too late. When the bell sounded two men in tuxedoes leaped into the ring and removed the blindfold. I found myself facing Tatlock, the biggest of the gang. I felt sick at my stomach. Hardly had the bell stopped ringing in my ears than it clanged again and I saw him moving swiftly toward me. Thinking of nothing else to do I hit him smash on the nose. He kept coming, bringing the rank sharp violence of stale sweat. His face was a black blank of a face, only his eyes alive—with hate of me and aglow with a feverish terror from what had happened to us all. I became anxious. I wanted to deliver my speech and he came at me as though he meant to beat it out of me. I smashed him again and again, taking his blows as they came. Then on a sudden impulse I struck him lightly and as we clinched, I whispered, "Fake like I knocked you out, you can have the prize."

"I'll break your behind," he whispered hoarsely.

"For *them?*"

"For *me,* sonofabitch!"

They were yelling for us to break it up and Tatlock spun me half around with a blow, and as a joggled camera sweeps in a reeling scene, I saw the howling red faces crouching tense beneath the cloud of blue-gray smoke. For a moment the world wavered, unraveled, flowed, then my head cleared and Tatlock bounced before me. That fluttering shadow before my eyes was his jabbing left hand. Then falling forward, my head against his damp shoulder, I whispered,

"I'll make it five dollars more."

"Go to hell!"

But his muscles relaxed a trifle beneath my pressure and I breathed, "Seven?"

"Give it to your ma," he said, ripping me beneath the heart.

And while I still held him I butted him and moved away. I felt myself bombarded with punches. I fought back with hopeless desperation. I wanted to deliver my speech more than anything else in the world, because I felt that only these men could judge truly my ability, and now this stupid clown was ruining my chances. I began fighting carefully now, moving in to punch him and out again with my greater speed. A lucky blow to his chin and I had him going too—until I heard a loud voice yell, "I got my money on the big boy."

Hearing this, I almost dropped my guard. I was confused: Should I try to win against the voice out there? Would not this go against my speech, and was not this a moment for humility, for nonresistance? A blow to my head as I danced about sent my right eye popping like a jack-in-the-box and settled my dilemma. The room went red as I fell. It was a dream fall, my body languid and fastidious as to where to land, until the floor became impatient and smashed up to meet me. A moment later I came to. An hypnotic voice said FIVE emphatically. And I lay there, hazily watching a dark red spot of my own blood shaping itself into a butterfly, glistening and soaking into the soiled gray world of the canvas.

When the voice drawled TEN I was lifted up and dragged to a chair. I sat dazed. My eye pained and swelled with each throb of my pounding heart and I wondered if now I would be allowed to speak. I was wringing wet, my mouth still bleeding. We were grouped along the wall now. The other boys ignored me as they congratulated Tatlock and speculated as to how much they would be paid. One boy whimpered over his smashed hand. Looking up front, I saw attendants in white jackets rolling the portable ring away and placing a small square rug in the vacant space surrounded by chairs. Perhaps, I thought, I will stand on the rug to deliver my speech.

Then the M.C. called to us, "Come on up here boys and get your money."

We ran forward to where the men laughed and talked in their chairs, waiting. Everyone seemed friendly now.

"There it is on the rug," the man said. I saw the rug covered with coins of all dimensions and a few crumpled bills. But what excited me, scattered here and there, were the gold pieces.

"Boys, it's all yours," the man said. "You get all you grab."

"That's right, Sambo," a blond man said, winking at me confidentially.

I trembled with excitement, forgetting my pain. I would get the gold and the bills, I thought. I would use both hands. I would throw my body against the boys nearest me to block them from the gold.

"Get down around the rug now," the man commanded, "and don't anyone touch it until I give the signal."

"This ought to be good," I heard.

As told, we got around the square rug on our knees. Slowly the man raised his freckled hand as we followed it upward with our eyes.

I heard, "These niggers look like they're about to pray!"

Then, "Ready," the man said. "Go!"

I lunged for a yellow coin lying on the blue design of the carpet, touching it and sending a surprised shriek to join those rising around me. I tried frantically to remove my hand but could not let go. A hot, violent force tore through my body, shaking me like a wet rat. The rug was electrified. The hair bristled up on my head as I shook myself free. My muscles jumped, my nerves jangled, writhed. But I saw that this was not stopping the other boys. Laughing in fear and embarrassment, some were holding back and scooping up the coins knocked off by the painful contortions of the others. The men roared above us as we struggled.

"Pick it up, goddamnit, pick it up!" someone called like a bass-voiced parrot. "Go on, get it!"

I crawled rapidly around the floor, picking up the coins, trying to avoid the coppers and to get greenbacks and the gold. Ignoring the shock by laughing, as I brushed the coins off quickly, I discovered that I could contain the electricity—a contradiction, but it works. Then the men began to push us onto the rug. Laughing embarrassedly, we struggled out of their hands and kept after the coins. We were all wet and slippery and hard to hold. Suddenly I saw a boy lifted into the air, glistening with sweat like a circus seal, and dropped, his wet back landing flush upon the charged rug, heard him yell and saw him literally dance upon his back, his elbows beating a frenzied tattoo upon the floor, his muscles twitching like the flesh of a horse stung by many flies. When he finally rolled off, his face was gray and no one stopped him when he ran from the floor amid booming laughter.

"Get the money," the M.C. called. "That's good hard American cash!"

And we snatched and grabbed, snatched and grabbed. I was careful not to come too close to the rug now, and when I felt the hot whiskey breath descend upon me like a cloud of foul air I reached out and grabbed the leg of a chair. It was occupied and I held on desperately.

"Leggo, nigger! Leggo!"

The huge face wavered down to mine as he tried to push me free. But my body was slippery and he was too drunk. It was Mr. Colcord, who owned a chain of movie houses and "entertainment palaces." Each time he grabbed me I slipped out of his hands. It became a real struggle. I feared the rug more than I did the drunk, so I held on, surprising myself for a moment by trying to topple *him* upon the rug. It was such an enormous idea that I found myself actually carrying it out. I tried not to be obvious, yet when I grabbed his leg, trying to tumble him out of the chair, he raised up roaring with laughter, and, looking at me with soberness dead in the eye, kicked me viciously in the chest. The chair leg flew out of my hand and I felt myself going and rolled. It was as though I had rolled through a bed of hot coals. It seemed a whole century would pass before I would roll free, a century in which I was seared through the deepest levels of my body to the fearful breath within me and the breath seared and heated to the point of explosion. It'll all be over in a flash, I thought as I rolled clear. It'll all be over in a flash.

But not yet, the men on the other side were waiting, red faces swollen as though from apoplexy as they bent forward in their chairs. Seeing their fingers coming toward me I rolled away as a fumbled football rolls off the receiver's fingertips, back into the coals. That time I luckily sent the rug sliding out of place and heard the coins ringing against the floor and the boys scuffling to pick them up and the M.C. calling, "All right, boys, that's all. Go get dressed and get your money."

I was limp as a dish rag. My back felt as though it had been beaten with wires.

When we had dressed the M.C. came in and gave us each five dollars, except Tatlock, who got ten for being last in the ring. Then he told us to leave. I was not to get a chance to deliver my speech, I thought. I was going out into the dim alley in despair when I was stopped and told to go back. I returned to the ballroom, where the men were pushing back their chairs and gathering in groups to talk.

The M.C. knocked on a table for quiet. "Gentlemen," he said, "we almost forgot an important part of the program. A most serious part, gentlemen. This boy was brought here to deliver a speech which he made at his graduation yesterday . . ."

"Bravo!"

"I'm told that he is the smartest boy we've got out there in Green-
wood. I'm told that he knows more big words than a pocket-sized
dictionary."

Much applause and laughter.

"So now, gentlemen, I want you to give him your attention."

There was still laughter as I faced them, my mouth dry, my eye
throbbing. I began slowly, but evidently my throat was tense, because
they began shouting, "Louder! Louder!"

"We of the younger generation extol the wisdom of that great leader
and educator," I shouted, "who first spoke these flaming words of wisdom:
'A ship lost at sea for many days suddenly sighted a friendly vessel. From
the mast of the unfortunate vessel was seen a signal: "Water, water; we
die of thirst!" The answer from the friendly vessel came back: "Cast
down your bucket where you are." The captain of the distressed vessel,
at last heeding the injunction, cast down his bucket, and it came up full of
fresh sparkling water from the mouth of the Amazon River.' And like him
I say, and in his words, 'To those of my race who depend upon bettering
their condition in a foreign land, or who underestimate the importance of
cultivating friendly relations with the Southern white man, who is his next-
door neighbor, I would say: "Cast down your bucket where you are"—
cast it down in making friends in every manly way of the people of all
races by whom we are surrounded . . .' "

I spoke automatically and with such fervor that I did not realize that
the men were still talking and laughing until my dry mouth, filling up with
blood from the cut, almost strangled me. I coughed, wanting to stop and go
to one of the tall brass, sand-filled spittoons to relieve myself, but a few of
the men, especially the superintendent, were listening and I was afraid. So I
gulped it down, blood, saliva and all, and continued. (What powers of
endurance I had during those days! What enthusiasm! What a belief in the
rightness of things!) I spoke even louder in spite of the pain. But still
they talked and still they laughed, as though deaf with cotton in dirty ears.
So I spoke with greater emotional emphasis. I closed my ears and swal-
lowed blood until I was nauseated. The speech seemed a hundred times as
long as before, but I could not leave out a single word. All had to be said,
each memorized nuance considered, rendered. Nor was that all. Whenever
I uttered a word of three or more syllables a group of voices would yell
for me to repeat it. I used the phrase "social responsibility" and they yelled:

"What's that word you say, boy?"

"Social responsibility," I said.

"What?"

"Social . . ."

"Louder."

". . . responsibility."

"More!"

"Respon—"

"Repeat!"

"—sibility."

The room filled with the uproar of laughter until, no doubt, distracted by having to gulp down my blood, I made a mistake and yelled a phrase I had often seen denounced in newspaper editorials, heard debated in private.

"Social . . ."

"What?" they yelled.

". . . equality—"

The laughter hung smokelike in the sudden stillness. I opened my eyes, puzzled. Sounds of displeasure filled the room. The M.C. rushed forward. They shouted hostile phrases at me. But I did not understand.

A small dry mustached man in the front row blared out, "Say that slowly, son!"

"What sir?"

"What you just said!"

"Social responsibility, sir," I said.

"You weren't being smart, were you, boy?" he said, not unkindly.

"No, sir!"

"You sure that about 'equality' was a mistake?"

"Oh, yes, sir," I said. "I was swallowing blood."

"Well, you had better speak more slowly so we can understand. We mean to do right by you, but you've got to know your place at all times. All right, now, go on with your speech."

I was afraid. I wanted to leave but I wanted also to speak and I was afraid they'd snatch me down.

"Thank you, sir," I said, beginning where I had left off, and having them ignore me as before.

Yet when I finished there was a thunderous applause. I was surprised to see the superintendent come forth with a package wrapped in white tissue paper, and, gesturing for quiet, address the men.

"Gentlemen, you see that I did not overpraise this boy. He makes a good speech and some day he'll lead his people in the proper paths. And I don't have to tell you that that is important in these days and times. This is a good, smart boy, and so to encourage him in the right direction, in the name of the Board of Education I wish to present him a prize in the form of this . . ."

He paused, removing the tissue paper and revealing a gleaming calf-skin brief case.

". . . in the form of this first-class article from Shad Whitmore's shop."

"Boy," he said, addressing me, "take this prize and keep it well. Consider it a badge of office. Prize it. Keep developing as you are and some day it will be filled with important papers that will help shape the destiny of your people."

I was so moved that I could hardly express my thanks. A rope of bloody saliva forming a shape like an undiscovered continent drooled upon the leather and I wiped it quickly away. I felt an importance that I had never dreamed.

"Open it and see what's inside," I was told.

My fingers a-tremble, I complied, smelling the fresh leather and finding an official-looking document inside. It was a scholarship to the state college for Negroes. My eyes filled with tears and I ran awkwardly off the floor.

I was overjoyed; I did not even mind when I discovered that the gold pieces I had scrambled for were brass pocket tokens advertising a certain make of automobile.

When I reached home everyone was excited. Next day the neighbors came to congratulate me. I even felt safe from grandfather, whose deathbed curse usually spoiled my triumphs. I stood beneath his photograph with my brief case in hand and smiled triumphantly into his stolid black peasant's face. It was a face that fascinated me. The eyes seemed to follow everywhere I went.

That night I dreamed I was at a circus with him and that he refused to laugh at the clowns no matter what they did. Then later he told me to open my brief case and read what was inside and I did, finding an official envelope stamped with the state seal; and inside the envelope I found another and another, endlessly, and I thought I would fall of weariness. "Them's years," he said. "Now open that one." And I did and in it I found an engraved document containing a short message in letters of gold. "Read it," my grandfather said. "Out loud."

"To Whom It May Concern," I intoned. "Keep This Nigger-Boy Running."

I awoke with the old man's laughter ringing in my ears.

(It was a dream I was to remember and dream again for many years after. But at that time I had no insight into its meaning. First I had to attend college.)

QUESTIONS FOR DISCUSSION

1) Writers are often among the foremost social analysts. Black writers, for example, have generally described as schizophrenic the state that white society pushes blacks towards. What evidence of this condition is contained in this excerpt from Ellison's novel?

2) Ellison relies heavily upon symbolism to communicate meaning in his novel. Discuss the significance of the symbols in this excerpt, particularly the dance of the blonde, the flag tattooed on her belly, the brass tokens, the hero's dream

at the end, and the free-for-all boxing match. Why are all the events of the evening ritualistic?

3) Why does the hero give his speech even though he has been tortured by his audience? What image does he have of himself? Why does his grandfather's death-bed speech haunt him in his dreams that night?

4) Why can it be said that the action of this excerpt demonstrates the fact that creativity sometimes brings heavy penalties along with its rewards?

VI. THE REVOLUTIONARY

Revolutionaries usually receive their greatest honors after they are dead. Perhaps they have been thinkers, and time is needed for the impact of their writings or sayings to become felt. Or their activities have been confined to a small area, and the world does not hear of them until later. Or, very often, angry forces of reaction will have made martyrs of them to be revered by later generations. For it is in the nature of their profession that revolutionaries must encounter resistance during their own lifetimes. They provide the leadership when the slow pace of human adaptation has lagged too far behind changing circumstances, and violent adjustment of governments, philosophies, economies, and societies is needed. And all who benefit from the status quo, with the help of many who think they do, will resist the proposed changes as long and as hard as they can. Thus revolutions are often bloody, and many more of them fail than succeed. We live in a time when new revolutions may be starting to brew. A minority of as yet uncertain size and strength clamors loudly for radical change. Would-be leaders are emerging who hope to guide this minority with new ideas and programs. We can only hope that these new leaders will be more creative than violent. Our society stands to gain from their ideas and their visions.

THE APOLOGY
OF SOCRATES*

Plato

How you, O Athenians, have been affected by my accusers, I cannot tell; but I know that they almost made me forget who I was—so persuasively did they speak; and yet they have hardly uttered a word of truth. But of the many falsehoods told by them, there was one which quite amazed me; —I mean when they said that you should be upon your guard and not allow yourselves to be deceived by the force of my eloquence. To say this, when they were certain to be detected as soon as I opened my lips and proved myself to be anything but a great speaker, did indeed appear to me most shameless—unless by the force of eloquence they mean the force of truth; for if such is their meaning, I admit that I am eloquent. But in how different a way from theirs! Well, as I was saying, they have scarcely spoken the truth at all; but from me you shall hear the whole truth: not, however, delivered after their manner in a set oration duly ornamented with words and phrases. No, by heaven! but I shall use the words and arguments which occur to me at the moment; for I am confident in the justice of my cause: at my time of life I ought not to be appearing before you, O men of Athens, in the character of a juvenile orator—let no one expect it of me. And I must beg of you to grant me a favour:—If I defend myself in my accustomed manner, and you hear me using the words which I have been in the habit of using in the agora, at the tables of the money-changers, or anywhere else, I would ask you not to be surprised, and not to interrupt me on this account. For I am more than seventy years of age, and appearing now for the first time in a court of law, I am quite a stranger to the language of the place; and therefore I would have you regard me as if I were really a stranger, whom you would excuse if he spoke in his native tongue, and after the fashion of his country:—Am I making an unfair request of you? Never mind the manner, which may or may not be good; but think only of the truth of my words, and give heed to that: let the speaker speak truly and the judge decide justly.

And first, I have to reply to the older charges and to my first accusers, and then I will go on to the later ones. For of old I have had many accusers, who have accused me falsely to you during many years; and I am more afraid of them than of Anytus and his associates, who are dangerous, too, in their own way. But far more dangerous are the others, who

* Translated by Benjamin Jowett.

began when you were children, and took possession of your minds with their falsehoods, telling of one Socrates, a wise man, who speculated about the heaven above, and searched into the earth beneath, and made the worse appear the better cause. The disseminators of this tale are the accusers whom I dread; for their hearers are apt to fancy that such enquirers do not believe in the existence of the gods. And they are many, and their charges against me are of ancient date, and they were made by them in the days when you were more impressible than you are now—in childhood, or it may have been in youth—and the cause when heard went by default, for there was none to answer. And hardest of all, I do not know and cannot tell the names of my accusers; unless in the chance case of a Comic poet. All who from envy and malice have persuaded you—some of them having first convinced themselves—all this class of men are most difficult to deal with; for I cannot have them up here, and cross-examine them, and therefore I must simply fight with shadows in my own defence, and argue when there is no one who answers. I will ask you then to assume with me, as I was saying, that my opponents are of two kinds; one recent, the other ancient: and I hope that you will see the propriety of my answering the latter first, for these accusations you heard long before the others, and much oftener.

Well, then, I must make my defence, and endeavor to clear away in a short time, a slander which has lasted a long time. May I succeed, if to succeed be for my good and yours, or likely to avail me in my cause! The task is not an easy one; I quite understand the nature of it. And so leaving the event with God, in obedience to the law I will now make my defence.

I will begin at the beginning, and ask what is the accusation which has given rise to the slander of me, and in fact has encouraged Meletus to prefer this charge against me. Well, what do the slanderers say? They shall be my prosecutors, and I will sum up their words in an affidavit: 'Socrates is an evil-doer, and a curious person, who searches into things under the earth and in heaven, and he makes the worse appear the better cause; and he teaches the aforesaid doctrines to others.' Such is the nature of the accusation: it is just what you have yourselves seen in the comedy of Aristophanes, who has introduced a man whom he calls Socrates, going about and saying that he walks in air, and talking a deal of nonsense concerning matters of which I do not pretend to know either much or little— not that I mean to speak disparagingly of any one who is a student of natural philosophy. I should be very sorry if Meletus could bring so grave a charge against me. But the simple truth is, O Athenians, that I have nothing to do with physical speculations. Very many of those here present are witnesses to the truth of this, and to them I appeal. Speak then, you who have heard me, and tell your neighbours whether any of you have ever known me hold forth in few words or in many upon such matters. . . . You hear their answer. And from what they say of this part of the charge you will be able to judge of the truth of the rest.

As little foundation is there for the report that I am a teacher, and take money; this accusation has no more truth in it than the other. Although, if a man were really able to instruct mankind, to receive money for giving instruction would, in my opinion, be an honour to him. There is Gorgias of Leontium, and Prodicus of Ceos, and Hippias of Elis, who go the round of the cities, and are able to persuade the young men to leave their own citizens by whom they might be taught for nothing, and come to them whom they not only pay, but are thankful if they may be allowed to pay them. There is at this time a Parian philosopher residing in Athens, of whom I have heard; and I came to hear of him in this way:—I came across a man who has spent a world of money on the Sophists, Callias, the son of Hipponicus, and knowing that he had sons, I asked him: 'Callias,' I said, 'if your two sons were foals or calves, there would be no difficulty in finding some one to put over them; we should hire a trainer of horses, or a farmer probably, who would improve and perfect them in their own proper virtue and excellence; but as they are human beings, whom are you thinking of placing over them? Is there any one who understands human and political virtue? You must have thought about the matter, for you have sons; is there any one?' 'There is,' he said. 'Who is he?' said I; 'and of what country? and what does he charge?' 'Evenus the Parian,' he replied; 'he is the man, and his charge is five minae.' Happy is Evenus, I said to myself; if he really has this wisdom, and teaches at such a moderate charge. Had I the same, I should have been very proud and conceited; but the truth is that I have no knowledge of the kind.

I dare say, Athenians, that some one among you will reply, 'Yes, Socrates, but what is the origin of these accusations which are brought against you; there must have been something strange which you have been doing? All these rumours and this talk about you would never have arisen if you had been like other men: tell us, then, what is the cause of them, for we should be sorry to judge hastily of you.' Now I regard this as a fair challenge, and I will endeavour to explain to you the reason why I am called wise and have such an evil fame. Please to attend then. And although some of you may think that I am joking, I declare that I will tell you the entire truth. Men of Athens, this reputation of mine has come of a certain sort of wisdom which I possess. If you ask me what kind of wisdom, I reply, wisdom such as may perhaps be attained by man, for to that extent I am inclined to believe that I am wise; whereas the persons of whom I was speaking have a superhuman wisdom, which I may fail to describe, because I have it not myself; and he who says that I have, speaks falsely, and is taking away my character. And here, O men of Athens, I must beg you not to interrupt me, even if I seem to say something extravagant. For the word which I will speak is not mine. I will refer you to a witness who is worthy of credit; that witness shall be the God of Delphi— he will tell you about my wisdom, if I have any, and of what sort it is. You must have known Chaerephon; he was early a friend of mine, and also a friend of yours, for he shared in the recent exile of the people, and returned with you. Well, Chaerephon, as you know, was very impetuous in all his doings, and he went to Delphi and boldly asked the oracle to tell him whether—as I was saying, I must beg you not to interrupt—he asked the oracle to tell him whether any one was wiser than I was, and the Pythian prophetess answered, that there was no man wiser. Chaerephon is dead himself; but his brother, who is in court, will confirm the truth of what I am saying.

Why do I mention this? Because I am going to explain to you why I have such an evil name. When I heard the answer, I said to myself, What can the god mean? and what is the interpretation of his riddle? for I know that I have no wisdom, small or great. What then can he mean when he says that I am the wisest of men? And yet he is a god, and cannot lie; that would be against his nature. After long consideration, I thought of a method of trying the question. I reflected that if I could only find a man wiser than myself, then I might go to the god with a refutation in my hand. I should say to him, 'Here is a man who is wiser than I am; but you said that I was the wisest.' Accordingly I went to one who had the reputation of wisdom, and observed him—his name I need not mention; he was a politician whom I selected for examination—and the result was as follows: When I began to talk with him, I could not help thinking that he was not really wise, although he was thought wise by many, and still wiser by himself; and thereupon I tried to explain to him that he thought himself wise, but was not really wise; and the consequence was that he hated me, and his enmity was shared by several who were present and heard me. So I left him, saying to myself, as I went away: Well, although I do not suppose that either of us knows anything really beautiful and good, I am better off than he is,—for he knows nothing, and thinks that he knows; I neither know nor think that I know. In this latter particular, then, I seem to have slightly the advantage of him. Then I went to another who had still higher pretensions to wisdom, and my conclusion was exactly the same. Whereupon I made another enemy of him, and of many others besides him.

Then I went to one man after another, being not unconscious of the enmity which I provoked, and I lamented and feared this: But necessity was laid upon me,—the word of God, I thought, ought to be considered first. And I said to myself, Go I must to all who appear to know, and find out the meaning of the oracle. And I swear to you, Athenians, by the dog I swear!—for I must tell you the truth—the result of my mission was just this: I found that the men most in repute were all but the most foolish; and that others less esteemed were really wiser and better. I will tell you the tale of my wanderings and of the 'Herculean' labours, as I may call them, which I endured only to find at last the oracle irrefutable. After the politicians, I went to the poets; tragic, dithyrambic, and all sorts. And there, I said to myself, you will be instantly detected; now you will find out that you are more ignorant than they are. Accordingly, I took them some of the most elaborate passages in their own writings, and asked what was the meaning of them—thinking that they would teach me something. Will you believe me? I am almost ashamed to confess the truth, but I must say that there is hardly a person present who would not have talked better about their poetry than they did themselves. Then I knew that not by wisdom do poets write poetry, but by a sort of genius and inspiration; they are like diviners or soothsayers who also say many fine things, but do not understand the meaning of them. The poets appeared to me to be much in the same case; and I further observed that upon the strength of their poetry they believed themselves to be the wisest of men in other things in which they were not wise. So I departed, conceiving myself to be superior to them for the same reason that I was superior to the politicians.

At last I went to the artisans, for I was conscious that I knew nothing at all, as I may say, and I was sure that they knew many fine things; and here I was not mistaken, for they did know many things of which I was ignorant, and in this they certainly were wiser than I was. But I observed that even the good artisans fell into the same error as the poets;—because they were good workmen they thought that they also knew all sorts of high matters, and this defect in them overshadowed their wisdom; and therefore I asked myself on behalf of the oracle, whether I would like to be as I was, neither having their knowledge nor their ignorance, or like them in both; and I made answer to myself and to the oracle that I was better off as I was.

This inquisition has led to my having many enemies of the worst and most dangerous kind, and has given occasion also to many calumnies. And I am called wise, for my hearers always imagine that I myself possess the wisdom which I find wanting in others: but the truth is, O men of Athens, that God only is wise; and by his answer he intends to show that the wisdom of men is worth little or nothing; he is not speaking of Socrates, he is only using my name by way of illustration, as if he said, He, O men, is the wisest, who, like Socrates, knows that his wisdom is in truth worth nothing. And so I go about the world, obedient to the god, and search and make enquiry into the wisdom of any one, whether citizen or stranger, who appears to be wise; and if he is not wise, then in vindication of the oracle I show him that he is not wise; and my occupation quite absorbs me, and I have no time to give either to any public matter of interest or to any concern of my own, but I am in utter poverty by reason of my devotion to the god.

There is another thing:—young men of the richer classes, who have not much to do, come about me of their own accord; they like to hear the pretenders examined, and they often imitate me, and proceed to examine others; there are plenty of persons, as they quickly discover, who think that they know something, but really know little or nothing; and then those who are examined by them instead of being angry with themselves are angry with me: This confounded Socrates, they say; this villainous mis-leader of youth!—and then if somebody asks them, Why, what evil does he practice or teach? they do not know, and cannot tell; but in order that they may not appear to be at a loss, they repeat the ready-made charges which are used against all philosophers about teaching things up in the clouds and under the earth, and having no gods, and making the worse appear the better cause; for they do not like to confess that their pretence of knowledge has been detected—which is the truth; and as they are numerous and ambitious and energetic, and are drawn up in battle array and have persuasive tongues, they have filled your ears with their loud and inveterate calumnies. And this is the reason why my three accusers, Mele-tus and Anytus and Lycon, have set upon me; Meletus, who has a quarrel with me on behalf of the poets; Anytus, on behalf of the craftsmen and politicians; Lycon, on behalf of the rhetoricians: and as I said at the be-ginning, I cannot expect to get rid of such a mass of calumny all in a moment. And this, O men of Athens, is the truth and the whole truth; I have concealed nothing, I have dissembled nothing. And yet, I know that my plainness of speech makes them hate me, and what is their hatred but a proof that I am speaking the truth?—Hence has arisen the prejudice against me; and this is the reason of it, as you will find out either in this or in any future enquiry.

I have said enough in my defence against the first class of my accusers; I turn to the second class. They are headed by Meletus, that good man and true lover of his country, as he calls himself. Against these, too, I must try to make a defence:—Let their affidavit be read: it contains something of this kind: It says that Socrates is a doer of evil, who corrupts the youth; and who does not believe in the gods of the state, but has other new divinities of his own. Such is the charge; and now let us examine the particular counts. He says that I am a doer of evil, and corrupt the youth; but I say, O men of Athens, that Meletus is a doer of evil, in that he pretends to be in earnest when he is only in jest, and is so eager to bring men to trial from a pretended zeal and interest about matters in which he really never had the smallest interest. And the truth of this I will endeavour to prove to you.

Come hither, Meletus, and let me ask a question of you. You think a great deal about the improvement of youth?

Yes, I do.

Tell the judges, then, who is their improver; for you must know, as you have taken the pains to discover their corrupter, and are citing and accusing me before them. Speak, then, and tell the judges who their im-prover is.—Observe, Meletus, that you are silent, and have nothing to say. But is not this rather disgraceful, and a very considerable proof of what I was saying, that you have no interest in the matter? Speak up, friend, and tell us who their improver is.

The laws.

But that, my good sir, is not my meaning. I want to know who the person is, who, in the first place, knows the laws.

The judges, Socrates, who are present in court.

What, do you mean to say, Meletus, that they are able to instruct and improve youth?

Certainly they are.

What, all of them, or some only and not others?

All of them.

By the goddess Herè, that is good news! There are plenty of improvers, then. And what do you say of the audience,—do they improve them?

Yes, they do.

And the senators?

Yes, the senators improve them.

But perhaps the members of the assembly corrupt them?—or do they too improve them?

They improve them.

Then every Athenian improves and elevates them; all with the exception of myself; and I alone am their corrupter? Is that what you affirm?

That is what I stoutly affirm.

I am very unfortunate if you are right. But suppose I ask you a question: How about horses? Does one man do them harm and all the world good? Is not the exact opposite the truth? One man is able to do them good, or at least not many;—the trainer of horses, that is to say, does them good, and others who have to do with them rather injure them? Is not that true, Meletus, of horses, or any other animals? Most assuredly it is; whether you and Anytus say yes or no. Happy indeed would be the condition of youth if they had one corrupter only, and all the rest of the world were their improvers. But you, Meletus, have sufficiently shown that you never had a thought about the young: your carelessness is seen in your not caring about the very things which you bring against me.

And now, Meletus, I will ask you another question—by Zeus I will: Which is better, to live among bad citizens, or among good ones? Answer, friend, I say; the question is one which may be easily answered. Do not the good do their neighbours good, and the bad do them evil?

Certainly.

And is there any one who would rather be injured than benefited by those who live with him? Answer, my good friend, the law requires you to answer—does any one like to be injured?

Certainly not.

And when you accuse me of corrupting and deteriorating the youth, do you allege that I corrupt them intentionally or unintentionally?

Intentionally, I say.

But you have just admitted that the good do their neighbours good, and evil do them evil. Now, is that a truth which your superior wisdom has recognized thus early in life, and am I, at my age, in such darkness and ignorance as not to know that if a man with whom I have to live is corrupted by me, I am very likely to be harmed by him; and yet I corrupt him, and intentionally, too—so you say, although neither I nor any other human being is ever likely to be convinced by you. But either I do not corrupt them, or I corrupt them unintentionally; and on either view of the case you lie. If my offence is unintentional, the law has no cognizance of unintentional offences; you ought to have taken me privately, and warned and admonished me; for if I had been better advised, I should have left off doing what I only did unintentionally—no doubt I should; but you would have nothing to say to me and refused to teach me. And now you bring me up in this court, which is not a place of instruction, but of punishment.

It will be very clear to you, Athenians, as I was saying, that Meletus has no care at all, great or small, about the matter. But still I should like to know, Meletus, in what I am affirmed to corrupt the young. I suppose you mean, as I infer from your indictment, that I teach them not to acknowledge the gods which the state acknowledges, but some other new divinities or spiritual agencies in their stead. These are the lessons by which I corrupt the youth, as you say.

Yes, that I say emphatically.

Then, by the gods, Meletus, of whom we are speaking, tell me and the court, in somewhat plainer terms, what you mean! for I do not as yet understand whether you affirm that I teach other men to acknowledge some gods, and therefore that I do believe in gods, and am not an entire atheist—this you do not lay to my charge,—but only you say that they are not the same gods which the city recognizes—the charge is that they are different gods. Or, do you mean that I am an atheist simply, and a teacher of atheism?

I mean the latter—that you are a complete atheist.

What an extraordinary statement! Why do you think so, Meletus? Do you mean that I do not believe in the godhead of the sun or moon, like other men?

I assure you, judges, that he does not: for he says that the sun is stone, and the moon earth.

Friend Meletus, you think that you are accusing Anaxagoras: and you have but a bad opinion of the judges, if you fancy them illiterate to such a degree as not to know that these doctrines are found in the books of Anaxagoras the Clazomenian, which are full of them. And so, forsooth, the youth are said to be taught them by Socrates, when there are not unfrequently exhibitions of them at the theatre (price of admission one drachma at the most); and they might pay their money, and laugh at Socrates if he pretends to father these extraordinary views. And so, Meletus, you really think that I do not believe in any god?

I swear by Zeus that you believe absolutely in none at all.

Nobody will believe you, Meletus, and I am pretty sure that you do not believe yourself. I cannot help thinking, men of Athens, that Meletus is reckless and impudent, and that he has written this indictment in a spirit of mere wantonness and youthful bravado. Has he not compounded a riddle, thinking to try me? He said to himself:—I shall see whether the wise Socrates will discover my facetious contradiction, or whether I shall be able to deceive him and the rest of them. For he certainly does appear to me to contradict himself in the indictment as much as if he said that Socrates is guilty of not believing in the gods, and yet of believing in them— but this is not like a person who is in earnest.

I should like you, O men of Athens, to join me in examining what I conceive to be his inconsistency; and do you, Meletus, answer. And I must remind the audience of my request that they would not make a disturbance if I speak in my accustomed manner:

Did ever man, Meletus, believe in the existence of human things, and not of human beings? . . . I wish, men of Athens, that he would answer, and not be always trying to get up an interruption. Did ever any man believe in horsemanship, and not in horses? or in flute-playing, and not in flute-players? No, my friend; I will answer to you and to the court, as you refuse to answer for yourself. There is no man who ever did. But now please to answer the next question: Can a man believe in spiritual and divine agencies, and not in spirits or demigods?

He cannot.

How lucky I am to have extracted that answer, by the assistance of the court! But then you swear in the indictment that I teach and believe in divine or spiritual agencies (new or old, no matter for that); at any rate, I believe in spiritual agencies,—so you say and swear in the affidavit; and yet if I believe in divine beings, how can I help believing in spirits or demigods;—must I not? To be sure I must; and therefore I may assume that your silence gives consent. Now what are spirits or demigods? are they not either gods or the sons of gods?

Certainly they are.

But this is what I call the facetious riddle invented by you: the demigods or spirits are gods, and you say first that I do not believe in gods, and then again that I do believe in gods; that is, if I believe in demigods. For if the demigods are the illegitimate sons of gods, whether by the nymphs or by any other mothers, of whom they are said to be the sons—what human being will ever believe that there are no gods if they are the sons of gods? You might as well affirm the existence of mules, and deny that of horses and asses. Such nonsense, Meletus, could only have been intended by you to make trial of me. You have put this into the indictment because you had nothing real of which to accuse me. But no one who has a particle of understanding will ever be convinced by you that the same men can believe in divine and superhuman things, and yet not believe that there are gods and demigods and heroes.

I have said enough in answer to the charge of Meletus: any elaborate defence is unnecessary; but I know only too well how many are the enmities which I have incurred, and this is what will be my destruction if I am destroyed;—not Meletus, nor yet Anytus, but the envy and detraction of the world, which has been the death of many good men, and will probably be the death of many more; there is no danger of my being the last of them.

Some one will say: And are you not ashamed, Socrates, of a course of life which is likely to bring you to an untimely end? To him I may fairly answer: There you are mistaken: a man who is good for anything ought not to calculate the chance of living or dying; he ought only to consider whether in doing anything he is doing right or wrong—acting the part of a good man or of a bad. Whereas, upon your view, the heroes who fell at Troy were not good for much, and the son of Thetis above all, who altogether despised danger in comparison with disgrace; and when he was so eager to slay Hector, his goddess mother said to him, that if he avenged his companion Patroclus, and slew Hector, he would die himself—'Fate,' she said, in these or the like words, 'waits for you next after Hector'; he, receiving this warning, utterly despised danger and death, and instead of fearing them, feared rather to live in dishonour, and not to avenge his friend. 'Let me die forthwith,' he replies, 'and be avenged of my enemy, rather than abide here by the beaked ships, a laughing-stock and a burden of the earth.' Had Achilles any thought of death and danger? For wherever a man's place is, whether the place which he has chosen or that in which he has been placed by a commander, there he ought to remain in hour of danger; he should not think of death or of anything but of disgrace. And this, O men of Athens, is a true saying.

Strange, indeed, would be my conduct, O men of Athens, if I who, when I was ordered by the generals whom you chose to command me at Potidaea and Amphipolis and Delium, remained where they placed me, like any other man, facing death—if now, when, as I conceive and imagine, God orders me to fulfil the philosopher's mission of searching into myself and other men, I were to desert my post through fear of death, or any other fear; that would indeed be strange, and I might justly be arraigned in court for denying the existence of the gods, if I disobeyed the oracle because I was afraid of death, fancying that I was wise when I was not wise. For the fear of death is indeed the pretence of wisdom, and not real wisdom, being a pretence of knowing the unknown; and no one knows whether death, which men in their fear apprehend to be the greatest evil, may not be the greatest good. Is not this ignorance of a disgraceful sort, the ignorance which is the conceit that man knows what he does not know? And in this respect only I believe myself to differ from men in general, and may perhaps claim to be wiser than they are:—that whereas I know but little of the world below, I do not suppose that I know: but I do know that injustice and disobedience to a better, whether God or man, is evil and dishonourable, and I will never fear or avoid a possible good rather than a certain evil. And therefore if you let me go now, and are not convinced by Anytus, who said that since I had been prosecuted I must be put to death (or if not that I ought never to have been prosecuted at all); and that if I escape now, your sons will all be utterly ruined by listening to my words —if you say to me, Socrates, this time we will not mind Anytus, and you shall be let off, but upon one condition, that you are not to enquire and speculate in this way any more, and that if you are caught doing so again you shall die:—if this was the condition on which you let me go, I should reply: Men of Athens, I honour and love you; but I shall obey God rather than you, and while I have life and strength I shall never cease from the practice and teaching of philosophy, exhorting any one whom I meet and saying to him after my manner: You, my friend,—a citizen of the great and mighty and wise city of Athens,—are you not ashamed of heaping up the greatest amount of money and honour and reputation, and caring so little about wisdom and truth and the greatest improvement of the soul, which you never regard or heed at all? And if the person with whom I am arguing, says: Yes, but I do care; then I do not leave him or let him go at once; but I proceed to interrogate and examine and cross-examine him, and if I think that he has no virtue in him, but only says that he has, I reproach him with undervaluing the greater, and overvaluing the less. And I shall repeat the same words to every one whom I meet, young and old, citizen and alien, but especially to the citizens, inasmuch as they are my brethren. For know that this is the command of God; and I believe that no greater good has ever happened in the state than my service to the God. For I do nothing but go about persuading you all, old and young alike, not to take thought for your persons or your properties, but first and chiefly to care about the greatest improvement of the soul. I tell you that virtue is not given by money, but that from virtue comes money and every other good of man, public as well as private. This is my teaching, and if this is the doctrine which corrupts the youth, I am a mischievous person. But if any one says that this is not my teaching, he is speaking an untruth. Wherefore, O men of Athens, I say to you, do as Anytus bids or not as Anytus bids, and either acquit me or not; but whichever you do, understand that I shall never alter my ways, not even if I have to die many times.

Men of Athens, do not interrupt, but hear me; there was an understanding between us that you should hear me to the end: I have something more to say, at which you may be inclined to cry out; but I believe that to hear me will be good for you, and therefore I beg that you will not cry out. I would have you know, that if you kill such an one as I am, you will injure yourselves more than you will injure me. Nothing will injure me, not Meletus nor yet Anytus—they cannot, for a bad man is not permitted to injure a better than himself. I do not deny that Anytus may, perhaps, kill him, or drive him into exile, or deprive him of civil rights; and he may imagine, and others may imagine, that he is inflicting a great injury upon him: but there I do not agree. For the evil of doing as he is doing—the evil of unjustly taking away the life of another—is greater far.

And now, Athenians, I am not going to argue for my own sake, as you may think, but for yours, that you may not sin against the God by condemning me, who am his gift to you. For if you kill me you will not easily find a successor to me, who, if I may use such a ludicrous figure of speech, am a sort of gadfly, given to the state by God; and the state is a great and noble steed who is tardy in his motions owing to his very size, and requires to be stirred into life. I am that gadfly which God has attached to the state, and all day long and in all places am always fastening upon you, arousing and persuading and reproaching you. You will not easily find another like me, and therefore I would advise you to spare me. I dare say that you may feel out of temper (like a person who is suddenly awakened from sleep), and you think that you might easily strike me dead as Anytus advises, and then you would sleep on for the remainder of your lives, unless God in his care of you sent you another gadfly. When I say that I am given to you by God, the proof of my mission is this:—if I had been like other men, I should not have neglected all my own concerns or patiently seen the neglect of them during all these years, and have been doing yours, coming to you individually like a father or elder brother, exhorting you to regard virtue; such conduct, I say, would be unlike human nature. If I had gained anything, or if my exhortations had been paid, there would have been some sense in my doing so; but now, as you will perceive, not even the impudence of my accusers dares to say that I have ever exacted or sought pay of any one; of that they have no witness. And I have a sufficient witness to the truth of what I say—my poverty.

Some one may wonder why I go about in private giving advice and busying myself with the concerns of others, but do not venture to come forward in public and advise the state. I will tell you why. You have heard me speak at sundry times and in divers places of an oracle or sign which comes to me, and is the divinity which Meletus ridicules in the indictment. This sign, which is a kind of voice, first began to come to me when I was a child; it always forbids but never commands me to do anything which I am going to do. This is what deters me from being a politician. And rightly, as I think. For I am certain, O men of Athens, that if I had engaged in politics, I should have perished long ago, and done no good either to you or to myself. And do not be offended at my telling you the truth: for the truth is, that no man who goes to war with you or any other multitude, honestly striving against the many lawless and unrighteous deeds which are done in a state, will save his life; he who will fight for the right, if he would live even for a brief space, must have a private station and not a public one.

I can give you convincing evidence of what I say, not words only, but what you value far more—actions. Let me relate to you a passage of my own life which will prove to you that I should never have yielded to injustice from any fear of death, and that 'as I should have refused to yield' I must have died at once. I will tell you a tale of the courts, not very interesting perhaps, but nevertheless true. The only office of state which I ever held, O men of Athens, was that of senator: the tribe Antiochis, which is my tribe, had the presidency at the trial of the generals who had not taken up the bodies of the slain after the battle of Arginusae; and you proposed to try them in a body, contrary to law, as you all thought afterwards; but at the time I was the only one of the Prytanes who was opposed to the illegality, and I gave my vote against you; and when the orators threatened to impeach and arrest me, and you called and shouted, I made up my mind that I would run the risk, having law and justice with me, rather than take part in your injustice because I feared imprisonment and death. This happened in the days of the democracy. But when the oligarchy of the Thirty was in power, they sent for me and four others into the rotunda, and bade us bring Leon the Salaminian from Salamis, as they wanted to put him to death. This was a specimen of the sort of commands which they were always giving with the view of implicating as many as possible in their crimes; and then I showed, not in word only but in deed, that, if I may be allowed to use such an expression, I cared not a straw for death, and that my great and only care was lest I should do an unrighteous or unholy thing. For the strong arm of that oppressive power did not frighten me into doing wrong; and when we came out of the rotunda the other four went to Salamis and fetched Leon, but I went quietly home. For which I might have lost my life, had not the power of the Thirty shortly afterwards come to an end. And many will witness to my words.

Now do you really imagine that I could have survived all these years, if I had led a public life, supposing that like a good man I had always maintained the right and had made justice, as I ought, the first thing? No indeed, men of Athens, neither I nor any other man. But I have been always the same in all my actions, public as well as private, and never have I yielded any base compliance to those who are slanderously termed my disciples, or to any other. Not that I have any regular disciples. But if any one likes to come and hear me while I am pursuing my mission, whether he be young or old, he is not excluded. Nor do I converse only with those who pay; but any one, whether he be rich or poor, may ask and answer me and listen to my words; and whether he turns out to be a bad man or a good one, neither result can be justly imputed to me; for I never taught or professed to teach him anything. And if any one says that he has ever learned or heard anything from me in private which all the world has not heard, let me tell you that he is lying.

But I shall be asked, Why do people delight in continually conversing with you? I have told you already, Athenians, the whole truth about this matter: they like to hear the cross-examination of the pretenders to wisdom; there is amusement in it. Now this duty of cross-examining other men has been imposed upon me by God; and has been signified to me by oracles, visions, and in every way in which the will of divine power was ever intimated to any one. This is true, O Athenians; or, if not true, would be soon refuted. If I am or have been corrupting the youth, those of them who are now grown up and become sensible that I gave them bad advice in the days of their youth should come forward as accusers, and take their revenge; or if they do not like to come themselves, some of their relatives, fathers, brothers, or other kinsmen, should say what evil their families have suffered at my hands. Now is their time. Many of them I see in the court. There is Crito, who is of the same age and of the same deme with myself, and there is Critobulus his son, whom I also see. Then again there is Lysanias of Sphettus, who is the father of Aeschines—he is present; and also there is Antiphon of Cephisus, who is the father of Epigenes; and there are the brothers of several who have associated with me. There is Nicostratus the son of Theosdotides, and the brother of Theodotus (now Theodotus himself is dead, and therefore he, at any rate, will not seek to stop him); and there is Paralus the son of Demodocus, who had a brother Theages; and Adeimantus the son of Ariston, whose brother Plato is present; and Aeantodorus, who is the brother of Apollodorus, whom I also see. I might mention a great many others, some of whom Meletus should have produced as witnesses in the course of his speech; and let him still produce them, if he has forgotten—I will make way for him. And let him say, if he has any testimony of the sort which he can produce. Nay, Athenians, the very opposite is the truth. For all these are ready to witness on behalf of the corrupter, of the injurer of their kindred, as Meletus and Anytus call me; not the corrupted youth only—there might have been a motive for that—but their uncorrupted elder relatives. Why should they too support me with their testimony? Why, indeed, except for the sake of truth and justice, and because they know that I am speaking the truth, and that Meletus is a liar.

Well, Athenians, this and the like of this is all the defence which I have to offer. Yet a word more. Perhaps there may be some one who is offended at me, when he calls to mind how he himself on a similar, or even a less serious occasion, prayed and entreated the judges with many tears, and how he produced his children in court, which was a moving spectacle, together with a host of relations and friends; whereas I, who am probably in danger of my life, will do none of these things. The contrast may occur to his mind, and he may be set against me, and vote in anger because he is displeased at me on this account. Now if there be such a person among you,—mind, I do not say that there is,—to him I may fairly reply: My friend, I am a man, and like other men, a creature of flesh and blood, and not 'of wood or stone,' as Homer says; and I have a family, yes, and sons, O Athenians, three in number, one almost a man, and two others who are still young; and yet I will not bring any of them hither in order to petition you for an acquittal. And why not? Not from any self-assertion or want of respect for you. Whether I am or am not afraid of death is another question, of which I will not now speak. But, having regard to public opinion,

I feel that such conduct would be discreditable to myself, and to you, and to the whole state. One who has reached my years, and who has a name for wisdom, ought not to demean himself. Whether this opinion of me be deserved or not, at any rate the world has decided that Socrates is in some way superior to other men. And if those among you who are said to be superior in wisdom and courage, and any other virtue, demean themselves in this way, how shameful is their conduct! I have seen men of reputation, when they have been condemned, behaving in the strangest manner: they seemed to fancy that they were going to suffer something dreadful if they died, and that they could be immortal if you only allowed them to live; and I think that such are a dishonour to the state, and that any stranger coming in would have said of them that the most eminent men of Athens, to whom the Athenians themselves give honour and command, are no better than women. And I say that these things ought not to be done by those of us who have a reputation; and if they are done, you ought not to permit them; you ought rather to show that you are far more disposed to condemn the man who gets up a doleful scene and makes the city ridiculous, than him who holds his peace.

But, setting aside the question of public opinion, there seems to be something wrong in asking a favour of a judge, and thus procuring an acquittal, instead of informing and convincing him. For his duty is, not to make a present of justice, but to give judgment; and he has sworn that he will judge according to the laws, and not according to his own good pleasure; and we ought not to encourage you, nor should you allow yourself to be encouraged, in this habit of perjury—there can be no piety in that. Do not then require me to do what I consider dishonourable and impious and wrong, especially now, when I am being tried for impiety on the indictment of Meletus. For if, O men of Athens, by force of persuasion and entreaty I could overpower your oaths, then I should be teaching you to believe that there are no gods, and in defending should simply convict myself of the charge of not believing in them. But that is not so—far otherwise. For I do believe that there are gods, and in a sense higher than that in which any of my accusers believe in them. And to you and to God I commit my cause, to be determined by you as is best for you and me.

There are many reasons why I am not grieved, O men of Athens, at the vote of condemnation. I expected it, and am only surprised that the votes are so nearly equal; for I had thought that the majority against me would have been far larger; but now, had thirty votes gone over to the other side, I should have been acquitted. And I may say, I think, that I have escaped Meletus. I may say more; for without the assistance of Anytus and Lycon, any one may see that he would not have had a fifth part of the votes, as the law requires, in which case he would have incurred a fine of a thousand drachmae.

And so he proposes death as the penalty. And what shall I propose on my part, O men of Athens? Clearly that which is my due. And what is my due? What return shall be made to the man who has never had the wit to be idle during his whole life; but has been careless of what the many care for—wealth, and family interests, and military offices, and speaking in the assembly, and magistracies, and plots, and parties. Reflecting that I was really too honest a man to be a politician and live, I did not go where I could do no good to you or to myself; but where I could do the greatest good privately to every one of you, thither I went, and sought to persuade every man among you that he must look to himself, and seek virtue and wisdom before he looks to his private interests, and look to the state before he looks to the interests of the state; and that this should be the order which he observes in all his actions. What shall be done to such an one? Doubtless some good thing, O men of Athens, if he has his reward; and the good should be of a kind suitable to him. What would be a reward suitable to a poor man who is your benefactor, and who desires leisure that he may instruct you? There can be no reward so fitting as maintenance in the Prytaneum, O men of Athens, a reward which he deserves far more than the citizen who has won the prize at Olympia in the horse or chariot race, whether the chariots were drawn by two horses or by many. For I am in want, and he has enough; and he only gives you the appearance of happiness, and I give you the reality. And if I am to estimate the penalty fairly, I should say that maintenance in the Prytaneum is the just return.

Perhaps you think that I am braving you in what I am saying now, as in what I said before about the tears and prayers. But this is not so. I speak rather because I am convinced that I never intentionally wronged any one, although I cannot convince you—the time has been too short; if there were a law at Athens, as there is in other cities, that a capital cause should not be decided in one day, then I believe that I should have convinced you. But I cannot in a moment refute great slander; and, as I am convinced that I never wronged another, I will assuredly not wrong myself. I will not say of myself that I deserve any evil, or propose any penalty. Why should I? Because I am afraid of the penalty of death which Meletus proposes? When I do not know whether death is a good or an evil, why should I propose a penalty which would certainly be an evil? Shall I say imprisonment? And why should I live in prison, and be the slave of the magistrates of the year—of the Eleven? Or shall the penalty be a fine, and imprisonment until the fine is paid? There is the same objection. I should have to lie in prison, for money I have none, and cannot pay. And if I say exile (and this may possibly be the penalty which you will affix), I must indeed be blinded by the love of life, if I am so irrational as to expect that when you, who are my own citizens, cannot endure my discourses and words, and have found them so grievous and odious that you will have no more of them, others are likely to endure me. No indeed, men of Athens, that is not very likely. And what a life should I lead, at my age, wandering from city to city, ever changing my place of exile, and always being driven out! For I am quite sure that wherever I go, there, as here, the young men will flock to me; and if I drive them away, their elders will drive me out at their request; and if I let them come, their fathers and friends will drive me out for their sakes.

Some one will say: Yes, Socrates, but cannot you hold your tongue, and then you may go into a foreign city, and no one will interfere with you? Now I have great difficulty in making you understand my answer to this. For if I tell you that to do as you say would be a disobedience to the God, and therefore that I cannot hold my tongue, you will not believe that I am serious; and if I say again that daily to discourse about virtue, and of those other things about which you hear me examining myself and others, is the greatest good of man, and that the unexamined life is not worth living, you are still less likely to believe me. Yet I say what is true, although a thing of which it is hard for me to persuade you. Also, I have never been accustomed to think that I deserve to suffer any harm. Had I money I might have estimated the offence at what I was able to pay, and not have been much the worse. But I have none, and therefore I must ask you to proportion the fine to my means. Well, perhaps I could afford a mina, and therefore I propose that penalty: Plato, Crito, Critobulus, and Appollodorus, my friends here, bid me say thirty minae, and they will be the sureties. Let thirty minae be the penalty; for which sum they will be ample security to you.

Not much time will be gained, O Athenians, in return for the evil name which you will get from the detractors of the city, who will say that you killed Socrates, a wise man; for they will call me wise, even although I am not wise, when they want to reproach you. If you had waited a little while, your desire would have been fulfilled in the course of nature. For I am far advanced in years, as you may perceive, and not far from death. I am speaking now not to all of you, but only to those who have condemned me to death. And I have another thing to say to them: You think that I was convicted because I had no words of the sort which would have procured my acquittal—I mean, if I had thought fit to leave nothing undone or unsaid. Not so; the deficiency which led to my conviction was not of words—certainly not. But I had not the boldness or impudence or inclination to address you as you would have liked me to do, weeping and wailing and lamenting, and saying and doing many things which you have been accustomed to hear from others, and which, as I maintain, are unworthy of me. I thought at the time that I ought not to do anything common or mean when in danger: nor do I now repent of the style of my defence; I would rather die having spoken after my manner, than speak in your manner and live. For neither in war nor yet at law ought I or any man to use every way of escaping death. Often in battle there can be no doubt that if a man will throw away his arms, and fall on his knees before his pursuers, he may escape death; and in other dangers there are other ways of escaping death, if a man is willing to say and do anything. The difficulty, my friends, is not to avoid death, but to avoid unrighteousness; for that runs faster than death. I am old and move slowly, and the slower runner has overtaken me, and my accusers are keen and quick, and the faster runner, who is unrighteousness, has overtaken them. And now I depart hence condemned by you to suffer the penalty of death,—they too go their ways condemned by the truth to suffer the penalty of villainy and wrong; and I must abide by my award—let them abide by theirs. I suppose that these things may be regarded as fated,—and I think that they are well.

And now, O men who have condemned me, I would fain prophesy to you; for I am about to die, and in the hour of death men are gifted with prophetic power. And I prophesy to you who are my murderers, that immediately after my departure punishment far heavier than you have inflicted on me will surely await you. Me you have killed because you wanted to escape the accuser, and not to give an account of your lives. But that will not be as you suppose: far otherwise. For I say that there will be more accusers of you than there are now; accusers whom hitherto I have restrained: and as they are younger they will be more inconsiderate with you, and you will be more offended at them. If you think that by killing men you can prevent some one from censuring your evil lives, you are mistaken; that is not a way of escape which is either possible or honourable; the easiest and the noblest way is not to be disabling others, but to be improving yourselves. This is the prophecy which I utter before my departure to the judges who have condemned me.

Friends, who would have acquitted me, I would like also to talk with you about the thing which has come to pass, while the magistrates are busy, and before I go to the place at which I must die. Stay then a little, for we may as well talk with one another while there is time. You are my friends, and I should like to show you the meaning of this event which has happened to me. O my judges—for you I may truly call judges—I should like to tell you of a wonderful circumstance. Hitherto the divine faculty of which the internal oracle is the source has constantly been in the habit of opposing me even about trifles, if I was going to make a slip or error in any matter; and now as you see there has come upon me that which may be thought, and is generally believed to be, the last and worst evil. But the oracle made no sign of opposition, either when I was leaving my house in the morning, or when I was on my way to the court, or while I was speaking, at anything which I was going to say; and yet I have often been stopped in the middle of a speech, but now in nothing I either said or did touching the matter in hand has the oracle opposed me. What do I take to be the explanation of this silence? I will tell you. It is an intimation that what has happened to me is a good, and that those of us who think that death is an evil are in error. For the customary sign would surely have opposed me had I been going to evil and not to good.

Let us reflect in another way, and we shall see that there is great reason to hope that death is a good; for one of two things—either death is a state of nothingness and utter unconsciousness, or, as men say, there is a change and migration of the soul from this world to another. Now if you suppose that there is no consciousness, but a sleep like the sleep of him who is undisturbed even by dreams, death will be an unspeakable gain. For if a person were to select the night in which his sleep was undisturbed even by dreams, and were to compare with this the other days and nights of his life, and then were to tell us how many days and nights he had passed in the course of his life better and more pleasantly than this one, I think that any man, I will not say a private man, but even the great king will not find many such days or nights, when compared with the others. Now if death be of such a nature, I say that to die is gain; for eternity is then only a single night. But if death is the journey to another place, and there, as men say, all the dead abide, what good, O my friends and judges, can be greater than this? If indeed when the pilgrim arrives in the world below, he is delivered from the professors of justice in this world, and finds the true judges who are said to give judgment there, Minos and Rhadamanthus and Aeacus and Triptolemus, and other sons of God who were righteous in their own life, that pilgrimage will be worth making. What would not a man give if he might converse with Orpheus and Musaeus and Hesiod and Homer? Nay, if this be true, let me die again and again. I myself, too, shall have a wonderful interest in there meeting and conversing with Palamedes, and Ajax the son of Telamon, and any other ancient hero who has suffered death through an unjust judgment; and there will be no small pleasure, as I think, in comparing my own sufferings with theirs. Above all, I shall then be able to continue my search into true and false knowledge; as in this world, so also in the next and I shall find out who is wise, and who pretends to be wise, and is not. What would not a man give, O judges, to be able to examine the leader of the great Trojan expedition; or Odysseus or Sisyphus, or numberless others, men and women too! What infinite delight would there be in conversing with them and asking them questions! In another world they do not put a man to death for asking questions: assuredly not. For besides being happier than we are, they will be immortal, if what is said is true.

Wherefore, O judges, be of good cheer about death, and know of a certainty, that no evil can happen to a good man, either in life or after death. He and his are not neglected by the gods; nor has my own approaching end happened by mere chance. But I see clearly that the time had arrived when it was better for me to die and be released from trouble; wherefore the oracle gave no sign. For which reason, also, I am not angry with my condemners, or with my accusers; they have done me no harm, although they did not mean to do me any good; and for this I may gently blame them.

Still I have a favour to ask of them. When my sons are grown up, I would ask you, O my friends, to punish them; and I would have you trouble them, as I have troubled you, if they seem to care about riches, or anything more than about virtue; or if they pretend to be something when they are really nothing,—then reprove them, as I have reproved you, for not caring about that for which they ought to care, and thinking that they are something when they are really nothing. And if you do this, both I and my sons will have received justice at your hands.

The hour of departure has arrived, and we go our ways—I to die, and you to live. Which is better God only knows.

QUESTIONS FOR DISCUSSION

1) Socrates, at the age of seventy, was brought to trial on a threefold charge of preaching false gods, denying the official gods of the state, and corrupting the young. These charges were untrue, but to save himself Socrates would have had to compromise his principles. He chose to mount an unconventional defense which failed to save him although the vote was close. This portion of his defense contains a sample of the Socratic method of question-and-answer and reviews the history of Socrates' service to Athens as a "sort of gadfly." How convincing is Socrates' questioning of Meletus? Is his analogy between himself as an improver of youth and the man who is a trainer of horses an apt one? How does he argue against the charge of intentionally injuring the youth of Athens? How does he demonstrate that he is not an atheist?

2) How does Socrates believe himself to differ from men in general? What was his message to the men of Athens?

3) "The unexamined life is not worth living." This is one of Socrates' most famous statements. Judging from what you have read in this book, to what extent do creative people lead the "examined" life? To what extent did Socrates himself lead a "creative" life? What did he create?

THE SERMON ON
THE MOUNT

23 And Jē'sŭs went about in all Găl'ĭ-lēe, teaching in their synagogues, and preaching the gospel of the kingdom, and healing all manner of disease and all manner of sickness among the people. 24 And the report of him went forth into all Sȳr'ĭ-à: and they brought unto him all that were sick, holden with divers diseases and torments, possessed with demons, and epileptic, and palsied; and he healed them. 25 And there followed him great multitudes from Găl'ĭ-lēe and Dĕ-căp'ŏ-lĭs and Jē-ru'så-lĕm and Jū-dæ'à and *from* beyond the Jordan.

5 And seeing the multitudes, he went up into the mountain: and when he had sat down, his disciples came unto him: 2 and he opened his mouth and taught them, saying,

3 Blessed are the poor in spirit: for theirs is the kingdom of heaven.

4 Blessed are they that mourn: for they shall be comforted.

5 Blessed are the meek: for they shall inherit the earth.

6 Blessed are they that hunger and thirst after righteousness: for they shall be filled.

7 Blessed are the merciful: for they shall obtain mercy.

8 Blessed are the pure in heart: for they shall see God.

9 Blessed are the peacemakers: for they shall be called sons of God.

10 Blessed are they that have been persecuted for righteousness' sake: for theirs is the kingdom of heaven. 11 Blessed are ye when *men* shall reproach you, and persecute you, and say all manner of evil against you falsely, for my sake. 12 Rejoice, and be exceeding glad: for great is your reward in heaven: for so persecuted they the prophets that were before you.

13 Ye are the salt of the earth: but if the salt have lost its savor, wherewith shall it be salted? it is thenceforth good for nothing, but to be cast out and trodden under foot of men. 14 Ye are the light of the world. A city set on a hill cannot be hid. 15 Neither do *men* light a lamp, and put it under the bushel, but on the stand; and it shineth unto all that are in the house. 16 Even so let your light shine before men; that they may see your good works, and glorify your Father who is in heaven.

17 Think not that I came to destroy the law or the prophets: I came not to destroy, but to fulfil. 18 For verily I say unto you, Till heaven and earth pass away, one jot or one tittle shall in no wise pass away from the law, till all things be accomplished. 19 Whosoever therefore shall break one of these least commandments, and shall teach men so, shall be called least in the kingdom of heaven: but whosoever shall do and teach them, he shall be called great in the kingdom of heaven. 20 For I say unto you,

that except your righteousness shall exceed *the righteousness* of the scribes and Phăr'ĭ-sēes, ye shall in no wise enter into the kingdom of heaven.

21 Ye have heard that it was said to them of old time, Thou shalt not kill; and whosoever shall kill shall be in danger of the judgment: 22 but I say unto you, that every one who is angry with his brother shall be in danger of the judgment; and whosoever shall say to his brother, Rā'cà, shall be in danger of the council; and whosoever shall say, Thou fool, shall be in danger of the hell of fire. 23 If therefore thou art offering thy gift at the altar, and there rememberest that thy brother hath aught against thee, 24 leave there thy gift before the altar, and go thy way, first be reconciled to thy brother, and then come and offer thy gift. 25 Agree with thine adversary quickly, while thou art with him in the way; lest haply the adversary deliver thee to the judge, and the judge deliver thee to the officer, and thou be cast into prison. 26 Verily I say unto thee, Thou shalt by no means come out thence, till thou have paid the last farthing.

27 Ye have heard that it was said, Thou shalt not commit adultery: 28 but I say unto you, that every one that looketh on a woman to lust after her hath committed adultery with her already in his heart. 29 And if thy right eye causeth thee to stumble, pluck it out, and cast it from thee: for it is profitable for thee that one of thy members should perish, and not thy whole body be cast into hell. 30 And if thy right hand causeth thee to stumble, cut it off, and cast it from thee: for it is profitable for thee that one of thy members should perish, and not thy whole body go into hell. 31 It was said also, Whosoever shall put away his wife, let him give her a writing of divorcement: 32 but I say unto you, that every one that putteth away his wife, saving for the cause of fornication, maketh her an adulteress: and whosoever shall marry her when she is put away committeth adultery.

33 Again, ye have heard that it was said to them of old time, Thou shalt not forswear thyself, but shalt perform unto the Lord thine oaths: 34 but I say unto you, Swear not at all; neither by the heaven, for it is the throne of God; 35 nor by the earth, for it is the footstool of his feet; nor by Jĕ-ru'sà-lĕm, for it is the city of the great King. 36 Neither shalt thou swear by thy head, for thou canst not make one hair white or black. 37 But let your speech be, Yea, yea; Nay, nay: and whatsoever is more than these is of the evil *one*.

38 Ye have heard that it was said, An eye for an eye, and a tooth for a tooth: 39 but I say unto you, Resist not him that is evil: but whosoever smiteth thee on thy right cheek, turn to him the other also. 40 And if any man would go to law with thee, and take away thy coat, let him have thy cloak also. 41 And whosoever shall compel thee to go one mile, go with him two. 42 Give to him that asketh thee, and from him that would borrow of thee turn not thou away.

43 Ye have heard that it was said, Thou shalt love thy neighbor, and hate thine enemy: 44 but I say unto you, Love your enemies, and pray

for them that persecute you; 45 that ye may be sons of your Father who is in heaven: for he maketh his sun to rise on the evil and the good, and sendeth rain on the just and the unjust. 46 For if ye love them that love you, what reward have ye? do not even the publicans the same? 47 And if ye salute your brethren only, what do ye more *than others?* do not even the Gĕn'tīles the same? 48 Ye therefore shall be perfect, as your heavenly Father is perfect.

6 Take heed that ye do not your righteousness before men, to be seen of them: else ye have no reward with your Father who is in heaven.

2 When therefore thou doest alms, sound not a trumpet before thee, as the hypocrites do in the synagogues and in the streets, that they may have glory of men. Verily I say unto you, They have received their reward. 3 But when thou doest alms, let not thy left hand know what thy right hand doeth: 4 that thine alms may be in secret: and thy Father who seeth in secret shall recompense thee.

5 And when ye pray, ye shall not be as the hypocrites: for they love to stand and pray in the synagogues and in the corners of the streets, that they may be seen of men. Verily I say unto you, They have received their reward. 6 But thou, when thou prayest, enter into thine inner chamber, and having shut thy door, pray to thy Father who is in secret, and thy Father who seeth in secret shall recompense thee. 7 And in praying use not vain repetitions, as the Gĕn'tīles do: for they think that they shall be heard for their much speaking. 8 Be not therefore like unto them: for your Father knoweth what things ye have need of, before ye ask him. 9 After this manner therefore pray ye: Our Father who art in heaven, Hallowed be thy name. 10 Thy kingdom come. Thy will be done, as in heaven, so on earth. 11 Give us this day our daily bread. 12 And forgive us our debts, as we also have forgiven our debtors. 13 And bring us not into temptation, but deliver us from the evil *one.* 14 For if ye forgive men their trespasses, your heavenly Father will also forgive you. 15 But if ye forgive not men their trespasses, neither will your Father forgive your trespasses.

16 Moreover when ye fast, be not, as the hypocrites, of a sad countenance: for they disfigure their faces, that they may be seen of men to fast. Verily I say unto you, They have received their reward. 17 But thou, when thou fastest, anoint thy head, and wash thy face; 18 that thou be not seen of men to fast, but of thy Father who is in secret: and thy Father, who seeth in secret, shall recompense thee.

19 Lay not up for yourselves treasures upon the earth, where moth and rust consume, and where thieves break through and steal: 20 but lay up for yourselves treasures in heaven, where neither moth nor rust doth consume, and where thieves do not break through nor steal: 21 for where thy treasure is, there will thy heart be also. 22 The lamp of the body is the eye: if therefore thine eye be single, thy whole body shall be full of light. 23 But if thine eye be evil, thy whole body shall be full of darkness. If therefore the light that is in thee be darkness, how great is the darkness!

24 No man can serve two masters: for either he will hate the one, and love the other; or else he will hold to one, and despise the other. Ye cannot serve God and mammon. 25 Therefore I say unto you, Be not anxious for your life, what ye shall eat, or what ye shall drink; nor yet for your body, what ye shall put on. Is not the life more than the food, and the body than the raiment? 26 Behold the birds of the heaven, that they sow not, neither do they reap, nor gather into barns; and your heavenly Father feedeth them. Are not ye of much more value than they? 27 And which of you by being anxious can add one cubit unto the measure of his life? 28 And why are ye anxious concerning raiment? Consider the lilies of the field, how they grow; they toil not, neither do they spin: 29 yet I say unto you, that even Sŏl'ŏ-mŏn in all his glory was not arrayed like one of these. 30 But if God doth so clothe the grass of the field, which to-day is, and to-morrow is cast into the oven, *shall he* not much more *clothe* you, O ye of little faith? 31 Be not therefore anxious, saying, What shall we eat? or, What shall we drink? or, Wherewithal shall we be clothed? 32 For after all these things do the Gĕn'tīles seek; for your heavenly Father knoweth that ye have need of all these things. 33 But seek ye first his kingdom, and his righteousness; and all these things shall be added unto you. 34 Be not therefore anxious for the morrow: for the morrow will be anxious for itself. Sufficient unto the day is the evil thereof.

7 Judge not, that ye be not judged. 2 For with what judgment ye judge, ye shall be judged: and with what measure ye mete, it shall be measured unto you. 3 And why beholdest thou the mote that is in thy brother's eye, but considerest not the beam that is in thine own eye? 4 Or how wilt thou say to thy brother, Let me cast out the mote out of thine eye; and lo, the beam is in thine own eye? 5 Thou hypocrite, cast out first the beam out of thine own eye; and then shalt thou see clearly to cast out the mote out of thy brother's eye.

6 Give not that which is holy unto the dogs, neither cast your pearls before the swine, lest haply they trample them under their feet, and turn and rend you.

7 Ask, and it shall be given you; seek, and ye shall find; knock, and it shall be opened unto you: 8 for every one that asketh receiveth; and he that seeketh findeth; and to him that knocketh it shall be opened. 9 Or what man is there of you, who, if his son shall ask him for a loaf, will give him a stone; 10 or if he shall ask for a fish, will give him a serpent? 11 If ye then, being evil, know how to give good gifts unto your children, how much more shall your Father who is in heaven give good things to them that ask him? 12 All things therefore whatsoever ye would that men should do unto you, even so do ye also unto them: for this is the law and the prophets.

13 Enter ye in by the narrow gate: for wide is the gate, and broad is the way, that leadeth to destruction, and many are they that enter in thereby. 14 For narrow is the gate, and straitened the way, that leadeth unto life, and few are they that find it.

15 Beware of false prophets, who come to you in sheep's clothing, but inwardly are ravening wolves. 16 By their fruits ye shall know them. Do *men* gather grapes of thorns, or figs of thistles? 17 Even so every good tree bringeth forth good fruit; but the corrupt tree bringeth forth evil fruit. 18 A good tree cannot bring forth evil fruit, neither can a corrupt tree bring forth good fruit. 19 Every tree that bringeth not forth good fruit is hewn down, and cast into the fire. 20 Therefore by their fruits ye shall know them. 21 Not every one that saith unto me, Lord, Lord, shall enter into the kingdom of heaven; but he that doeth the will of my Father who is in heaven. 22 Many will say to me in that day, Lord, Lord, did we not prophesy by thy name, and by thy name cast out demons, and by thy name do many mighty works? 23 And then will I profess unto them, I never knew you: depart from me, ye that work iniquity.

24 Every one therefore that heareth these words of mine, and doeth them, shall be likened unto a wise man, who built his house upon the rock: 25 and the rain descended, and the floods came, and the winds blew, and beat upon that house; and it fell not: for it was founded upon the rock. 26 And every one that heareth these words of mine, and doeth them not, shall be likened unto a foolish man, who built his house upon the sand: 27 and the rain descended, and the floods came, and the winds blew, and smote upon that house; and it fell: and great was the fall thereof.

28 And it came to pass, when Jē'sŭs had finished these words, the multitudes were astonished at his teaching: 29 for he taught them as *one* having authority, and not as their scribes.

QUESTIONS FOR DISCUSSION

1) Some of the commandments in this most famous of all orations might be considered revolutionary, others not. Make a list of the more important revolutionary statements. Why are they so, and do they still qualify as such?

2) The heart of Jesus' message is contained in the passage where he says "Resist not him that is evil: but whosoever smiteth thee on thy right cheek, turn to him the other also." Human beings have never obeyed this injunction on any grand scale. Is it possible that they could learn to do so? Explain.

3) Can "good" and "evil" be adequately defined, not by means of examples but in an abstract sense? Explain.

4) In what sense can Jesus be considered a "creative" person? By virtue of his teachings? By virtue of his example? Or both? Is "creative" an appropriate word to describe a person who has had such an impact on Western civilization? Explain.

from
THE COMMUNIST MANIFESTO

Karl Marx and Friedrich Engels

A spectre is haunting Europe—the spectre of Communism. All the powers of old Europe have entered into a holy alliance to exorcise this spectre: Pope and Tsar, Metternich and Guizot, French Radicals and German police-spies.

Where is the party in opposition that has not been decried as communistic by its opponents in power? Where is the Opposition that has not hurled back the branding reproach of Communism, against the more advanced opposition parties, as well as against its reactionary adversaries?

Two things result from this fact:

1. Communism is already acknowledged by all European powers to be itself a power.

2. It is high time that Communists should openly, in the face of the whole world, publish their views, their aims, their tendencies, and meet this nursery tale of the spectre of Communism with a manifesto of the party itself.

To this end, Communists of various nationalities have assembled in London, and sketched the following manifesto, to be published in the English, French, German, Italian, Flemish and Danish languages:

I: BOURGEOIS AND PROLETARIANS

The history of all hitherto existing society is the history of class struggles.

Freeman and slave, patrician and plebeian, lord and serf, guild-master and journeyman, in a word, oppressor and oppressed, stood in constant opposition to one another, carried on an uninterrupted, now hidden, now open fight, a fight that each time ended, either in a revolutionary reconstitution of society at large, or in the common ruin of the contending classes.

In the earlier epochs of history, we find almost everywhere a complicated arrangement of society into various orders, a manifold gradation of social rank. In ancient Rome we have patricians, knights, plebeians, slaves; in the Middle Ages, feudal lords, vassals, guild-masters, journeymen, apprentices, serfs; in almost all of these classes, again, subordinate gradations.

The modern bourgeois society that has sprouted from the ruins of feudal society has not done away with class antagonisms. It has but established new classes, new conditions of oppression, new forms of struggle in place of the old ones.

Our epoch, the epoch of the bourgeoisie, possesses, however, this distinctive feature: it has simplified the class antagonisms. Society as a whole is more and more splitting up into two great hostile camps, into two great classes directly facing each other—bourgeoisie and proletariat.

From the serfs of the Middle Ages sprang the chartered burghers of the earliest towns. From these burgesses the first elements of the bourgeoisie were developed.

The discovery of America, the rounding of the Cape, opened up fresh ground for the rising bourgeoisie. The East-Indian and Chinese markets, the colonisation of America, trade with the colonies, the increase in the means of exchange and in commodities generally, gave to commerce, to navigation, to industry, an impulse never before known, and thereby, to the revolutionary element in the tottering feudal society, a rapid development.

The feudal system of industry, in which industrial production was monopolised by closed guilds, now no longer sufficed for the growing wants of the new markets. The manufacturing system took its place. The guild-masters were pushed aside by the manufacturing middle class; division of labour between the different corporate guilds vanished in the face of division of labour in each single workshop.

Meantime the markets kept ever growing, the demand ever rising. Even manufacture no longer sufficed. Thereupon, steam and machinery revolutionised industrial production. The place of manufacture was taken by the giant, modern industry, the place of the industrial middle class, by industrial millionaires, the leaders of whole industrial armies, the modern bourgeois.

Modern industry has established the world market, for which the discovery of America paved the way. This market has given an immense development to commerce, to navigation, to communication by land. This development has, in its turn, reacted on the extension of industry; and in proportion as industry, commerce, navigation, railways extended, in the same proportion the bourgeoisie developed, increased its capital, and pushed into the background every class handed down from the Middle Ages.

We see, therefore, how the modern bourgeoisie is itself the product of a long course of development, of a series of revolutions in the modes of production and of exchange.

Each step in the development of the bourgeoisie was accompanied by a corresponding political advance of that class. An oppressed class under the sway of the feudal nobility, an armed and self-governing association in the mediaeval commune; here independent urban republic (as in Italy and

Germany), there taxable "third estate" of the monarchy (as in France); afterwards, in the period of manufacture proper, serving either the semi-feudal or the absolute monarchy as a counterpoise against the nobility, and, in fact, corner stone of the great monarchies in general, the bourgeoisie has at last, since the establishment of Modern Industry and of the world market, conquered for itself, in the modern representative State, exclusive political sway. The executive of the modern State is but a committee for managing the common affairs of the whole bourgeoisie.

The bourgeoisie, historically, has played a most revolutionary part.

The bourgeoisie, wherever it has got the upper hand, has put an end to all feudal, patriarchal, idyllic relations. It has pitilessly torn asunder the motley feudal ties that bound man to his "natural superiors," and has left no other nexus between man and man than naked self-interest, than callous "cash payment." It has drowned the most heavenly ecstasies of religious fervour, of chivalrous enthusiasm, of philistine sentimentalism, in the icy water of egotistical calculation. It has resolved personal worth into exchange value, and in place of the numberless indefeasible chartered freedoms, has set up that single, unconscionable freedom—Free Trade. In one word, for exploitation, veiled by religious and political illusions, it has substituted naked, shameless, direct, brutal exploitation.

The bourgeoisie has stripped of its halo every occupation hitherto honoured and looked up to with reverent awe. It has converted the physician, the lawyer, the priest, the poet, the man of science, into its paid wage-labourers.

The bourgeoisie has torn away from the family its sentimental veil, and has reduced the family relation to a mere money relation.

The bourgeoisie has disclosed how it came to pass that the brutal display of vigour in the Middle Ages, which reactionaries so much admire, found its fitting complement in the most slothful indolence. It has been the first to show what man's activity can bring about. It has accomplished wonders far surpassing Egyptian pyramids, Roman aqueducts, and Gothic cathedrals; it has conducted expeditions that put in the shade all former Exoduses of nations and crusades.

The bourgeoisie cannot exist without constantly revolutionising the instruments of production, and thereby the relations of production, and with them the whole relations of society. Conservation of the old modes of production in unaltered form, was, on the contrary, the first condition of existence for all earlier industrial classes. Constant revolutionising of production, uninterrupted disturbance of all social conditions, everlasting uncertainty and agitation distinguished the bourgeois epoch from all earlier ones. All fixed, fast-frozen relations, with their train of ancient and venerable prejudices and opinions, are swept away, all new-formed ones become antiquated before they can ossify. All that is solid melts into air, all that is holy is profaned, and man is at last compelled to face with sober senses his real conditions of life and his relations with his kind.

The need of a constantly expanding market for its products chases the bourgeoisie over the whole surface of the globe. It must nestle everywhere, settle everywhere, establish connections everywhere.

The bourgeoisie has through its exploitation of the world market given a cosmopolitan character to production and consumption in every country. To the great chagrin of reactionaries, it has drawn from under the feet of industry the national ground on which it stood. All old-established national industries have been destroyed or are daily being destroyed. They are dislodged by new industries, whose introduction becomes a life and death question for all civilised nations, by industries that no longer work up indigenous raw material, but raw material drawn from the remotest zones; industries whose products are consumed, not only at home, but in every quarter of the globe. In place of the old wants, satisfied by the production of the country, we find new wants, requiring for their satisfaction the products of distant lands and climes. In place of the old local and national seclusion and self-sufficiency, we have intercourse in every direction, universal inter-dependence of nations. And as in material, so also in intellectual production. The intellectual creations of individual nations become common property. National one-sidedness and narrow-mindedness become more and more impossible, and from the numerous national and local literatures there arises a world literature.

The bourgeoisie, by the rapid improvement of all instruments of production, by the immensely facilitated means of communication, draws all, even the most barbarian, nations into civilisation. The cheap prices of its commodities are the heavy artillery with which it batters down all Chinese walls, with which it forces the barbarians' intensely obstinate hatred of foreigners to capitulate. It compels all nations, on pain of extinction, to adopt the bourgeois modes of production; it compels them to introduce what it calls civilisation into their midst, i.e., to become bourgeois themselves. In one word, it creates a world after its own image.

The bourgeoisie has subjected the country to the rule of the towns. It has created enormous cities, has greatly increased the urban population as compared with the rural, and has thus rescued a considerable part of the population from the idiocy of rural life. Just as it has made the country dependent on the towns, so it has made barbarian and semi-barbarian countries dependent on the civilised ones, nations of peasants on nations of bourgeois, the East on the West.

The bourgeoisie keeps more and more doing away with the scattered state of the population, of the means of production, and of property. It has agglomerated population, centralised means of production, and has concentrated property in a few hands. The necessary consequence of this was political centralisation. Independent, or but loosely connected provinces, with separate interests, laws, governments and systems of taxation, became lumped together into one nation, with one government, one code of laws, one national class interest, one frontier and one customs tariff.

The bourgeoisie, during its rule of scarce one hundred years, has created more massive and more colossal productive forces than have all preceding generations together. Subjection of nature's forces to man, machinery, application of chemistry to industry and agriculture, steam-navigation, railways, electric telegraphs, clearing of whole continents for cultivation, canalisation of rivers, whole populations conjured out of the ground—what earlier century had even a presentiment that such productive forces slumbered in the lap of social labour?

We see then; the means of production and of exchange, on whose foundation the bourgeoisie built itself up, were generated in feudal society. At a certain stage in the development of these means of production and of exchange, the conditions under which feudal society produced and exchanged, the feudal organisation of agriculture and manufacturing industry, in one word, the feudal relations of property became no longer compatible with the already developed productive forces; they became so many fetters. They had to be burst asunder; they were burst asunder.

Into their place stepped free competition, accompanied by a social and political constitution adapted to it, and by the economical and political sway of the bourgeois class.

A similar movement is going on before our own eyes. Modern bourgeois society with its relations of production, of exchange and of property, a society that has conjured up such gigantic means of production and of exchange, is like the sorcerer who is no longer able to control the powers of the nether world whom he has called up by his spells. For many a decade past the history of industry and commerce is but the history of the revolt of modern productive forces against modern conditions of production, against the property relations that are the conditions for the existence of the bourgeoisie and of its rule. It is enough to mention the commercial crises that by their periodical return put the existence of the entire bourgeois society on its trial, each time more threateningly. In these crises a great part not only of the existing products, but also of the previously created productive forces, are periodically destroyed. In these crises there breaks out an epidemic that, in all earlier epochs, would have seemed an absurdity—the epidemic of over-production. Society suddenly finds itself put back into a state of momentary barbarism; it appears as if a famine, a universal war of devastation had cut off the supply of every means of subsistence; industry and commerce seem to be destroyed. And why? Because there is too much civilisation, too much means of subsistence, too much industry, too much commerce. The productive forces at the disposal of society no longer tend to further the development of the conditions of bourgeois property; on the contrary, they have become too powerful for these conditions, by which they are fettered, and so soon as they overcome these fetters, they bring disorder into the whole of bourgeois society, endanger the existence of bourgeois property. The conditions of bourgeois society are too narrow to comprise the wealth created by them. And how does the bourgeoisie get over these crises? On the one hand by enforced destruction of a mass of productive forces; on the other, by the conquest of new markets, and by the more thorough exploitation of the old ones. That is to say, by paving the way for more extensive and more destructive crises, and by diminishing the means whereby crises are prevented.

The weapons with which the bourgeoisie felled feudalism to the ground are now turned against the bourgeoisie itself.

But not only has the bourgeoisie forged the weapons that bring death to itself; it has also called into existence the men who are to wield those weapons—the modern working class—the proletarians.

In proportion as the bourgeoisie, i.e., capital, is developed, in the same proportion is the proletariat, the modern working class, developed—a class of labourers, who live only so long as they find work, and who find work only so long as their labour increases capital. These labourers, who must sell themselves piecemeal, are a commodity, like every other article of commerce, and are consequently exposed to all the vicissitudes of competition, to all the fluctuations of the market.

Owing to the extensive use of machinery and to division of labour, the work of the proletarians has lost all individual character, and, consequently, all charm for the workman. He becomes an appendage of the machine, and it is only the most simple, most monotonous, and most easily acquired knack, that is required of him. Hence, the cost of production of a workman is restricted, almost entirely, to the means of subsistence that he requires for his maintenance, and for the propagation of his race. But the price of a commodity, and therefore, also of labour, is equal to its cost of production. In proportion, therefore, as the repulsiveness of the work increases, the wage decreases. Nay, more, in proportion as the use of machinery and division of labour increases, in the same proportion the burden of toil also increases, whether by prolongation of the working hours, by increase of the work exacted in a given time, or by increased speed of the machinery, etc.

Modern industry has converted the little workshop of the patriarchal master into the great factory of the industrial capitalist. Masses of labourers, crowded into the factory, are organised like soldiers. As privates of the industrial army they are placed under the command of a perfect hierarchy of officers and sergeants. Not only are they slaves of the bourgeois class, and of the bourgeois state; they are daily and hourly enslaved by the machine, by the over-looker, and, above all, by the individual bourgeois manufacturer himself. The more openly this despotism proclaims gain to be its end and aim, the more petty, the more hateful and the more embittering it is.

The less the skill and exertion of strength implied in manual labour, in other words, the more modern industry becomes developed, the more is the labour of men superseded by that of women. Differences of age and sex have no longer any distinctive social validity for the working class. All are instruments of labour, more or less expensive to use, according to their age and sex.

No sooner is the exploitation of the labourer by the manufacturer so far at an end that he receives his wages in cash than he is set upon by the other portions of the bourgeoisie, the landlord, the shopkeeper, the pawn-broker, etc. The lower strata of the middle class—the small tradespeople, shopkeepers, and retired tradesmen generally, the handicraftsmen and peasants—all these sink gradually into the proletariat, partly because their diminutive capital does not suffice for the scale on which modern industry is carried on, and is swamped in the competition with the large capitalists, partly because their specialised skill is rendered worthless by new methods of production. Thus the proletariat is recruited from all classes of the population.

The proletariat goes through various stages of development. With its birth begins its struggle with the bourgeoisie. At first the contest is carried on by individual labourers, then by the work people of a factory, then by the operatives of one trade, in one locality, against the individual bourgeois who directly exploits them. They direct their attacks not against the bour-geois conditions of production, but against the instruments of production themselves; they destroy imported wares that compete with their labour, they smash to pieces machinery, they set factories ablaze, they seek to restore by force the vanished status of the workman of the Middle Ages.

At this stage the labourers still form an incoherent mass scattered over the whole country, and broken up by their mutual competition. If anywhere they unite to form more compact bodies, this is not yet the conse-quence of their own active union, but of the union of the bourgeoisie, which class, in order to attain its own political ends, is compelled to set the whole proletariat in motion, and is moreover yet, for a time, able to do so. At this stage, therefore, the proletarians do not fight their enemies, but the enemies of their enemies, the remnants of absolute monarchy, the land-owners, the non-industrial bourgeois, the petty bourgeoisie. Thus the whole historical movement is concentrated in the hands of the bourgeoisie; every victory so obtained is a victory for the bourgeoisie.

But with the development of industry the proletariat not only in-creases in number; it becomes concentrated in greater masses, its strength grows, and it feels that strength more. The various interests and con-ditions of life within the ranks of the proletariat are more and more equal-ised, in proportion as machinery obliterates all distinctions of labour, and nearly everywhere reduces wages to the same low level. The growing com-petition among the bourgeois, and the resulting commercial crises, make the wages of the workers ever more fluctuating. The unceasing improve-ment of machinery, ever more rapidly developing, makes their livelihood more and more precarious; the collisions between individual workmen and individual bourgeois take more and more the character of collisions be-tween two classes. Thereupon the workers begin to form combinations (trades' unions) against the bourgeois; they club together in order to keep up the rate of wages; they found permanent associations in order to make provision beforehand for these occasional revolts. Here and there the contest breaks out into riots.

Now and then the workers are victorious, but only for a time. The real fruit of their battles lies, not in the immediate result, but in the ever expanding union of the workers. This union is helped on by the improved means of communication that are created by modern industry, and that place the workers of different localities in contact with one another. It was just this contact that was needed to centralise the numerous local struggles, all of the same character, into one national struggle between classes. But every class struggle is a political struggle. And that union, to attain which the burghers of the Middle Ages, with their miserable highways, required centuries, the modern proletarians, thanks to railways, achieve in a few years.

This organisation of the proletarians into a class, and consequently into a political party, is continually being upset again by the competition between the workers themselves. But it ever rises up again, stronger, firmer, mightier. It compels legislative recognition of particular interests of the workers, by taking advantage of the divisions among the bourgoisie itself. Thus the ten-hours' bill in England was carried.

Altogether, collisions between the classes of the old society further in many ways the course of development of the proletariat. The bourgeoisie finds itself involved in a constant battle. At first with the aristocracy; later on, with those portions of the bourgeoisie itself, whose interests have become antagonistic to the progress of industry; at all times with the bourgeoisie of foreign countries. In all these battles it sees itself compelled to appeal to the proletariat, to ask for its help, and thus to drag it into the political arena. The bourgeoisie itself, therefore, supplies the proletariat with its own elements of political and general education, in other words, it furnishes the proletariat with weapons for fighting the bourgeoisie.

Further, as we have already seen, entire sections of the ruling classes are, by the advance of industry, precipitated into the proletariat, or are at least threatened in their conditions of existence. These also supply the proletariat with fresh elements of enlightenment and progress.

Finally, in times when the class struggle nears the decisive hour, the process of dissolution going on within the ruling class, in fact within the whole range of old society, assumes such a violent, glaring character that a small section of the ruling class cuts itself adrift and joins the revolutionary class, the class that holds the future in its hands. Just as, therefore, at an earlier period, a section of the nobility went over to the bourgeoisie, so now a portion of the bourgeoisie goes over to the proletariat, and, in particular, a portion of the bourgeois ideologists, who have raised themselves to the level of comprehending theoretically the historical movement as a whole.

Of all the classes that stand face to face with the bourgeoisie to-day, the proletariat alone is a really revolutionary class. The other classes decay and finally disappear in the face of modern industry; the proletariat is its special and essential product.

The lower middle class, the small manufacturer, the shopkeeper, the artisan, the peasant, all these fight against the bourgeoisie, to save from extinction their existence as fractions of the middle class. They are therefore not revolutionary but conservative. Nay, more, they are reactionary, for they try to roll back the wheel of history. If by chance they are revolutionary, they are so only in view of their impending transfer into the proletariat; they thus defend not their present, but their future interests; they desert their own standpoint to place themselves at that of the proletariat.

The "dangerous class," the social scum, that passively rotting mass thrown off by the lowest layers of old society, may, here and there, be swept into the movement by a proletarian revolution; its conditions of life, however, prepare it far more for the part of a bribed tool of reactionary intrigue.

In the conditions of the proletariat, those of old society at large are already virtually swamped. The proletarian is without property; his relation to his wife and children has no longer anything in common with the bourgeois family relations; modern industrial labour, modern subjection to capital, the same in England as in France, in America as in Germany, has stripped him of every trace of national character. Law, morality, religion, are to him so many bourgeois prejudices, behind which lurk in ambush just as many bourgeois interests.

All the preceding classes that got the upper hand, sought to fortify their already acquired status by subjecting society at large to their conditions of appropriation. The proletarians cannot become masters of the productive forces of society, except by abolishing their own previous mode of appropriation, and thereby also every other previous mode of appropriation. They have nothing of their own to secure and to fortify; their mission is to destroy all previous securities for, and insurances of, individual property.

All previous historical movements were movements of minorities, or in the interest of minorities. The proletarian movement is the self-conscious, independent movement of the immense majority, in the interest of the immense majority. The proletariat, the lowest stratum of our present society, cannot stir, cannot raise itself up, without the whole superincumbent strata of official society being sprung into the air.

Though not in substance, yet in form, the struggle of the proletariat with the bourgeoisie is at first a national struggle. The proletariat of each country must, of course, first of all settle matters with its own bourgeoisie.

In depicting the most general phases of the development of the proletariat, we traced the more or less veiled civil war, raging within existing society, up to the point where that war breaks out into open revolution, and where the violent overthrow of the bourgeoisie lays the foundation for the sway of the proletariat.

Hitherto, every form of society has been based, as we have already seen, on the antagonism of oppressing and oppressed classes. But in order to oppress a class, certain conditions must be assured to it under which it can, at least, continue its slavish existence. The serf, in the period of serfdom, raised himself to membership in the commune, just as the petty bourgeois, under the yoke of feudal absolutism, managed to develop into a bourgeois. The modern labourer, on the contrary, instead of rising with the progress of industry, sinks deeper and deeper below the conditions of existence of his own class. He becomes a pauper, and pauperism develops more rapidly than population and wealth. And here it becomes evident that the bourgeoisie is unfit any longer to be the ruling class in society and to impose its conditions of existence upon society as an over-riding law. It is unfit to rule because it is incompetent to assure an existence to its slave within his slavery, because it cannot help letting him sink into such a state, that it has to feed him, instead of being fed by him. Society can no longer live under this bourgeoisie; in other words, its existence is no longer compatible with society.

The essential condition for the existence and for the sway of the bourgeois class is the formation and augmentation of capital; the condition for capital is wage-labour. Wage-labour rests exclusively on competition between the labourers. The advance of industry, whose involuntary promoter is the bourgeoisie, replaces the isolation of the labourers, due to competition, by their revolutionary combination, due to association. The development of modern industry, therefore, cuts from under its feet the very foundation on which the bourgeoisie produces and appropriates products. What the bourgeoisie therefore produces, above all, are its own grave-diggers. Its fall and the victory of the proletariat are equally inevitable.

The Communists everywhere support every revolutionary movement against the existing social and political order of things.

In all these movements they bring to the front, as the leading question in each, the property question, no matter what its degree of development at the time.

Finally, they labour everywhere for the union and agreement of the democratic parties of all countries.

The Communists disdain to conceal their views and aims. They openly declare that their ends can be attained only by the forcible overthrow of all existing social conditions. Let the ruling classes tremble at a Communist revolution. The proletarians have nothing to lose but their chains. They have a world to win.

Working men of all countries, unite!

QUESTIONS FOR DISCUSSION

1) Contemporary Marxists still see the struggle between economic classes as the germ of history, and they continue to press for thoroughgoing redistribution of wealth and reorganization of power in favor of the workers. Do you agree with this general theory of history and historical change? Explain.

2) How did the middle class—what Marx and Engels call the bourgeoisie—rise to power? Who are the bourgeoisie in America today? Are they the same class Marx was referring to?

3) Marx says that the bourgeoisie "has drowned the most heavenly ecstasies of religious fervor, of chivalrous enthusiasm, of philistine sentimentalism, in the icy water of egotistical calculation." Following this quotation, the Manifesto details the creative upsurge which bourgeois industrialism brought about. How and why did this happen? Is there any balance between the good and evil created by the bourgeoisie, or does one far outweigh the other?

4) Marx and Engels contend that the bourgeoisie itself created the weapon of its downfall—the workers, or proletariat. In a similar way, can it be said that men, considered individually as well as in groups, are frequently endangered by the products of their own creativity? Discuss.

5) To what extent would you say "The Communist Manifesto" was a "creative" view of history? Similarly, is the writer of history—even revolutionary history—in any way similar, in terms of creativity, to the writer of poems or stories? Or do historians simply deal with "facts"? Explain.

THE POLITICS OF "THE MOVEMENT"

Tom Hayden

My own disenchantment with American society was not caused by its racial bigotry, its warlike posturing, its supreme respect for money. All these might be understood as irrationalities which could be struck from the national character if only rational men were mobilized more effectively. But when events prove this assumption false, then disenchantment really begins—with the understanding that the most respected and enlightened Americans are among the most barbarous.

Take just two examples. There is a conventional notion that the Southern racial crisis is caused and prolonged by "white trash"—an isolated and declining remnant in our society. We are told that rational men are attempting, within the framework of due process, to educate these minority elements to a more progressive social outlook. But this picture is shattered every day by events in the Black Belt. There the murderers of civil rights workers again and again include men like Byron de la Beckwith, the respected downtown businessman who shot Medgar Evers in the back. They are middle class and enjoy the broad support of their local communities.

When this is pointed out, of course, we are told that respectable men are murderers only in places like Mississippi. By national standards the Black Belt killers are not respectable. But is Mississippi an isolated part of America? If not, who at the national level is responsible for the state of terror in Mississippi? Part of the answer, I am afraid, is that leading Northerners buttress the Southern status quo. Without dozens of companies owned from the North, plus the billions provided by defense contracts and agricultural subsidies, Mississippi could not have survived the postwar period as a racist state. Mississippi Power and Light, for example, many of whose personnel are connected with the White Citizens Council, is owned and controlled by the same men who play leading roles in another corporation known for its enlightenment, Harvard University.

A second example: we are told that the United States is on the side of the new nations and the exploited and impoverished peoples of the third world. But once again the facts have nothing to do with this happy picture—as the affairs of an American businessman like Charles Engelhard of New Jersey suggest. In his mid-forties, Engelhard is already renowned in business circles and has become an important political figure in the liberal wing of the Democratic Party. He was sent by the President to represent the U.S. at occasions as vital as the celebration of Algerian independence. He was a friend of John F. Kennedy; Lyndon Johnson praises him as a "great humanitarian." How did he become so famous? Presumably because he owns the controlling interest in the mines of the Republic of South Africa. But aren't those mines a blasphemy against the values of the free world? And is Engelhard an isolated and unrespectable member of that world?

This is civilized barbarism—pernicious, sophisticated, subtly concealed from public view, massively protected from political attack. The barbaric America is invisible to the majority of its people, who are lodged in occupations and social positions which form a desensitizing trap. They are at the bottom, or in the middle, of organizations whose official purposes are justified in abstract terms. Their views, inherited from their families or implanted by the school system, and fed every day by the mass media, permit them to screen out threatening information or alternative ways of seeing the world.

The usual way to "escape" the trapped condition of ordinary Americans is to ascend to higher levels of influence and knowledge in some key institution. But while an overview of society is gained from these positions, a new trap is waiting. For entry into higher organizational circles depends upon accepting their general design and purpose. This means that people in "responsible" positions are most often blind to immoral consequences of their work. Their blindness is intensified by the belief that they are close to people's problems and that administrative remedies exist for whatever arises. This is the usual attitude among public servants, from police to administrators of the War on Poverty.

II

This national trance depends upon one crucial assumption: that American society is being improved domestically. The legitimacy gained by the industrial unions, the liberal welfare legislation which was passed in the thirties and forties, and now the civil rights and anti-poverty reforms of the sixties—these are seen as part of a long sweep toward a society of economic and social justice. But there is, in fact, little evidence to justify the view that the social reforms of the past thirty years actually improved the quality of American life in a lasting way. And there is much evidence which suggests that the reforms gained were illusory or token, serving chiefly to sharpen the capacity of the system for manipulation and oppression.

Look closely for a moment at the social legislation upon which the notion of domestic improvement is based. The Wagner Act was supposed to effect unionization of workers; but today the unionized labor force is shrinking with the automation of the mass-production industries, and millions of other workers, never organized, are without any protection. The Social Security laws were supposed to support people in distress, but today many are still not covered, and those with coverage can barely make ends meet. Unemployment compensation policies were supposed to aid men in need of jobs, but today many are still without coverage, while benefits represent a smaller and smaller share of the cost of living. The 1946 Full Employment Act was supposed to guarantee federal action to provide a job for every American who needed one, but today the official (understated) unemployment rate is close to 6 per cent. The 1949 Public Housing Act, sponsored by conservative Robert Taft, was to create 800,000 low-cost units by 1953, but today less than half that number are constructed, many of them beyond reach of the poor. The difficult struggle to enact even a token policy of public medical care, the hollow support for public education, the stagnation and starvation of broader programs for health, recreation, and simple city services—all this evidence for a simple truth: *the welfare state is a myth.*

Seen in the context of a history of unkept promises, the 1965 antipoverty program should evoke no optimism. The amount of money allocated is a pittance; most of it is going to local politicians, school boards, welfare agencies, housing authorities, professional personnel, and even to the police; its main thrust is to shore up sagging organizational machinery, not to shift the distribution of income and influence in the direction of the poor. Some of the more sophisticated liberals understand that the "involvement of the poor" is essential to an effective program, but this is seen in capitalist-psychological terms, stressing the need to "repair" the defeatist self-image which supposedly excludes the poor from sharing in the enterprise system. A few people, including members of the Administration, see "involvement" in political terms as well. But this participation is frustrated by the poverty planners' undeviating allegiance to existing power centers. In reality, then, the poor only *flavor* the program. A few are co-opted into it, but only as atomized individuals. They do not have independent organizational strength, as do the machines and social agencies.

But the quality of the welfare state is best illustrated by the sluggish way in which it responds to pressure for civil rights reform. It required the slaughter of little girls, a near blood bath in Birmingham, violence toward Northern whites, students and ministers, an outbreak of riots across the North, and the organization of an independent political party in Mississippi before the Administration began to move on the civil rights front. And that motion gives little hope of real progress. Indeed, the 1965 Voting Rights Bill actually shrinks the existing powers of the federal government (as established in such codes as Section 242, Title 18, which provides for criminal prosecution of people acting under cover of law to violate others' constitutional rights). It leaves the decision to take action to the Attorney General; it involves complicated and time-consuming procedures for local Negroes; it provides no protection against intimidation for civil rights workers or local people.

In all these areas, from the Wagner Act to the newest civil rights legislation, my criticism has been narrowed to the question: did the legislation achieve, or does it offer some hope of achieving, its stated purposes? The tragedy, however, is not simply that these programs fall short of their goals. Rather, the goals themselves are far from desirable to anyone interested in greater democracy and a richer quality of social life. Welfare and public housing policies, for instance, are creating a new and public kind of authoritarianism. Public relief clients and tenants, lacking any protective organizations, are subject to the caprice and cruelty of supervisors, investigators, and local machine politicians. Similarly, labor and civil rights legislation creates tools for government intervention at moments of sharp social conflict, without really changing the tyrannical conditions in which millions of workers and Negroes live. The full employment and anti-poverty acts, along with the relief measures of the thirties, give the government power to cushion the economic situation just short of the point of mass unemployment. Programs such as urban renewal serve as the major domestic outlet for investment capital and, consciously or not, as a means of demoralizing and politically fragmenting the poor. The national government thus becomes the chief force for stabilizing the private economy and for managing social crisis. Its interests, institutions, and personnel have merged with those of high finance and industry.

The traditional left expectation of irreconcilable and clashing class interests has been defied. Still assuming such antagonisms, however, many leftists tend to view each piece of social legislation as a victory which strengthens the "progressive" forces. They see a step-by-step transformation of society as the result of pushing for one "politically acceptable" reform after another. But it appears that the American elite has discovered a long-term way to stabilize or cushion the contradictions of our society. It does this through numerous forms of state intervention, the use of our abundant capacity for material gratification, and the ability to condition nearly all the information which people receive. And if this is the case, then more changes of the New Deal variety will not be "progressive" at all. Except for temporarily boosting income for a few people, this entire reformist trend has weakened the poor under the pretense of helping them and strengthened elite rule under the slogan of curbing private enterprise. In fostering a "responsible" Negro and labor leadership and bringing it into the pseudo-pluralist system of bargaining and rewards, a way has been found to contain and paralyze the disadvantaged and voiceless people.

III

Why have liberal strategies failed to secure substantial reforms over the last three decades? The answer can only be grasped by looking at the general organizing concepts of American liberal and labor leaders. These begin with the view that the American masses are "apathetic" and can only be roused because of simple material needs or during short periods of great enthusiasm. The masses most likely to move, it is said, are those who have gained something already: the unionized workers, registered voters, property owners. Those less likely to move are the people on the absolute bottom with nothing to lose, for they are too damaged to be the real motor of change.

From this rough description of the masses, liberals go on to argue the need for certain sorts of organizations. The masses need skilled and responsible leaders, they insist. It is best if these leaders have rank-and-file experience and operate within a formally democratic system. But this grass-roots flavor must not obscure the necessity for leaders to lead, that is, put forward a program, a set of answers that guides The Movement. And because they monopolize leadership experience, it soon appears to these leaders that they alone are qualified to maintain the organization.

The perilous position of The Movement, owing to attacks from centralized business and political forces, adds a further incentive for a top-down system of command. The need for alliances with other groups, created in large part through the trust which sets of leaders develop for each other, also intensifies the trend toward vertical organization. Finally, the leaders see a need to screen out anyone with "communist-oriented" views, since such individuals are presumably too skilled to be allowed to operate freely within The Movement. Slowly an elite is formed, calling itself the liberal-labor community. It treats the rank and file as a mass to be molded; sometimes thrust forward into action, sometimes held back. A self-fulfilling pattern emerges: because the nature of the organization is elitist, many people react to it with disinterest or suspicion, giving the leadership the evidence it needs to call the masses apathetic.

The pressures which influence these leaders come, not primarily from below, but from the top, from the most powerful men in the country. Sometimes bluntly and sometimes subtly, the real elite grooms responsible trade union and civil rights leaders. The leaders' existence comes to depend upon the possibility of receiving attention from the President or some top aide, and they judge organizational issues with an eye on this possibility. There is usually no question about the leaders' primary loyalty to the "national interest" as defined by the Administration, even though they always believe their judgments are independently made. Thus most of the civil rights leadership in 1964, fearing the Goldwater movement and hoping for civil rights legislation from a victorious Johnson Administration, called for a "moratorium" on mass demonstrations. The labor leadership performed the same function for the same reasons during World War II; the irony is that their critics in that period included A. Philip Randolph and Bayard Rustin, two Negroes who pushed for the 1964 moratorium.

A recent incident clarified the political role of this leadership and pointed towards the possibility of an alternative strategy. This was the challenge posed by the Mississippi Freedom Democratic Party and the

Student Nonviolent Coordinating Committee at the 1964 Democratic National Convention.

Members of the FDP trooped into Atlantic City to argue for their rightful control of the Mississippi Democratic seats. They found substantial support from rank-and-file members of Northern delegations who favored their modest demand for at least equal treatment with the racist party at the convention. Here was a chance, it was thought, to end Southern obstruction of the Johnson administration's program. But then the Democratic leadership let its position be known: the FDP was morally sound, but "illegal" and "not qualified." Support within the delegations wavered. The FDP's last chance for success depended on rallying national liberal-labor leaders to support its demand for a floor debate, in front of the television cameras. But some Negro leaders worked against the Mississippi party, others took a vacillating position, and no one would stand firmly with them. To do so, the leaders claimed, would jeopardize Humphrey's chance at the vice-presidency, strengthen Goldwater's hand, and split the FDP from its "allies" in the liberal-labor world. The FDP members decided that the fate of Humphrey and Goldwater depended, in fact, upon the same power structure that was determining their own fate. Not wanting the kind of "allies" and "victories" being offered, they went home. Their real allies were the poor people waiting in the Delta; and their real victory was in being able to maintain fidelity to those allies. This was a victory because it kept the movement alive and gave its members some real understanding of what was needed to change the national situation.

IV

The Mississippi challenge to the convention points toward a new kind of politics and a new kind of organizing, which has at least an outside chance of truly changing American society. This stirring we call The Movement.

The Movement tries to oppose American barbarism with new structures and opposing identities. These are created by people whose need to understand their society and govern their own existence has somehow not been canceled out by the psychological damage they have received. For different reasons such needs survive among the poor, among students and other young people, and finally among millions of other Americans not easily grouped except by their modest individual resistance to the system's inhumanity. It is from these ranks that The Movement is being created. What kind of people, more exactly, are they, and what kind of organizational strategy might they develop?

1. *An interracial movement of the poor.* The Mississippi sharecroppers are the most visible and inspiring representatives of an awakening that is taking place among the poor in America. Their perspective centers on Negro freedom, of course, but they are committed deeply to the idea of a

movement of all the powerless and exploited. In certain ways theirs is a radicalism unique because of Black Belt conditions. Their strength comes from a stable system of family life and work. Politics is new and fresh for them; they have not experienced the hollow promises of an opportunistic liberal-Negro machine. Their opposition's naked brutality keeps them constantly in a crisis framework. The broadening of their movement into Arkansas, Alabama, Louisiana, Georgia, the Carolinas, and Virginia, already under way, can be expected to challenge fundamentally the national coalition directing the Democratic Party. Already the Democrats are trying to groom moderate and liberal politicians to provide an "alternative" to the segregationists and the independent FDP. Probably this effort will succeed, in the sense that political moderates will begin to compete for electoral power and leadership of the civil rights forces, mostly basing their strength in the cities, among privileged Negroes. The FDP, as a structure, may be absorbed into the national party, if only because it has no other, more effective place to go. But since the new Southern power structure will not solve the problems of poverty and race which have plagued the North for generations, there is very little chance that this movement of poor people will be entirely co-opted or crushed.

In the black ghettos of the North, The Movement faces heavier obstacles. There work is often deadening, family life distorted; "proper" political channels are sewers; people are used to, and tired of, party organizers exploiting them. The civil rights movement does not touch these hundreds of ghettos in any significant way because of the middle-class nature of its program and leadership. However, the Harlem rent strikes and the activities of Malcolm X were clear evidence that there are in the ghettos people prepared to take action. Some of them are of Southern background; some are housewives with wasted talents; some are youth with no future for their energy; some are junkies and numbers men with little loyalty to their particular game. Different as the forms of their discontent may be, the discontent itself is general to the ghetto and can be the mainspring for action. Under present conditions political movements among these people are likely to be based on a race consciousness which is genuine and militant —and which is also vital because of the failure of whites to act in favor of equal rights. The ghetto race consciousness, however, is intertwined with the consciousness of being both poor and powerless. Almost of necessity, the demands that the ghetto poor put forward are also in the interest of the white poor, as well as of middle-class professionals who depend on the expansion of the public sectors of the economy.

But will white working-class and poor people take up these issues, which the "Negro problem" by its nature tends to raise? The negative evidence is plentiful. Poor whites, such as those in parts of the South who are truly irrelevant to the modern economy, tend to see their plight (sometimes with accuracy) as personal rather than social: a function of sickness, bad luck, or psychological disorder. Poverty is not seen clearly as the fate of a whole interracial class, but only as the fate of individuals, each shamed into self-blame by their Protestant ideology. Working-class whites, on the other hand, are more likely to be conscious of their problems as a group, but they tend to defend their scarce privileges—jobs, wages, education for their children—against what they see as the onslaught of Negro competition. While "backlash" did not split the alliance of white working people with the Democratic Party in 1964, it does serve as a barrier to an alliance with the Negro poor. But it is foolish to be rigid about these notions. Whites *are* being organized, on a mass basis, in areas of Appalachia where there exists a common culture and an industrial union tradition, and where the blame for misery can be laid to the coal operators, the conservative United Mine Workers, and the government. They also have been organized in Cleveland, where they face the "welfare situation" together.

But these organizing efforts were led by local people or independent organizers outside the structure of the labor movement. Today there are millions of workers trapped by the organizational framework of the AFL-CIO. Their unrest at times moves the international unions slightly, but the internationals are more dependent on government and business than on their own members, and, in addition, they seem to possess effective techniques for curbing shop revolts. It is not simply the "better objective conditions" which split the white from the Negro poor but the existence of trade unions which actively distort the better aspirations of their members. Economic and social conditions, of course, are not improving and workers' discontent is evidenced by the recent wave of rank-and-file revolts. But whether or not this discontent spurs a coalition of poor whites with Negroes depends, most of all, on whether a way can be found to organize workers independent of AFL-CIO routines. Concretely, that means democratic control by the workers of their union locals, and the entry of those locals into political activities and coalitions on the community level. It also means community action and organization among the millions of low-paid workers presently outside the labor movement.

The crucial importance of community work can be grasped only if one understands the sorts of ideas the American poor have about themselves. They operate with a kind of split consciousness. On the one hand, poor people know they are victimized from every direction. The facts of life always break through to expose the distance between American ideals and personal realities. This kind of knowledge, however, is kept undeveloped and unused because of another knowledge imposed on the poor, a keen sense of dependence on the oppressor. This is the source of that universal fear which leads poor people to act and even to think subserviently. Seeing themselves to blame for their situation, they rule out the possibility that they might be qualified to govern themselves and their own organizations. Besides fear, it is their sense of inadequacy and embarrassment which destroys the possibility of revolt. At the same time this set of contradictory feelings results in indirect forms of protest all the time: styles of dress and language, withdrawal from political life, defiance of the boss's or the welfare worker's rules and regulations.

There can be no poor people's movement in any form unless the poor can overcome their fear and embarrassment. I think the release comes from a certain kind of organizing which tries to make people understand their own worth and dignity. This work depends on the existence of "material issues" as a talking and organizing point—high rents, voting rights, unpaved roads, and so on—but it moves from there into the ways such issues are related to personal life. The organizer spends hours and hours in the community, listening to people, drawing out their own ideas, rejecting their tendency to depend on him for solutions. Meetings are organized at which people with no "connections" can be given a chance to talk and work out problems together—usually for the first time. All this means fostering in *everyone* that sense of decision-making power which American society works to destroy. Only in this way can a movement be built which the Establishment can neither buy off nor manage, a movement too vital ever to become a small clique of spokesmen.

An organizational form that suggests the style of such a movement is the "community union," involving working-class and poor people in local insurgency. Open and democratic, the community union offers a real alternative to the kind of participation permitted in civil rights groups, trade unions, and Democratic Party machines. It might take a variety of forms: block clubs, housing committees, youth groups, etc. The union's insistence on the relevance of "little people," as well as its position outside and against the normal channels, would create a rooted sense of independence among the members.

The problem of politics among the poor is severe. In the first place, their potential electoral power is low because of their location in gerrymandered political districts, their rapid movement from house to house, and the complicated and discriminatory electoral procedures in many cities. Beyond these problems lies the obvious and well-grounded cynicism of the poor about elections. Given all these conditions, it is barely conceivable that a poor person could be elected to an important political office. Even were this possible, it would be on a token basis, and the elected official would be under strong pressure to conform to the rules of the game. Thus the orthodox idea of politics is contradictory to building a movement. The Movement needs to discover a politics of its own. This might be done by electing people who will see their office as a community organizing tool, letting community people participate directly in decisions about how the office should be used. This experiment is being made in Atlanta where a SNCC field secretary, Julian Bond, was elected in June 1965 to the state legislature. What might be done is to contest the basic class and racial injustices of American politics, demanding that poverty areas be granted political representation, or running freedom elections to dramatize the lack of representation for the boxed-in poor. This sort of thing would probably mobilize more poor people than orthodox electoral activity. The mobilization would be "practical" from the standpoint of getting modest reforms; more importantly, it would point toward the need to rearrange American political institutions to fit the needs of excluded people.

2. *A student movement.* If poor people are in The Movement because they have nothing to gain in the status system, students are in it because, in a sense, they have gained too much. Most of the active student radicals today come from middle- to upper-middle-class professional homes. They were born with status and affluence as facts of life, not goals to be striven for. In their upbringing, their parents stressed the right of children to question and make judgments, producing perhaps the first generation of young people both affluent and independent of mind. And then these students so often encountered social institutions that denied them their independence and betrayed the democratic ideals they were taught. They saw that men of learning were careerists; that school administrators and ministers almost never discussed the realities the students lived with; that even their parents were not true to the ideals they taught the young.

It was against this background of tension that young people became concerned in the early sixties about war, racism, and inequality. By now the empty nature of existing vocational alternatives has pushed several hundreds of these students into community organizing. Working in poor communities is a concrete task in which the split between job and values can be healed. It is also a position from which to expose the whole structure of pretense, status, and glitter that masks the country's real human problems. And, finally, it is a way to find people who want to change the country, and possibly can do so.

When a student comes into a community there are countless obstacles in his way. He is an outsider, he is overeducated, he has nothing concrete to offer people, and often he is white in a Negro ghetto. At the same time, however, he brings something with him: the very presence of students suggests to the poor that their more activist notions may be right after all. The student alone can say, "Look, I come from the world that says you are not qualified, and I know that is a lie. I come to you because you can teach me as much as I can teach you." Students can also make the poverty problem visible and threatening because they create resources previously unimaginable. Parents and universities become energized; money can be raised; contacts can be set up with other people's organizations around the country. Finally, students and poor people make each other feel real. What has flowed from this connection is most of the vitality of the civil rights and anti-poverty movements over the past five years.

Now it appears that students are finding ways to organize effectively around other problems too: university reform and peace. The Berkeley "uprising" and the April March of 20,000 against the war in Vietnam were major departures from the inconsequential student politics of the old days. On many campuses students are beginning to form unions of their own, as well as independent seminars pointed toward the eventual organization of a "free university." In addition, they are beginning to mobilize community action against the Vietnamese war—thereby encountering their friends already at work among the poor. These efforts may thread the several protest movements in the country into a grass-roots coalition.

3. *Middle-class insurgents.* A centralized and commercial society wastes the talents and energies of millions of individuals. Some of these are women who are excluded from male-dominated vocations. Some are people with human values who cannot assert them effectively within organizations attached to the Cold War consensus. Some were politically active in the thirties but faded away when popular movements declined. Some are part of the postwar generation that missed the experience of a radical movement altogether, and who are lodged uncomfortably in publishing houses, universities, and labor bureaucracies.

The new movements are opening great possibilities for participation by such middle-class people. Their activity often includes vital financial support, but it can and does go further. Insurgency within American institutions is spreading: professors fighting their administrations, lawyers against the bar association, welfare workers against the political machine, muckrakers against the press establishments. This insurgency is bound to increase as the new generation of student activists graduates into the professions. And it is an insurgency which needs a movement of poor people, insistently demanding new social purposes from the professionals.

To summarize: The Movement is a community of insurgents sharing the same radical values and identity, seeking an independent base of power wherever they are. It aims at a transformation of society led by the most excluded and "unqualified" people. Primarily, this means building institutions outside the established order which seek to become the genuine institutions of the total society. Community unions, freedom schools, experimental universities, community-formed police review boards, people's own anti-poverty organizations fighting for federal money, independent union locals —all can be "practical" pressure points from which to launch reform in the conventional institutions while at the same time maintaining a separate base and pointing toward a new system. Ultimately this Movement might lead to a Continental Congress called by all the people who feel excluded from the higher circles of decision making in the country. This Congress might even become a kind of second government, receiving taxes from its supporters, establishing contact with other nations, holding debates on American foreign and domestic policy, dramatizing the plight of all groups that suffer from the American system.

If it is hard to imagine this kind of revolutionary process in the United States, it might be because no previous model of revolution seems appropriate to this most bloated and flexible of the advanced societies. There may be no way to change this country. At least there is no way we can bank on. Both technological change and social reform seem to rationalize the power of the system to drain the heart of protest. The Movement at least suggests that we bank on our own consciousness, what there is of our own humanity, and begin to work.

QUESTIONS FOR DISCUSSION

1) Contemporary critics of Marxism consider it a discredited philosophy with no cause left to champion since the working class has not descended into "pauperism" and has not revolted on a world-wide scale. However, in the last ten years, the "left" has begun to gain back some of its old vigor. Tom Hayden's article sets forth the concerns and programs of this "New Left." What similarity, implicit or explicit, do you find between "The Communist Manifesto" (p. 297) and Hayden's article? Discuss.

2) Hayden begins by attempting to prove two propositions. The first is that the American ruling class is barbaric. The second is that the American people have not gained as much as they think they have from liberal legislation. How convincing are Hayden's arguments supporting these two propositions? Explain.

3) Why, according to Hayden, are labor leaders more sensitive to the wishes of their business and political counterparts than to those of their own rank and file?

4) Hayden stresses the importance for the poor of gaining enough confidence and hope to become active and innovative themselves, to find their own solutions to their problems. What are the advantages and disadvantages of this approach?

5) Can you think of other ways besides those mentioned by Hayden for channeling the nation's creative energies toward the solution of its social, economic, and political problems? Hayden's basic response to this challenge is "The Movement." Comment on its chances for success or failure.

6) Is "radical" political action always "creative"?

THE WALL

Jean-Paul Sartre

They pushed us into a big white room and I began to blink because the light hurt my eyes. Then I saw a table and four men behind the table, civilians, looking over the papers. They had bunched another group of prisoners in the back and we had to cross the whole room to join them. There were several I knew and some others who must have been foreigners. The two in front of me were blond with round skulls; they looked alike. I supposed they were French. The smaller one kept hitching up his pants; nerves.

It lasted about three hours; I was dizzy and my head was empty; but the room was well heated and I found that pleasant enough: for the past 24 hours we hadn't stopped shivering. The guards brought the prisoners up to the table, one after the other. The four men asked each one his name and occupation. Most of the time they didn't go any further—or they would simply ask a question here and there: "Did you have anything to do with the sabotage of munitions?" Or "Where were you the morning of the 9th and what were you doing?" They didn't listen to the answers or at least didn't seem to. They were quiet for a moment and then looking straight in front of them began to write. They asked Tom if it were true he was in the International Brigade; Tom couldn't tell them otherwise because of the papers they found in his coat. They didn't ask Juan anything but they wrote for a long time after he told them his name.

"My brother José is the anarchist," Juan said, "you know he isn't here any more. I don't belong to any party, I never had anything to do with politics."

They didn't answer. Juan went on, "I haven't done anything. I don't want to pay for somebody else."

His lips trembled. A guard shut him up and took him away. It was my turn.

"Your name is Pablo Ibbieta?"

"Yes."

The man looked at the papers and asked me, "Where's Ramon Gris?"

"I don't know."

"You hid him in your house from the 6th to the 19th."

"No."

They wrote for a minute and then the guards took me out. In the corridor Tom and Juan were waiting between two guards. We started walking. Tom asked one of the guards, "So?"

"So what?" the guard said.

"Was that the cross-examination or the sentence?"

"Sentence," the guard said.

"What are they going to do with us?"

The guard answered dryly, "Sentence will be read in your cell."

As a matter of fact, our cell was one of the hospital cellars. It was terrifically cold there because of the drafts. We shivered all night and it wasn't much better during the day. I had spent the previous five days in a cell in a monastery, a sort of hole in the wall that must have dated from the middle ages: since there were a lot of prisoners and not much room, they locked us up anywhere. I didn't miss my cell; I hadn't suffered too much from the cold but I was alone; after a long time it gets irritating. In the cellar I had company. Juan hardly ever spoke: he was afraid and he was too young to have anything to say. But Tom was a good talker and he knew Spanish well.

There was a bench in the cellar and four mats. When they took us back we sat and waited in silence. After a long moment, Tom said, "We're screwed."

"I think so too," I said, "but I don't think they'll do anything to the kid."

"They don't have a thing against him," said Tom. "He's the brother of a militiaman and that's all."

I looked at Juan: he didn't seem to hear. Tom went on, "You know what they do in Saragossa? They lay the men down on the road and run over them with trucks. A Moroccan deserter told us that. They said it was to save ammunition."

"It doesn't save gas," I said.

I was annoyed at Tom: he shouldn't have said that.

"Then there's officers walking along the road," he went on, "supervising it all. They stick their hands in their pockets and smoke cigarettes. You think they finish off the guys? Hell no. They let them scream. Sometimes for an hour. The Moroccan said he damned near puked the first time."

"I don't believe they'll do that here," I said. "Unless they're really short on ammunition."

Day was coming in through four airholes and a round opening they had made in the ceiling on the left, and you could see the sky through it. Through this hole, usually closed by a trap, they unloaded coal into the cellar. Just below the hole there was a big pile of coal dust; it had been used to heat the hospital but since the beginning of the war the patients were evacuated and the coal stayed there, unused; sometimes it even got rained on because they had forgotten to close the trap.

Tom began to shiver. "Good Jesus Christ I'm cold," he said. "Here it goes again."

He got up and began to do exercises. At each movement his shirt opened on his chest, white and hairy. He lay on his back, raised his legs in the air and bicycled. I saw his great rump trembling. Tom was husky but he had too much fat. I thought how rifle bullets or the sharp points of bayonets would soon be sunk into this mass of tender flesh as in a lump of butter. It wouldn't have made me feel like that if he'd been thin.

I wasn't exactly cold, but I couldn't feel my arms and shoulders any more. Sometimes I had the impression I was missing something and began to look around for my coat and then suddenly remembered they hadn't given me a coat. It was rather uncomfortable. They took our clothes and gave them to their soldiers leaving us only our shirts—and those canvas pants that hospital patients wear in the middle of summer. After a while Tom got up and sat next to me, breathing heavily.

"Warmer?"

"Good Christ, no. But I'm out of wind."

Around eight o'clock in the evening a major came in with two *falangistas*. He had a sheet of paper in his hand. He asked the guard, "What are the names of those three?"

"Steinbock, Ibbieta and Mirbal," the guard said.

The major put on his eyeglasses and scanned the list: "Steinbock . . . Steinbock . . . Oh yes . . . You are sentenced to death. You will be shot tomorrow morning." He went on looking. "The other two as well."

"That's not possible," Juan said. "Not me."

The major looked at him amazed. "What's your name?"

"Juan Mirbal," he said.

"Well, your name is there," said the major. "You're sentenced."

"I didn't do anything," Juan said.

The major shrugged his shoulders and turned to Tom and me.

"You're Basque?"

"Nobody is Basque."

He looked annoyed. "They told me there were three Basques. I'm not going to waste my time running after them. Then naturally you don't want a priest?"

We didn't even answer.

He said, "A Belgian doctor is coming shortly. He is authorized to spend the night with you." He made a military salute and left.

"What did I tell you," Tom said. "We get it."

"Yes," I said, "it's a rotten deal for the kid."

I said that to be decent but I didn't like the kid. His face was too thin and fear and suffering had disfigured it, twisting all his features. Three days before he was a smart sort of kid, not too bad; but now he looked like an old fairy and I thought how he'd never be young again, even if they were to let him go. It wouldn't have been too hard to have a little pity for him but pity disgusts me, or rather it horrifies me. He hadn't said anything more but he had turned grey; his face and hands were both grey. He sat down again and looked at the ground with round eyes. Tom was good hearted, he wanted to take his arm, but the kid tore himself away violently and made a face.

"Let him alone," I said in a low voice, "you can see he's going to blubber."

Tom obeyed regretfully; he would have liked to comfort the kid, it would have passed his time and he wouldn't have been tempted to think about himself. But it annoyed me: I'd never thought about death because I never had any reason to, but now the reason was here and there was nothing to do but think about it.

Tom began to talk. "So you think you've knocked guys off, do you?" he asked me. I didn't answer. He began explaining to me that he had knocked off six since the beginning of August; he didn't realize the situation and I could tell he didn't *want* to realize it. I hadn't quite realized it myself, I wondered if it hurt much, I thought of bullets, I imagined their burning hail through my body. All that was beside the real question; but I was calm: we had all night to understand. After a while Tom stopped talking and I watched him out of the corner of my eye; I saw he too had turned grey and he looked rotten; I told myself "Now it starts." It was almost dark, a dim glow filtered through the airholes and the pile of coal and made a big stain beneath the spot of sky; I could already see a star through the hole in the ceiling: the night would be pure and icy.

The door opened and two guards came in, followed by a blonde man in a tan uniform. He saluted us. "I am the doctor," he said. "I have authorization to help you in these trying hours."

He had an agreeable and distinguished voice. I said, "What do you want here?"

"I am at your disposal. I shall do all I can to make your last moments less difficult."

"What did you come here for? There are others, the hospital's full of them."

"I was sent here," he answered with a vague look. "Ah! Would you like to smoke?" he added hurriedly, "I have cigarettes and even cigars."

He offered us English cigarettes and *puros,* but we refused. I looked him in the eyes and he seemed irritated. I said to him, "You aren't here on an errand of mercy. Besides, I know you. I saw you with the fascists in the barracks yard the day I was arrested."

I was going to continue, but something surprising suddenly happened to me; the presence of this doctor no longer interested me. Generally when I'm on somebody I don't let go. But the desire to talk left me completely; I shrugged and turned my eyes away. A little later I raised my head; he was watching me curiously. The guards were sitting on a mat. Pedro, the tall thin one, was twiddling his thumbs, the other shook his head from time to time to keep from falling asleep.

"Do you want a light?" Pedro suddenly asked the doctor. The other nodded "Yes": I think he was about as smart as a log, but he surely wasn't bad. Looking in his cold blue eyes it seemed to me that his only sin was lack of imagination. Pedro went out and came back with an oil lamp which he set on the corner of the bench. It gave a bad light but it was better than nothing: they had left us in the dark the night before. For a long time I watched the circle of light the lamp made on the ceiling. I was fascinated. Then suddenly I woke up, the circle of light disappeared and I felt myself crushed under an enormous weight. It was not the thought of death, or fear; it was nameless. My cheeks burned and my head ached.

I shook myself and looked at my two friends. Tom had hidden his face in his hands. I could only see the fat white nape of his neck. Little Juan was the worst, his mouth was open and his nostrils trembled. The doctor went to him and put his hand on his shoulder to comfort him: but his eyes stayed cold. Then I saw the Belgian's hand drop stealthily along Juan's arm, down to the wrist. Juan paid no attention. The Belgian took his wrist between three fingers, distractedly, the same time drawing back a little and turning his back to me. But I leaned backward and saw him take a watch from his pocket and look at it for a moment, never letting go of the wrist. After a minute he let the hand fall inert and went and leaned his back against the wall, then, as if he suddenly remembered something very important which had to be jotted down on the spot, he took a notebook from his pocket and wrote a few lines. "Bastard," I thought angrily, "let him come and take my pulse. I'll shove my fist in his rotten face."

He didn't come but I felt him watching me. I raised my head and returned his look. Impersonally, he said to me, "Doesn't it seem cold to you here?" He looked cold, he was blue.

"I'm not cold," I told him.

He never took his hard eyes off me. Suddenly I understood and my hands went to my face: I was drenched in sweat. In this cellar, in the midst of winter, in the midst of drafts, I was sweating. I ran my hands through my hair, gummed together with perspiration; at the same time I saw my shirt was damp and sticking to my skin: I had been dripping for an hour and hadn't felt it. But that swine of a Belgian hadn't missed a thing; he had seen the drops rolling down my cheeks and thought: this is the manifestation of an almost pathological state of terror; and he had felt normal and proud of being alive because he was cold. I wanted to stand up and smash his face but no sooner had I made the slightest gesture than my rage and shame were wiped out; I fell back on the bench with indifference.

I satisfied myself by rubbing my neck with my handkerchief because now I felt the sweat dropping from my hair onto my neck and it was unpleasant. I soon gave up rubbing, it was useless; my handkerchief was already soaked and I was still sweating. My buttocks were sweating too and my damp trousers were glued to the bench.

Suddenly Juan spoke. "You're a doctor?"

"Yes," the Belgian said.

"Does it hurt . . . very long?"

"Huh? When . . . ? Oh, no," the Belgian said paternally. "Not at all. It's over quickly." He acted as though he were calming a cash customer.

"But I . . . they told me . . . sometimes they have to fire twice."

"Sometimes," the Belgian said, nodding. "It may happen that the first volley reaches no vital organs."

"Then they have to reload their rifles and aim all over again?" He thought for a moment and then added hoarsely, "That takes time!"

He had a terrible fear of suffering, it was all he thought about: it was his age. I never thought much about it and it wasn't fear of suffering that made me sweat.

I got up and walked to the pile of coal dust. Tom jumped up and threw me a hateful look: I had annoyed him because my shoes squeaked. I wondered if my face looked as frightened as his: I saw he was sweating too. The sky was superb, no light filtered into the dark corner and I had only to raise my head to see the Big Dipper. But it wasn't like it had been: the night before I could see a great piece of sky from my monastery cell and each hour of the day brought me a different memory. Morning, when the sky was a hard, light blue, I thought of beaches on the Atlantic; at noon I saw the sun and I remembered a bar in Seville where I drank *manzanilla* and ate olives and anchovies; afternoons I was in the shade and I thought of the deep shadow which spreads over half a bull-ring leaving the other half shimmering in sunlight; it was really hard to see the whole world reflected in the sky like that. But now I could watch the sky as much as I pleased, it no longer evoked anything in me. I liked that better. I came back and sat near Tom. A long moment passed.

Tom began speaking in a low voice. He had to talk, without that he wouldn't have been able to recognize himself in his own mind. I thought he was talking to me but he wasn't looking at me. He was undoubtedly afraid to see me as I was, grey and sweating: we were alike and worse than mirrors of each other. He watched the Belgian, the living.

"Do you understand?" he said. "I don't understand."

I began to speak in a low voice too. I watched the Belgian. "Why? What's the matter?"

"Something is going to happen to us that I can't understand."

There was a strange smell about Tom. It seemed to me I was more sensitive than usual to odors. I grinned. "You'll understand in a while."

"It isn't clear," he said obstinately. "I want to be brave but first I have to know . . . Listen, they're going to take us into the courtyard. Good. They're going to stand up in front of us. How many?"

"I don't know. Five or eight. Not more."

"All right. There'll be eight. Someone'll holler 'aim!' and I'll see eight rifles looking at me. I'll think how I'd like to get inside the wall, I'll push against it with my back . . . with every ounce of strength I have, but the wall will stay, like in a nightmare. I can imagine all that. If you only knew how well I can imagine it."

"All right, all right!" I said, "I can imagine it too."

"It must hurt like hell. You know, they aim at the eyes and the mouth to disfigure you," he added mechanically. "I can feel the wounds already; I've had pains in my head and in my neck for the past hour. Not real pains. Worse. This is what I'm going to feel tomorrow morning. And then what?"

I well understood what he meant but I didn't want to act as if I did. I had pains too, pains in my body like a crowd of tiny scars. I couldn't get used to it. But I was like him, I attached no importance to it. "After," I said, "you'll be pushing up daisies."

He began to talk to himself: he never stopped watching the Belgian. The Belgian didn't seem to be listening. I knew what he had come to do; he wasn't interested in what we thought; he came to watch our bodies, bodies dying in agony while yet alive.

"It's like a nightmare," Tom was saying. "You want to think something, you always have the impression that it's all right, that you're going to understand and then it slips, it escapes you and fades away. I tell myself there will be nothing afterwards. But I don't understand what it means. Sometimes I almost can . . . and then it fades away and I start thinking about the pains again, bullets, explosions. I'm a materialist, I swear it to you; I'm not going crazy. But something's the matter. I see my corpse; that's not hard but *I'm* the one who sees it, with *my* eyes. I've got to think . . . think that I won't see anything anymore and the world will go on for the others. We aren't made to think that, Pablo. Believe me: I've already stayed up a whole night waiting for something. But this isn't the same: this will creep up behind us, Pablo, and we won't be able to prepare for it."

"Shut up," I said, "Do you want me to call a priest?"

He didn't answer. I had already noticed he had the tendency to act like a prophet and call me Pablo, speaking in a toneless voice. I didn't like that: but it seems all the Irish are that way. I had the vague impression he smelled of urine. Fundamentally, I hadn't much sympathy for Tom and I didn't see why, under the pretext of dying together, I should have any more. It would have been different with some others. With Ramon Gris, for example. But I felt alone between Tom and Juan. I liked that better, anyhow: with Ramon I might have been more deeply moved. But I was terribly hard just then and I wanted to stay hard.

He kept on chewing his words, with something like distraction. He certainly talked to keep himself from thinking. He smelled of urine like an old prostate case. Naturally, I agreed with him, I could have said everything he said: it isn't *natural* to die. And since I was going to die, nothing seemed natural to me, not this pile of coal dust, or the bench, or Pedro's ugly face. Only it didn't please me to think the same things as Tom. And I knew that, all through the night, every five minutes, we would keep on thinking things at the same time. I looked at him sideways and for the first time he seemed strange to me: he wore death on his face. My pride was wounded: for the past 24 hours I had lived next to Tom, I had listened to him, I had spoken to him and I knew we had nothing in common. And now we looked as much alike as twin brothers, simply because we were going to die together. Tom took my hand without looking at me.

"Pablo, I wonder . . . I wonder if it's really true that everything ends."

I took my hand away and said, "Look between your feet, you pig."

There was a big puddle between his feet and drops fell from his pants-leg.

"What is it," he asked, frightened.

"You're pissing in your pants," I told him.

"It isn't true," he said furiously. "I'm not pissing. I don't feel anything."

The Belgian approached us. He asked with false solicitude, "Do you feel ill?"

Tom did not answer. The Belgian looked at the puddle and said nothing.

"I don't know what it is," Tom said ferociously. "But I'm not afraid. I swear I'm not afraid."

The Belgian did not answer. Tom got up and went to piss in a corner. He came back buttoning his fly, and sat down without a word. The Belgian was taking notes.

All three of us watched him because he was alive. He had the motions of a living human being, the cares of a living human being; he shivered in the cellar the way the living are supposed to shiver; he had an obedient, well-fed body. The rest of us hardly felt ours—not in the same way anyhow. I wanted to feel my pants between my legs but I didn't dare; I watched the Belgian, balancing on his legs, master of his muscles, someone who could think about tomorrow. There we were, three bloodless shadows; we watched him and we sucked his life like vampires.

Finally he went over to little Juan. Did he want to feel his neck for some professional motive or was he obeying an impulse of charity? If he was acting by charity it was the only time during the whole night.

He caressed Juan's head and neck. The kid let himself be handled, his eyes never leaving him, then suddenly, he seized the hand and looked at it strangely. He held the Belgian's hand between his own two hands and there was nothing pleasant about them, two grey pincers gripping this fat and reddish hand. I suspected what was going to happen and Tom must have suspected it too: but the Belgian didn't see a thing, he smiled paternally. After a moment the kid brought the fat red hand to his mouth and tried to bite it. The Belgian pulled away quickly and stumbled back against the wall. For a second he looked at us with horror, he must have suddenly understood that we were not men like him. I began to laugh and one of the guards jumped up. The other was asleep, his wide open eyes were blank.

I felt relaxed and over-excited at the same time. I didn't want to think any more about what would happen at dawn, at death. It made no sense. I only found words or emptiness. But as soon as I tried to think of anything else I saw rifle barrels pointing at me. Perhaps I lived through my execution twenty times; once I even thought it was for good: I must have slept a minute. They were dragging me to the wall and I was struggling; I was asking for mercy. I woke up with a start and looked at the Belgian: I was afraid I might have cried out in my sleep. But he was stroking his moustache, he hadn't noticed anything. If I had wanted to, I think I could have slept a while; I had been awake for 48 hours. I was at the end of my rope. But I didn't want to lose two hours of life: they would come to wake me up at dawn, I would follow them, stupefied with sleep and I would have croaked without so much as an "Oof!"; I didn't want that, I didn't want to die like an animal, I wanted to understand. Then I was afraid of having nightmares. I got up, walked back and forth, and, to change my ideas, I began to think about my past life. A crowd of memories came back to me pell-mell. There were good and bad ones—or at least I called them that *before*. There were faces and incidents. I saw the face of a little *novillero* who was gored in Valencia during the *Feria,* the face of one of my uncles, the face of Ramon Gris. I remembered my whole life: how I was out of work for three months in 1926, how I almost starved to death. I remembered a night I spent on a bench in Grenada: I hadn't eaten for three days. I was angry, I didn't want to die. That made me smile. How madly I ran after happiness, after women, after liberty. Why? I wanted to free Spain, I admired Pi y Margall, I joined the anarchist movement, I spoke in public meetings: I took everything as seriously as if I were immortal.

At that moment I felt that I had my whole life in front of me and I thought, "It's a damned lie." It was worth nothing because it was finished. I wondered how I'd been able to walk, to laugh with the girls: I wouldn't have moved so much as my little finger if I had only imagined I would die like this. My life was in front of me, shut, closed, like a bag and yet everything inside of it was unfinished. For an instant I tried to judge it. I wanted to tell myself, this is a beautiful life. But I couldn't pass judgment on it; it was only a sketch; I had spent my time counterfeiting eternity, I had understood nothing. I missed nothing: there were so many things I could have missed, the taste of *manzanilla* or the baths I took in summer in a little creek near Cadiz; but death had disenchanted everything.

The Belgian suddenly had a bright idea. "My friends," he told us, "I will undertake—if the military administration will allow it—to send a message for you, a souvenir to those who love you . . ."

Tom mumbled, "I don't have anybody."

I said nothing. Tom waited an instant then looked at me with curiosity. "You don't have anything to say to Concha?"

"No."

I hated this tender complicity: it was my own fault, I had talked about Concha the night before, I should have controlled myself. I was with her for a year. Last night I would have given an arm to see her again for five minutes. That was why I talked about her, it was stronger than I was. Now I had no more desire to see her, I had nothing more to say to her. I would not even have wanted to hold her in my arms: my body filled me with horror because it was grey and sweating—and I wasn't sure that her body didn't fill me with horror. Concha would cry when she found out I was dead, she would have no taste for life for months afterward. But I was still the one who was going to die. I thought of her soft, beautiful eyes. When she looked at me something passed from her to me. But I knew it was over: if she looked at me *now* the look would stay in her eyes, it wouldn't reach me. I was alone.

Tom was alone too but not in the same way. Sitting cross-legged, he had begun to stare at the bench with a sort of smile, he looked amazed. He put out his hand and touched the wood cautiously as if he were afraid of breaking something, then drew back his hand quickly and shuddered. If I had been Tom I wouldn't have amused myself by touching the bench; this was some more Irish nonsense, but I too found that objects had a funny look: they were more obliterated, less dense than usual. It was enough for me to look at the bench, the lamp, the pile of coal dust, to feel that I was going to die. Naturally I couldn't think clearly about my death but I saw it everywhere, on things, in the way things fell back and kept their distance, discreetly, as people who speak quietly at the bedside of a dying man. It was *his* death which Tom had just touched on the bench.

In the state I was in, if someone had come and told me I could go home quietly, that they would leave me my life whole, it would have left me cold: several hours or several years of waiting is all the same when you have lost the illusion of being eternal. I clung to nothing, in a way I was calm. But it was a horrible calm—because of my body; my body, I saw with its eyes, I heard with its ears, but it was no longer me; it sweated and trembled by itself and I didn't recognize it any more. I had to touch it and look at it to find out what was happening, as if it were the body of someone else. At times I could still feel it, I felt sinkings, and fallings, as when you're in a plane taking a nosedive, or I felt my heart beating. But that didn't reassure me. Everything that came from my body was all cockeyed. Most of the time it was quiet and I felt no more than a sort of weight, a filthy presence against me; I had the impression of being tied to an enormous vermin. Once I felt my pants and I felt they were damp; I didn't know whether it was sweat or urine, but I went to piss on the coal pile as a precaution.

The Belgian took out his watch, looked at it. He said, "It is three-thirty."

Bastard! He must have done it on purpose. Tom jumped; we hadn't noticed time was running out; night surrounded us like a shapeless, somber mass, I couldn't even remember that it had begun.

Little Juan began to cry. He wrung his hands, pleaded, "I don't want to die. I don't want to die."

He ran across the whole cellar waving his arms in the air then fell sobbing on one of the mats. Tom watched him with mournful eyes, without the slightest desire to console him. Because it wasn't worth the trouble: the kid made more noise than we did, but he was less touched: he was like a sick man who defends himself against his illness by fever. It's much more serious when there isn't any fever.

He wept: I could clearly see he was pitying himself; he wasn't thinking about death. For one second, one single second, I wanted to weep myself, to weep with pity for myself. But the opposite happened: I glanced at the kid, I saw his thin sobbing shoulders and I felt inhuman: I could pity neither the others nor myself. I said to myself, "I want to die cleanly."

Tom had gotten up, he placed himself just under the round opening and began to watch for daylight. I was determined to die cleanly and I only thought of that. But ever since the doctor told us the time, I felt time flying, flowing away drop by drop.

It was still dark when I heard Tom's voice: "Do you hear them?"

Men were marching in the courtyard.

"Yes."

"What the hell are they doing? They can't shoot in the dark."

After a while we heard no more. I said to Tom, "It's day."

Pedro got up, yawning, and came to blow out the lamp. He said to his buddy, "Cold as hell."

The cellar was all grey. We heard shots in the distance.

"It's starting," I told Tom. "They must do it in the court in the rear."

Tom asked the doctor for a cigarette. I didn't want one; I didn't want cigarettes or alcohol. From that moment on they didn't stop firing.

"Do you realize what's happening," Tom said.

He wanted to add something but kept quiet, watching the door. The door opened and a lieutenant came in with four soldiers. Tom dropped his cigarette.

"Steinbock?"

Tom didn't answer. Pedro pointed him out.

"Juan Mirbal?"

"On the mat."

"Get up," the lieutenant said.

Juan did not move. Two soldiers took him under the arms and set him on his feet. But he fell as soon as they released him.

The soldiers hesitated.

"He's not the first sick one," said the lieutenant. "You two carry him; they'll fix it up down there."

He turned to Tom. "Let's go."

Tom went out between two soldiers. Two others followed, carrying the kid by the armpits. He hadn't fainted; his eyes were wide open and tears ran down his cheeks. When I wanted to go out the lieutenant stopped me.

"You Ibbieta?"

"Yes."

"You wait here; they'll come for you later."

They left. The Belgian and the two jailers left too, I was alone. I did not understand what was happening to me but I would have liked it better if they had gotten it over with right away. I heard shots at almost regular intervals; I shook with each one of them. I wanted to scream and tear out my hair. But I gritted my teeth and pushed my hands in my pockets because I wanted to stay clean.

After an hour they came to get me and led me to the first floor, to a small room that smelt of cigars and where the heat was stifling. There were two officers sitting smoking in the armchairs, papers on their knees.

"You're Ibbieta?"

"Yes."

"Where is Ramon Gris?"

"I don't know."

The one questioning me was short and fat. His eyes were hard behind his glasses. He said to me, "Come here."

I went to him. He got up and took my arms, staring at me with a look that should have pushed me into the earth. At the same time he pinched my biceps with all his might. It wasn't to hurt me, it was only a game: he wanted to dominate me. He also thought he had to blow his stinking breath square in my face. We stayed for a moment like that, and I almost felt like laughing. It takes a lot to intimidate a man who is going to die; it didn't work. He pushed me back violently and sat down again. He said, "It's his life against yours. You can have yours if you tell us where he is."

These men dolled up with their riding crops and boots were still going to die. A little later than I, but not too much. They busied themselves looking for names in their crumpled papers, they ran after other men to imprison or suppress them; they had opinions on the future of Spain and on other subjects. Their little activities seemed shocking and burlesqued to me; I couldn't put myself in their place, I thought they were insane. The little man was still looking at me, whipping his boots with the riding crop. All his gestures were calculated to give him the look of a live and ferocious beast.

"So? You understand?"

"I don't know where Gris is," I answered. "I thought he was in Madrid."

The other officer raised his pale hand indolently. This indolence was also calculated. I saw through all their little schemes and I was stupefied to find there were men who amused themselves that way.

"You have a quarter of an hour to think it over," he said slowly. "Take him to the laundry, bring him back in fifteen minutes. If he still refuses he will be executed on the spot."

They knew what they were doing: I had passed the night in waiting; then they had made me wait an hour in the cellar while they shot Tom and Juan and now they were locking me up in the laundry; they must have prepared their game the night before. They told themselves that nerves eventually wear out and they hoped to get me that way.

They were badly mistaken. In the laundry I sat on a stool because I felt very weak and I began to think. But not about their proposition. Of course I knew where Gris was; he was hiding with his cousins, four kilometers from the city. I also knew that I would not reveal his hiding place unless they tortured me (but they didn't seem to be thinking about that). All that was perfectly regulated, definite and in no way interested me. Only I would have liked to understand the reasons for my conduct. I would rather die than give up Gris. Why? I didn't like Ramon Gris any more. My friendship for him had died a little while before dawn at the same time as my love for Concha, at the same time as my desire to live. Undoubtedly I thought highly of him: he was tough. But it was not for this reason that I consented to die in his place; his life had no more value than mine; no life had value. They were going to slap a man up against a wall and shoot at him till he died, whether it was I or Gris or somebody else made no difference. I knew he was more useful than I to the cause of Spain but I thought to hell with Spain and anarchy; nothing was important. Yet I was there, I could save my skin and give up Gris and I refused to do it. I found that somehow comic; it was obstinacy. I thought, "I must be stubborn!" And a droll sort of gaiety spread over me.

They came for me and brought me back to the two officers. A rat ran out from under my feet and that amused me. I turned to one of the *falangistas* and said, "Did you see the rat?"

He didn't answer. He was very sober, he took himself seriously. I wanted to laugh but I held myself back because I was afraid that once I got started I wouldn't be able to stop. The *falangista* had a moustache. I said to him again, "You ought to shave off your moustache, idiot." I thought it funny that he would let the hairs of his living being invade his face. He kicked me without great conviction and I kept quiet.

"Well," said the fat officer, "have you thought about it?"

I looked at them with curiosity, as insects of a very rare species. I told them, "I know where he is. He is hidden in the cemetery. In a vault or in the gravediggers' shack."

It was a farce. I wanted to see them stand up, buckle their belts and give orders busily.

They jumped to their feet. "Let's go. Molés, go get fifteen men from Lieutenant Lopez. You," the fat man said, "I'll let you off if you're telling the truth, but it'll cost you plenty if you're making monkeys out of us."

They left in a great clatter and I waited peacefully under the guard of *falangistas*. From time to time I smiled, thinking about the spectacle they would make. I felt stunned and malicious. I imagined them lifting up tombstones, opening the doors of the vaults one by one. I represented this situation to myself as if I had been someone else: this prisoner obstinately playing the hero, these grim *falangistas* with their moustaches and their men in uniform running among the graves; it was irresistibly funny. After half an hour the little fat man came back alone. I thought he had come to give the orders to execute me. The others must have stayed in the cemetery.

The officer looked at me. He didn't look at all sheepish. "Take him into the big courtyard with the others," he said. "After the military operations a regular court will decide what happens to him."

"Then they're not . . . not going to shoot me? . . ."

"Not now, anyway. What happens afterwards is none of my business."

I still didn't understand. I asked, "But why . . . ?"

He shrugged his shoulders without answering and the soldiers took me away. In the big courtyard there were about a hundred prisoners, women, children and a few old men. I began walking around the central grass-plot, I was stupefied. At noon they let us eat in the mess hall. Two or three people questioned me. I must have known them, but I didn't answer: I didn't even know where I was.

Around evening they pushed about ten new prisoners into the court. I recognized Garcia, the baker. He said, "What damned luck you have! I didn't think I'd see you alive."

"They sentenced me to death," I said, "and then they changed their minds. I don't know why."

"They arrested me at two o'clock," Garcia said.

"Why?" Garcia had nothing to do with politics.

"I don't know," he said. "They arrest everybody who doesn't think the way they do." He lowered his voice. "They got Gris."

I began to tremble. "When?"

"This morning. He messed it up. He left his cousin's on Tuesday because they had an argument. There were plenty of people to hide him but he didn't want to owe anything to anybody. He said, 'I'd go and hide in Ibbieta's place, but they got him, so I'll go hide in the cemetery.' "

"In the cemetery?"

"Yes. What a fool. Of course they went by there this morning, that was sure to happen. They found him in the gravediggers' shack. He shot at them and they got him."

"In the cemetery!"

Everything began to spin and I found myself sitting on the ground: I laughed so hard I cried.

QUESTIONS FOR DISCUSSION

1) All is not glory and lofty words in revolution. This story of the Spanish Civil War dramatically illustrates the collapse of meaning which is always part of the revolutionary situation. Sartre's philosophy of existentialism, which emphasizes individual responsibility and choice and "the absurd," grew out of the political and societal breakdowns in Europe during the thirties and forties. Why does Sartre include no revolutionary or philosophical doctrines in this story? Is "The Wall" an apt title? Explain.

2) What is it that Pablo fears most? Why is the Belgian doctor included in the story?

3) Should this story be called "anti-revolutionary"? What is the meaning of the surprise ending?

4) Would it appear from this story that Sartre considers life or death the more "creative" act? Explain.

VII. THE INDIVIDUAL

We arrive finally at ourselves—to find that, without exception, each and every one of us is a reasonable person with the best of intentions. We all want to make the most of our potentialities, we're all willing to work hard, and we all think it only fair that we be rewarded with happy, successful lives. But fair or not, the statistics on everything from tranquilizers to alcoholism, from insomnia to suicide, suggest that many of us just aren't making it. And there is a strong possibility that the problem lies in the hard work part of the equation. Much of human unhappiness certainly stems from the stifling of the creative urge, the need to express ourselves. But perhaps the most important lesson of this book is the terrible difficulty of creativity, of self-expression. To overcome those formidable blocks within ourselves and those strong opposing forces without is the hardest kind of hard work. Many these days preach a virtual religion of creativity: as if homage to this new deity could save us all. The present authors, mindful of the great difficulties always in the way of genuine creativity, make a more modest claim. Those who can recognize and stand by their own needs to produce and create, and tackle the obstacles of laziness, fear, ritual, envy, and false praise, will have a good chance of finding satisfaction with themselves and their environments. Those who give up the struggle can have no one else but themselves to blame if they end up part of one dreary statistic or another.

THE LOST DIMENSION IN RELIGION

Paul Tillich

"*. . . Is there an answer? . . .*"

Every observer of our Western civilization is aware of the fact that something has happened to religion. It especially strikes the observer of the American scene. Everywhere he finds symptoms of what one has called religious revival, or more modestly, the revival of interest in religion. He finds them in the churches with their rapidly increasing membership. He finds them in the mushroomlike growth of sects. He finds them on college campuses and in the theological faculties of universities. Most conspicuously, he finds them in the tremendous success of men like Billy Graham and Norman Vincent Peale, who attract masses of people Sunday after Sunday, meeting after meeting. The facts cannot be denied, but how should they be interpreted? It is my intention to show that these facts must be seen as expressions of the predicament of Western man in the second half of the twentieth century. But I would even go a step further. I believe that the predicament of man in our period gives us also an important insight into the predicament of man generally—at all times and in all parts of the earth.

There are many analyses of man and society in our time. Most of them show important traits in the picture, but few of them succeed in giving a general key to our present situation. Although it is not easy to find such a key, I shall attempt it and, in so doing, will make an assertion which may be somewhat mystifying at first hearing. The decisive element in the predicament of Western man in our period is his loss of the dimension of depth. Of course, "dimension of depth" is a metaphor. It is taken from the spatial realm and applied to man's spiritual life. What does it mean?

It means that man has lost an answer to the question: What is the meaning of life? Where do we come from, where do we go to? What shall we do, what should we become in the short stretch between birth and death? Such questions are not answered or even asked if the "dimension of depth" is lost. And this is precisely what has happened to man in our period of history. He has lost the courage to ask such questions with an infinite seriousness—as former generations did—and he has lost the courage to receive answers to these questions, wherever they may come from.

I suggest that we call the dimension of depth the religious dimension in man's nature. Being religious means asking passionately the question of the meaning of our existence and being willing to receive answers, even if the answers hurt. Such an idea of religion makes religion universally human, but it certainly differs from what is usually called religion. It does not describe religion as the belief in the existence of gods or one God, and as a set of activities and institutions for the sake of relating oneself to these beings in thought, devotion and obedience. No one can deny that the religions which have appeared in history are religions in this sense. Nevertheless, religion in its innermost nature is more than religion in this narrower sense. It is the state of being concerned about one's own being and being universally.

There are many people who are ultimately concerned in this way who feel far removed, however, from religion in the narrower sense, and therefore from every historical religion. It often happens that such people take the question of the meaning of their life infinitely seriously and reject any historical religion just for this reason. They feel that the concrete religions fail to express their profound concern adequately. They are religious while rejecting the religions. It is this experience which forces us to distinguish the meaning of religion as living in the dimension of depth from particular expressions of one's ultimate concern in the symbols and institutions of a concrete religion. If we now turn to the concrete analysis of the religious situation of our time, it is obvious that our key must be the basic meaning of religion and not any particular religion, not even Christianity. What does this key disclose about the predicament of man in our period?

If we define religion as the state of being grasped by an infinite concern we must say: Man in our time has lost such infinite concern. And the resurgence of religion is nothing but a desperate and mostly futile attempt to regain what has been lost.

How did the dimension of depth become lost? Like any important event, it has many causes, but certainly not the one which one hears often mentioned from ministers' pulpits and evangelists' platforms, namely that a widespread impiety of modern man is responsible. Modern man is neither more pious nor more impious than man in any other period. The loss of the dimension of depth is caused by the relation of man to his world and to himself in our period, the period in which nature is being subjected scientifically and technically to the control of man. In this period, life in the dimension of depth is replaced by life in the horizontal dimension. The driving forces of the industrial society of which we are a part go ahead horizontally and not vertically. In popular terms this is expressed in phrases like "better and better," "bigger and bigger," "more and more." One should not disparage the feeling which lies behind such speech. Man is right in feeling that he is able to know and transform the world he encounters without a foreseeable limit. He can go ahead in all directions without a definite boundary.

A most expressive symbol of this attitude of going ahead in the horizontal dimension is the breaking through of the space which is controlled by the gravitational power of the earth into the world-space. It is interesting that one calls this world-space simply "space" and speaks, for instance, of space travel, as if every trip were not travel into space. Perhaps one feels that the true nature of space has been discovered only through our entering into indefinite world-space. In any case, the predominance of the horizontal dimension over the dimension of depth has been immensely increased by the opening up of the space beyond the space of the earth.

If we now ask what does man do and seek if he goes ahead in the horizontal dimension, the answer is difficult. Sometimes one is inclined to say that the mere movement ahead without an end, the intoxication with speeding forward without limits, is what satisfies him. But this answer is by no means sufficient. For on his way into space and time man changes the world he encounters. And the changes made by him change himself. He transforms everything he encounters into a tool; and in doing so he himself becomes a tool. But if he asks, a tool for what, there is no answer.

One does not need to look far beyond everyone's daily experience in order to find examples to describe this predicament. Indeed our daily life in office and home, in cars and airplanes, at parties and conferences, while reading magazines and watching television, while looking at advertisements and hearing radio, are in themselves continuous examples of a life which has lost the dimension of depth. It runs ahead, every moment is filled with something which must be done or seen or said or planned. But no one can experience depth without stopping and becoming aware of himself. Only if he has moments in which he does not care about what comes next can he experience the meaning of this moment here and now and ask himself about the meaning of his life. As long as the preliminary, transitory concerns are not silenced, no matter how interesting and valuable and important they may be, the voice of the ultimate concern cannot be heard. This is the deepest root of the loss of the dimension of depth in our period— the loss of religion in its basic and universal meaning.

If the dimension of depth is lost, the symbols in which life in this dimension has expressed itself must also disappear. I am speaking of the great symbols of the historical religions in our Western world, of Judaism and Christianity. The reason that the religious symbols became lost is not primarily scientific criticism, but it is a complete misunderstanding of their meaning; and only because of this misunderstanding was scientific critique able, and even justified, in attacking them. The first step toward the non-religion of the Western world was made by religion itself. When it defended its great symbols, not as symbols, but as literal stories, it had already lost the battle. In doing so the theologians (and today many religious laymen) helped to transfer the powerful expressions of the dimension of depth into objects or happenings on the horizontal plane. There the symbols lose their power and meaning and become an easy prey to physical, biological and historical attack.

If the symbol of creation which points to the divine ground of everything is transferred to the horizontal plane, it becomes a story of events in a removed past for which there is no evidence, but which contradicts every piece of scientific evidence. If the symbol of the Fall of Man, which points to the tragic estrangement of man and his world from their true being is transferred to the horizontal plane, it becomes a story of a human couple a few thousand years ago in what is now present-day Iraq. One of the most profound psychological descriptions of the general human predicament becomes an absurdity on the horizontal plane. If the symbols of the Saviour and the salvation through Him which point to the healing power in history and personal life are transferred to the horizontal plane, they become stories of a half-divine being coming from a heavenly place and returning to it. Obviously, in this form, they have no meaning whatsoever for people whose view of the universe is determined by scientific astronomy.

If the idea of God (and the symbols applied to Him) which expresses man's ultimate concern is transferred to the horizontal plane, God becomes a being among others whose existence or nonexistence is a matter of inquiry. Nothing, perhaps, is more symptomatic of the loss of the dimension of depth than the permanent discussion about the existence or nonexistence of God—a discussion in which both sides are equally wrong, because the discussion itself is wrong and possible only after the loss of the dimension of depth.

When in this way man has deprived himself of the dimension of depth and the symbols expressing it, he then becomes a part of the horizontal plane. He loses his self and becomes a thing among things. He becomes an element in the process of manipulated production and manipulated consumption. This is now a matter of public knowledge. We have become aware of the degree to which everyone in our social structure is managed, even if one knows it and even if one belongs himself to the managing group. The influence of the gang mentality on adolescents, of the corporation's demands on the executives, of the conditioning of everyone by public communication, by propaganda and advertising under the guidance of motivation research, et cetera, have all been described in many books and articles.

Under these pressures, man can hardly escape the fate of becoming a thing among the things he produces, a bundle of conditioned reflexes without a free, deciding and responsible self. The immense mechanism, set up by man to produce objects for his use, transforms man himself into an object used by the same mechanism of production and consumption.

But man has not ceased to be man. He resists this fate anxiously, desperately, courageously. He asks the question, for what? And he realizes that there is no answer. He becomes aware of the emptiness which is covered by the continuous movement ahead and the production of means for ends which become means again without an ultimate end. Without knowing what has happened to him, he feels that he has lost the meaning of life, the dimension of depth.

Out of this awareness the religious question arises and religious answers are received or rejected. Therefore, in order to describe the contemporary attitude toward religion, we must first point to the places where the awareness of the predicament of Western man in our period is most sharply expressed. These places are the great art, literature and, partly at least, the philosophy of our time. It is both the subject matter and the style of these creations which show the passionate and often tragic struggle about the meaning of life in a period in which man has lost the dimension of depth. This art, literature, philosophy is not religious in the narrower sense of the word; but it asks the religious question more radically and more profoundly than most directly religious expressions of our time.

It is the religious question which is asked when the novelist describes a man who tries in vain to reach the only place which could solve the problem of his life, or a man who disintegrates under the memory of a guilt which persecutes him, or a man who never had a real self and is pushed by his fate without resistance to death, or a man who experiences a profound disgust of everything he encounters.

It is the religious question which is asked when the poet opens up the horror and the fascination of the demonic regions of his soul, or if he leads us into the deserts and empty places of our being, or if he shows the physical and moral mud under the surface of life, or if he sings the song of transitoriness, giving words to the ever-present anxiety of our hearts.

It is the religious question which is asked when the playwright shows the illusion of a life in a ridiculous symbol, or if he lets the emptiness of a life's work end in self-destruction, or if he confronts us with the inescapable bondage to mutual hate and guilt, or if he leads us into the dark cellar of lost hopes and slow disintegration.

It is the religious question which is asked when the painter breaks the visible surface into pieces, then reunites them into a great picture which has little similarity with the world at which we normally look, but which expresses our anxiety and our courage to face reality.

It is the religious question which is asked when the architect, in creating office buildings or churches, removes the trimmings taken over from past styles because they cannot be considered an honest expression of our own period. He prefers the seeming poverty of a purpose-determined style to the deceptive richness of imitated styles of the past. He knows that he gives no final answer, but he does give an honest answer.

The philosophy of our time shows the same hiddenly religious traits. It is divided into two main schools of thought, the analytic and the existentialist. The former tries to analyze logical and linguistic forms which are always used and which underlie all scientific research. One may compare them with the painters who dissolve the natural forms of bodies into cubes, planes and lines; or with those architects who want the structural "bones" of their buildings to be conspicuously visible and not hidden by covering features. This self-restriction produces the almost monastic poverty and seriousness of this philosophy. It is religious—without any contact with religion in its method—by exercising the humility of "learned ignorance."

In contrast to this school the existentialist philosophers have much to say about the problems of human existence. They bring into rational concepts what the writers and poets, the painters and architects, are expressing in their particular material. What they express is the human predicament in time and space, in anxiety and guilt and the feeling of meaninglessness. From Pascal in the seventeenth century to Heidegger and Sartre in our time, philosophers have emphasized the contrast between human dignity and human misery. And by doing so, they have raised the religious question. Some have tried to answer the question they have asked. But if they did so, they turned back to past traditions and offered to our time that which does not fit our time. Is it possible for our time to receive answers which are born out of our time?

Answers given today are in danger of strengthening the present situation and with it the questions to which they are supposed to be the answers. This refers to some of the previously mentioned major representatives of the so-called resurgence of religion, as for instance the evangelist Billy Graham and the counseling and healing minister, Norman Vincent Peale. Against the validity of the answers given by the former, one must say that, in spite of his personal integrity, his propagandistic methods and his primitive theological fundamentalism fall short of what is needed to give an answer to the religious question of our period. In spite of all his seriousness, he does not take the radical questions of our period seriously.

The effect that Norman Peale has on large groups of people is rooted in the fact that he confirms the situation which he is supposed to help overcome. He heals people with the purpose of making them fit again for the demands of the competitive and conformist society in which we are living. He helps them to become adapted to the situation which is characterized by the loss of the dimension of depth. Therefore, his advice is valid on this level; but it is the validity of this level that is the true religious question of our time. And this question he neither raises nor answers.

In many cases the increase of church membership and interest in religious activities does not mean much more than the religious consecration of a state of things in which the religious dimension has been lost. It is the desire to participate in activities which are socially strongly approved and give internal and a certain amount of external security. This is not necessarily bad, but it certainly is not an answer to the religious question of our period.

Is there an answer? There is always an answer, but the answer may not be available to us. We may be too deeply steeped in the predicament out of which the question arises to be able to answer it. To acknowledge this is certainly a better way toward a real answer than to bar the way to it by deceptive answers. And it may be that in this attitude the real answer (within available limits) is given. The real answer to the question of how to regain the dimension of depth is not given by increased church member-ship or church attendance, nor by conversion or healing experiences. But it is given by the awareness that we have lost the decisive dimension of life, the dimension of depth, and that there is no easy way of getting it back. Such awareness is in itself a state of being grasped by that which is symbol-ized in the term, dimension of depth. He who realizes that he is separated from the ultimate source of meaning shows by this realization that he is not only separated but also reunited. And this is just our situation. What we need above all—and partly have—is the radical realization of our pre-dicament, without trying to cover it up by secular or religious ideologies. The revival of religious interest would be a creative power in our culture if it would develop into a movement of search for the lost dimension of depth.

This does not mean that the traditional religious symbols should be dismissed. They certainly have lost their meaning in the literalistic form into which they have been distorted, thus producing the critical reaction against them. But they have not lost their genuine meaning, namely, of an-swering the question which is implied in man's very existence in powerful, revealing and saving symbols. If the resurgence of religion would produce a new understanding of the symbols of the past and their relevance for our situation, instead of premature and deceptive answers, it would become a creative factor in our culture and a saving factor for many who live in estrangement, anxiety and despair. The religious answer has always the character of "in spite of." In spite of the loss of dimension of depth, its power is present, and most present in those who are aware of the loss and are striving to regain it with ultimate seriousness.

QUESTIONS FOR DISCUSSION

1) Observing what seemed a religious revival in the 1950's, the theologian Paul Tillich argued that the new interest in religion proved anew that the American society has lost religion, not that it has found religion again. The dimension of depth is characteristic of true religion, and the new interest in religion is not very deep; nor is the answering approach of the popular men of religion such as Billy Graham and Norman Vincent Peale very deep. What is the distinguishing characteristic of religion in *depth?* How does this kind of religion differ from "practiced" religion?

2) Tillich sees two main causes of the loss of religion in depth. What are they?

3) Why does Tillich judge contemporary literature, drama, painting, archi-tecture, and philosophy (all acts of "creation") to be more "religious" than contemporary religion?

4) Why are the religious answers provided by men like Billy Graham and Norman Vincent Peale ultimately unsatisfactory, according to Tillich?

5) Does Tillich see the solution to our religious problem as coming eventually from the individual or from the religious institutions? Explain.

6) Is a religious life necessarily a creative life? Discuss.

THE DAEMONIC:
LOVE & DEATH

Rollo May

Death and delight, anguish and joy, anxiety and the pangs of birth—these are the warp and woof of which the fabric of human love is woven. Creation and destruction both are there, inescapably intermingled, always vital, and ever the anxiety-creating elements of love.

In the early Greek account of creation, Eros—Love—creates life upon the earth. He seizes his life-giving arrows and pierces the cold bosom of the earth, and immediately the brown surface is covered with luxuriant verdure. Before, all was silent, bare, and motionless. Now, all is life, joy, and motion. He then breathes into the nostrils of the clay forms of man and woman and gives them the spirit of life.

And yet Eros destroys as he creates. The bow of Eros shoots poisoned arrows which pierce hearts to their death or to their healing and delight. The Greeks knew an eternal truth. Hesiod, in his 750 B.C. cosmogony, says that it is Eros, "handsomest among all immortals, who breaks the limbs' strength; who in all gods, in all human beings, overpowers the intelligence in the breast, and all their shrewd planning." In *The Symposium,* that beautiful dialogue devoted entirely to a discussion of love, Plato tells us that "Eros is a daimon. He is neither mortal nor immortal, but a mean between the two. . . . He is a great spirit (daimon) and like all spirits he is intermediate between the divine and the mortal. He is the mediator between men and gods, and therefore in him all is bound together."

I define the *daemonic* as any natural function in the individual which has the power of taking over the whole person. In my definition, Eros is the daemon which constitutes man's creative spirit, the drive that not only impels him to sexual union and to other forms of love, but also incites in him the yearning for knowledge and drives him to seek union with the truth, to become poet, or artist, or scientist. Sex and eros, anger and rage, and the craving for power are daemonic and thus *either* creative or destructive. When this power goes awry, and one element takes over the total personality, we see *"daemon possession,"* the traditional term through history for psychosis. Then we see the destructive activities of the daemonic which are the reverse side of its constructive vitality.

Most fascinating and compelling of all is the relationship of the daemonic to love. In real love, it is always present. When we *fall* in love, as the expressive verb puts it, the world shakes and changes around us, not only in the way it looks but in our whole experience of what we are doing in the world. The shaking generally is felt consciously in its positive aspects—as a wonderful new universe which love, with its miracle, suddenly has produced. Love is the answer, we sing. But our Western culture seems to be engaged in a desperate—albeit romantic—conspiracy to enforce the illusion that this is *all* there is to eros. The very strength of the effort to support the illusion betrays the strong presence of the repressed, opposing pole.

This element we deny is the consciousness of death. For death is always in the shadow of the delight of love. In the shadows, too, is the dread, haunting question: will this new relationship destroy us? When we love, we give up the center of ourselves. We are thrown from our previous state of existence into a void, and though we hope for a new world, and for a new existence, we can never be sure. Nothing looks the same and may never look the same again. Our world is annihilated. How can we know whether it will ever be built up again? We give, and give up, our own center. How shall we know that we will get it back? We wake to find the whole world shaking. Where or when will it come to rest?

The most excruciating joy is accompanied by the consciousness of the imminence of death—and with the same intensity. And it seems that one is not possible without the other.

This experience of annihilation is an inward one and, as the myth rightly puts it, is essentially what *eros* does to us. It is not simply what another person does to us. This intensity of consciousness has something in common with the ecstasy of the mystic in his union with God. Just as he can never be *sure* God is there, love carries us to an intensity of consciousness where we have no guarantee of security.

The relationship between death and love has an impressive history in literature. In Italian writing, there always was the common play upon the words—*amore,* love; with *morte,* death. The connection also has its biological analogies in nature. The male bee dies after inseminating the queen. More vivid is the sex life of the praying mantis. The female bites off the head of the male as he copulates, and his death throes unite with his copulatory spasms to make them stronger. Then, inseminated, the female eats the male to store up food for the new offspring.

In our common human experience, this relationship between death and love perhaps is most clear to people when they have children. A man may have thought—and prided himself on it—very little about death, until he becomes a father. The Cruel Impostor can at any moment take away the object of his love—his child. In this sense, love is an experience of increased vulnerability. It is a reminder of our own mortality.

When we love, we open ourselves to the possibility of grief, sorrow, and disappointment, as well as of joy, fulfillment, and an intensity of consciousness we did not believe possible. Some of us never know deep love until we experience, at someone's death, the preciousness of a human relationship that was.

This razor's edge, this dizzy balance of anxiety and joy, has much to do with the exciting quality of physical love. The dread joy is not just the question of whether the love we give will be returned in kind. Indeed, the real dialectic is within the lover himself, and the anxiety is not essentially quieted if the loved one *does* respond. Paradoxically, the lover sometimes is more anxious when love is returned than when it is not.

If one loves unrequitedly—which is even the aim in some love writing —or from a safe distance like Dante and the whole *style nouveau* movement in Italian literature, one can at least go on about his customary daily tasks, writing his *Divine Comedy,* or sonnets, or novels. It is when love *is* realized that eros literally may "break the limbs' strength," as with Antony when he loved Cleopatra, or with Paris and Helen, or Heloise and Abelard.

Love's effect can parallel that of the artificial agency, LSD. Both break down the walls of our customary world and crumble our defenses, leaving us naked and vulnerable. In LSD, the experience may be one of paranoid reactions, with no delight. Yet that parallel, too, holds in love. Jealousy, envy, suspicion, rage, and even hatred can be more powerful when love is present. Many couples stay together, ostensibly motivated more by hatred than by love. As in Edward Albee's *Who's Afraid of Virginia Woolf,* it is sometimes very hard to tell whether hatred masks love, or the reverse.

The relationship between death and love certainly is clear in the sex act. Every kind of mythology relates the sex act itself to dying. Every therapist comes to see the relationship ever more clearly through his patients. A patient of mine whose problem was sexual frigidity and who had never experienced an orgasm in intercourse, told me of a dream which dramatically illustrates this sex and death theme. In her dream, she experienced herself for the first time in her own identity as a woman. Then, still in the dream, she had the strange conviction that she would have to jump into the river and drown. That night in sexual intercourse she had an orgasm for the first time. The capacity for surrender, for giving one's self up, must exist in love-making if there is to be the spontaneity for orgasm.

Something very basic had taken place in this woman's dream—the capacity to confront death, a capacity which is a prerequisite to growth. I take the orgasm here as a psychophysical symbol. It is not by accident that the orgasm often appears symbolically as death and rebirth. The myth of going underwater, of being drowned and born again, has been passed down through history in different religions and different cultures—to be drowned, to die, to be baptized in order to be born again.

Mythology, that treasure house of the revelations of man's self-interpretation of his inner experience and his world down through the ages, has been clear, eloquent, and profound about the relationship of love to anxiety, and to death. Joseph Campbell, our most comprehensive contemporary scholar of mythology, points out on the basis of the whole

Aegean prehistoric mythology that the goddess Aphrodite and her son, Eros, are "exactly the great cosmic mother and her son—the ever-dying, ever-living god." All myths on the parentage of Eros point to such a background, Campbell says. "He is hatched from the egg of Night. He is the son, now of Gaea and Uranus, now of Artemis and Hermes, now of Iris and Zephyrus: all transformations of the same mythological background, pointing without exception to the timeless catalogue of themes with which we are now familiar—of that willing victim in whose death is our life, whose flesh is our meat and blood; our drink; the victim present in the young embracing couple of the primitive ritual of the love-death, who at the moment of ecstasy are killed, to be sacramentally roasted and consumed; the victim present in Attis or Adonis slain by a boar, Osiris slain by Seth. . . . In the later allegories of Eros (Cupid) and his victim, the god is in the role of the dark enemy—the rushing boar, the dark brother Seth . . . and the lover is the incarnate, dying god."

What a different light this throws on the human problems in love than does all our glib talk about the art of loving, about love as the answer to all our needs, love as instant self-actualization, love as contentment, or love as a mail-order technique! No wonder we try to reduce eros to purely physiological sex or try to avoid the whole dilemma by playing it cool, by using sex to drug and vaccinate ourselves against the anxiety-creating effects of eros.

It may seem possible to have sexual intercourse without any particular anxiety. But to do this in casual encounters, we block off, by definition, our eros. Eros stands for passion as opposed to mere sensation, and for authentic participation, imagination, and personal significance. We assume that we can have sex without love and thus escape the daemonic anxiety known throughout the ages as an inseparable part of human love. And we further use sexual activity itself as an escape from the commitments eros demands of us, in our hope that we have gained an airtight defense against anxiety!

But in doing so, we are in danger of losing exactly what makes sex so desirable. When human sexuality is separated from the dimension of the daemonic and becomes simply a matter of reduction of tension, it is no different from what is done better by the birds and the bees. For there is then no human mind to tangle up the machinery with fantasy and memories, no heart to long for tenderness, no imagination that yearns for a touch of ecstasy worth remembering.

Otto Rank once remarked that practically all the women who came to him for therapy had problems because their husbands were not aggressive enough. This sounds vastly oversimplified, but it contains a telling point: our effete cultivation of sex can make us so arbitrary and detached that the power of the sexual act evaporates, and women lose the vital elemental pleasure of being taken, of being transported. This aspect of the constructive use of the daemonic may be seen when we remind ourselves that through assertion of one's own individuality in relation to another person, one always skates on the edge of daemonic exploitation of the partner. Nevertheless, the daemonic is necessary and always exists in any deep relationship.

Every person, as a separate individual, experiences aloneness. And so we strive actively to overcome our aloneness by some form of love. And sexual love requires self-assertion. If we cannot be individuals in our own right, we have nothing to give, nothing to relate *with*. Unable to assert ourselves, we cannot participate genuinely in a relationship.

Biologically, this is expressed most vividly in the male by the erection —a phenomenon which in itself has bewitching, erotic seductiveness for a woman as she realizes it is occurring, if she is already interested. (If she is not, she is of course repulsed, which simply proves in reverse that the erection of the penis exerts emotional power.) The erection is a powerful daemonic symbol. But this daemonic assertion, though perhaps less biologically obvious, is still present and necessary in the woman—in her capacity to have outright desire for her man, to lust for him, and to let him feel that she wants him. Both man and woman need this self-assertion to bridge their separateness and to achieve union with each other.

There is insight, therefore, in the vernacular expresssions like "letting yourself go" and "being taken." I am not in the slightest arguing here for a return to primitive sexuality. Nor do I want to comfort the still infantile man or woman who interprets aggression as blunt insistence upon his or her demands of the sexual partner. I am using aggression in its healthy sense as rooted in strength, not weakness, and allied inseparably with the capacities for sensitivity and tenderness. But I am arguing that we have amputated significant aspects of our sexuality in overcultivation of sexual love, and so we run the risk of losing exactly what we set out to achieve.

The daemonic element always has its biological base. So says Goethe, whose *Faust* demonstrates keen understanding of modern man's daemonic urge: "The daemon is the power of nature." One of the two most important characteristics of the daemonic is that this one element within us which has its rightful function as part of the personality can itself usurp power over the *whole* self and thus drive us into disintegrative behavior. The erotic-sexual urge pushes us toward physical union with our partners. But it may, when it takes total command, drive us in many diverse directions and into all kinds of relationships without regard for the integration of the self. The Karamazov father has intercourse with the idiot woman in the ditch, and it is their son who later murders the father.

The creative reverse is equally important. The daemonic is also the origin of ethical sensitivity. When Socrates, in *The Apologia,* tells the Athenian court how he came to his decision to die rather than to recant, he explains that he has consulted his "daemon . . . that tells me what to do."

The daemon gives individual guidance in particular situations. It is parallel to the *genii* or *jinni,* an original symbol in Roman religion from which our word *genius,* and which originally meant a tutelar deity, a spirit presiding over a person's destiny, and later became a particular mental endowment or talent. Genius has its roots in the Latin verb, *genere,* which means to generate or to beget. And so it is synonymous to this sense of the daemonic, which is also the voice of the creative process that produces the poet and the artist. Given the highly developed self-consciousness of Socrates, it is not surprising that he should experience his daemon as the voice of his own being. The daemon speaks in dreams, and to the sensitive person in conscious meditation and self-questioning. Aristotle believed that dreams may be called daemonic, "for nature is daemonic."

Freud expresses the daemonic dimension in his emphasis on fate and destiny, in his writings, and in his concepts of libido, thanatos, and Trieb. These words are, of course, loaded and mean many things, but there is contained in each one of them the implication that powers reside in us which can seize us. Not to come to terms with this inescapable psycho-biological phenomenon leads to pathology, Freud says. This is a constructive emphasis, especially when we see it against the background of Victorian separation of the self from nature. Freud's sense of the relentlessness of life, his humility in the face of destiny, and his refusal to pander to man's need to be reassured about himself stem not from that pessimism of which he is so often accused, but from a sense of the finite quality of human existence and of the finality of death—both bespeaking a genuine sense of the daemonic.

The daemonic is vital in psychotherapy, for eros is also the push toward health and is necessary if there is to be any vitality in therapy. The fatal error in much psychotherapy is to narcotize the daemon. The poet, Rainer Maria Rilke, withdrew from this kind of anaesthesia-therapy after learning its purpose, saying: "If my devils leave me, I am afraid my angels will take flight as well."

It is well to consider carefully the daemonic force, and particularly eros, because this has portentous, even ominous, implications for the rise and fall of civilizations. The Eros who had been the powerful creator in Hesiod's time, and who caused the barren earth to spring up with green trees and breathed the spirit of life into men, deteriorated in late Greece into a child—the rosy, chubby, playful Cupid, sometimes a mere fat infant playing with his bow and arrows. It is time to face the parallel with our present culture: eros has lost passion and has become insipid, childish, and banal.

As is so often the case, the mythic degeneration reveals a critical conflict in the very roots of human experience—true for the Greeks and true for us! We flee from Eros, the once-powerful, original source of being, to sex, the mischievous plaything. Eros is demoted to the function of serving grapes and wine. He stands not for the creative use of power—sexual, procreative, and otherwise—but for the immediacy of gratification. And, *mirabile dictu,* we discover that the myth proclaims exactly what we have seen happening in our own day: Eros then even loses interest in sex. In one version of the myth, Aphrodite tries to find him to get him up and about his business of spreading love with his bow and arrows. And, teenage loafer that he has become, he is off gambling with Ganymede and cheating at the cards. Gone are the life-giving arrows, gone the creature who could breathe spirit into man and woman, gone the powerful Dionysian festivals, gone the frenzied dancing and the mysteries that moved the initiates more than the vaunted drugs of our mechanical age, gone even the bucolic intoxication. Oh, miserable Eros, now playboy indeed! Bacchanal with Pepsi-cola!

Is this what civilization always must do—tame Eros to make him fit the needs of the society to perpetuate itself? Must we ever change him from the power that brings to birth new being and ideas and passion, and weaken him till he no longer is the creative force that breaks old forms asunder to make new ones? And must we tame him until he stands for the goals of perpetual ease and dalliance—and ultimately of apathy?

We face a new problem in history if we are to avoid this disintegrative process in our Western culture. That problem is the war between eros and technology. There is no war between sex and technology: our inventions help make sex safe, available, and efficient. We have "the pill" and an endless supply of sexual how-to-do-it books. Sex and technology join to *achieve* our adjustment, and with the full release of tension over the weekend, we then assume we can work better in the button-down world on Monday. Sexual needs are not at war with technology, at least not in any immediate sense. Whether they are in the long run is another question!

But it is not at all clear that technology and eros are compatible or can ever live without perpetual warfare. Eros breaks existing forms and creates new ones—and that naturally is a threat to technology. Technology requires regularity and predictability and runs by the clock. Eros transcends all concepts and confines of time.

Eros is the essence of building civilizations. But there comes a point —and this is a critical challenge now facing modern technological Western man—when the cult of technique destroys feeling, undermines passion, and blots out personal identity. The technologically efficient lover ultimately is defeated in the contradiction which is copulation without eros. He loses the power to be carried away. It is at this point that technology *diminishes* consciousness and *demolishes* eros.

Asking the final question—Must civilization always tame Eros in the interest of stabilization?—is also asking—Must Toynbee be right? Hesiod lived in the strongly fomenting, archaic eighth century B.C., near the sources of culture and the moments of gestation and birth when the procreative powers were at work and man had to live with chaos and form it into something new. Then the need for stabilization grew, and the daemonic power of eros was buried.

Insight into the downfall of civilizations is revealed here. We see effete Athens set up for the more primitive Macedonians, they in turn for the Romans, and the Romans in turn for the Huns. And we for the yellow and black races?

Eros and the daemonic form are the center of the vitality of a culture, and its heart and soul. And when release of tension takes the place of this creative force, the downfall of the civilization is assured.

QUESTIONS FOR DISCUSSION

1) This article presents the reader with a theory not only of love, but of creativity, the search for knowledge, and even the rise and fall of civilizations. Why does May's concept of Eros enable him to do this with relative ease?

2) When is any natural function "daemonic," according to May's definition of the term? Why is "daemonic" a synonym for "creative" in May's thinking?

3) In contrast to the popular conception of love as being merely delightful, May believes that love in all its stages is daemonic and therefore creative. For evidence he asks that we consider the effect of love upon one's awareness. What kind of awareness overtakes a person newly "in love"? Why is this awareness creative?

4) While exalting love expressed, May yet believes that physical love is not "the answer to all our needs." Why?

5) Is it an oversimplification of May's statements to say that creativity is an expression of the sex drive? Is it an oversimplification of the truth? How and why?

6) Comment on the following statement: "Rollo May leaves no hope for the survival of our civilization. Our technological advances, always aimed at maximizing security and efficiency, are about to stifle our creative energies, enabling more vigorous peoples to overrun us."

WHY ALL OF US MAY BE HIPPIES SOMEDAY

Fred Davis

> *And thus in love we have declared the purpose of our hearts plainly, without flatterie, expecting love, and the same sincerity from you, without grumbling, or quarreling, being Creatures of your own image and mould, intending no other matter herein, but to observe the Law of righteous action, endeavoring to shut out of the Creation, the cursed thing, called Particular Propriety, which is the cause of all wars, bloud-shed, theft, and enslaving Laws, that hold the people under miserie.*
>
> *Signed for and in behalf of all the poor oppressed people of England, and the whole world.*
>
> Gerrard Winstanley and others
> June 1, 1649

This quotation is from the leader of the Diggers, a millenarian sect of communistic persuasion that arose in England at the time of Oliver Cromwell. Today in San Francisco's hippie community, the Haight-Ashbury district, a group of hippies naming themselves after this sect distributes free food to fellow hippies (and all other takers, for that matter) who congregate at about four o'clock every afternoon in the district's Panhandle, an eight-block strip of urban green, shaded by towering eucalyptus trees, that leads into Golden Gate Park to the west. On the corner of a nearby street, the "Hashbury" Diggers operate their Free Store where all —be they hip, straight, hostile, curious, or merely in need—can avail themselves (free of charge, no questions asked) of such used clothing, household articles, books, and second-hand furniture as find their way into the place on any particular day. The Diggers also maintained a large flat in the district where newly arrived or freshly dispossessed hippies could stay without charge for a night, a week, or however long they wished— until some months ago, when the flat was condemned by the San Francisco Health Department. Currently, the Diggers are rehabilitating a condemned skid-row hotel for the same purpose.

Not all of Haight-Ashbury's 7500 hippies are Diggers, although no formal qualifications bar them; nor, in one sense, are the several dozen Diggers hippies. What distinguishes the Diggers—an amorphous, shifting, and sometimes contentious amalgam of ex-political radicals, psychedelic mystics, Ghandians, and Brechtian avant-garde thespians—from the area's "ordinary" hippies is their ideological brio, articulateness, good works, and flair for the dramatic event. (Some are even rumored to be over 30.) In the eyes of many Hashbury hippies, therefore, the Diggers symbolize what is best, what is most persuasive and purposive, about the surrounding, more variegated hippie subculture—just as, for certain radical social critics of the American scene, the hippies are expressing, albeit elliptically, what is best about a seemingly ever-broader segment of American youth: its openness to new experience, puncturing of cant, rejection of bureaucratic regimentation, aversion to violence, and identification with the exploited and disadvantaged. That this is not the whole story barely needs saying. Along with the poetry and flowers, the melancholy smile at passing and ecstatic clasp at greeting, there is also the panicky incoherence of the bad LSD trip, the malnutrition, a startling rise in V.D. and hepatitis, a seemingly phobic reaction to elementary practices of hygiene and sanitation, and—perhaps most disturbing in the long run—a casualness about the comings and goings of human relationships that must verge on the grossly irresponsible.

But, then, social movements—particularly of this expressive-religious variety—are rarely of a piece, and it would be unfortunate if social scientists, rather than inquiring into the genesis, meaning, and future of the hippie movement, too soon joined ranks (as many are likely to, in any case) with solid burghers in an orgy of research into the "pathology" of it all: the ubiquitous drug use (mainly marihuana and LSD, often amphetamines, rarely heroin or other opiates), the easy attitudes toward sex ("If two people are attracted to each other, what better way of showing it than to make love?"), and the mocking hostility toward the middle-class values of pleasure-deferral, material success, and—ultimately—the whole mass-media-glamorized round of chic, deodorized, appliance-glutted suburban existence.

THE HIP SCENE IS THE MESSAGE

Clearly, despite whatever real or imagined "pathology" middle-class spokesmen are ready to assign to the hippies, it is the middle-class scheme of life that young hippies are reacting against, even though in their ranks are to be found some youth of working-class origin who have never enjoyed the affluence that their peers now so heartily decry. To adulterate somewhat the slogan of Marshall McLuhan, one of the few non-orientalized intellectuals whom hippies bother to read at all, *the hip scene is the message,* not the elements whence it derives or the meanings that can be assigned to it verbally. (Interestingly, this fusion of disparate classes does not appear to include any significant number of the Negro youths who reside with their families in the integrated Haight-Ashbury district or in the adjoining Negro ghetto, the Fillmore district. By and large, Negroes view with bewilderment and ridicule the white hippies who flaunt, to the extent of begging on the streets, their rejection of what the Negroes have had scant opportunity to attain. What more revealing symbol of the Negro riots in our nation's cities than the carting off of looted TV sets, refrigerators, and washing machines? After all, aren't these things what America is all about?)

But granting that the hippie scene is a reaction to middle-class values, can the understanding of any social movement—particularly one that just in the process of its formation is so fecund of new art forms, new styles of dress and demeanor, and (most of all) new ethical bases for human relationships—ever be wholly reduced to its reactive aspect? As Ralph Ellison has eloquently observed in his critique of the standard sociological explanation of the American Negro's situation, a people's distinctive way of life is never solely a reaction to the dominant social forces that have oppressed, excluded, or alienated them from the larger society. The cumulative process of reaction and counterreaction, in its historical unfolding, creates its own ground for the emergence of new symbols, meanings, purposes, and social discoveries, none of which are ever wholly contained in embryo, as it were, in the conditions that elicited the reaction. It is, therefore, less with an eye toward explaining "how it came to be" than toward explaining what it may betoken of life in the future society that I now want to examine certain facets of the Hashbury hippie subculture. (Of course, very similar youth movements, subcultures, and settlements are found nowadays in many parts of the affluent Western world—Berkeley's Telegraph Avenue teeny-boppers; Los Angeles' Sunset Strippers; New York's East Village hippies; London's mods; Amsterdam's Provos; and the summer *Wandervögel* from all over Europe who chalk the pavement of Copenhagen's main shopping street, the Strøget, and sun themselves on the steps of Stockholm's Philharmonic Hall. What is culturally significant about the Haight-Ashbury hippies is, I would hazard, in general significant about these others as well, with—to be sure—certain qualifications. Indeed, a certain marvelous irony attaches itself to the fact that perhaps the only genuine cross-national culture found in the world today builds on the rag-tag of beards, bare feet, bedrolls, and beads, not on the cultural-exchange programs of governments and universities, or tourism, or—least of all—ladies' clubs' invocations for sympathetic understanding of one's foreign neighbors.)

What I wish to suggest here is that there is, as Max Weber would have put it, an *elective affinity* between prominent styles and themes in the hippie subculture and certain incipient problems of identity, work, and leisure that loom ominously as Western industrial society moves into an epoch of accelerated cybernation, staggering material abundance, and historically-unprecedented mass opportunities for creative leisure and enrichment of the human personality. This is not to say that the latter are the *hidden causes* or tangible *motivating forces* of the former. Rather, the point is that the hippies, in their collective, yet radical, break with the constraints of our present society, are—whether they know it or not (some clearly do intuit a connection)—already rehearsing *in vivo* a number of possible cultural solutions to central life problems posed by the emerging society of the future. While other students of contemporary youth culture could no doubt cite many additional emerging problems to which the hippie subculture is, willy-nilly, addressing itself (marriage and family organization, the character of friendship and personal loyalties, the forms of political participation), space and the kind of observations I have been able to make require that I confine myself to three: the problems of *compulsive consumption,* of *passive spectatorship,* and of the *time-scale of experience.*

COMPULSIVE CONSUMPTION

What working attitude is man to adopt toward the potential glut of consumer goods that the new technology will make available to virtually all members of the future society? Until now, modern capitalist society's traditional response to short-term conditions of overproduction has been to generate—through government manipulation of fiscal devices—greater purchasing power for discretionary consumption. At the same time, the aim has been to cultivate the acquisitive impulse—largely through mass advertising, annual styling changes, and planned obsolescence—so that, in the economist's terminology, a high level of aggregate demand could be sustained. Fortunately, given the great backlog of old material wants and the technologically-based creation of new wants, these means have, for the most part, worked comparatively well—both for advancing (albeit unequally) the mass standard of living and ensuring a reasonably high rate of return to capital.

But, as Walter Weisskopf, Robert Heilbroner, and other economists have wondered, will these means prove adequate for an automated future society in which the mere production of goods and services might easily outstrip man's desire for them, or his capacity to consume them in satisfying ways? Massive problems of air pollution, traffic congestion, and waste disposal aside, is there no psychological limit to the number of automobiles, TV sets, freezers, and dishwashers that even a zealous consumer can aspire to, much less make psychic room for in his life space? The specter that haunts post-industrial man is that of a near worker-less economy in which most men are constrained, through a variety of economic and political sanctions, to frantically purchase and assiduously use up the cornucopia of consumer goods that a robot-staffed factory system (but one still harnessed to capitalism's rationale of pecuniary profit) regurgitates upon the populace. As far back as the late 1940s sociologists like David Riesman were already pointing to the many moral paradoxes of work, leisure, and interpersonal relations posed by a then only nascent society of capitalist mass abundance. How much more perplexing the paradoxes if, using current technological trends, we extrapolate to the year 2000?

Hippies, originating mainly in the middle classes, have been nurtured at the boards of consumer abundance. Spared their parents' vivid memories of economic depression and material want, however, they now, with what to their elders seems like insulting abandon, declare unshamefacedly that the very quest for "the good things of life" and all that this entails—the latest model, the third car, the monthly credit payments, the right house in the right neighborhood—are a "bad bag." In phrases redolent of nearly all utopian thought of the past, they proclaim that happiness and a meaningful life are not to be found in things, but in the cultivation of the self and by an intensive exploration of inner sensibilities with like-minded others.

Extreme as this antimaterialistic stance may seem, and despite its probable tempering should hippie communities develop as a stable feature on the American landscape, it nonetheless points a way to a solution of the problem of material glut; to wit, the simple demonstration of the ability to live on less, thereby calming the acquisitive frenzy that would have to be sustained, and even accelerated, if the present scheme of capitalist production and distribution were to remain unchanged. Besides such establishments as the Diggers' Free Store, gleanings of this attitude are even evident in the street panhandling that so many hippies engage in. Unlike the street beggars of old, there is little that is obsequious or deferential about their manner. On the contrary, their approach is one of easy, sometimes condescending casualness, as if to say, "You've got more than enough to spare, I need it, so let's not make a degrading charity scene out of my asking you." The story is told in the Haight-Ashbury of the patronizing tourist who, upon being approached for a dime by a hippie girl in her late teens, took the occasion to deliver a small speech on how delighted he would be to give it to her—provided she first told him what she needed it for. Without blinking an eye she replied, "It's my menstrual period and that's how much a sanitary napkin costs."

PASSIVE SPECTATORSHIP

As social historians are forever reminding us, modern man has—since the beginnings of the industrial revolution—become increasingly a spectator and less a participant. Less and less does he, for example, create or play music, engage in sports, dance or sing; instead he watches professionally-trained others, vastly more accomplished than himself, perform their acts while he, perhaps, indulges in Mitty-like fantasies of hidden graces and talents. Although this bald statement of the spectator thesis has been challenged in recent years by certain social researchers—statistics are cited of the growing numbers taking guitar lessons, buying fishing equipment, and painting on Sunday—there can be little doubt that "doing" kinds of expressive pursuits, particularly of the collective type, no longer bear the same *integral* relationship to daily life that they once did, or still do in primitive societies. The mere change in how they come to be perceived, from what one does in the ordinary course of life to one's "hobbies," is in itself of profound historical significance. Along with this, the virtuoso standards that once were the exclusive property of small aristocratic elites, rather than being undermined by the oft-cited revolutions in mass communications and mass education, have so diffused through the class structure as to even cause the gifted amateur *at play* to apologize for his efforts with some remark as, "I only play at it." In short, the cult of professionalism, in the arts as elsewhere, has been institutionalized so intensively in Western society that the ordinary man's sense of expressive adequacy and competence has progressively atrophied. This is especially true of the college-educated, urban middle classes, which—newly exposed to the lofty aesthetic standards of high culture—stand in reverent, if passive, awe of them.

Again, the problem of excessive spectatorship has not proved particularly acute until now, inasmuch as most men have had other time-consuming demands to fill their lives with, chiefly work and family life, leavened by occasional vacations and mass-produced amusements. But what of the future when, according to such social prognosticators as Robert Theobald and Donald Michael, all (except a relatively small cadre of professionals and managers) will be faced with a surfeit of leisure time? Will the mere extension of passive spectatorship and the professional's monopoly of expressive pursuits be a satisfactory solution?

Here, too, hippies are opening up new avenues of collective response to life issues posed by a changing socio-technological environment. They are doing so by rejecting those virtuoso standards that stifle participation in high culture; by substituting an extravagantly eclectic (and, according to traditional aestheticians, reckless) admixture of materials, styles, and motifs from a great diversity of past and present human cultures; and, most of all, by insisting that every man can find immediate expressive fulfillment provided he lets the socially-suppressed spirit within him ascend into vibrant consciousness. The manifesto is: All men are artists, and who cares that some are better at it than others; we can all have fun! Hence, the deceptively crude antisophistication of hippie art forms, which are, perhaps, only an apparent reversion to primitivism. One has only to encounter the lurid *art nouveau* contortions of the hippie posters and their

Beardsleyan exoticism, or the mad mélange of hippie street costume—
Greek-sandaled feet peeking beneath harem pantaloons encased in a
fringed American Indian suede jacket, topped by pastel floral decorations
about the face—or the sitar-whining cacophony of the folk-rock band, to
know immediately that one is in the presence of *expressiveness* for its own
sake.

In more mundane ways, too, the same readiness to let go, to participate, to create and perform without script or forethought is everywhere
evident in the Hashbury. Two youths seat themselves on the sidewalk or
in a store entranceway; bent beer can in hand, one begins scratching a
bongo-like rhythm on the pavement while the other tattoos a bell-like accompaniment by striking a stick on an empty bottle. Soon they are joined,
one by one, by a tambourinist, a harmonica player, a penny-whistler or
recorder player, and, of course, the ubiquitous guitarist. A small crowd
collects and, at the fringes, some blanket-bedecked boys and girls begin
twirling about in movements vaguely resembling a Hindu dance. The wailing, rhythmic beating and dancing, alternately rising to peaks of intensity
and subsiding, may last for as little as five minutes or as long as an hour,
players and dancers joining in and dropping out as whim moves them. At
some point—almost any—a mood takes hold that "the happening is over";
participants and onlookers disperse as casually as they had collected.

Analogous scenes of "participation unbound" are to be observed almost every night of the week (twice on Sunday) at the hippies' Parnassus,
the Fillmore Auditorium, where a succession of name folk-rock bands,
each more deafening than the one before, follow one another in hour-long
sessions. Here, amidst the electric guitars, the electric organs, and the
constantly metamorphizing show of lights, one can see the gainly and the
graceless, the sylph bodies and rude stompers, the crooked and straight—
all, of whatever condition or talent, *dance* as the flickering of a strobe light
reduces their figures in silhouette to egalitarian spastic bursts. The recognition dawns that this, at last, is dancing of utterly free form, devoid of fixed
sequence or step, open to all and calling for no Friday after-school classes
at Miss Martha's or expensive lessons from Arthur Murray. The sole requisite is to tune in, take heart, and let go. What follows must be "beautiful" (a favorite hippie word) because it is *you* who are doing and feeling,
not another to whom you have surrendered the muse.

As with folk-rock dancing, so (theoretically, at least) with music,
poetry, painting, pottery, and the other arts and crafts: expression over
performance, impulse over product. Whether the "straight world" will in
time heed this message of the hippies is, to be sure, problematical. Also,
given the lavish financial rewards and prestige heaped upon more talented
hippie artists by a youth-dominated entertainment market, it is conceivable that high standards of professional performance will develop here as
well (listen to the more recent Beatles' recordings), thus engendering perhaps as great a participative gulf between artist and audience as already

exists in the established arts. Despite the vagaries of forecasting, however, the hippies—as of now, at least—are responding to the incipient plenitude of leisure in ways far removed from the baleful visions of a Huxley or an Orwell.

THE TIME-SCALE OF EXPERIENCE

In every society, certain activities are required to complete various tasks and to achieve various goals. These activities form a sequence—they may be of short duration and simple linkage (boiling an egg); long duration and complex linkage (preparing for a profession); or a variety of inter-mediate combinations (planting and harvesting a crop). And the activity sequences needed to complete valued tasks and to achieve valued goals in a society largely determine how the people in that society will subjectively experience *time*.

The distinctive temporal bent of industrial society has been toward the second of these arrangements, long duration and complex linkage. As regards the subjective experience of time, this has meant what the anthropologist Florence Kluckhohn has termed a strong "future orientation" on the part of Western man, a quality of sensibility that radically distinguishes him from his peasant and tribal forebears. The major activities that fill the better part of his life acquire their meaning less from the pleasure they may or may not give at the moment than from their perceived relevance to some imagined future state of being or affairs, be it salvation, career achievement, material success, or the realization of a more perfect social order. Deprived of the pursuit of these temporally distant, complexly modulated goals, we would feel that life, as the man in the street puts it, is without meaning.

This subjective conception of time and experience is, of course, admirably suited to the needs of post-18th century industrial society, needs that include a stable labor force; work discipline; slow and regular accumulation of capital with which to plan and launch new investments and to expand; and long, arduous years of training to provide certain people with the high levels of skill necessary in so many professions and technical fields. If Western man had proved unable to defer present gratifications for future rewards (that is, if he had not been a future-oriented being), nothing resembling our present civilization, as Freud noted, could have come to pass.

Yet, paradoxically, it is the advanced technology of computers and servo-mechanisms, not to overlook nuclear warfare, that industrial civilization has carried us to that is raising grave doubts concerning this temporal ordering of affairs, this optimistic, pleasure-deferring, and magically rationalistic faith in converting present effort to future payoff. Why prepare, if there will be so few satisfying jobs to prepare for? Why defer, if there will be a superabundance of inexpensively-produced goods to choose from? Why plan, if all plans can disintegrate into nuclear dust?

Premature or exaggerated as these questions may seem, they are being asked, especially by young people. And merely to ask them is to prompt a radical shift in time-perspective—from what *will be* to what *is,* from future promise to present fulfillment, from the mundane discounting of present feeling and mood to a sharpened awareness of their contours and their possibilities for instant alteration. Broadly, it is to invest present experience with a new cognitive status and importance: a lust to extract from the living moment its full sensory and emotional potential. For if the present is no longer to be held hostage to the future, what other course than to ravish it at the very instant of its apprehension?

There is much about the hippie subculture that already betokens this alteration of time-perspective and concomitant reconstitution of the experienced self. Hippie argot—some of it new, much of it borrowed with slight connotative changes from the Negro, jazz, homosexual, and addict subcultures—is markedly skewed toward words and phrases in the active present tense: "happening," "where it's at," "turn on," "freak out," "grooving," "mind-blowing," "be-in," "cop out," "split," "drop acid" (take LSD), "put on," "uptight" (anxious and tense), "trip out" (experience the far-out effects of a hallucinogenic drug). The very concept of a happening signifies immediacy: Events are to be actively engaged in, improvised upon, and dramatically exploited for their own sake, with little thought about their origins, duration, or consequences. Thus, almost anything—from a massive be-in in Golden Gate Park to ingesting LSD to a casual street conversation to sitting solitarily under a tree—is approached with a heightened awareness of its happening potential. Similarly, the vogue among Hashbury hippies for astrology, tarot cards, I Ching, and other forms of thaumaturgic prophecy (a hippie conversation is as likely to begin with "What's your birthday?" as "What's your name?") seems to be an attempt to denude the future of its temporal integrity—its unknowability and slow unfoldingness—by fusing it indiscriminately with present dispositions and sensations. The hippie's structureless round-of-day ("hanging loose"), his disdain for appointments, schedules, and straight society's compulsive parceling out of minutes and hours, are all implicated in his intense reverence for the possibilities of the present and uninterest in the future. Few wear watches, and as a colleague who has made a close participant-observer study of one group of hippies remarked, "None of them ever seems to know what time it is."

It is, perhaps from this vantage point that the widespread use of drugs by hippies acquires its cultural significance, above and beyond the fact that drugs are easily available in the subculture or that their use (especially LSD) has come to symbolize a distinctive badge of membership in that culture. Denied by our Protestant-Judaic heritage the psychological means for experiencing the moment intensively, for parlaying sensation and exoticizing mundane consciousness, the hippie uses drugs where untutored imagination fails. Drugs impart to the present—or so it is alleged by the hippie psychedelic religionists—an aura of aliveness, a sense of union with fellow man and nature, which—we have been taught—can be apprehended, if not in the afterlife that few modern men still believe in, then only after the deepest reflection and self-knowledge induced by protracted experience.

A topic of lively debate among hippie intellectuals is whether drugs represent but a transitory phase of the hippie subculture to be discarded once other, more self-generating, means are discovered by its members for extracting consummatory meaning from present time, or whether drugs are the *sine qua non* of the subculture. Whatever the case, the hippies' experiment with ways to recast our notions of time and experience is deserving of close attention.

THE HIPPIES' FUTURE

As of this writing, it is by no means certain that Haight-Ashbury's "new community," as hippie spokesmen like to call it, can survive much beyond early 1968. Although the "great summer invasion" of émigré hippies fell far short of the 100,000 to 500,000 forecast, the influx of youth from California's and the nation's metropolitan suburbs was, despite considerable turnover, large enough to place a severe strain on the new community's meager resources. "Crash pads" for the night were simply not available in sufficient quantity; the one daily meal of soup or stew served free by the Diggers could hardly appease youthful appetites; and even the lure of free love, which to young minds might be construed as a substitute for food, tarnished for many—boys outnumbered girls by at least three to one, if not more. Besides, summer is San Francisco's most inclement season, the city being shrouded in a chilling, wind-blown fog much of the time. The result was hundreds of youths leading a hand-to-mouth existence, wandering aimlessly on the streets, panhandling, munching stale doughnuts, sleeping in parks and autos and contracting virulent upper-respiratory infections. In this milieu cases of drug abuse, notably involving Methedrine and other "body-wrecking" amphetamines, have showed an alarming increase, beginning about mid-summer and continuing up to the present. And, while the city fathers were not at first nearly so repressive as many had feared, they barely lifted a finger to ameliorate the situation in the Haight-Ashbury. Recently, however, with the upcoming city elections for Mayor and members of the Board of Supervisors, they have given evidence of taking a "firmer" attitude toward the hippies: Drug arrests are on the increase, many more minors in the area are being stopped for questioning and referral to juvenile authorities, and a leading Haight Street hippie cultural establishment, the Straight Theatre, has been denied a dance permit.

It has not, therefore, been solely the impact of sheer numbers that has subjected the new community to a difficult struggle for survival. A variety of forces, internal and external, appear to have conjoined to crush it. To begin with, there is the hippies' notorious, near-anarchic aversion to sustained and organized effort toward reaching some goal. Every man "does his own thing for as long as he likes" until another thing comes along to distract or delight him, whereupon the hippie ethos enjoins him to drop the first thing. (Shades of the early, utopian Karl Marx: ". . . in the communist society it [will be] possible for me to do this today and that tomorrow, to hunt in the morning, to fish in the afternoon, to raise cattle in the evening, to be a critic after dinner, just as I feel at the moment; without ever being a hunter, fisherman, herdsman, or critic." From *The German Ideology*.) Even with such groups as the Diggers, projects are abandoned almost as soon as they are begun. One of the more prominent examples: An ongoing pastoral idyll of summer cultural happenings, proclaimed with great fanfare in May by a group calling itself the Council for the Summer of Love, was abandoned in June when the Council's leader decided one morning to leave town. Add to this the stalling and ordinance-juggling of a city bureaucracy reluctant to grant hippies permits and licenses for their pet enterprises, and very little manages to get off the ground. With only a few notable exceptions, therefore, like the Haight-Ashbury Free Medical Clinic, which—though closed temporarily—managed through its volunteer staff to look after the medical needs of thousands of hippies during the summer, the new community badly failed to provide for the hordes of youth drawn by its paeans of freedom, love, and the new life. Perhaps there is some ultimate wisdom to "doing one's own thing"; it was, however, hardly a practical way to receive a flock of kinsmen.

Exacerbating the "uptightness" of the hippies is a swelling stream of encounters with the police and courts, ranging from panhandling misdemeanors to harboring runaway minors ("contributing to the delinquency of a minor") to, what is most unnerving for hip inhabitants, a growing pattern of sudden mass arrests for marihuana use and possession in which as many as 25 youths may be hauled off in a single raid on a flat. (Some hippies console themselves with the thought that if enough middle-class youths get "busted for grass," such a hue and cry will be generated in respectable quarters that the marihuana laws will soon be repealed or greatly liberalized.) And, as if the internal problems of the new community were not enough, apocalyptic rumors sprung up, in the wake of the Newark and Detroit riots, that "the Haight is going to be burned to the ground" along with the adjoining Fillmore Negro ghetto. There followed a series of ugly street incidents between blacks and whites—assaults, sexual attacks, window smashings—which palpably heightened racial tensions and fed the credibility of the rumors.

Finally, the area's traffic-choked main thoroughfare, Haight Street, acquired in the space of a few months so carnival and Dantesque an atmosphere as to defy description. Hippies, tourists, drug peddlers, Hell's Angels, drunks, speed freaks (people high on Methedrine), panhandlers, pamphleteers, street musicians, crackpot evangelists, photographers, TV camera crews, reporters (domestic and foreign), researchers, ambulatory schizophrenics, and hawkers of the underground press (at least four such papers are produced in the Haight-Ashbury alone) jostled, put-on, and taunted one another through a din worthy of the Tower of Babel. The street-milling was incessant, and all heads remained cocked for "something to happen" to crystallize the disarray. By early summer, so repugnant had this atmosphere become for the "old" hippies (those residing there before —the origins of Hashbury's new community barely go back two years) that many departed; those who remained did so in the rapidly fading hope that the area might revert to its normal state of abnormality following the expected post-Labor Day exodus of college and high-school hippies. And, while the exodus of summer hippies has indeed been considerable, the consensus among knowledgeable observers of the area is that it has not regained its former, less frenetic, and less disorganized ambience. The transformations wrought by the summer influx—the growing shift to Methedrine as *the* drug of choice, the more general drift toward a wholly drug-oriented subculture, the appearance of hoodlum and thrill-seeking elements, the sleazy tourist shops, the racial tensions—persist, only on a lesser scale.

But though Haight-Ashbury's hippie community may be destined to soon pass from the scene, the roots upon which it feeds run deep in our culture. These are not only of the long-term socio-historic kind I have touched on here, but of a distinctly contemporary character as well, the pain and moral duplicity of our Vietnam involvement being a prominent wellspring of hippie alienation. As the pressures mount on middle-class youth for ever greater scholastic achievement (soon a graduate degree may be mandatory for middle-class status, as a high-school diploma was in the 1940s), as the years of adolescent dependence are further prolonged, and as the accelerated pace of technological change aggravates the normal social tendency to intergenerational conflict, an increasing number of young people can be expected to drop out, or opt out, and drift into the hippie subculture. It is difficult to foresee how long they will remain there and what the consequences for later stages of their careers will be, inasmuch as insufficient time has passed for even a single age cohort of hippies to make the transition from early to middle adulthood. However, even among those youths who "remain in" conventional society in some formal sense, a very large number can be expected to hover so close to the margins of the hippie subculture as to have their attitudes and outlooks substantially modified. Indeed, it is probably through some such muted, gradual, and indirect process of social conversion that the hippie subculture will make a lasting impact on American society, if it is to have any at all.

At the same time, the hippie rebellion gives partial, as yet ambiguous, evidence of a massiveness, a universality, and a density of existential texture, all of which promise to transcend the narrowly-segregated confines of age, occupation, and residence that characterized most bohemias of the past (Greenwich Village, Bloomsbury, the Left Bank). Some hippie visionaries already compare the movement to Christianity sweeping the Roman Empire. We cannot predict how far the movement can go toward enveloping the larger society, and whether as it develops it will—as have nearly all successful social movements—significantly compromise the visions that animate it with the practices of the reigning institutional system. Much depends on the state of future social discontent, particularly within the middle classes, and on the viable political options governments have for assuaging this discontent. Judging, however, from the social upheavals and mass violence of recent decades, such options are, perhaps inevitably, scarce indeed. Just possibly, then, by opting out and making their own kind of cultural waves, the hippies are telling us more than we can now imagine about our future selves.

QUESTIONS FOR DISCUSSION

1) Aided by the mass media, the hippie subculture has penetrated to every corner of the land. Because it represents, as Dr. Davis points out, both a sharp divergence with conventional middle-class modes and a fresh response to some troubling problems, its impact is heavy and it may be here to stay. One question that may be asked, however, is this: Is the hippie really an individual or is he too much a member of a mass-movement, careful to be like his peers in his "differentness" from conventional society?

2) Explain the problems of compulsive consumption, passive spectatorship, and the time-scale of experience. What is the hippie contribution in each of these areas? Is it a "creative" contribution? Do you think any or all of these contributions have spread and may become permanent?

3) How does Dr. Davis explain the fact that the hippie subculture is part of an international revolt of the young?

4) What factors caused the decline of the hippie community in the Haight-Ashbury? Are such factors likely to operate in all hippie communities, thus preventing them from ever taking root? Explain.

5) The theologian Paul Tillich, in "The Lost Dimension in Religion," argues that depth has disappeared from religion in contemporary America. The psychiatrist Rollo May argues that depth has also disappeared from love in

America, from the earthly love that is or should be a shadow of divine love. With neither religion nor love, a person is forsaken to boredom and frustration, like the tragic hero in T. S. Eliot's "The Love Song of J. Alfred Prufrock." It might be said that the hippie subculture affords a new quest for the satisfactions of religion and of love. Why is this movement like a religion? What is its prevailing attitude toward love?

ECSTATIC LIVING

Thad and Rita Ashby

In the daytime, we want a tree-top house that admits all possible light so the walls and the floor move slowly in motion, in harmony with what we know of the structure of atomic physics. Everything is flowing, breathing; Heraclitus is our philosopher for reality. The house should always be changing, the light should always be dazzling.

Then for our nighttime hours, we want another kind of room in the house, one that is the very opposite of the tree-tops, in the greenhouse. We want a WOMB. Tim Leary has some womb rooms at Millbrook; there is an Indian cloth on the ceiling and the walls, Indian rugs on the floor, and an altar and pillows spread around. The purpose of the womb room is exactly opposite from the purpose of the tree-top room; one opens out into the air and light, and the other is a return to the womb of the universe.

Everything in it should be soft. If you drape cloths along the wall and on the ceiling, and turn on an electric fan or an air conditioning blower the walls tend to undulate with the air. If you have a stroboscopic light or any little revolving light, you can create the effect of the walls flowing, of their consisting of liquid.

Everyone should invest in a little electric motor of the kind that revolves things from the ceiling. Then you can take a large tin can and puncture it with holes and cause it to revolve around a light bulb and it shines little bits of starlight all over the room.

In addition to the little electric motor for throwing lights and shadows around the room we might also have a little revolving stage of the kind you see in jewelry store windows. I'm suggesting something anyone can build. It would consist of a little revolving stage, covered with bits of mirror. You usually see them with wrist watches on them in a jewelry store window. Cover this with any visionary object. For a list of visionary objects, you can read Huxley's *The Doors of Perception* or *Heaven and Hell*.

We can create jewels without a very heavy investment. It can be costume jewelry, or it can be little bits of plastic. Put them on this revolving stage, and then surround the little stage with a black cloth that would drape down in a circle around the stage so that you can't see it. Cut holes in the cloth at about eye level for a chair, and insert a teleidoscope in the hole. Sit in a circle around this thing. You can't see what's in there. You can't see the jewels and bits of junk, except through the teleidoscope.

Live in this kind of room at night and then in the daytime live in a kind of greenhouse with lots of plants surrounding you and lots of just natural funky, earthy smells, and lots of light coming in flickering and dazzling everything. It will change your life!

We want to emphasize everything that's organic in this room. We want to have lots of animals and lots of anything that lives. You can meditate more easily on a flower or a gold fish, I think, than you can on a statue of the Buddha.

If we think of reality as hard, as the generation of our parents think of reality, then we'll build hard wall houses. When we think of reality as flowing, as dynamic, as growing, then we begin to build houses that are more like flowers, more like buds. Imagine, for example, the absolute ecstasy of living inside a big orange flower about a block wide. We'd ride around on large, trained butterflies.

The image of the world, that organic unity, is something we can achieve in our house or in a simple little room. These things that I'm talking about don't cost anything. To put them into practice, all you need in mind to start with is a visionary experience. We can reproduce it with twenty-five cents worth of metal foil and a dollar's worth of colored ribbons and maybe five dollars worth of lights and light cords. We'd begin with a pile of junk and we'd end with a reproduction of the universe.

If each of us would change his own house, it would gradually change the entire moral tone of our country. We would begin to think of the earth as a visionary garden. We would become caretakers of the trees and the animals, and the flowers. We would think of ourselves as creatures in a garden who are all being grown for some great, great cosmic enjoyment.

If everyone built such a home, with a treehouse room for daylight, and a womb-like room for the night, it would effect the same kind of transformation in our society as it does in the Buddhist countries where they tend to make their decisions slowly and refer everything to, say, the Hour of the Tea Ceremony, or the Hour of Meditation. You ask them a direct question and ask them for an immediate decision; they give you an indirect answer and postpone the decision until they've gone into their little private temple and thought about it from every angle. When they come up with an answer it's usually something very subtle, and something that transcends the conflict of opposites.

QUESTIONS FOR DISCUSSION

1) This brief article suggests the wealth of creative new ideas flowing from the hippie subculture. Notice the specific rejection of the "hardwall houses" of the "generation of our parents." Can you visualize the appearance of the type of house the Ashbys advocate? What is its main purpose?

2) To suit their various moods, the Ashbys will not have all the rooms of their dream house under the same roof. Why should one room be in a tree-top and another in a green-house? What will be the main impression created by each of these rooms?

3) "If each of us would change his own house, it would gradually change the entire moral tone of our country." What changes do the authors desire? Can change in living quarters produce moral change? Explain.

THE SECOND TREE
FROM THE CORNER

E. B. White

"Ever have any bizarre thoughts?" asked the doctor.

Mr. Trexler failed to catch the word. "What kind?" he said.

"Bizarre," repeated the doctor, his voice steady. He watched his patient for any slight change of expression, any wince. It seemed to Trexler that the doctor was not only watching him closely but was creeping slowly toward him, like a lizard toward a bug. Trexler shoved his chair back an inch and gathered himself for a reply. He was about to say "Yes" when he realized that if he said yes the next question would be unanswerable. Bizarre thoughts, bizarre thoughts? Ever have any bizarre thoughts? What kind of thoughts *except* bizarre had he had since the age of two?

Trexler felt the time passing, the necessity for an answer. These psychiatrists were busy men, overloaded, not to be kept waiting. The next patient was probably already perched out there in the waiting room, lonely, worried, shifting around on the sofa, his mind stuffed with bizarre thoughts and amorphous fears. Poor bastard, thought Trexler. Out there all alone in that misshapen antechamber, staring at the filing cabinet and wondering whether to tell the doctor about that day on the Madison Avenue bus.

Let's see, bizarre thoughts. Trexler dodged back along the dreadful corridor of the years to see what he could find. He felt the doctor's eyes upon him and knew that time was running out. Don't be so conscientious, he said to himself. If a bizarre thought is indicated here, just reach into the bag and pick anything at all. A man as well supplied with bizarre thoughts as you are should have no difficulty producing one for the record. Trexler darted into the bag, hung for a moment before one of his thoughts, as a hummingbird pauses in the delphinium. No, he said, not that one. He darted to another (the one about the rhesus monkey), paused, considered. No, he said, not that.

Trexler knew he must hurry. He had already used up pretty nearly four seconds since the question had been put. But it was an impossible situation—just one more lousy, impossible situation such as he was always getting himself into. When, he asked himself, are you going to quit maneuvering yourself into a pocket? He made one more effort. This time he stopped at the asylum, only the bars were lucite—fluted, retractable. Not here, he said. Not this one.

He looked straight at the doctor. "No," he said quietly. "I never have any bizarre thoughts."

The doctor sucked in on his pipe, blew a plume of smoke toward the rows of medical books. Trexler's gaze followed the smoke. He managed to make out one of the titles, *The Genito-Urinary System*. A bright wave of fear swept cleanly over him and he winced under the first pain of kidney stones. He remembered when he was a child, the first time he ever entered a doctor's office, sneaking a look at the titles of the books—and the flush of fear, the shirt wet under the arms, the book on t.b., the sudden knowledge that he was in the advanced stages of consumption, the quick vision of the hemorrhage. Trexler sighed wearily. Forty years, he thought, and I still get thrown by the title of a medical book. Forty years and I still can't stay on life's little bucky horse. No wonder I'm sitting here in this dreary joint at the end of this woebegone afternoon, lying about my bizarre thoughts to a doctor who looks, come to think of it, rather tired.

The session dragged on. After about twenty minutes, the doctor rose and knocked his pipe out. Trexler got up, knocked the ashes out of his brain, and waited. The doctor smiled warmly and stuck out his hand. "There's nothing the matter with you—you're just scared. Want to know how I know you're scared?"

"How?" asked Trexler.

"Look at the chair you've been sitting in! See how it has moved back away from my desk? You kept inching away from me while I asked you questions. That means you're scared."

"Does it?" said Trexler, faking a grin. "Yeah, I suppose it does."

They finished shaking hands. Trexler turned and walked out uncertainly along the passage, then into the waiting room and out past the next patient, a ruddy pin-striped man who was seated on the sofa twirling his hat nervously and staring straight ahead at the files. Poor, frightened guy, thought Trexler, he's probably read in the *Times* that one American male out of every two is going to die of heart disease by twelve o'clock next Thursday. It says that in the paper almost every morning. And he's also probably thinking about that day on the Madison Avenue bus.

A week later, Trexler was back in the patient's chair. And for several weeks thereafter he continued to visit the doctor, always toward the end of the afternoon, when the vapors hung thick above the pool of the mind and darkened the whole region of the East Seventies. He felt no better as time went on, and he found it impossible to work. He discovered that the visits were becoming routine and that although the routine was one to which he certainly did not look forward, at least he could accept it with cool resignation, as once, years ago, he had accepted a long spell with a dentist who had settled down to a steady fooling with a couple of dead teeth. The visits, moreover, were now assuming a pattern recognizable to the patient.

Each session would begin with a resumé of symptoms—the dizziness in the streets, the constricting pain in the back of the neck, the apprehensions, the tightness of the scalp, the inability to concentrate, the despondency and the melancholy times, the feeling of pressure and tension, the anger at not being able to work, the anxiety over work not done, the gas on the stomach. Dullest set of neurotic symptoms in the world, Trexler would think, as he obediently trudged back over them for the doctor's benefit. And then, having listened attentively to the recital, the doctor would spring his question: "Have you ever found anything that gives you relief?" And Trexler would answer, "Yes. A drink." And the doctor would nod his head knowingly.

As he became familiar with the pattern Trexler found that he increasingly tended to identify himself with the doctor, transferring himself into the doctor's seat—probably (he thought) some rather slick form of escapism. At any rate, it was nothing new for Trexler to identify himself with other people. Whenever he got into a cab, he instantly became the driver, saw everything from the hackman's angle (and the reaching over with the right hand, the nudging of the flag, the pushing it down, all the way down along the side of the meter), saw everything—traffic, fare, everything—through the eyes of Anthony Rocco, or Isidore Freedman, or Matthew Scott. In a barbershop, Trexler was the barber, his fingers curled around the comb, his hand on the tonic. Perfectly natural, then, that Trexler should soon be occupying the doctor's chair, asking the questions, waiting for the answers. He got quite interested in the doctor, in this way. He liked him, and he found him a not too difficult patient.

It was on the fifth visit, about halfway through, that the doctor turned to Trexler and said, suddenly, "What do you want?" He gave the word "want" special emphasis.

"I d'know," replied Trexler uneasily. "I guess nobody knows the answer to that one."

"Sure they do," replied the doctor.

"Do *you* know what *you* want?" asked Trexler narrowly.

"Certainly," said the doctor. Trexler noticed that at this point the doctor's chair slid slightly backward, away from him. Trexler stifled a small, internal smile. Scared as a rabbit, he said to himself. Look at him scoot!

"What *do* you want?" continued Trexler, pressing his advantage, pressing it hard.

The doctor glided back another inch away from his inquisitor. "I want a wing on the small house I own in Westport. I want more money, and more leisure to do the things I want to do."

Trexler was just about to say, "And what are those things you want to do, Doctor?" when he caught himself. Better not go too far, he mused. Better not lose possession of the ball. And besides, he thought, what the hell goes on here, anyway—me paying fifteen bucks a throw for these séances and then doing the work myself, asking the questions, weighing the answers. So he wants a new wing! There's a fine piece of theatrical gauze for you! A new wing.

Trexler settled down again and resumed the role of patient for the rest of the visit. It ended on a kindly, friendly note. The doctor reassured him that his fears were the cause of his sickness, and that his fears were unsubstantial. They shook hands, smiling.

Trexler walked dizzily through the empty waiting room and the doctor followed along to let him out. It was late; the secretary had shut up shop and gone home. Another day over the dam. "Good-bye," said Trexler. He stepped into the street, turned west toward Madison, and thought of the doctor all alone there, after hours, in that desolate hole—a man who worked longer hours than his secretary. Poor, scared, over-worked bastard, thought Trexler. And that new wing!

It was an evening of clearing weather, the Park showing green and desirable in the distance, the last daylight applying a high lacquer to the brick and brownstone walls and giving the street scene a luminous and intoxicating splendor. Trexler meditated, as he walked, on what he wanted. "What do you want?" he heard again. Trexler knew what he wanted, and what, in general, all men wanted; and he was glad in a way, that it was both inexpressible and unattainable, and that it wasn't a wing. He was satisfied to remember that it was deep, formless, enduring, and impossible of fulfillment, and that it made men sick, and that when you sauntered along Third Avenue and looked through the doorways into the dim saloons, you could sometimes pick out from the unregenerate ranks the ones who had not forgotten, gazing steadily into the bottoms of the glasses on the long chance that they could get another little peek at it. Trexler found himself renewed by the remembrance that what he wanted was at once great and microscopic, and that although it borrowed from the nature of large deeds and of youthful love and of old songs and early intimations, it was not any one of these things, and that it had not been isolated or pinned down, and that a man who attempted to define it in the privacy of a doctor's office would fall flat on his face.

Trexler felt invigorated. Suddenly his sickness seemed health, his dizziness stability. A small tree, rising between him and the light, stood there saturated with the evening, each gilt-edged leaf perfectly drunk with excellence and delicacy. Trexler's spine registered an ever so slight tremor as it picked up this natural disturbance in the lovely scene. "I want the second tree from the corner, just as it stands," he said, answering an imaginary question from an imaginary physician. And he felt a slow pride in realizing that what he wanted none could bestow, and that what he had none could take away. He felt content to be sick, unembarrassed at being afraid; and in the jungle of his fear he glimpsed (as he had so often glimpsed them before) the flashy tail feathers of the bird courage.

Then he thought once again of the doctor, and of his being left there all alone, tired, frightened. (The poor, scared guy, thought Trexler.) Trexler began humming "Moonshine Lullaby," his spirit reacting instantly to the hypodermic of Merman's healthy voice. He crossed Madison, boarded a downtown bus, and rode all the way to Fifty-second Street before he had a thought that could rightly have been called bizarre.

QUESTIONS FOR DISCUSSION

1) Many of the writers in this book have emphasized that anxiety is a necessary accompaniment to the creative impulse. Some writers have shown that this impulse, with its consequent anxieties, follows from the experiences of religion or love. Some have shown how it can be produced by the external powers that direct our lives—like parents or teachers. Yet, not every person seized by religious or romantic ecstasy becomes creative. And under external pressure, many people find their talent crushed and their will dissolved by anxiety. Thus, the deepest springs of creativity remain a mystery. However, a glimpse into the secret workings of creativity is offered in this story. What does the young man realize about himself that permits this personal triumph?

2) White does not draw a very favorable picture of the psychotherapeutic process. In your opinion, or from your experience, can psychotherapy be "creative"? Explain.

3) In the light of White's story and the other articles you have read in this book, comment on the following statement: "Man's finest creation is himself."